CROSSW

SIMONE STAGGS

CROSSWIND™

CO-CREATORS

CAT STAGGS // Illustrator

GAIL SIMONE // Writer

SIMON BOWLAND // Letterer

CAREY HALL // Production

IMAGE COMICS, INC.
Robert Kirkman—Chief Operating Officer
Erik Larsen—Chief Financial Officer
Todd McFarlane—President
Marc Silvestri—Chief Executive Officer
Jim Valentino—Vice President

Eric Stephenson—Publisher
Corey Hart—Director of Sales
Jeff Boison—Director of Publishing Planning & Book Trade Sales
Chris Ross—Director of Digital Sales
Jeff Stang—Director of Specialty Sales
Kat Salazar—Director of PR & Marketing
Drew Gill—Art Director
Heather Doornink—Production Director
Branwyn Bigglestone—Controller
IMAGECOMICS.COM

CROSSWIND, VOL. 1. First printing. February 2018. Published by Image Comics, Inc. Office of publication: 2701 NW Vaughn St., Suite 780, Portland, OR 97210. ISBN: 978-1-5343-0474-1.

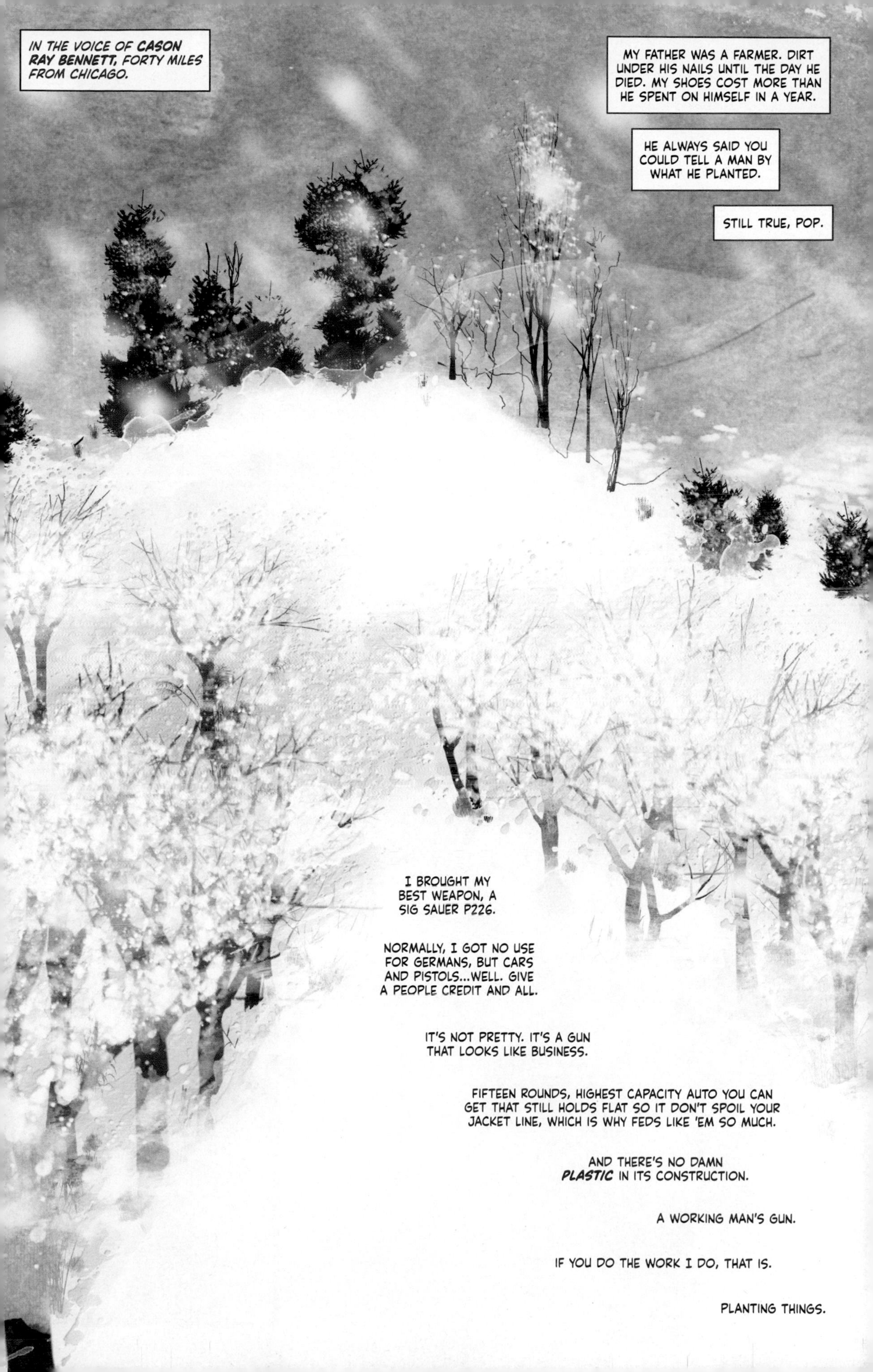
IN THE VOICE OF **CASON RAY BENNETT**, FORTY MILES FROM CHICAGO.
MY FATHER WAS A FARMER. DIRT UNDER HIS NAILS UNTIL THE DAY HE DIED. MY SHOES COST MORE THAN HE SPENT ON HIMSELF IN A YEAR.
HE ALWAYS SAID YOU COULD TELL A MAN BY WHAT HE PLANTED.
STILL TRUE, POP.
I BROUGHT MY BEST WEAPON, A SIG SAUER P226.
NORMALLY, I GOT NO USE FOR GERMANS, BUT CARS AND PISTOLS...WELL. GIVE A PEOPLE CREDIT AND ALL.
IT'S NOT PRETTY. IT'S A GUN THAT LOOKS LIKE BUSINESS.
FIFTEEN ROUNDS, HIGHEST CAPACITY AUTO YOU CAN GET THAT STILL HOLDS FLAT SO IT DON'T SPOIL YOUR JACKET LINE, WHICH IS WHY FEDS LIKE 'EM SO MUCH.
AND THERE'S NO DAMN ***PLASTIC*** IN ITS CONSTRUCTION.
A WORKING MAN'S GUN.
IF YOU DO THE WORK I DO, THAT IS.
PLANTING THINGS.

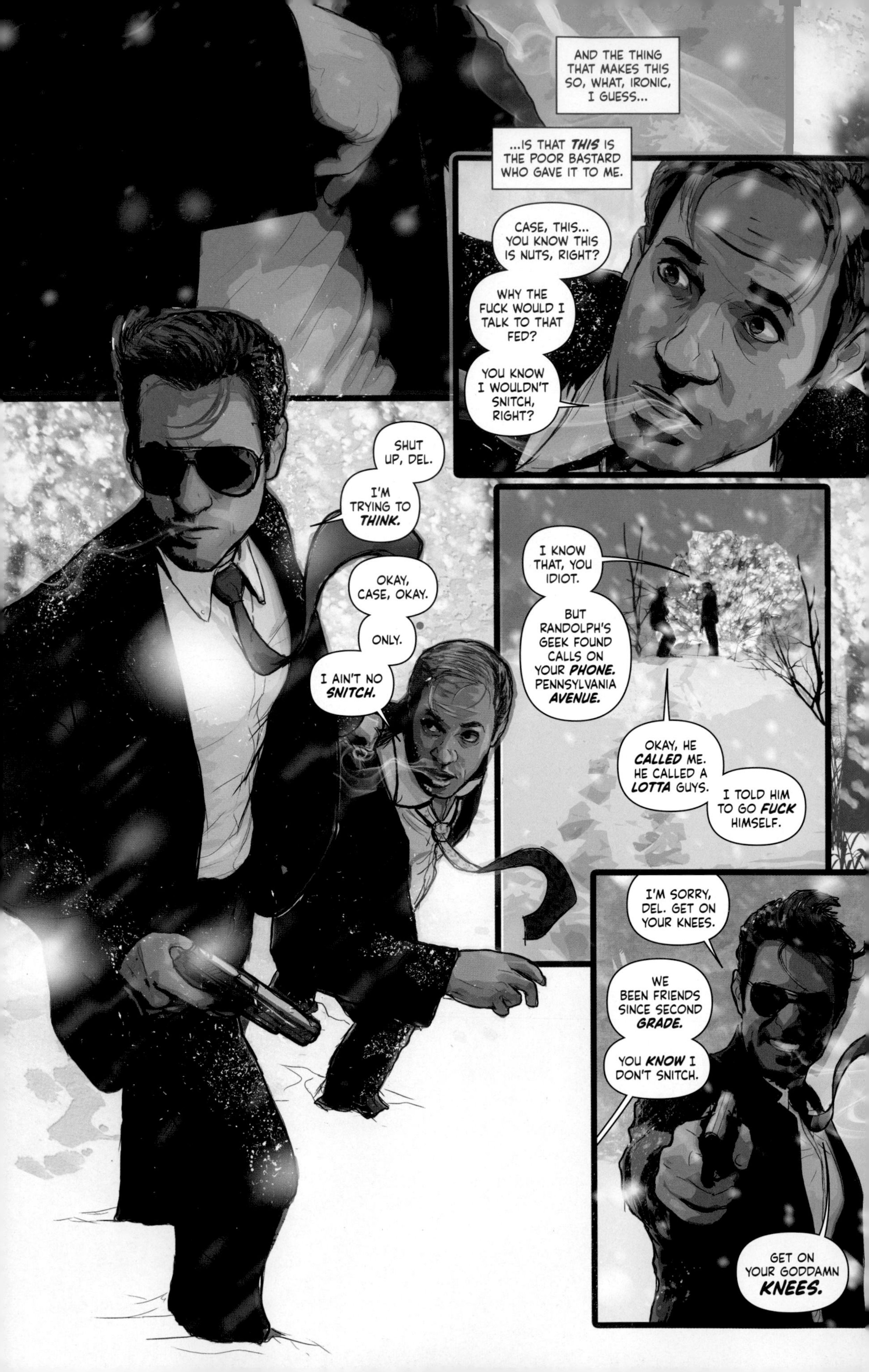
AND THE THING THAT MAKES THIS SO, WHAT, IRONIC, I GUESS...
...IS THAT ***THIS*** IS THE POOR BASTARD WHO GAVE IT TO ME.
CASE, THIS... YOU KNOW THIS IS NUTS, RIGHT?
WHY THE FUCK WOULD I TALK TO THAT FED?
YOU KNOW I WOULDN'T SNITCH, RIGHT?
SHUT UP, DEL.
I'M TRYING TO ***THINK.***
OKAY, CASE, OKAY.
ONLY.
I AIN'T NO ***SNITCH.***
I KNOW THAT, YOU IDIOT.
BUT RANDOLPH'S GEEK FOUND CALLS ON YOUR ***PHONE.*** PENNSYLVANIA ***AVENUE.***
OKAY, HE ***CALLED*** ME. HE CALLED A ***LOTTA*** GUYS.
I TOLD HIM TO GO ***FUCK*** HIMSELF.
I'M SORRY, DEL. GET ON YOUR KNEES.
WE BEEN FRIENDS SINCE SECOND ***GRADE.***
YOU ***KNOW*** I DON'T SNITCH.
GET ON YOUR GODDAMN ***KNEES.***

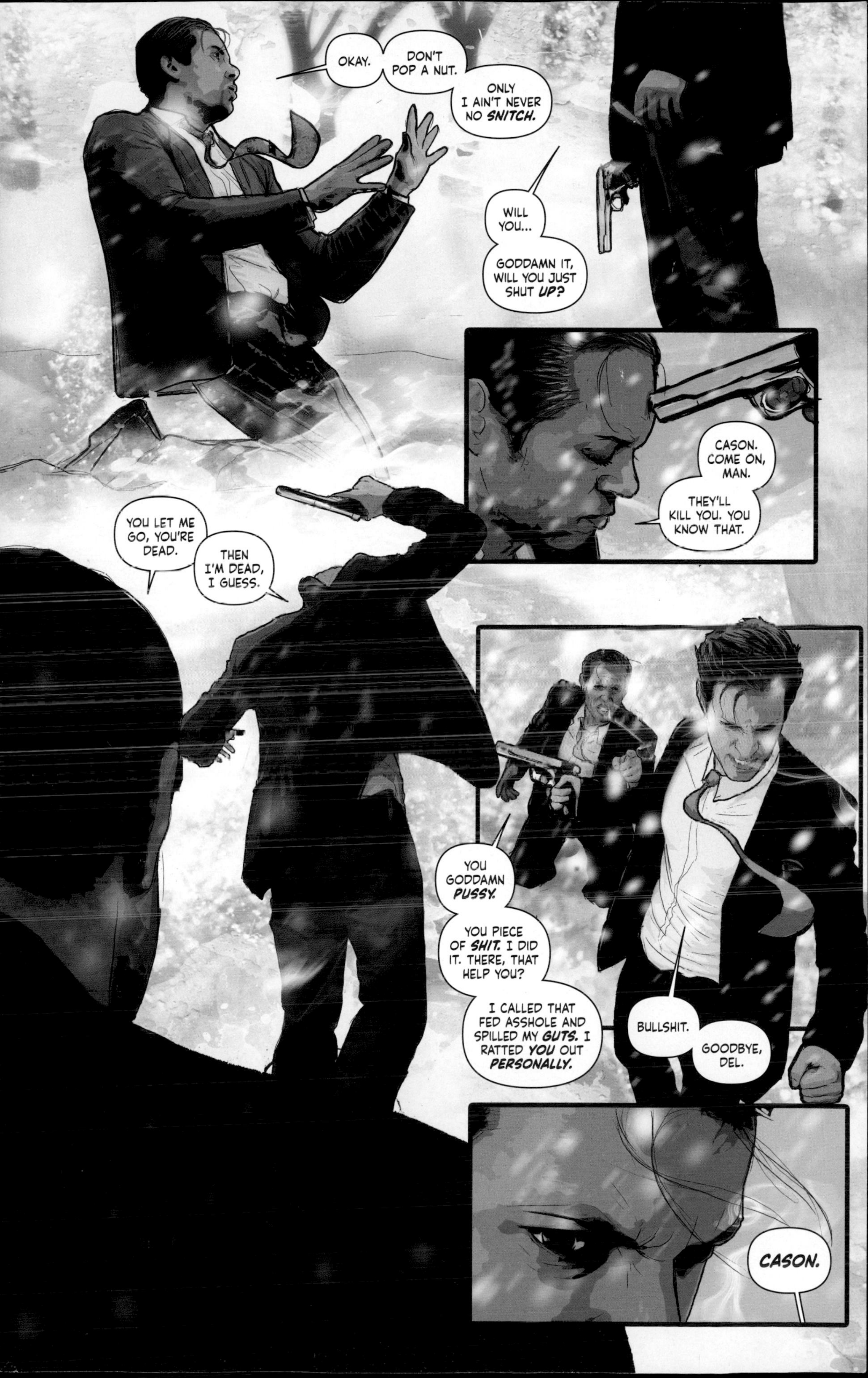
OKAY.
DON'T POP A NUT.
ONLY I AIN'T NEVER NO SNITCH.
WILL YOU...
GODDAMN IT, WILL YOU JUST SHUT UP?
CASON. COME ON, MAN.
THEY'LL KILL YOU. YOU KNOW THAT.
YOU LET ME GO, YOU'RE DEAD.
THEN I'M DEAD, I GUESS.
YOU GODDAMN PUSSY.
YOU PIECE OF SHIT. I DID IT. THERE, THAT HELP YOU?
I CALLED THAT FED ASSHOLE AND SPILLED MY GUTS. I RATTED YOU OUT PERSONALLY.
BULLSHIT.
GOODBYE, DEL.
CASON.

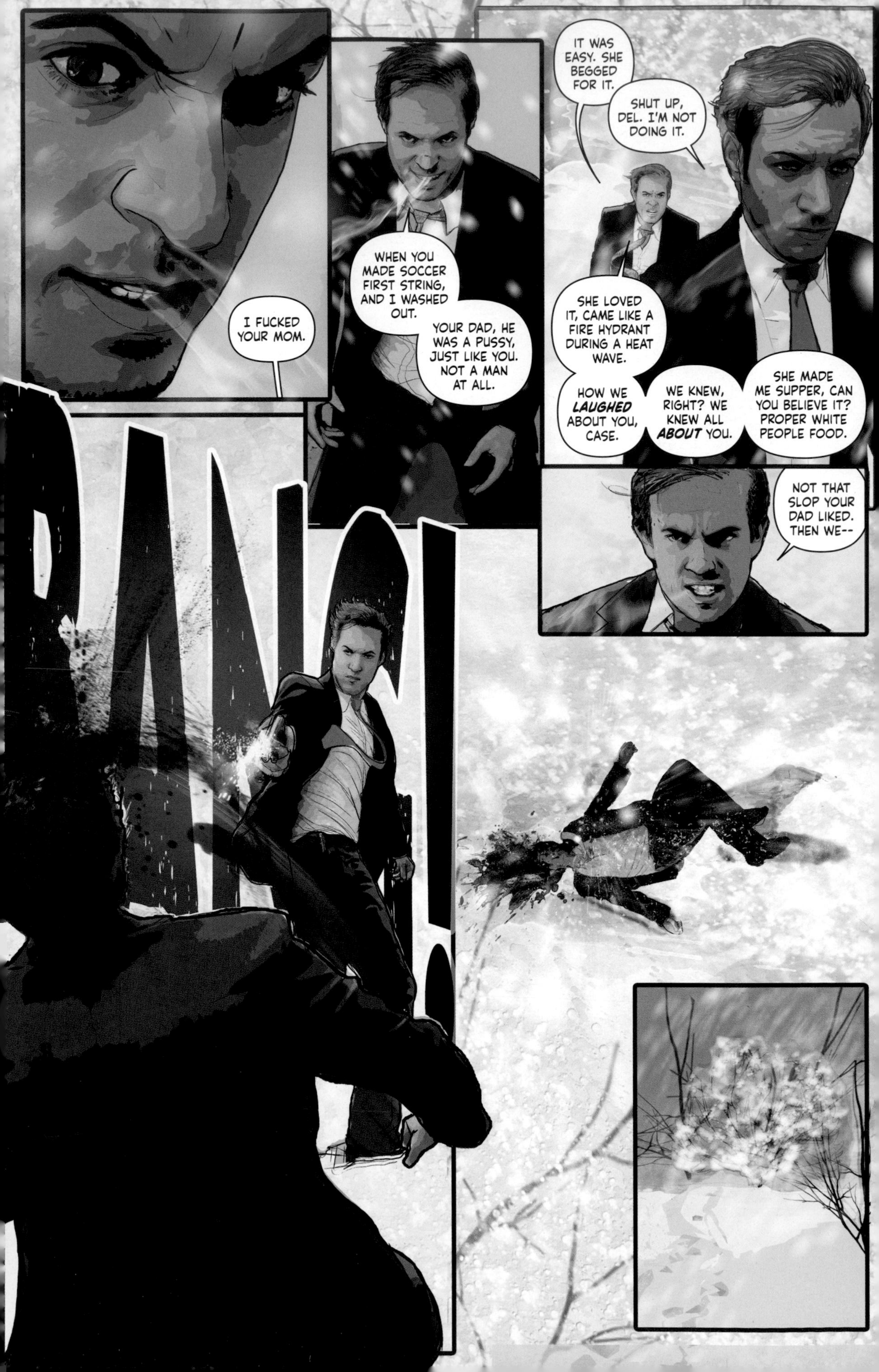
I FUCKED YOUR MOM.
WHEN YOU MADE SOCCER FIRST STRING, AND I WASHED OUT.
YOUR DAD, HE WAS A PUSSY, JUST LIKE YOU. NOT A MAN AT ALL.
IT WAS EASY. SHE BEGGED FOR IT.
SHUT UP, DEL. I'M NOT DOING IT.
SHE LOVED IT, CAME LIKE A FIRE HYDRANT DURING A HEAT WAVE.
HOW WE *LAUGHED* ABOUT YOU, CASE.
WE KNEW, RIGHT? WE KNEW ALL *ABOUT* YOU.
SHE MADE ME SUPPER, CAN YOU BELIEVE IT? PROPER WHITE PEOPLE FOOD.
NOT THAT SLOP YOUR DAD LIKED. THEN WE--
BANG!

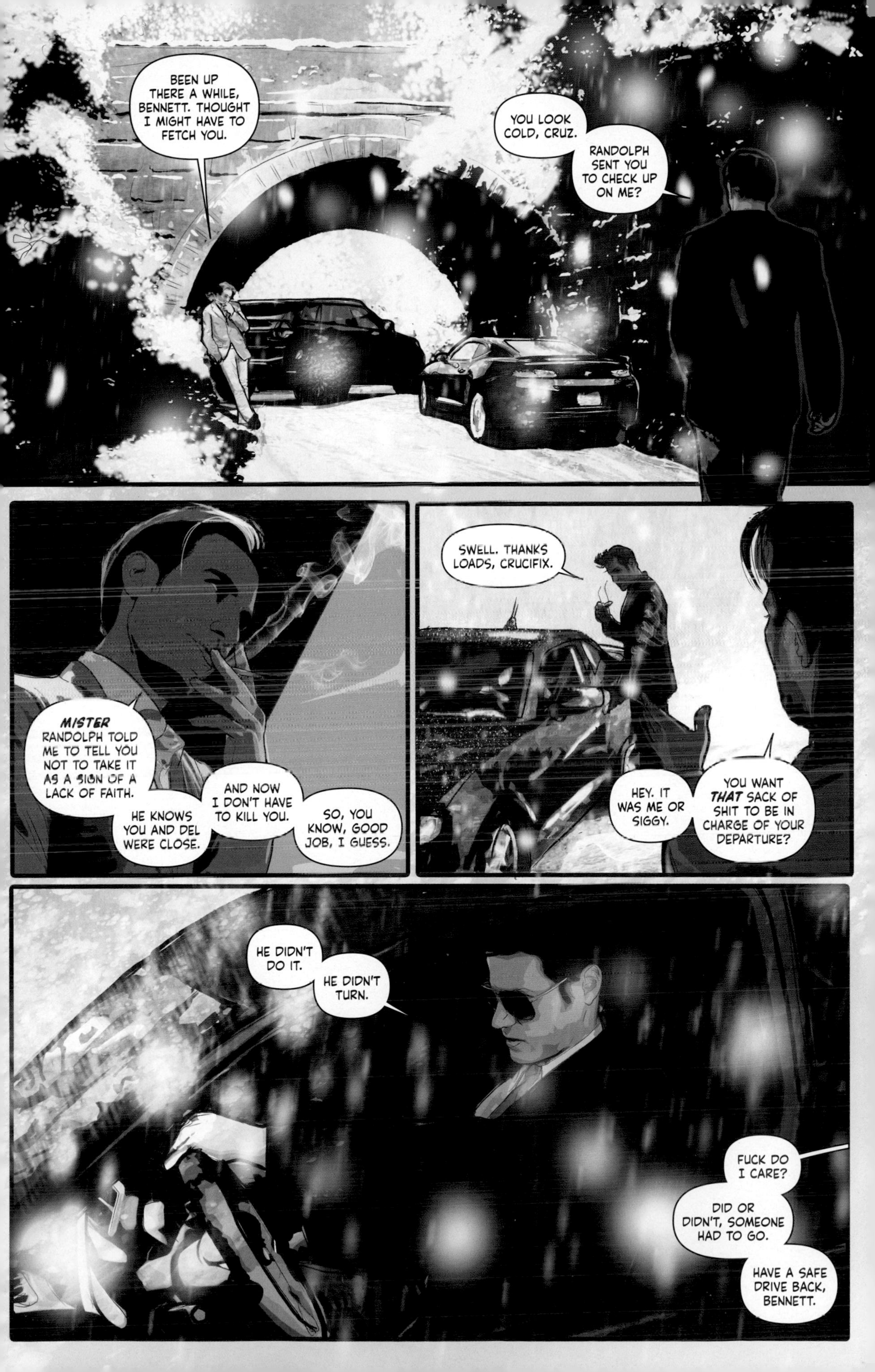
BEEN UP THERE A WHILE, BENNETT. THOUGHT I MIGHT HAVE TO FETCH YOU.
YOU LOOK COLD, CRUZ.
RANDOLPH SENT YOU TO CHECK UP ON ME?
MISTER RANDOLPH TOLD ME TO TELL YOU NOT TO TAKE IT AS A SIGN OF A LACK OF FAITH.
HE KNOWS YOU AND DEL WERE CLOSE.
AND NOW I DON'T HAVE TO KILL YOU.
SO, YOU KNOW, GOOD JOB, I GUESS.
SWELL. THANKS LOADS, CRUCIFIX.
HEY. IT WAS ME OR SIGGY.
YOU WANT THAT SACK OF SHIT TO BE IN CHARGE OF YOUR DEPARTURE?
HE DIDN'T DO IT.
HE DIDN'T TURN.
FUCK DO I CARE?
DID OR DIDN'T, SOMEONE HAD TO GO.
HAVE A SAFE DRIVE BACK, BENNETT.

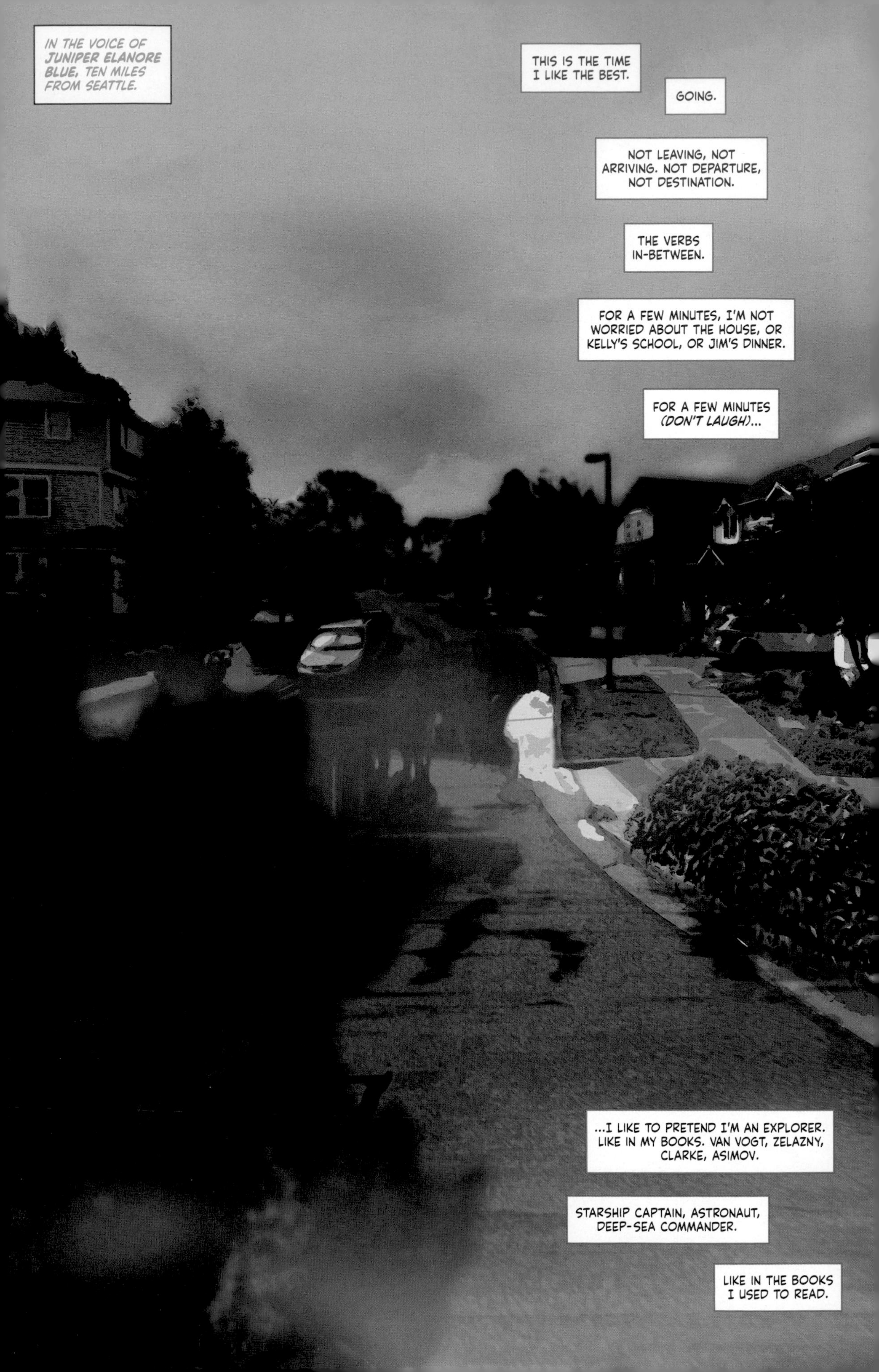
IN THE VOICE OF JUNIPER ELANORE BLUE, TEN MILES FROM SEATTLE.
THIS IS THE TIME I LIKE THE BEST.
GOING.
NOT LEAVING, NOT ARRIVING. NOT DEPARTURE, NOT DESTINATION.
THE VERBS IN-BETWEEN.
FOR A FEW MINUTES, I'M NOT WORRIED ABOUT THE HOUSE, OR KELLY'S SCHOOL, OR JIM'S DINNER.
FOR A FEW MINUTES (DON'T LAUGH)...
...I LIKE TO PRETEND I'M AN EXPLORER. LIKE IN MY BOOKS. VAN VOGT, ZELAZNY, CLARKE, ASIMOV.
STARSHIP CAPTAIN, ASTRONAUT, DEEP-SEA COMMANDER.
LIKE IN THE BOOKS I USED TO READ.

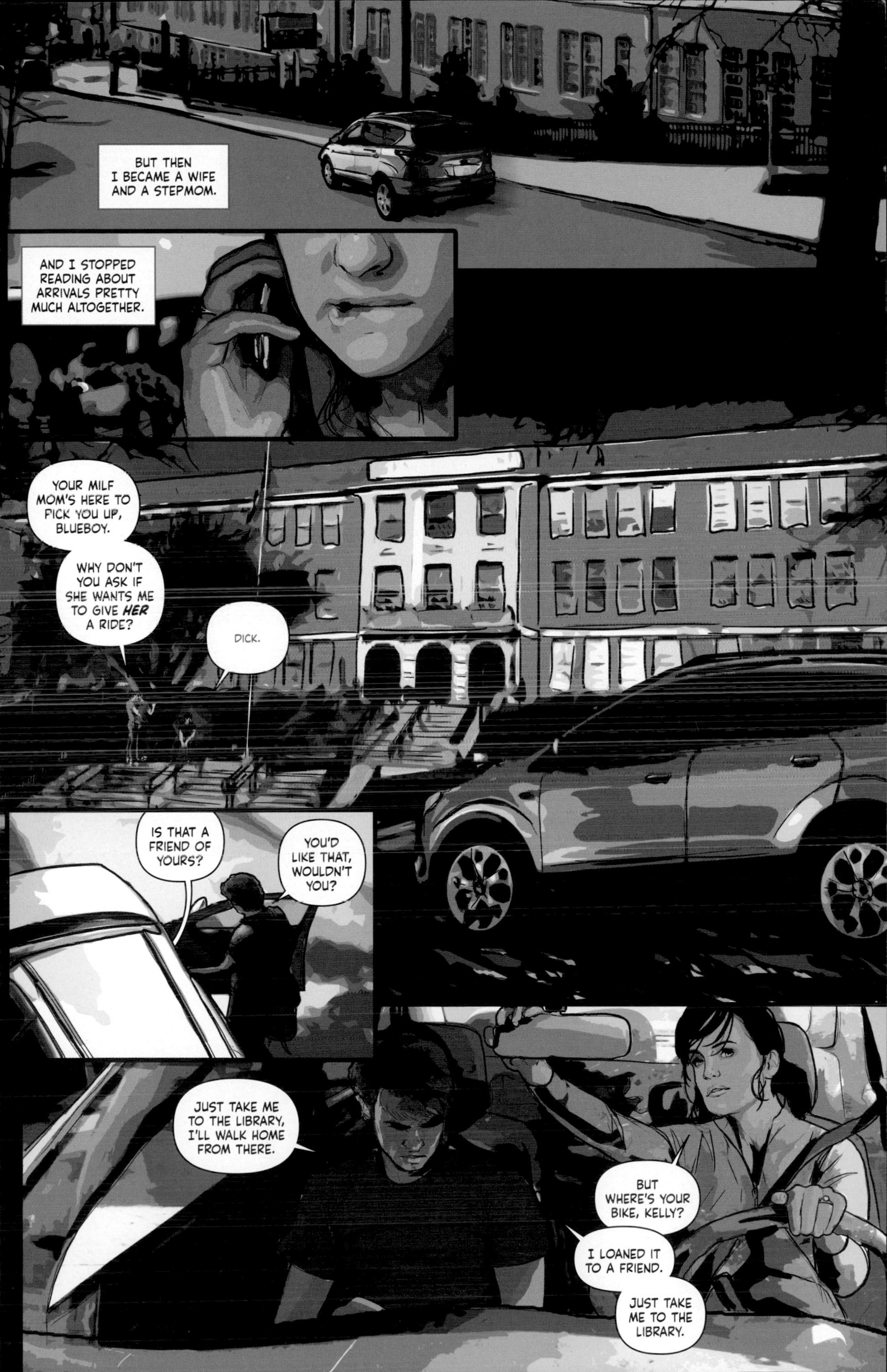
BUT THEN I BECAME A WIFE AND A STEPMOM.
AND I STOPPED READING ABOUT ARRIVALS PRETTY MUCH ALTOGETHER.
YOUR MILF MOM'S HERE TO PICK YOU UP, BLUEBOY.
WHY DON'T YOU ASK IF SHE WANTS ME TO GIVE *HER* A RIDE?
DICK.
IS THAT A FRIEND OF YOURS?
YOU'D LIKE THAT, WOULDN'T YOU?
JUST TAKE ME TO THE LIBRARY, I'LL WALK HOME FROM THERE.
BUT WHERE'S YOUR BIKE, KELLY?
I LOANED IT TO A FRIEND.
JUST TAKE ME TO THE LIBRARY.

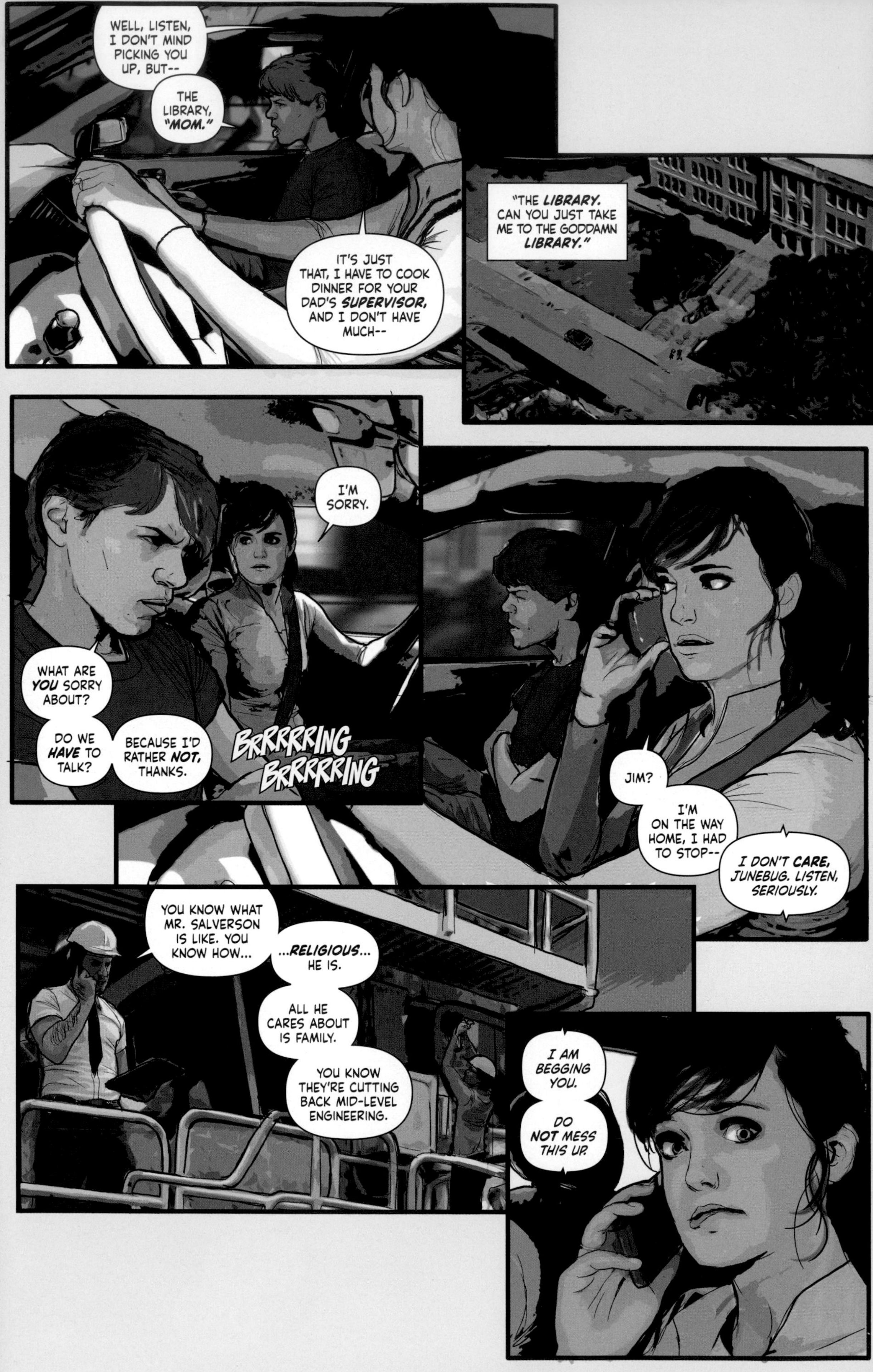
WELL, LISTEN, I DON'T MIND PICKING YOU UP, BUT--
THE LIBRARY, "MOM."
IT'S JUST THAT, I HAVE TO COOK DINNER FOR YOUR DAD'S SUPERVISOR, AND I DON'T HAVE MUCH--
"THE LIBRARY. CAN YOU JUST TAKE ME TO THE GODDAMN LIBRARY."
I'M SORRY.
WHAT ARE YOU SORRY ABOUT?
DO WE HAVE TO TALK?
BECAUSE I'D RATHER NOT, THANKS.
BRRRRRING BRRRRRING
JIM?
I'M ON THE WAY HOME, I HAD TO STOP--
I DON'T CARE, JUNEBUG. LISTEN, SERIOUSLY.
YOU KNOW WHAT MR. SALVERSON IS LIKE. YOU KNOW HOW...
...RELIGIOUS... HE IS.
ALL HE CARES ABOUT IS FAMILY.
YOU KNOW THEY'RE CUTTING BACK MID-LEVEL ENGINEERING.
I AM BEGGING YOU.
DO NOT MESS THIS UP.

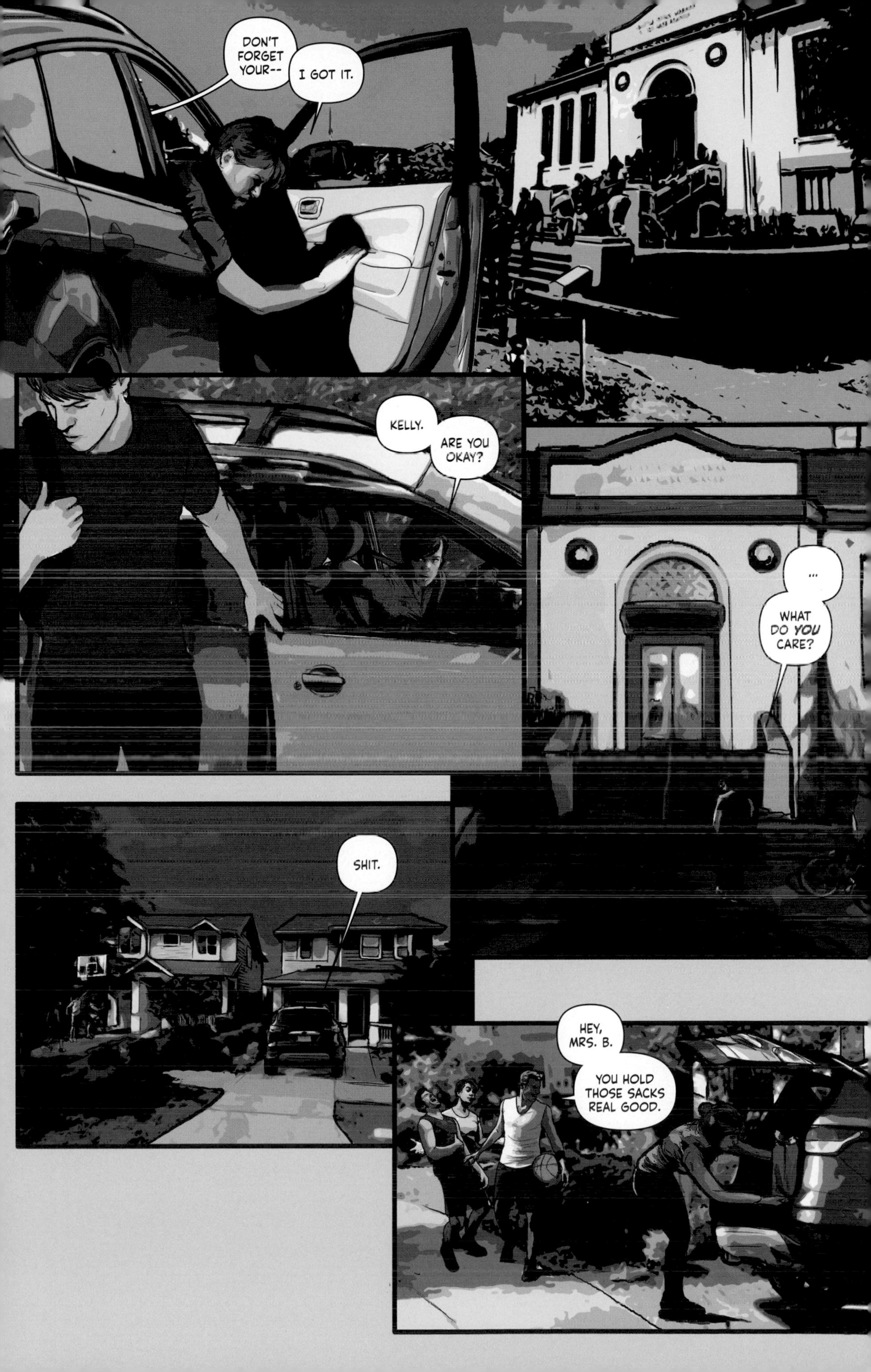
DON'T FORGET YOUR--
I GOT IT.
KELLY.
ARE YOU OKAY?
...
WHAT DO *YOU* CARE?
SHIT.
HEY, MRS. B.
YOU HOLD THOSE SACKS REAL GOOD.

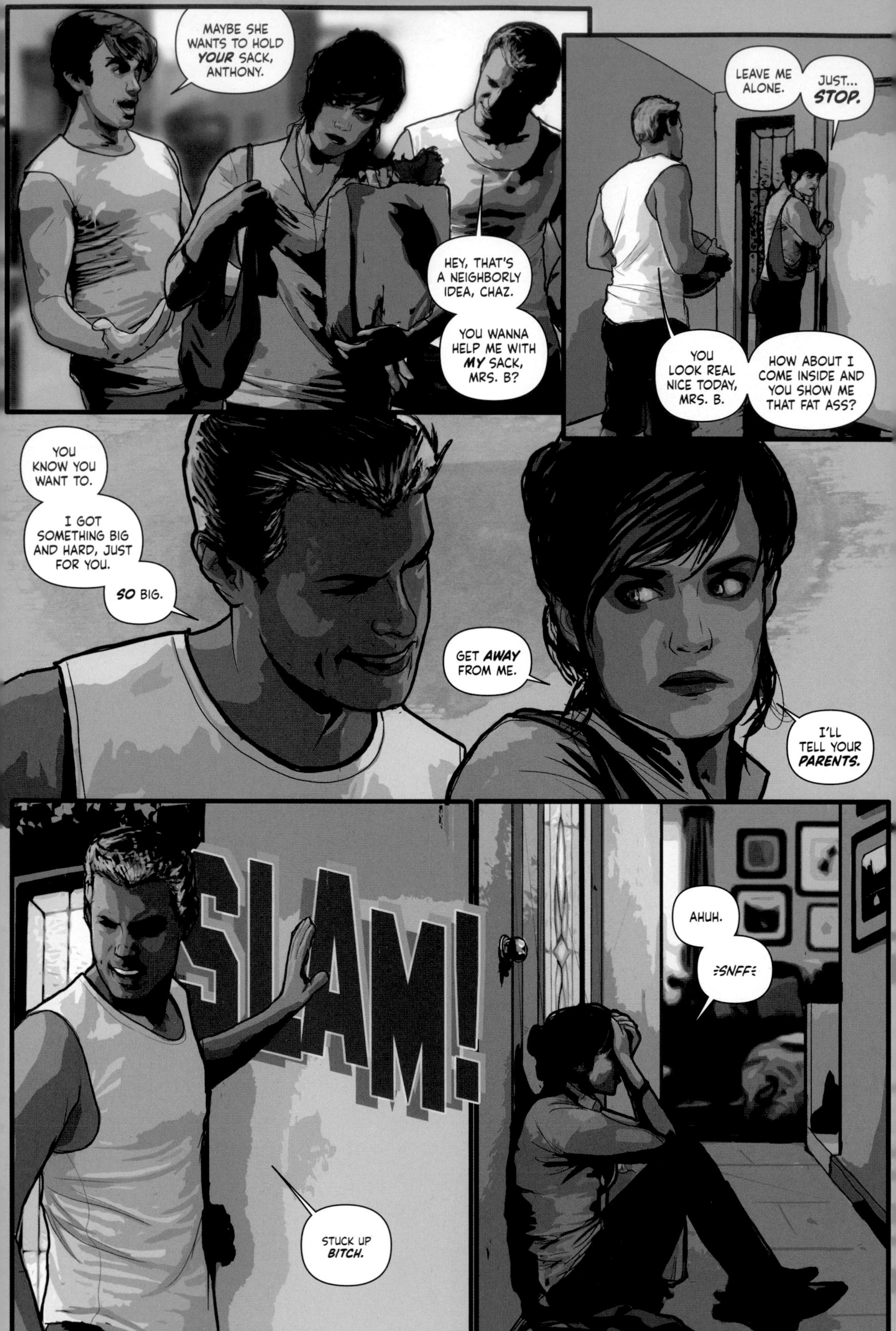
MAYBE SHE WANTS TO HOLD YOUR SACK, ANTHONY.
HEY, THAT'S A NEIGHBORLY IDEA, CHAZ.
YOU WANNA HELP ME WITH MY SACK, MRS. B?
LEAVE ME ALONE.
JUST... STOP.
YOU LOOK REAL NICE TODAY, MRS. B.
HOW ABOUT I COME INSIDE AND YOU SHOW ME THAT FAT ASS?
YOU KNOW YOU WANT TO.
I GOT SOMETHING BIG AND HARD, JUST FOR YOU.
SO BIG.
GET AWAY FROM ME.
I'LL TELL YOUR PARENTS.
SLAM!
STUCK UP BITCH.
AHUH.
SNFF

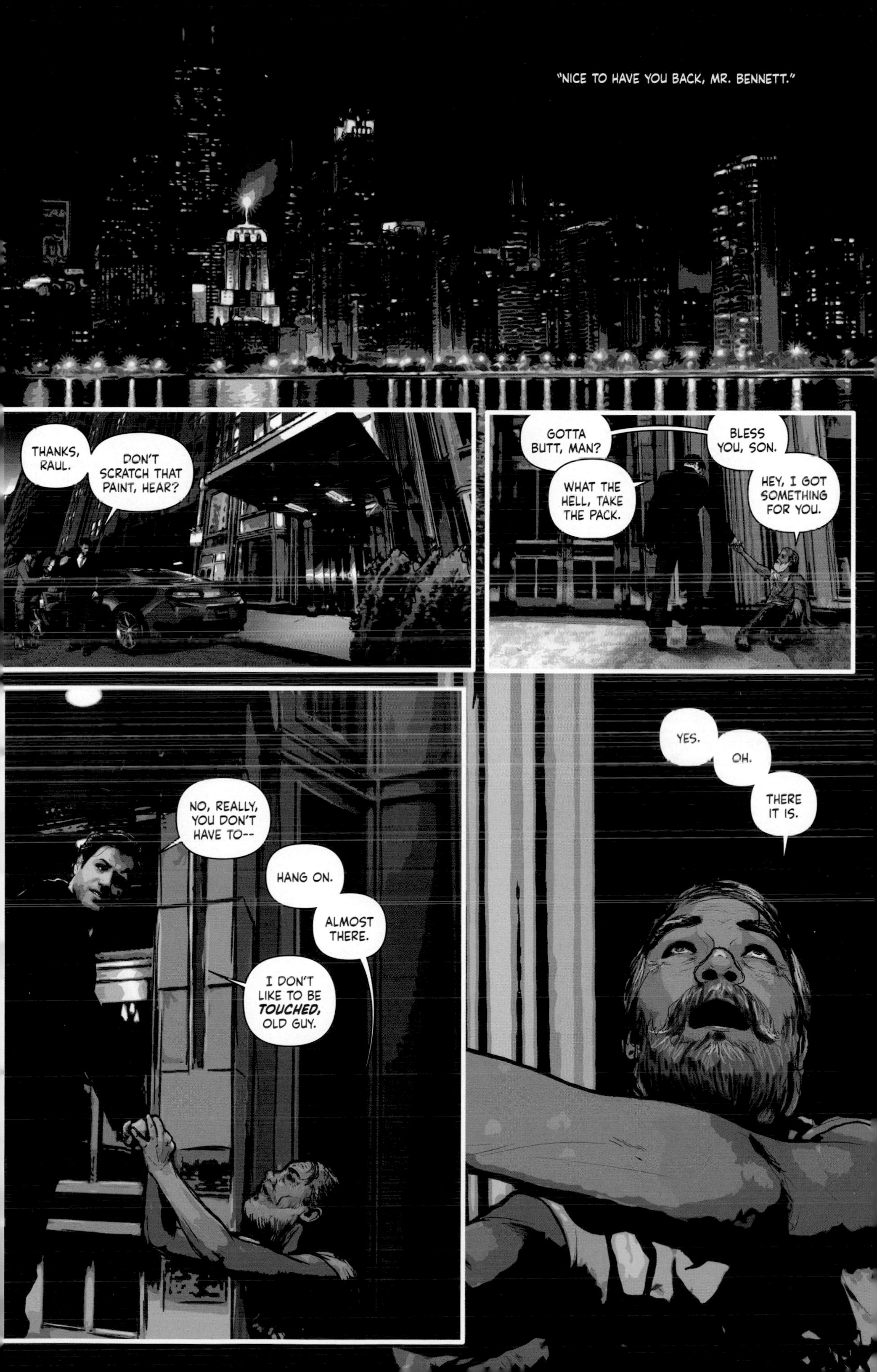
"NICE TO HAVE YOU BACK, MR. BENNETT."
THANKS, RAUL.
DON'T SCRATCH THAT PAINT, HEAR?
GOTTA BUTT, MAN?
WHAT THE HELL, TAKE THE PACK.
BLESS YOU, SON.
HEY, I GOT SOMETHING FOR YOU.
NO, REALLY, YOU DON'T HAVE TO--
HANG ON.
ALMOST THERE.
I DON'T LIKE TO BE *TOUCHED,* OLD GUY.
YES.
OH.
THERE IT IS.

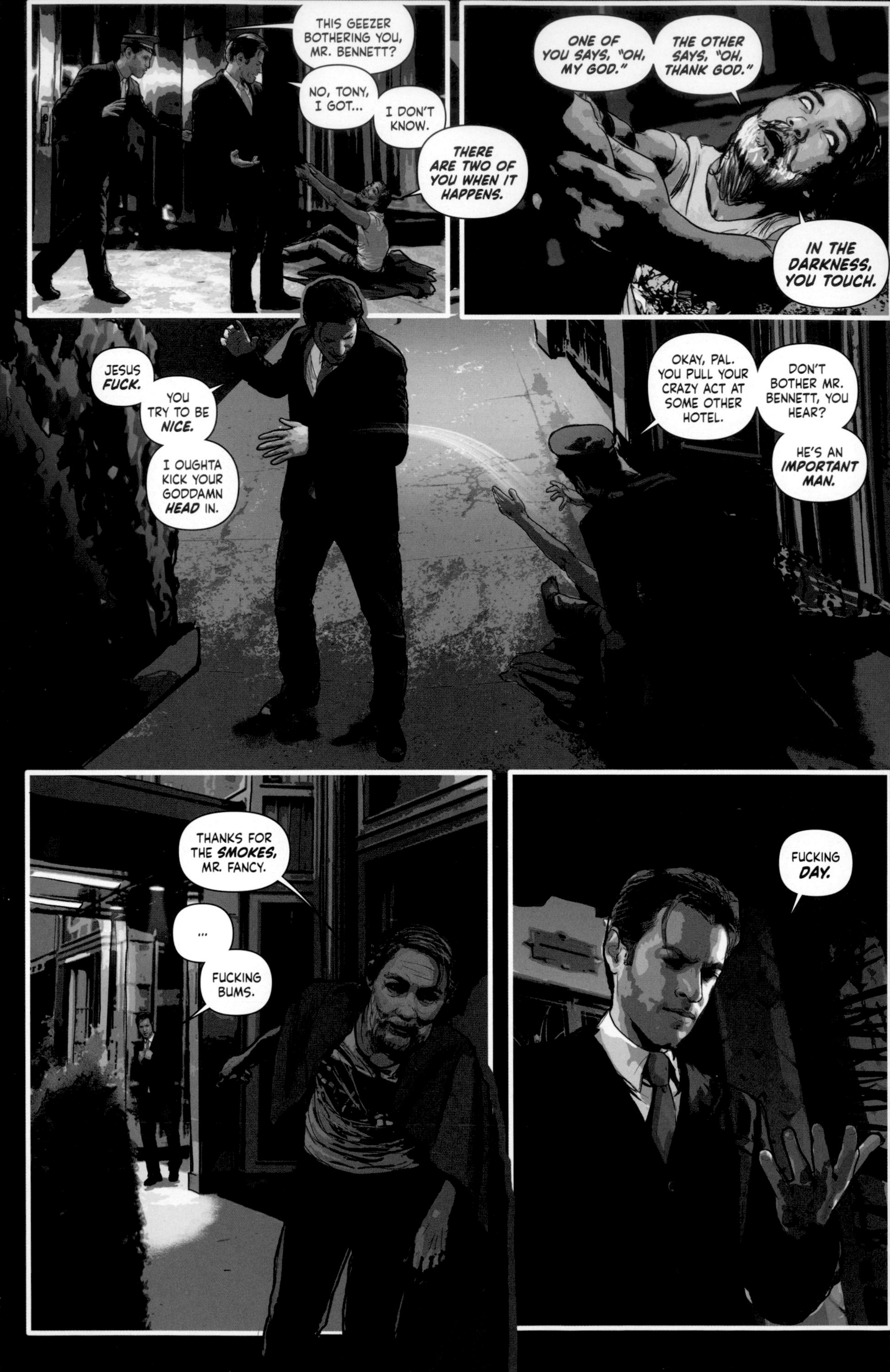
THIS GEEZER BOTHERING YOU, MR. BENNETT?
NO, TONY, I GOT...
I DON'T KNOW.
THERE ARE TWO OF YOU WHEN IT HAPPENS.
ONE OF YOU SAYS, "OH, MY GOD."
THE OTHER SAYS, "OH, THANK GOD."
IN THE DARKNESS, YOU TOUCH.
JESUS FUCK.
YOU TRY TO BE NICE.
I OUGHTA KICK YOUR GODDAMN HEAD IN.
OKAY, PAL. YOU PULL YOUR CRAZY ACT AT SOME OTHER HOTEL.
DON'T BOTHER MR. BENNETT, YOU HEAR?
HE'S AN IMPORTANT MAN.
THANKS FOR THE SMOKES, MR. FANCY.
...
FUCKING BUMS.
FUCKING DAY.

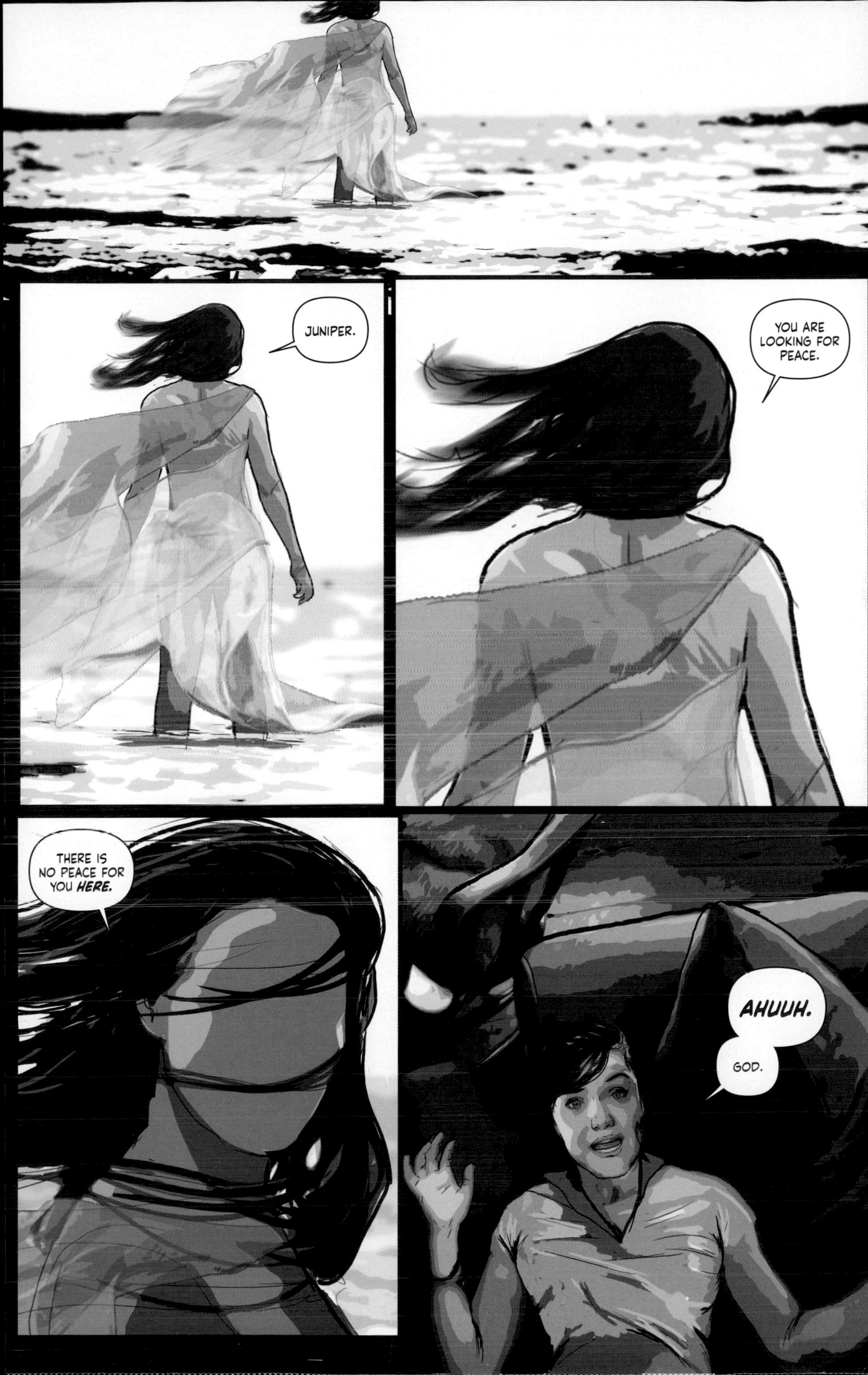
JUNIPER.
YOU ARE LOOKING FOR PEACE.
THERE IS NO PEACE FOR YOU *HERE.*
AHUUH.
GOD.

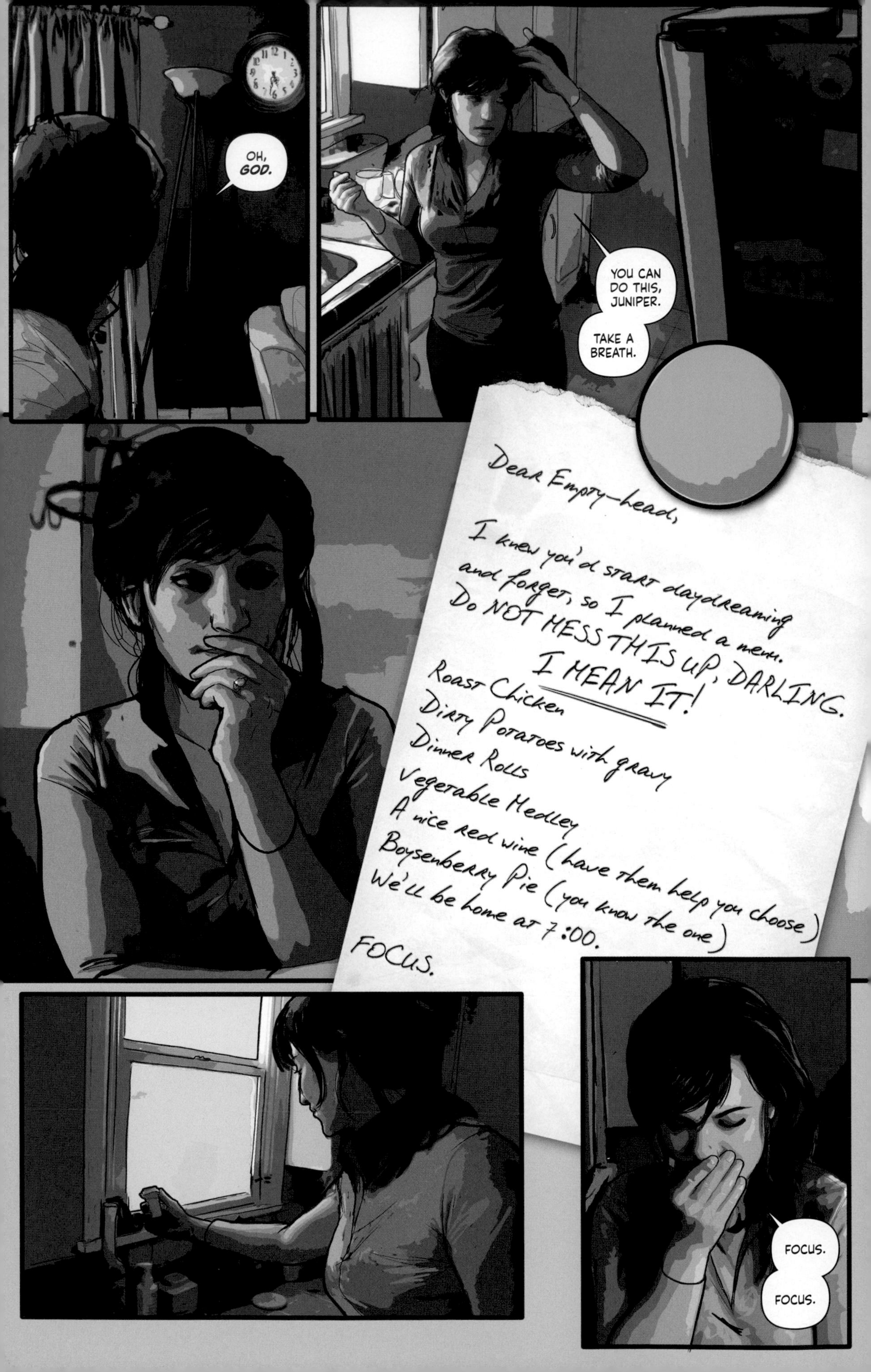
OH, GOD.
YOU CAN DO THIS, JUNIPER.
TAKE A BREATH.
Dear Empty-head,
I knew you'd start daydreaming and forget, so I planned a menu.
Do NOT MESS THIS UP, DARLING.
I MEAN IT!
Roast Chicken
Dirty Potatoes with gravy
Dinner Rolls
Vegetable Medley
A nice red wine (have them help you choose)
Boysenberry Pie (you know the one)
We'll be home at 7:00.
FOCUS.
FOCUS.
FOCUS.

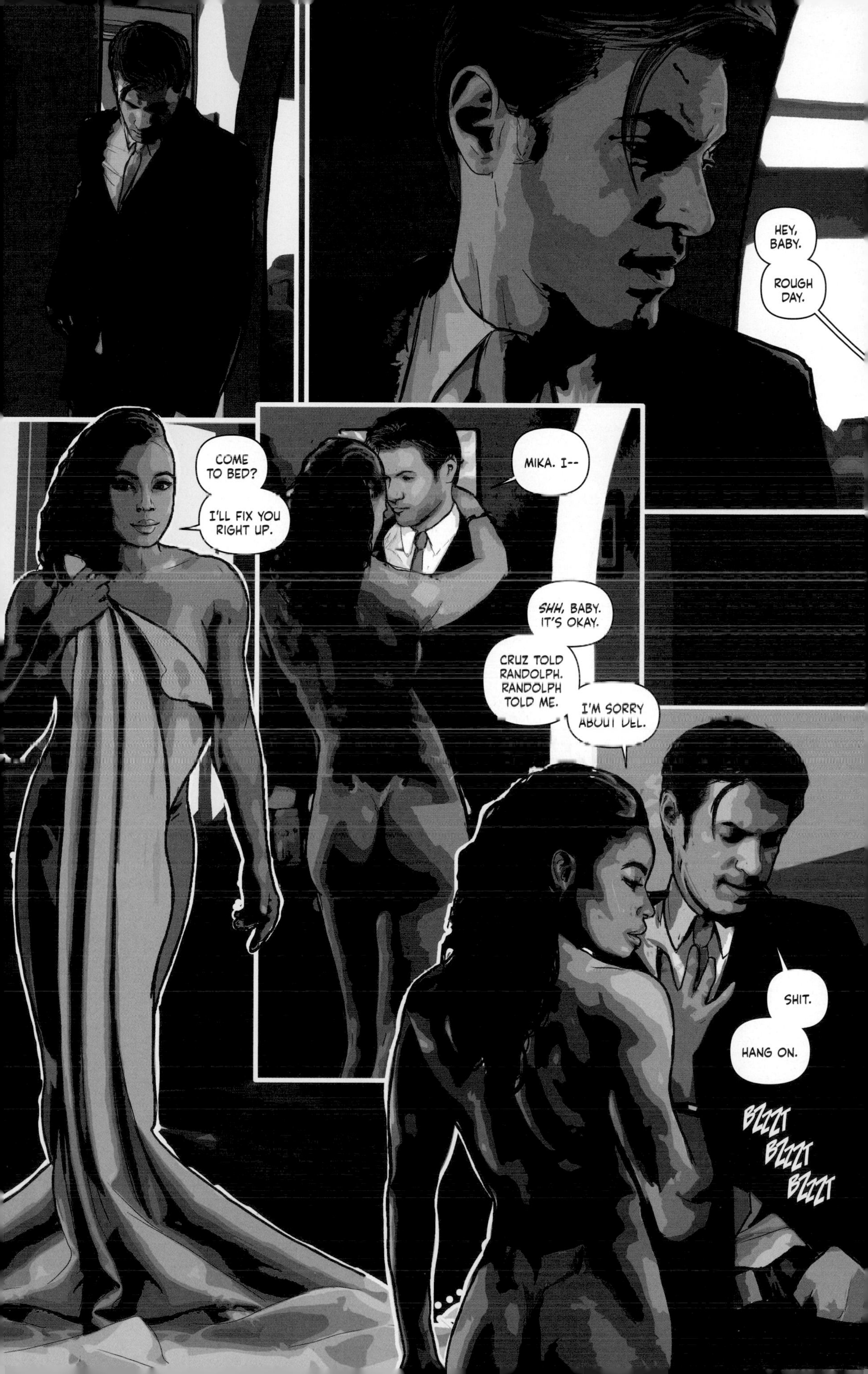
HEY, BABY.
ROUGH DAY.
COME TO BED?
I'LL FIX YOU RIGHT UP.
MIKA. I--
SHH, BABY. IT'S OKAY.
CRUZ TOLD RANDOLPH. RANDOLPH TOLD ME.
I'M SORRY ABOUT DEL.
SHIT.
HANG ON.
BZZZT
BZZZT
BZZZT

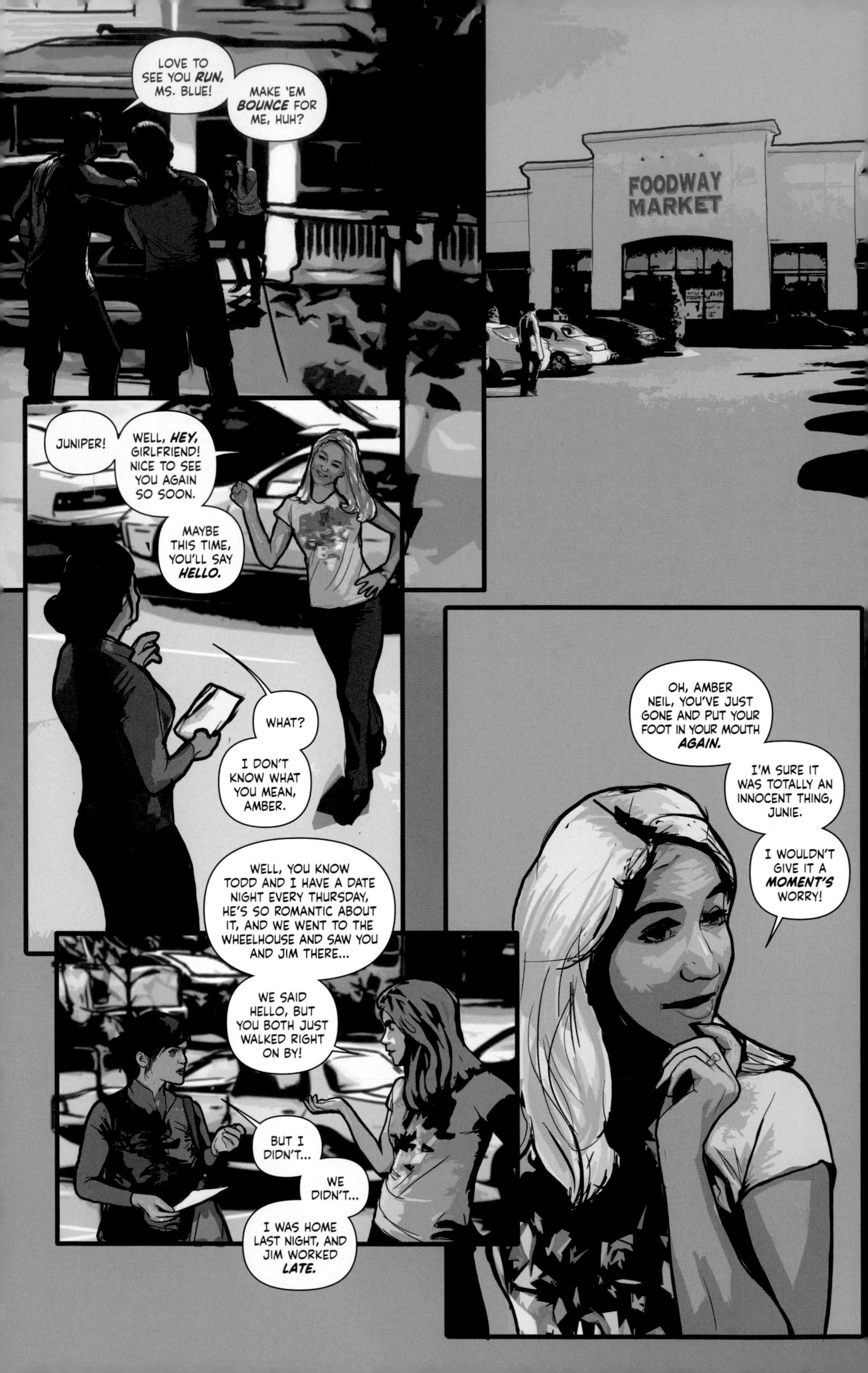
LOVE TO SEE YOU RUN, MS. BLUE!
MAKE 'EM BOUNCE FOR ME, HUH?
FOODWAY MARKET
JUNIPER!
WELL, HEY, GIRLFRIEND! NICE TO SEE YOU AGAIN SO SOON.
MAYBE THIS TIME, YOU'LL SAY HELLO.
WHAT?
I DON'T KNOW WHAT YOU MEAN, AMBER.
WELL, YOU KNOW TODD AND I HAVE A DATE NIGHT EVERY THURSDAY, HE'S SO ROMANTIC ABOUT IT, AND WE WENT TO THE WHEELHOUSE AND SAW YOU AND JIM THERE...
WE SAID HELLO, BUT YOU BOTH JUST WALKED RIGHT ON BY!
BUT I DIDN'T...
WE DIDN'T...
I WAS HOME LAST NIGHT, AND JIM WORKED LATE.
OH, AMBER NEIL, YOU'VE JUST GONE AND PUT YOUR FOOT IN YOUR MOUTH AGAIN.
I'M SURE IT WAS TOTALLY AN INNOCENT THING, JUNIE.
I WOULDN'T GIVE IT A MOMENT'S WORRY!

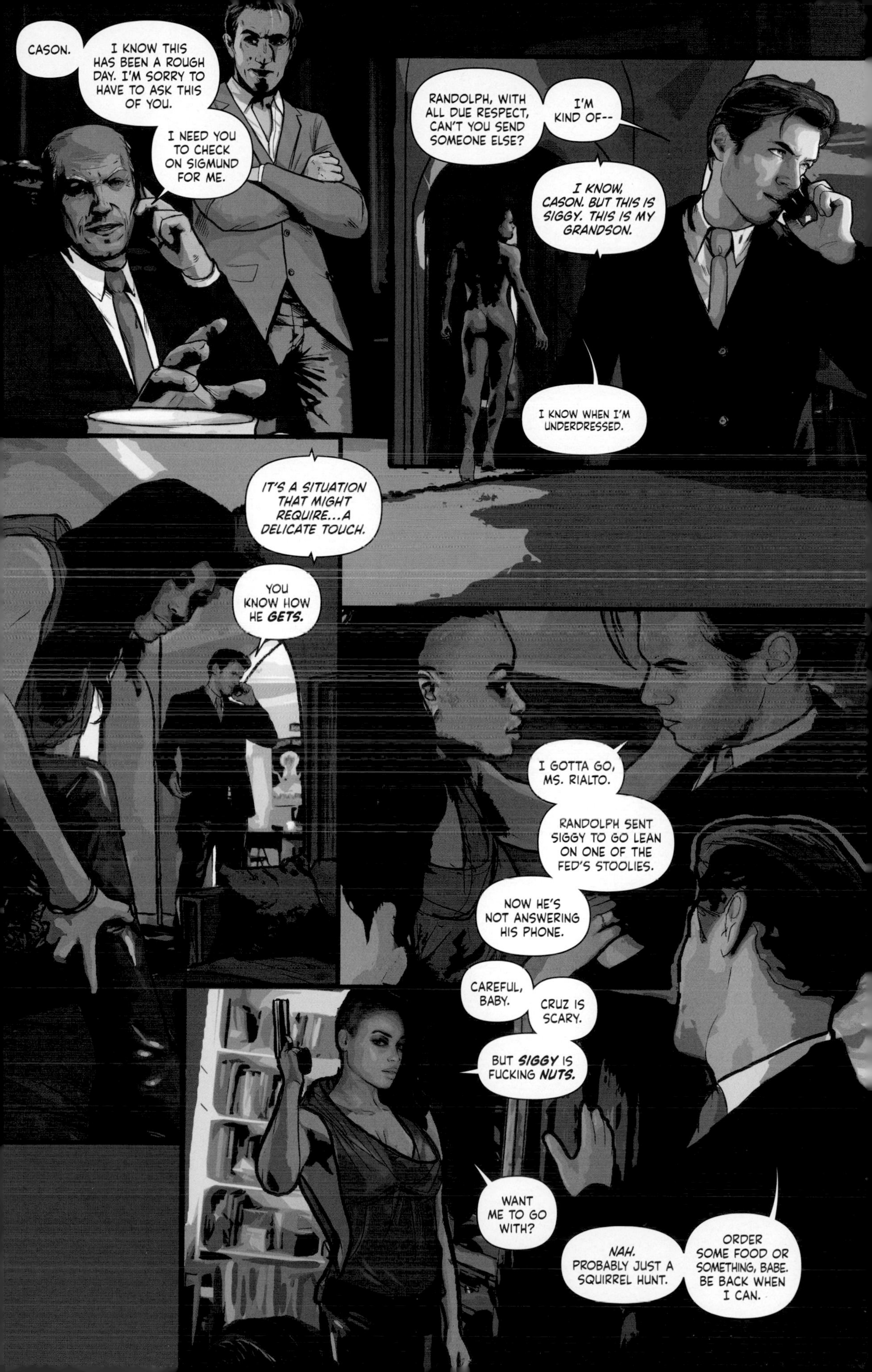
CASON.
I KNOW THIS HAS BEEN A ROUGH DAY. I'M SORRY TO HAVE TO ASK THIS OF YOU.
I NEED YOU TO CHECK ON SIGMUND FOR ME.
RANDOLPH, WITH ALL DUE RESPECT, CAN'T YOU SEND SOMEONE ELSE?
I'M KIND OF--
I KNOW, CASON. BUT THIS IS SIGGY. THIS IS MY GRANDSON.
I KNOW WHEN I'M UNDERDRESSED.
IT'S A SITUATION THAT MIGHT REQUIRE...A DELICATE TOUCH.
YOU KNOW HOW HE GETS.
I GOTTA GO, MS. RIALTO.
RANDOLPH SENT SIGGY TO GO LEAN ON ONE OF THE FED'S STOOLIES.
NOW HE'S NOT ANSWERING HIS PHONE.
CAREFUL, BABY.
CRUZ IS SCARY.
BUT SIGGY IS FUCKING NUTS.
WANT ME TO GO WITH?
NAH. PROBABLY JUST A SQUIRREL HUNT.
ORDER SOME FOOD OR SOMETHING, BABE. BE BACK WHEN I CAN.

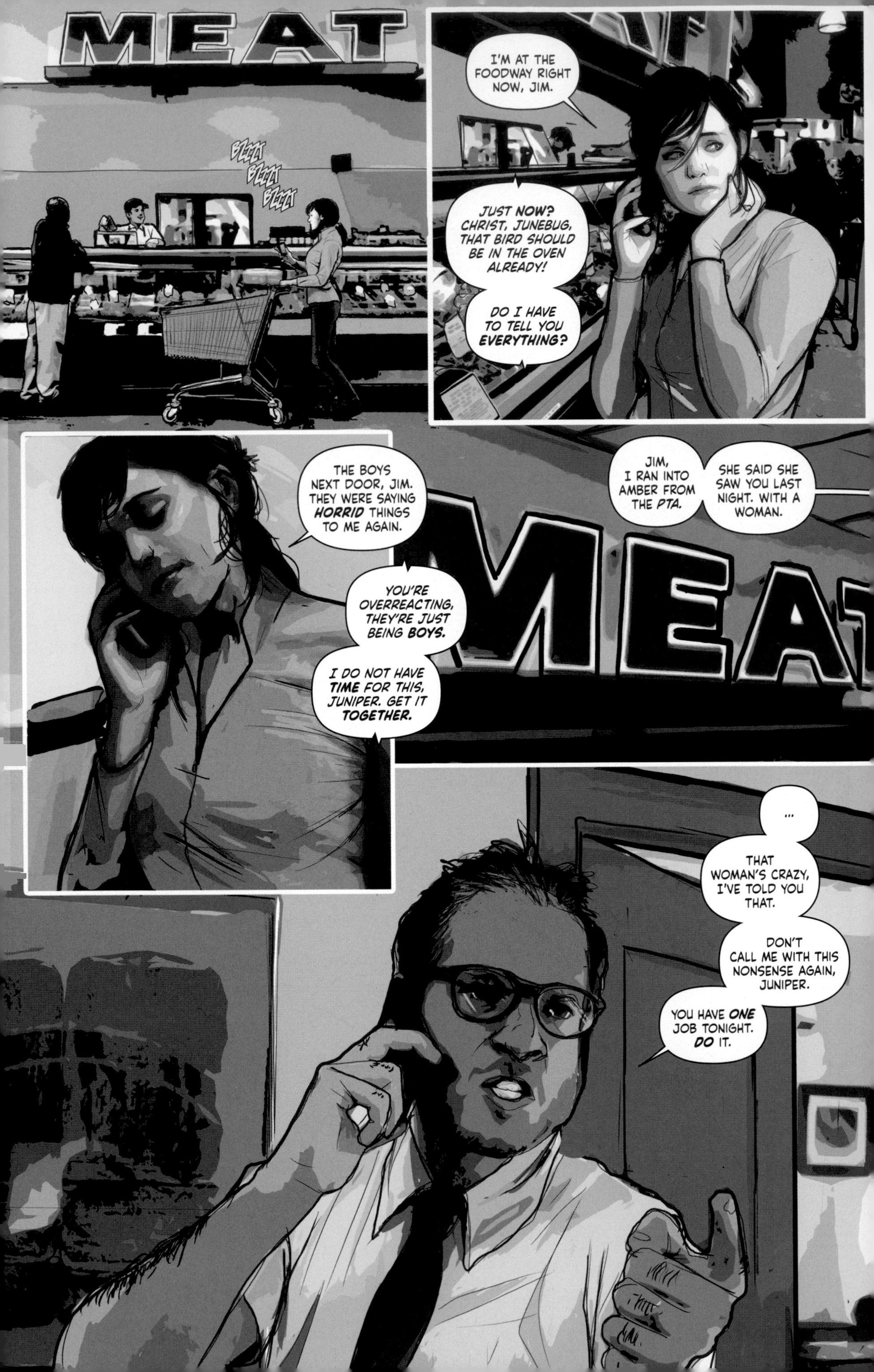
MEAT
BZZZT BZZZT BZZZT
I'M AT THE FOODWAY RIGHT NOW, JIM.
JUST NOW? CHRIST, JUNEBUG, THAT BIRD SHOULD BE IN THE OVEN ALREADY!
DO I HAVE TO TELL YOU EVERYTHING?
THE BOYS NEXT DOOR, JIM. THEY WERE SAYING HORRID THINGS TO ME AGAIN.
YOU'RE OVERREACTING, THEY'RE JUST BEING BOYS.
I DO NOT HAVE TIME FOR THIS, JUNIPER. GET IT TOGETHER.
JIM, I RAN INTO AMBER FROM THE PTA.
SHE SAID SHE SAW YOU LAST NIGHT. WITH A WOMAN.
MEAT
...
THAT WOMAN'S CRAZY, I'VE TOLD YOU THAT.
DON'T CALL ME WITH THIS NONSENSE AGAIN, JUNIPER.
YOU HAVE ONE JOB TONIGHT. DO IT.

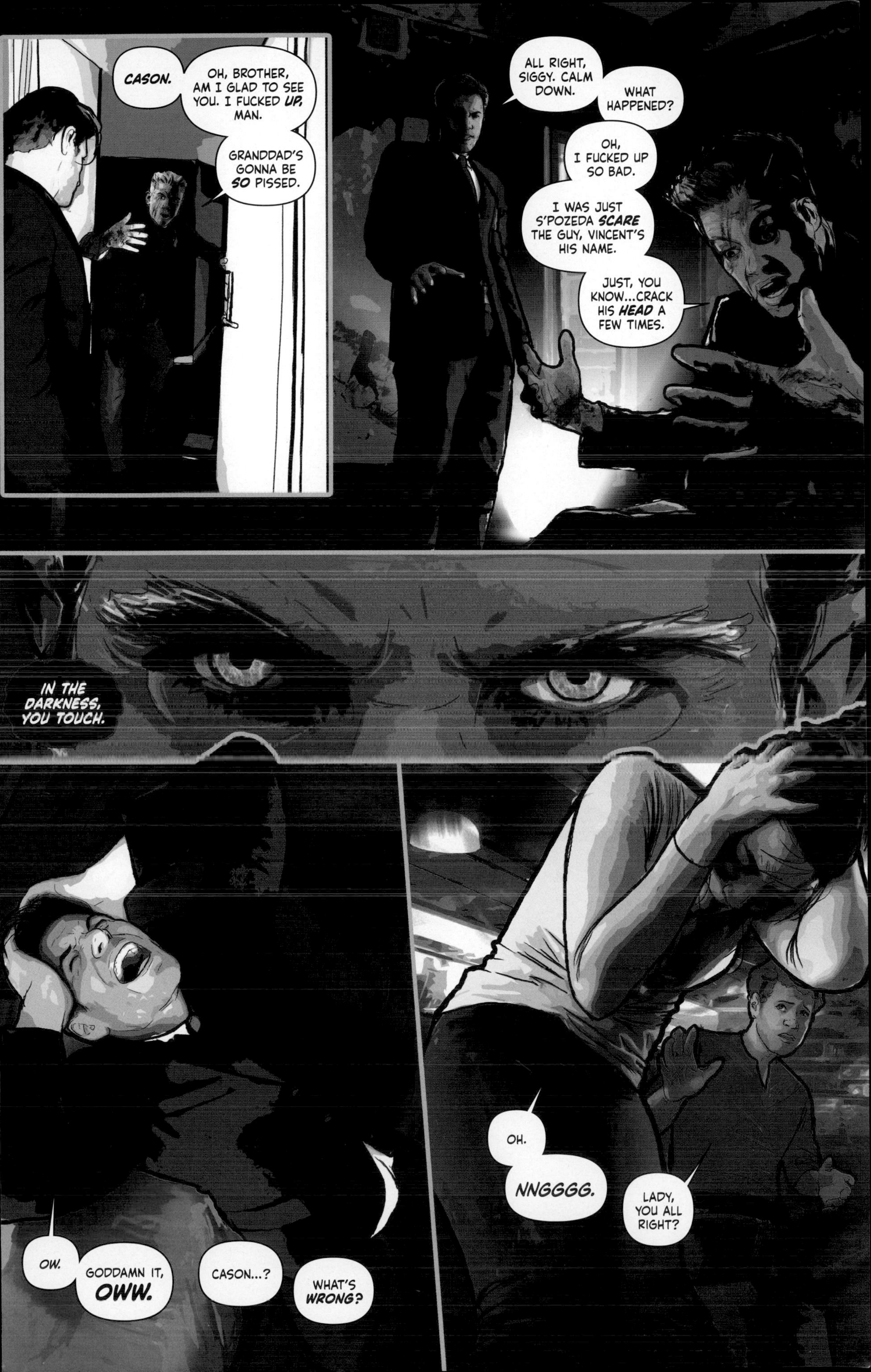
CASON.
OH, BROTHER, AM I GLAD TO SEE YOU. I FUCKED UP, MAN.
GRANDDAD'S GONNA BE SO PISSED.
ALL RIGHT, SIGGY. CALM DOWN.
WHAT HAPPENED?
OH, I FUCKED UP SO BAD.
I WAS JUST S'POZEDA SCARE THE GUY, VINCENT'S HIS NAME.
JUST, YOU KNOW...CRACK HIS HEAD A FEW TIMES.
IN THE DARKNESS, YOU TOUCH.
OW.
GODDAMN IT, OWW.
CASON...?
WHAT'S WRONG?
OH.
NNGGGG.
LADY, YOU ALL RIGHT?

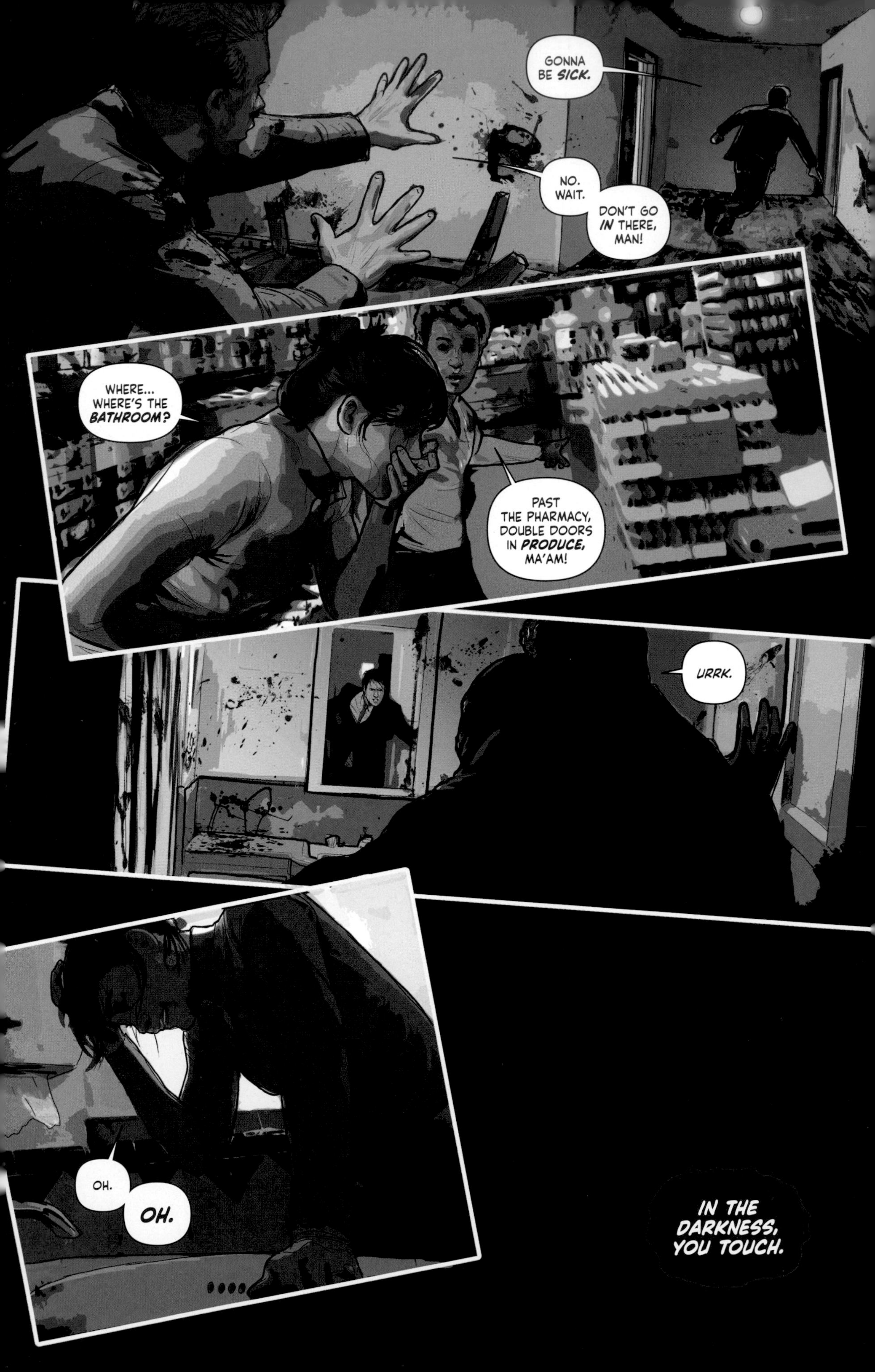
GONNA BE SICK.
NO. WAIT.
DON'T GO IN THERE, MAN!
WHERE... WHERE'S THE BATHROOM?
PAST THE PHARMACY, DOUBLE DOORS IN PRODUCE, MA'AM!
URRK.
OH.
OH.
IN THE DARKNESS, YOU TOUCH.

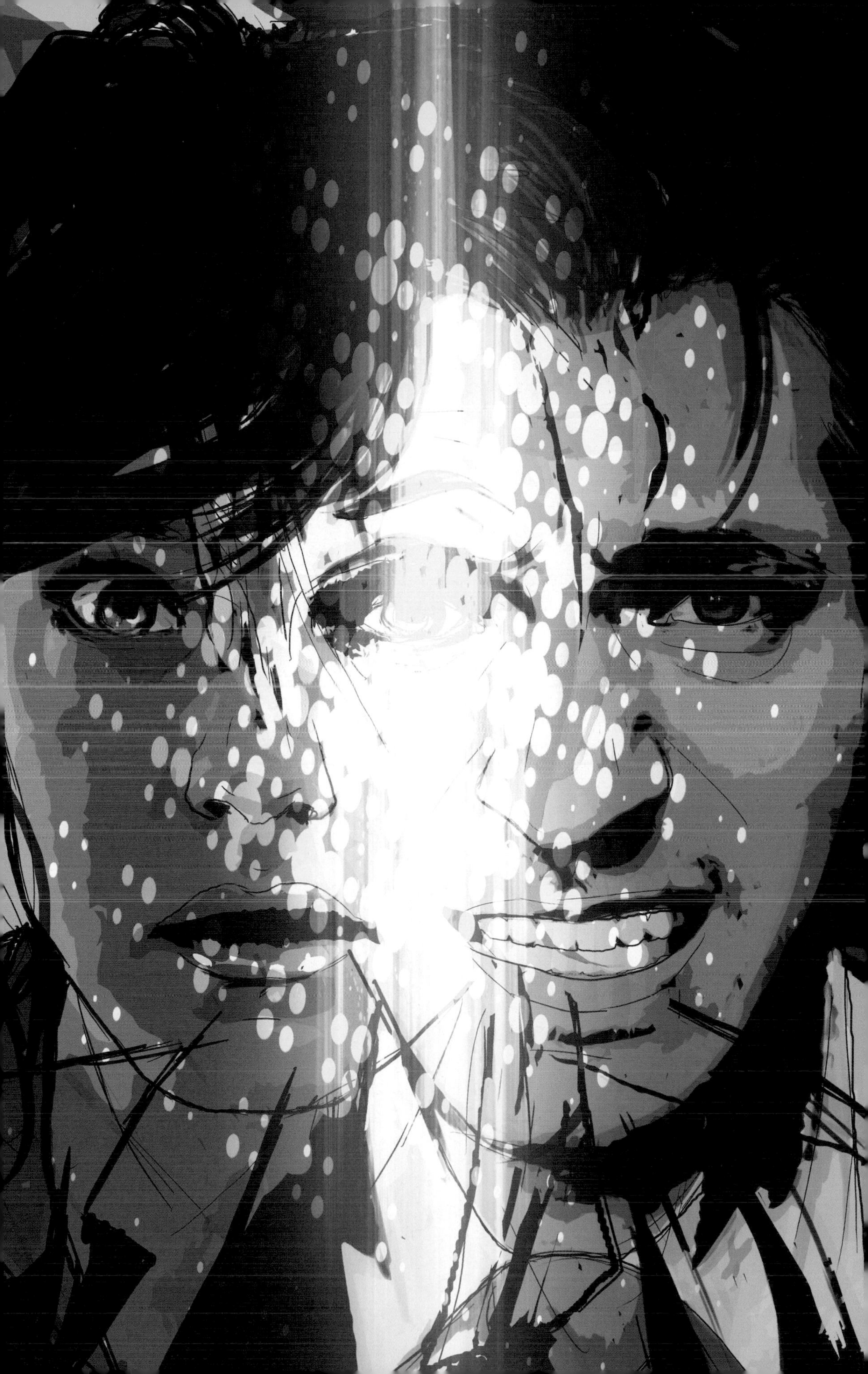

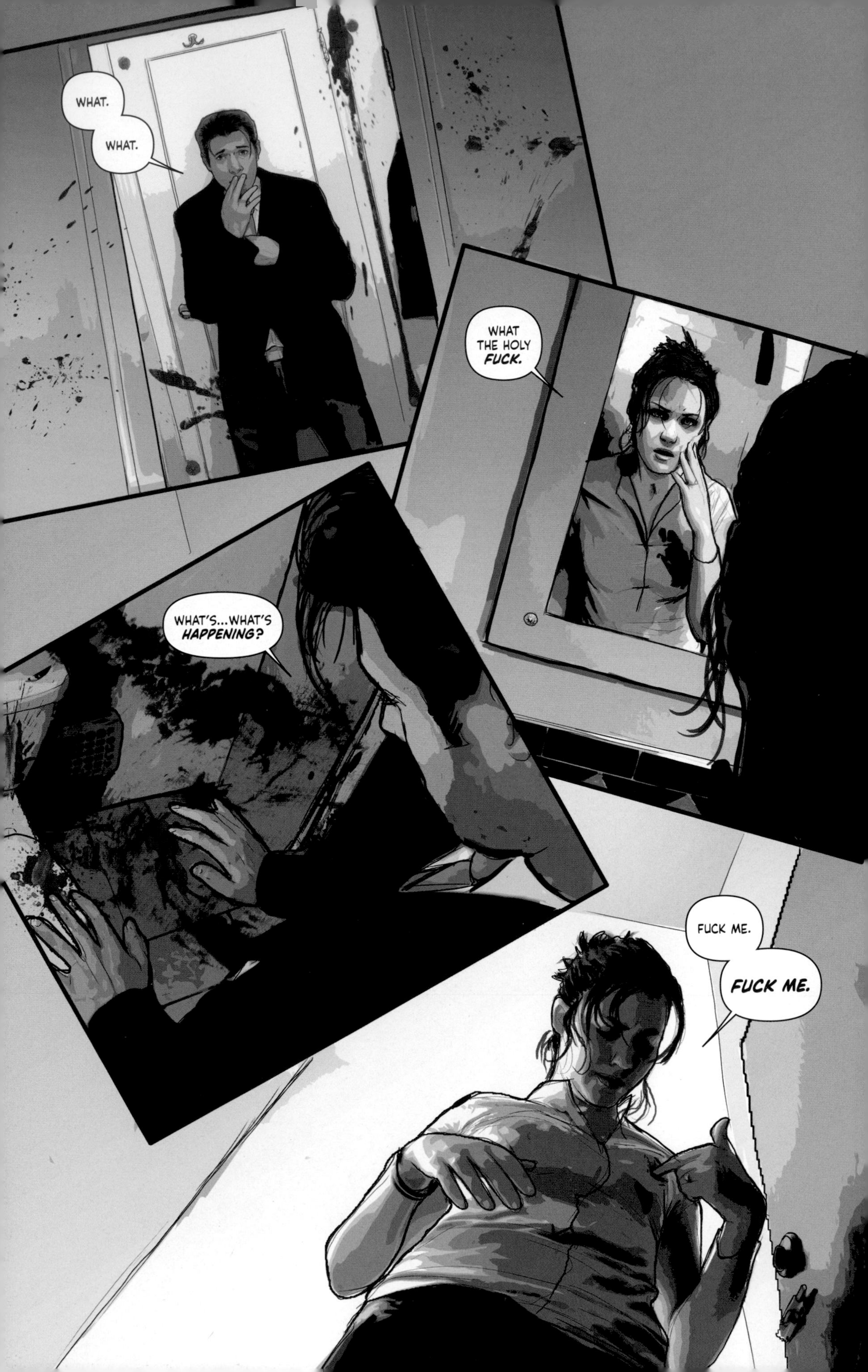
WHAT.
WHAT.
WHAT THE HOLY FUCK.
WHAT'S...WHAT'S HAPPENING?
FUCK ME.
FUCK ME.

AND ONE SAID,
"OH, MY GOD."

AND THE OTHER SAID,
"OH, THANK GOD."

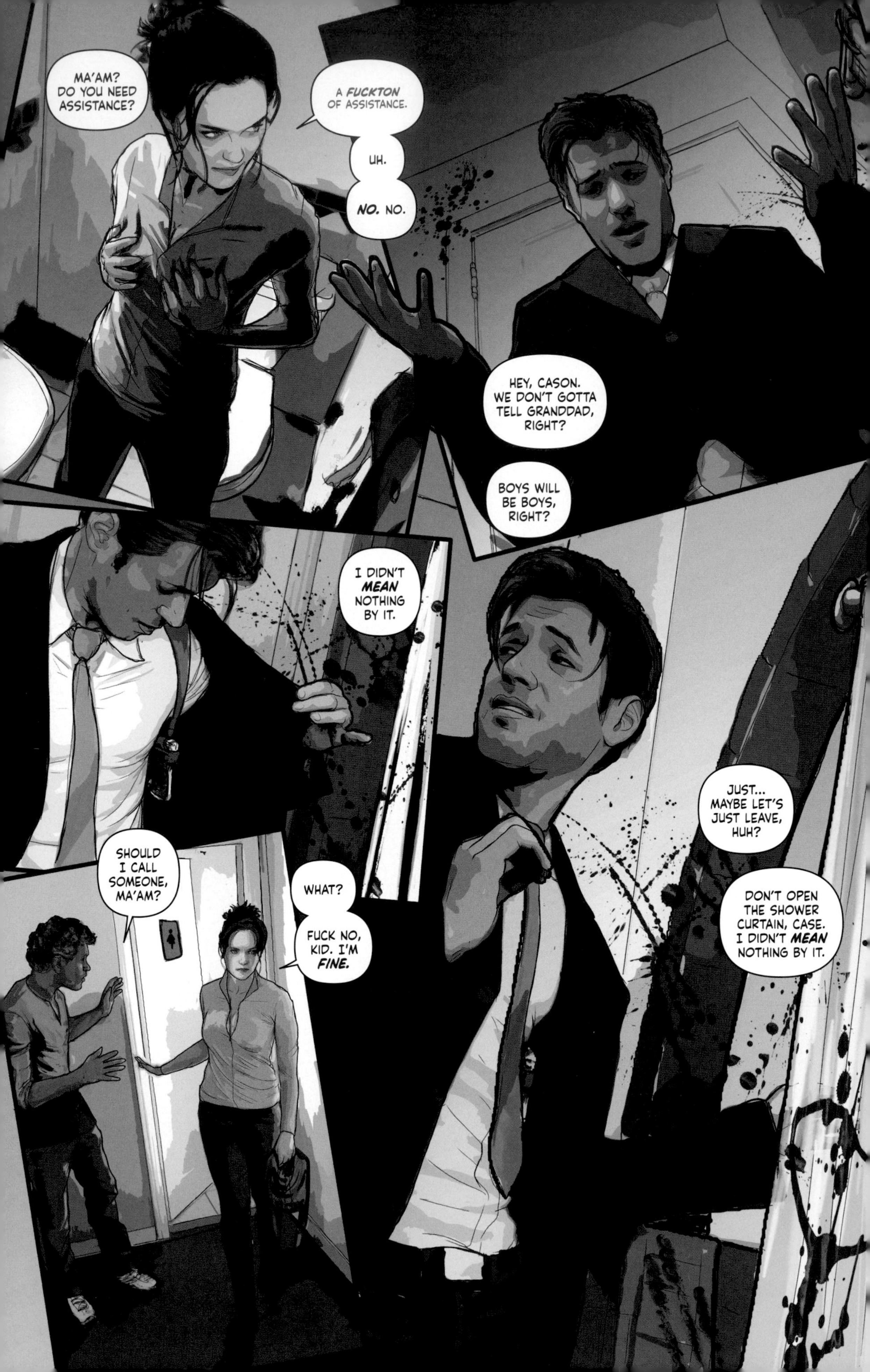
MA'AM? DO YOU NEED ASSISTANCE?
A *FUCKTON* OF ASSISTANCE.
UH.
NO. NO.
HEY, CASON. WE DON'T GOTTA TELL GRANDDAD, RIGHT?
BOYS WILL BE BOYS, RIGHT?
I DIDN'T *MEAN* NOTHING BY IT.
JUST... MAYBE LET'S JUST LEAVE, HUH?
DON'T OPEN THE SHOWER CURTAIN, CASE. I DIDN'T *MEAN* NOTHING BY IT.
SHOULD I CALL SOMEONE, MA'AM?
WHAT?
FUCK NO, KID. I'M *FINE.*

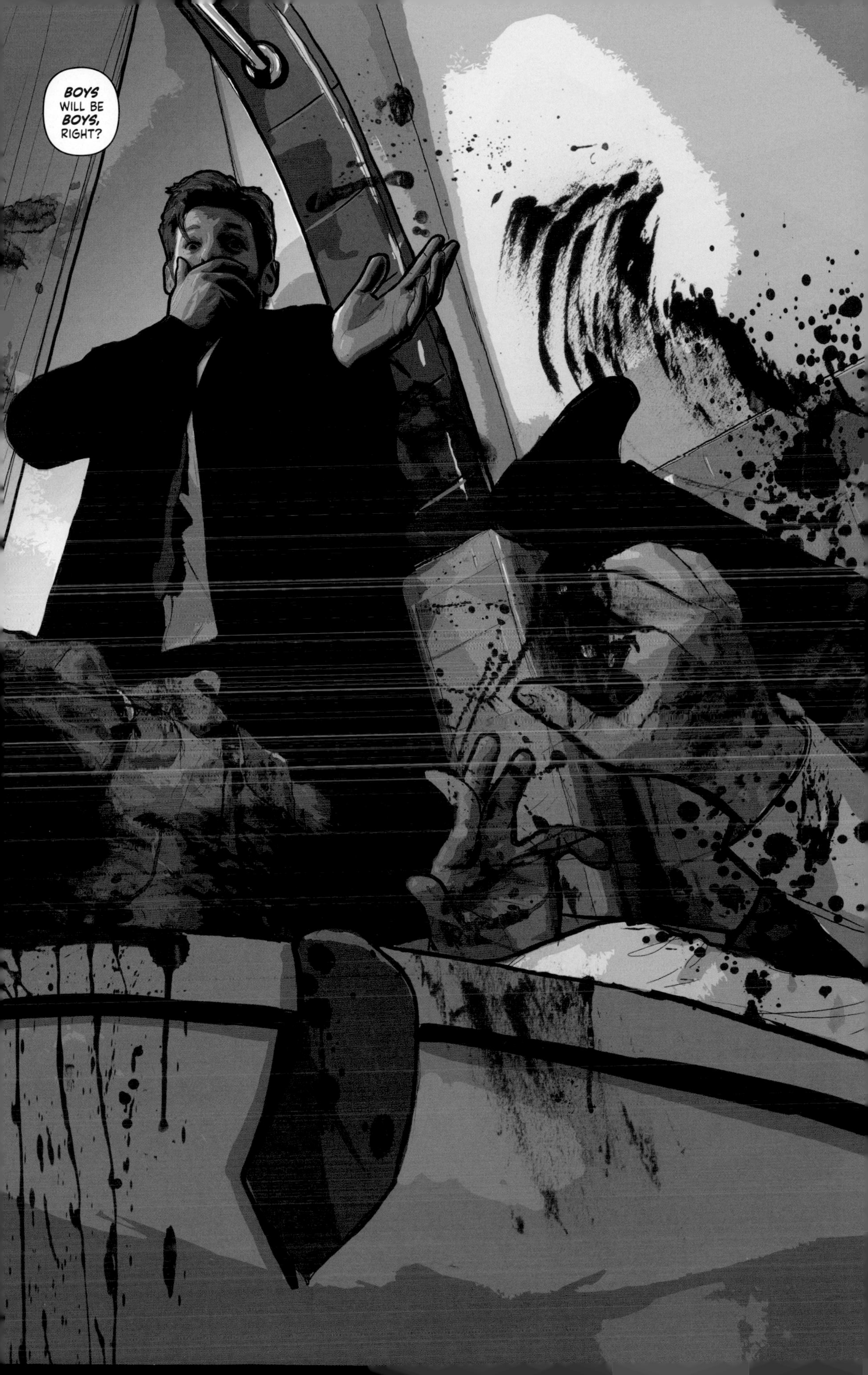
BOYS WILL BE BOYS, RIGHT?

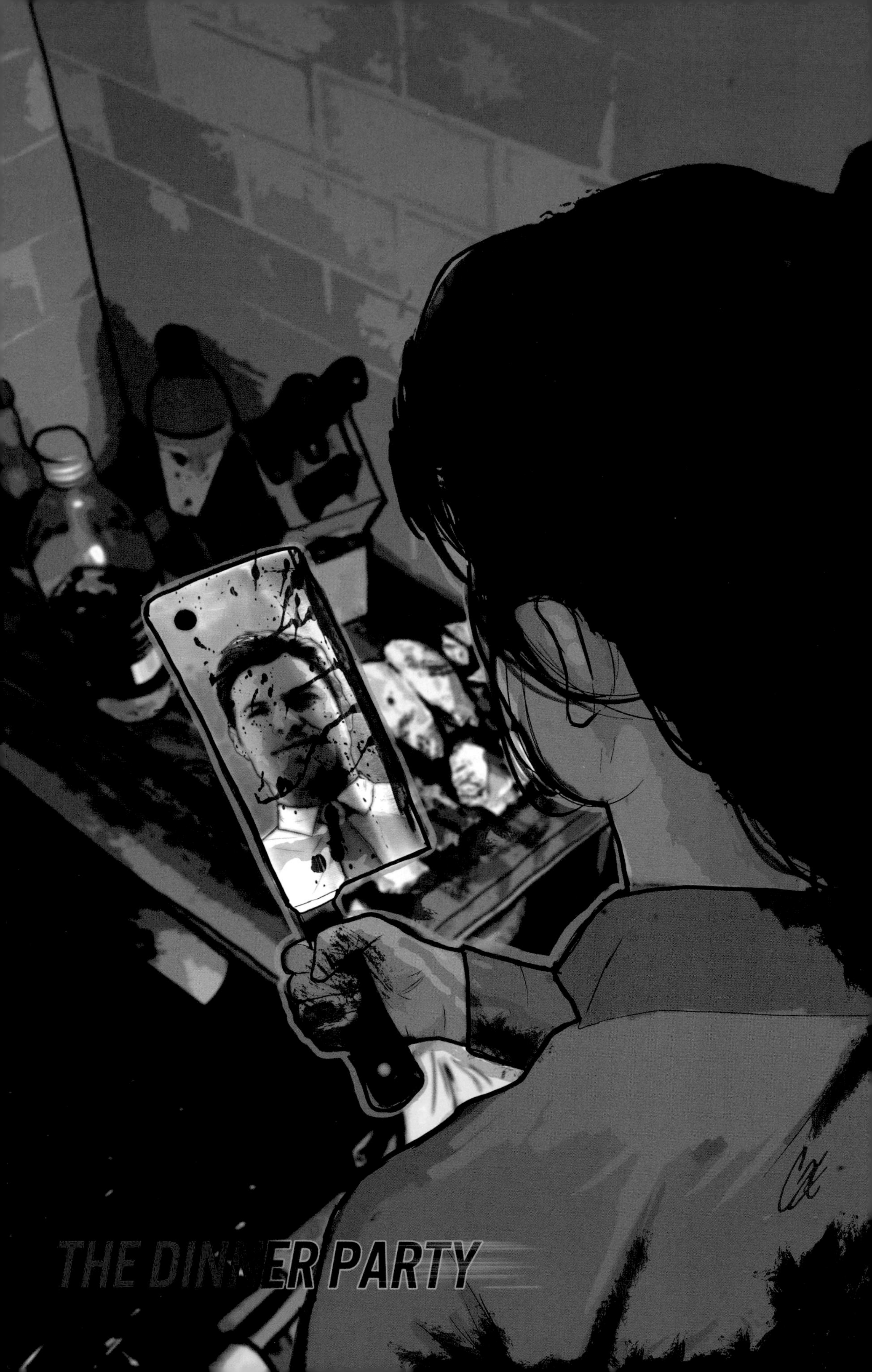
THE DINNER PARTY

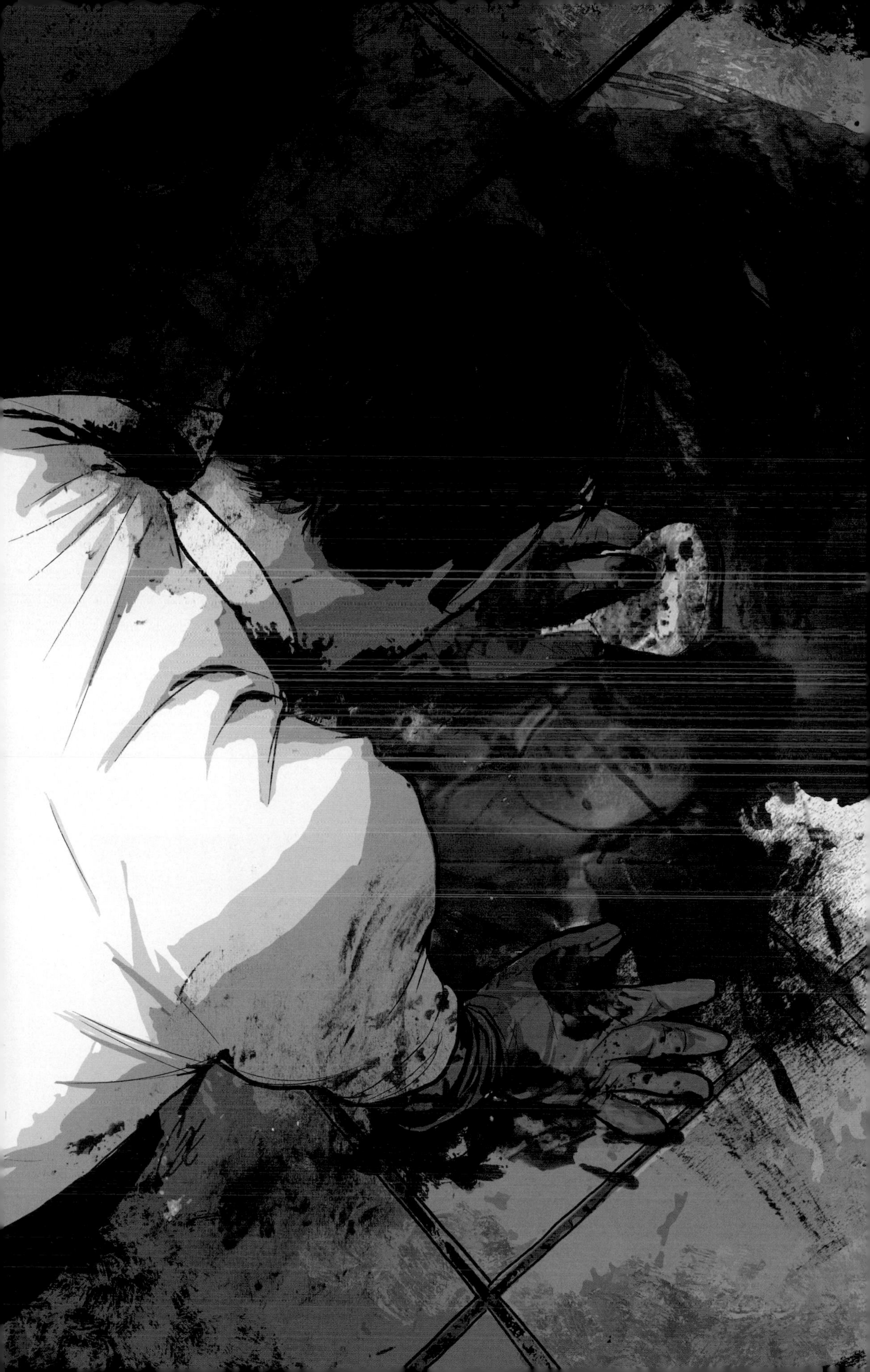

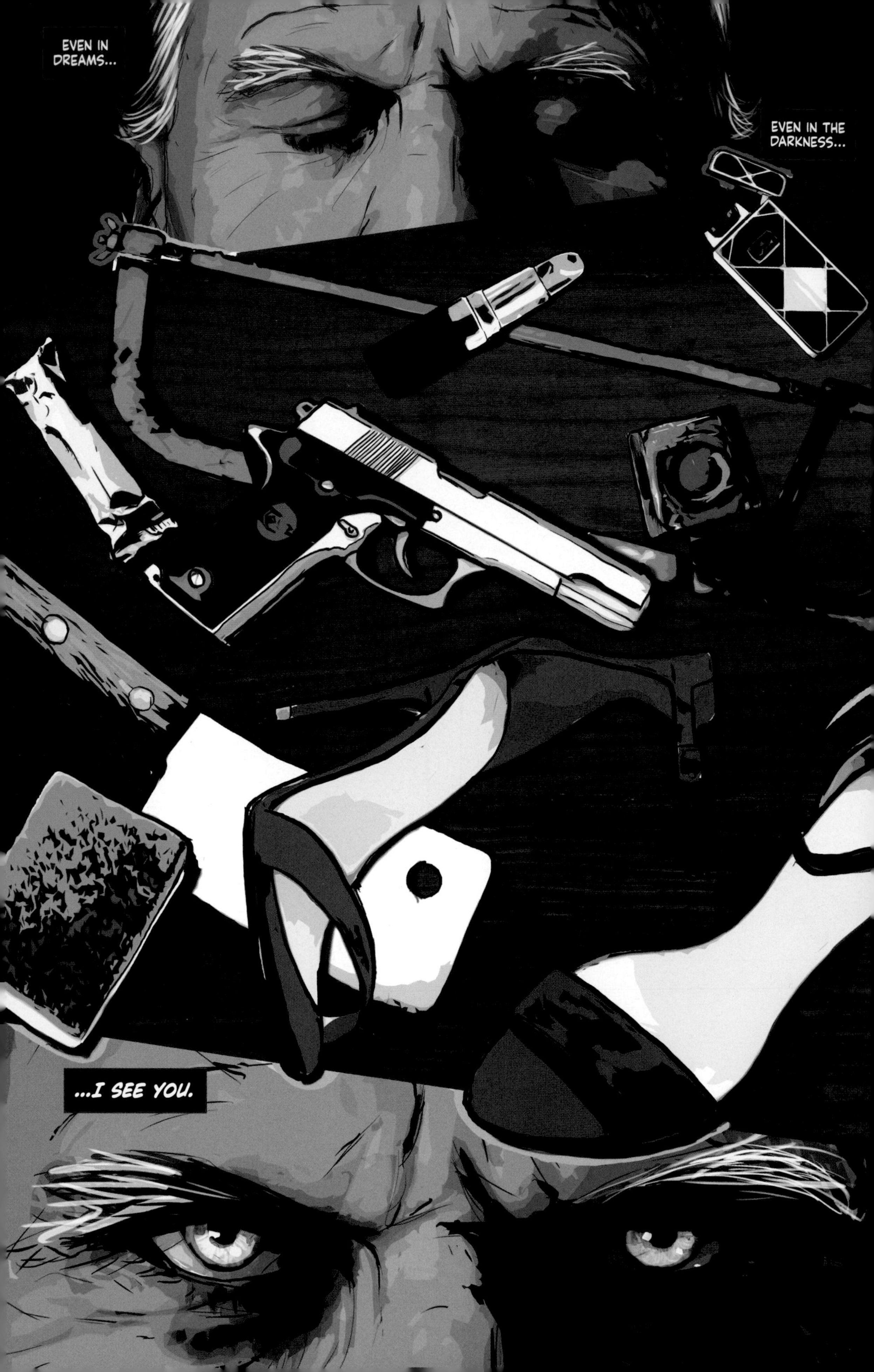
EVEN IN DREAMS...
EVEN IN THE DARKNESS...
...I SEE YOU.

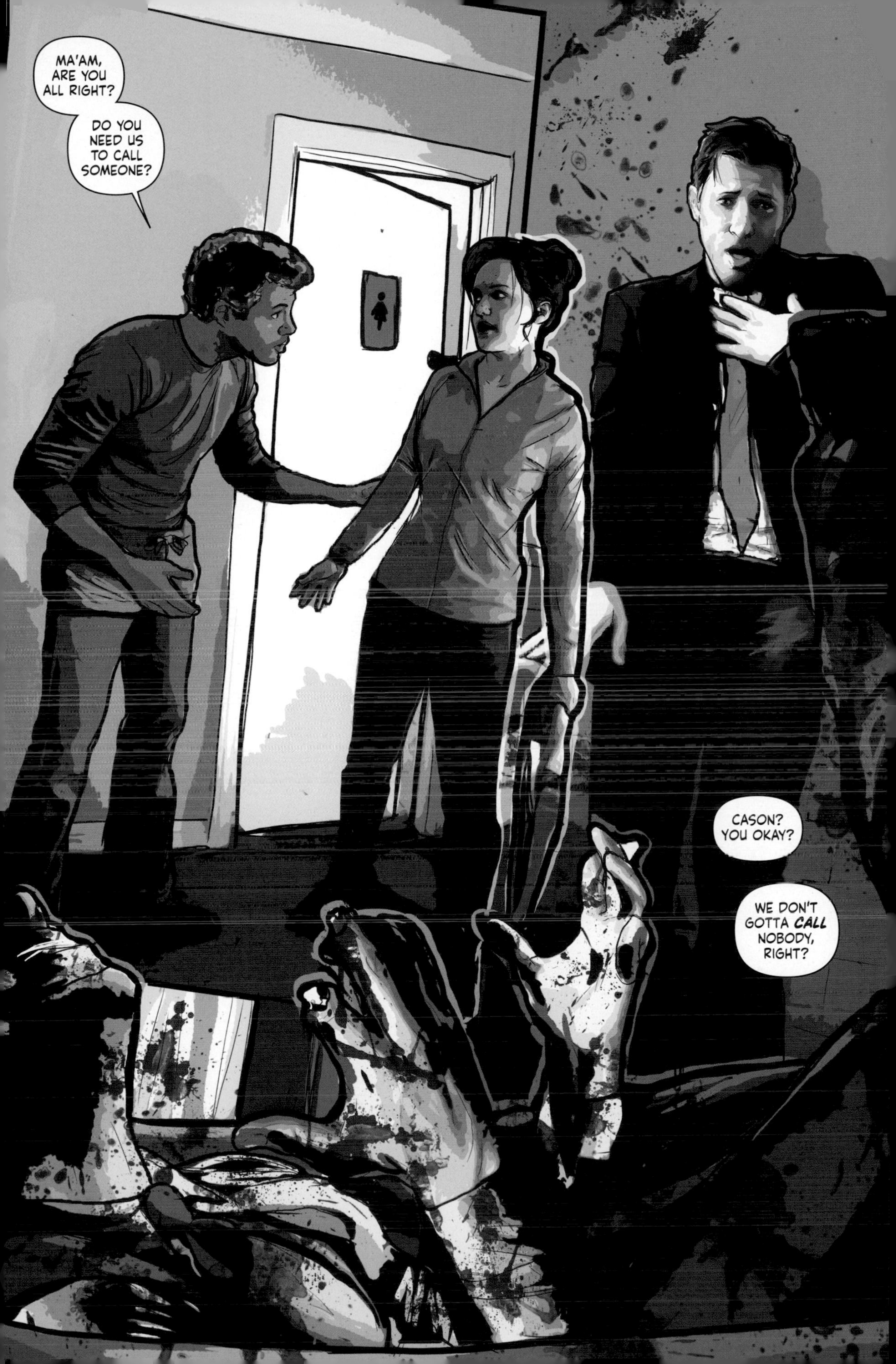
MA'AM, ARE YOU ALL RIGHT?
DO YOU NEED US TO CALL SOMEONE?
CASON? YOU OKAY?
WE DON'T GOTTA **CALL** NOBODY, RIGHT?

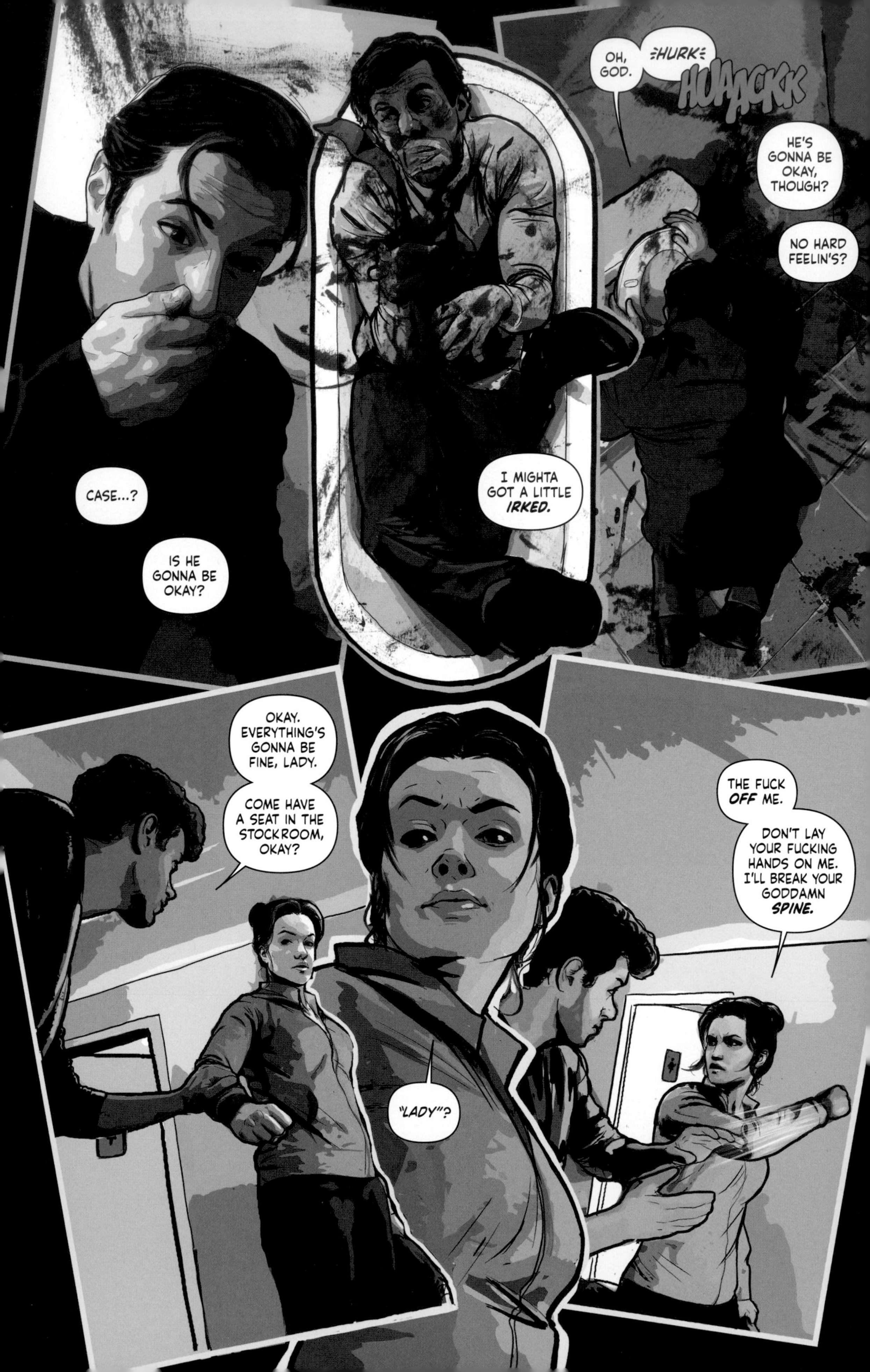
OH, GOD.
HURK
HUAACKK
HE'S GONNA BE OKAY, THOUGH?
NO HARD FEELIN'S?
CASE...?
IS HE GONNA BE OKAY?
I MIGHTA GOT A LITTLE IRKED.
OKAY. EVERYTHING'S GONNA BE FINE, LADY.
COME HAVE A SEAT IN THE STOCKROOM, OKAY?
"LADY"?
THE FUCK OFF ME.
DON'T LAY YOUR FUCKING HANDS ON ME. I'LL BREAK YOUR GODDAMN SPINE.

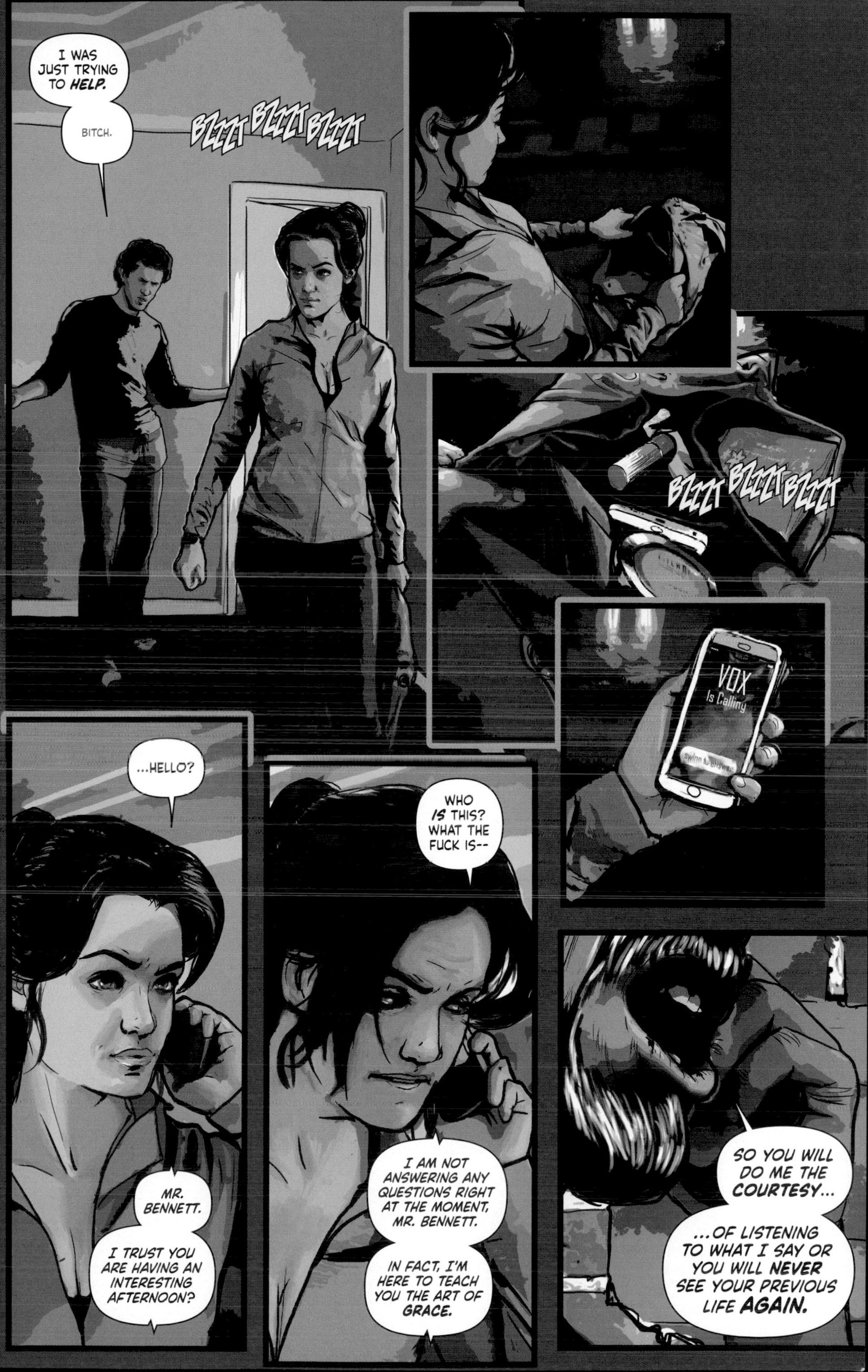
I WAS JUST TRYING TO HELP.
BITCH.
BZZZT BZZZT BZZZT
BZZZT BZZZT BZZZT
VOX
Is Calling
...HELLO?
MR. BENNETT.
I TRUST YOU ARE HAVING AN INTERESTING AFTERNOON?
WHO IS THIS? WHAT THE FUCK IS--
I AM NOT ANSWERING ANY QUESTIONS RIGHT AT THE MOMENT, MR. BENNETT.
IN FACT, I'M HERE TO TEACH YOU THE ART OF GRACE.
SO YOU WILL DO ME THE COURTESY...
...OF LISTENING TO WHAT I SAY OR YOU WILL NEVER SEE YOUR PREVIOUS LIFE AGAIN.

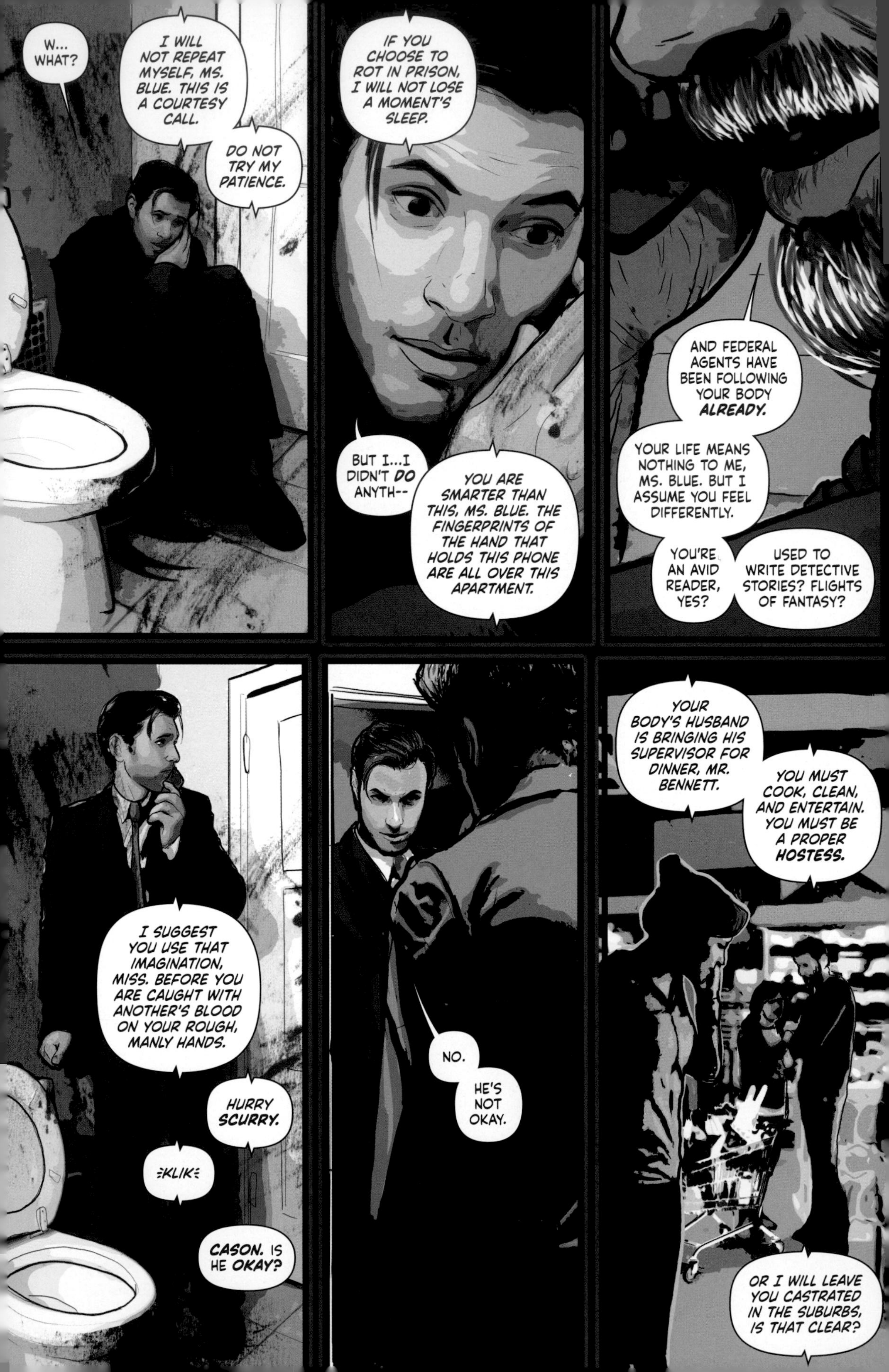
W... WHAT?
I WILL NOT REPEAT MYSELF, MS. BLUE. THIS IS A COURTESY CALL.
DO NOT TRY MY PATIENCE.
IF YOU CHOOSE TO ROT IN PRISON, I WILL NOT LOSE A MOMENT'S SLEEP.
BUT I...I DIDN'T *DO* ANYTH--
YOU ARE SMARTER THAN THIS, MS. BLUE. THE FINGERPRINTS OF THE HAND THAT HOLDS THIS PHONE ARE ALL OVER THIS APARTMENT.
AND FEDERAL AGENTS HAVE BEEN FOLLOWING YOUR BODY ***ALREADY.***
YOUR LIFE MEANS NOTHING TO ME, MS. BLUE. BUT I ASSUME YOU FEEL DIFFERENTLY.
YOU'RE AN AVID READER, YES?
USED TO WRITE DETECTIVE STORIES? FLIGHTS OF FANTASY?
I SUGGEST YOU USE THAT IMAGINATION, MISS. BEFORE YOU ARE CAUGHT WITH ANOTHER'S BLOOD ON YOUR ROUGH, MANLY HANDS.
HURRY ***SCURRY.***
KLIK
CASON. IS HE ***OKAY?***
NO.
HE'S NOT OKAY.
YOUR BODY'S HUSBAND IS BRINGING HIS SUPERVISOR FOR DINNER, MR. BENNETT.
YOU MUST COOK, CLEAN, AND ENTERTAIN. YOU MUST BE A PROPER ***HOSTESS.***
OR I WILL LEAVE YOU CASTRATED IN THE SUBURBS, IS THAT CLEAR?

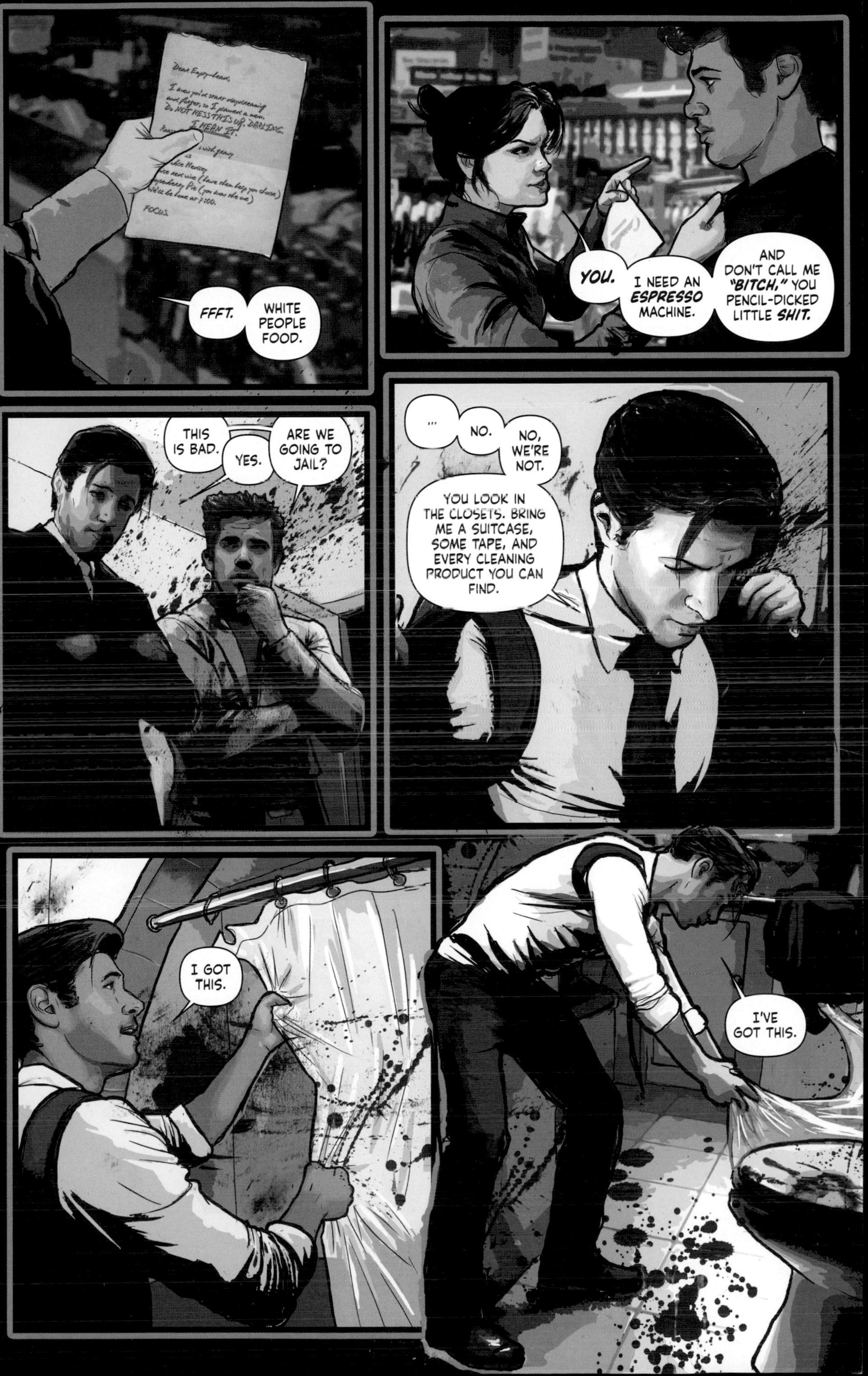

Dear Empty-head,
I knew you'd start daydreaming
and forget, so I planned a menu.
Do NOT MESS THIS UP, DARLING.
I MEAN IT.
We'll be home at 7:00.
FOCUS.
FFFT.
WHITE PEOPLE FOOD.
YOU.
I NEED AN ESPRESSO MACHINE.
AND DON'T CALL ME "BITCH," YOU PENCIL-DICKED LITTLE SHIT.
THIS IS BAD.
YES.
ARE WE GOING TO JAIL?
...
NO.
NO, WE'RE NOT.
YOU LOOK IN THE CLOSETS. BRING ME A SUITCASE, SOME TAPE, AND EVERY CLEANING PRODUCT YOU CAN FIND.
I GOT THIS.
I'VE GOT THIS.

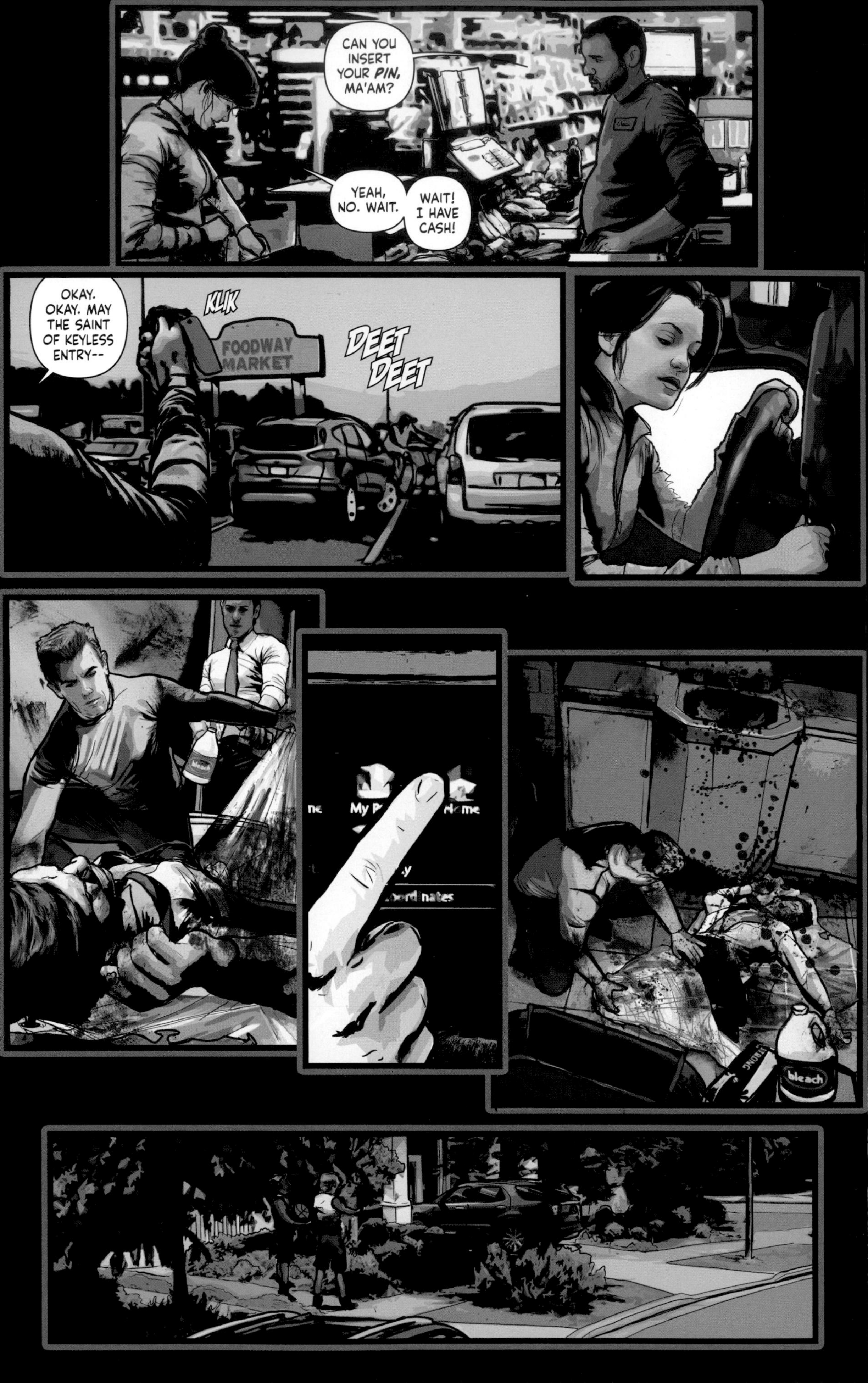
CAN YOU INSERT YOUR PIN, MA'AM?
YEAH, NO. WAIT.
WAIT! I HAVE CASH!
OKAY. OKAY. MAY THE SAINT OF KEYLESS ENTRY--
KLIK
FOODWAY MARKET
DEET DEET
bleach

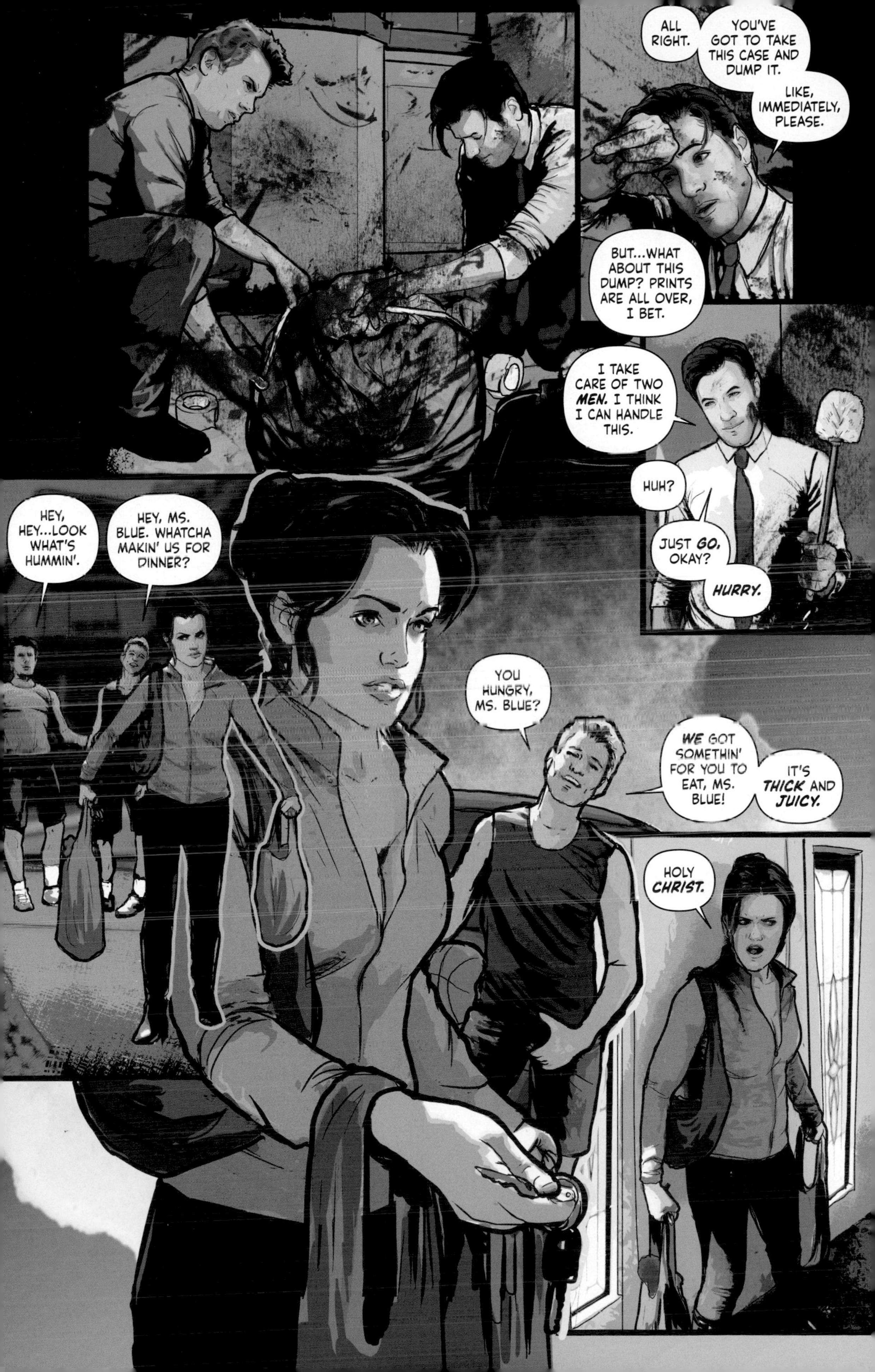
ALL RIGHT.
YOU'VE GOT TO TAKE THIS CASE AND DUMP IT.
LIKE, IMMEDIATELY, PLEASE.
BUT...WHAT ABOUT THIS DUMP? PRINTS ARE ALL OVER, I BET.
I TAKE CARE OF TWO MEN. I THINK I CAN HANDLE THIS.
HUH?
JUST GO, OKAY?
HURRY.
HEY, HEY...LOOK WHAT'S HUMMIN'.
HEY, MS. BLUE. WHATCHA MAKIN' US FOR DINNER?
YOU HUNGRY, MS. BLUE?
WE GOT SOMETHIN' FOR YOU TO EAT, MS. BLUE!
IT'S THICK AND JUICY.
HOLY CHRIST.

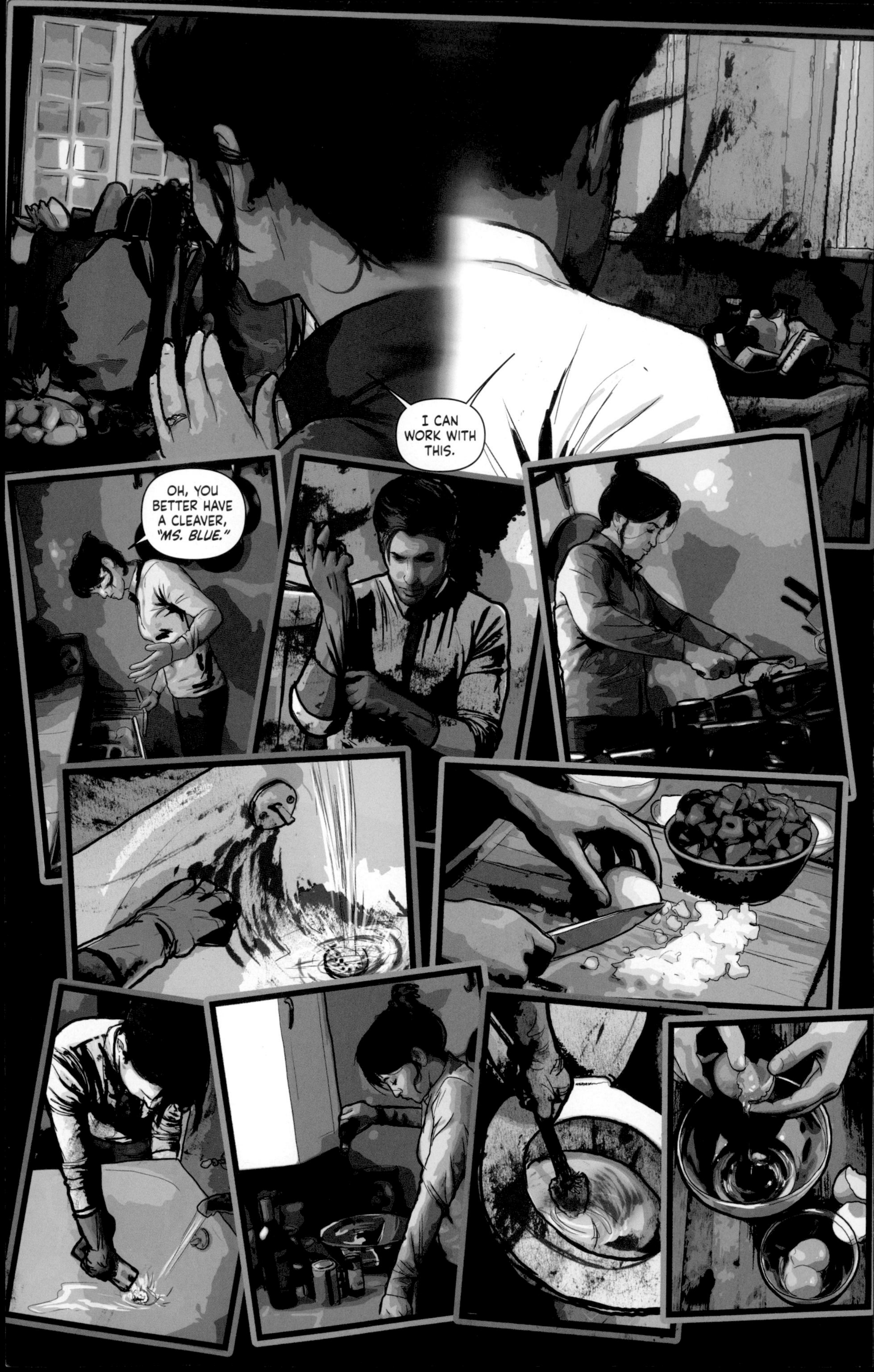
I CAN WORK WITH THIS.
OH, YOU BETTER HAVE A CLEAVER, "MS. BLUE."

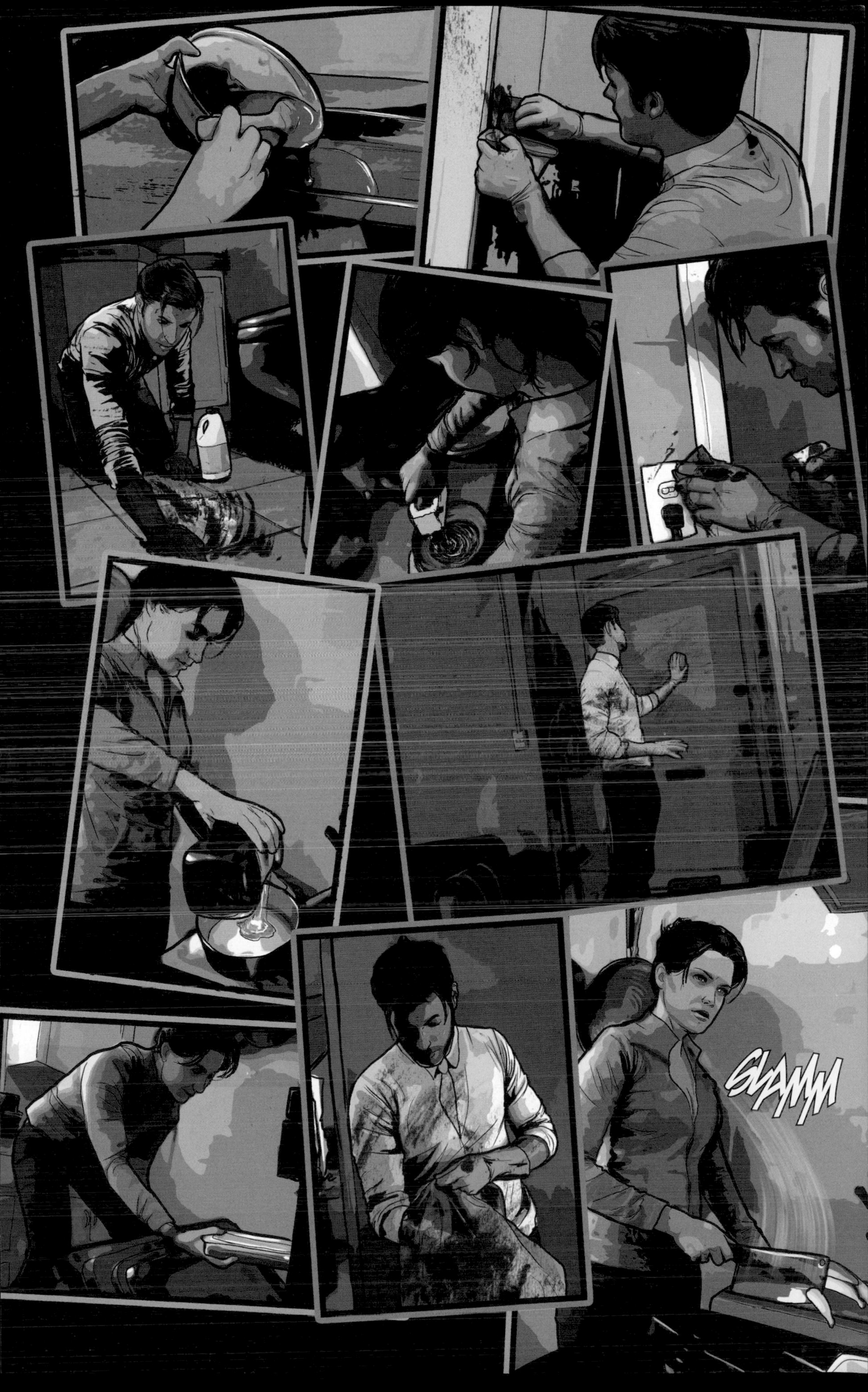
SLAMM

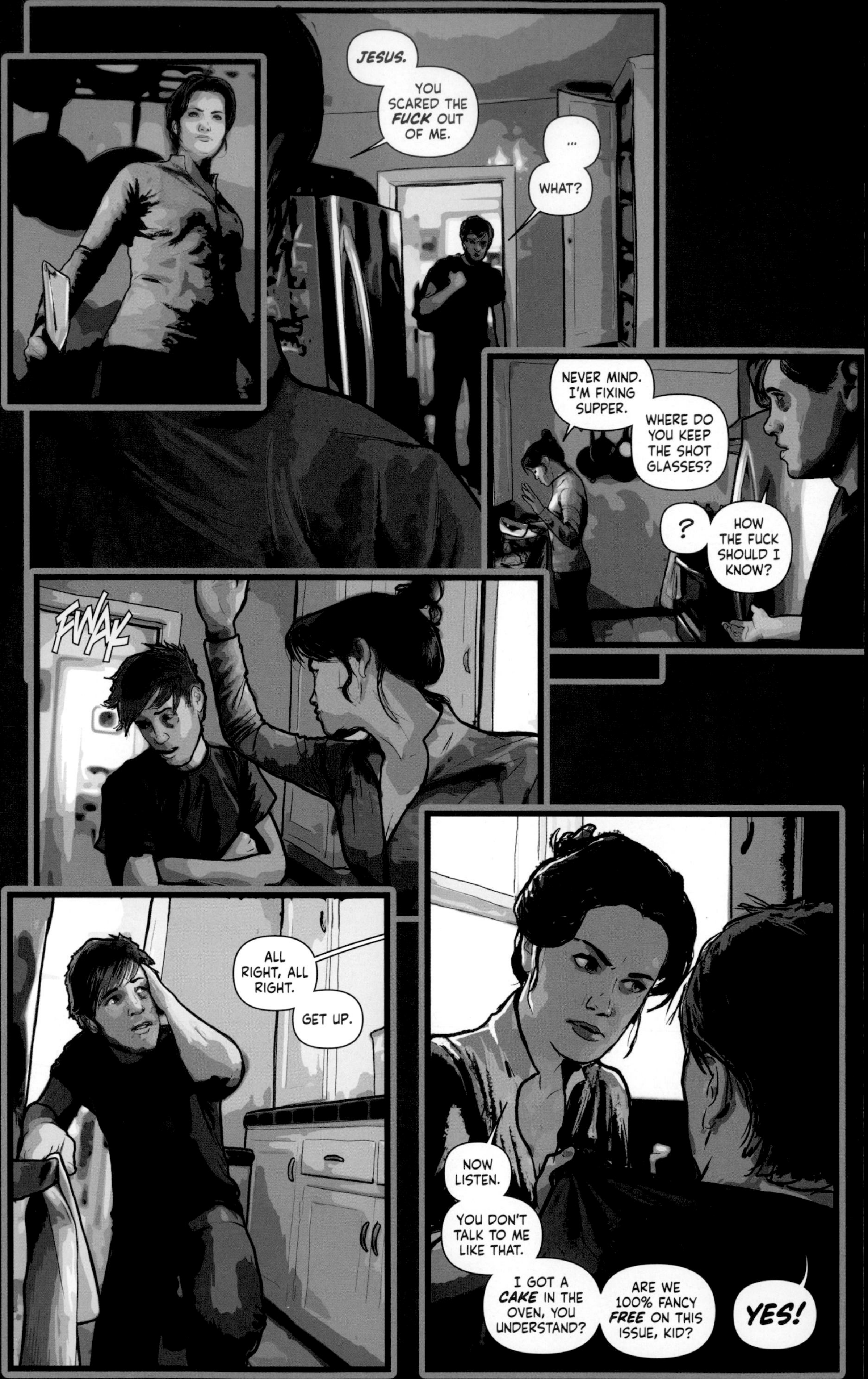
JESUS.
YOU SCARED THE FUCK OUT OF ME.
...
WHAT?
NEVER MIND. I'M FIXING SUPPER.
WHERE DO YOU KEEP THE SHOT GLASSES?
?
HOW THE FUCK SHOULD I KNOW?
FWAK
ALL RIGHT, ALL RIGHT.
GET UP.
NOW LISTEN.
YOU DON'T TALK TO ME LIKE THAT.
I GOT A CAKE IN THE OVEN, YOU UNDERSTAND?
ARE WE 100% FANCY FREE ON THIS ISSUE, KID?
YES!

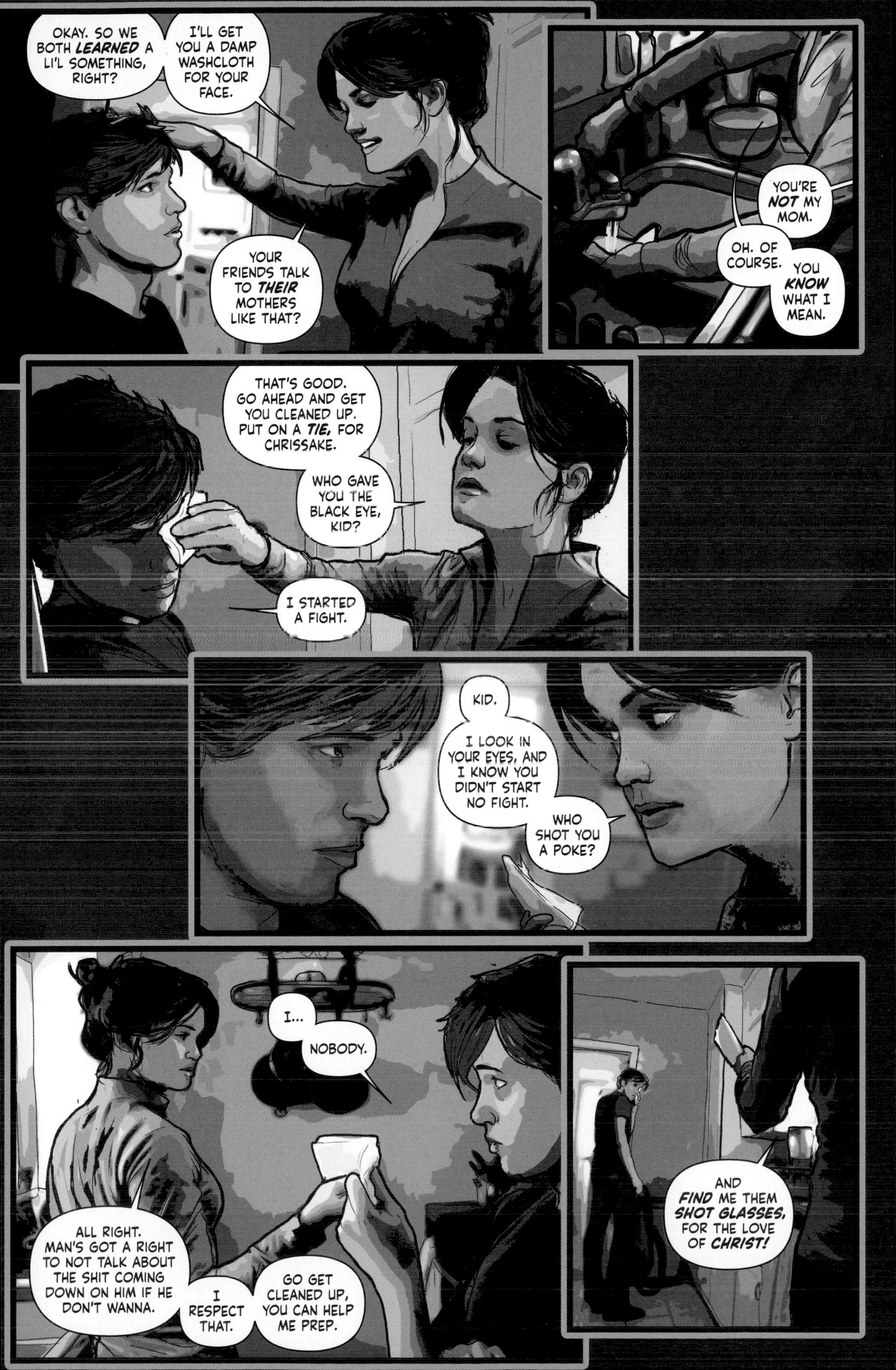

OKAY. SO WE BOTH LEARNED A LI'L SOMETHING, RIGHT?
I'LL GET YOU A DAMP WASHCLOTH FOR YOUR FACE.
YOUR FRIENDS TALK TO THEIR MOTHERS LIKE THAT?
YOU'RE NOT MY MOM.
OH. OF COURSE.
YOU KNOW WHAT I MEAN.
THAT'S GOOD. GO AHEAD AND GET YOU CLEANED UP. PUT ON A TIE, FOR CHRISSAKE.
WHO GAVE YOU THE BLACK EYE, KID?
I STARTED A FIGHT.
KID.
I LOOK IN YOUR EYES, AND I KNOW YOU DIDN'T START NO FIGHT.
WHO SHOT YOU A POKE?
I...
NOBODY.
ALL RIGHT. MAN'S GOT A RIGHT TO NOT TALK ABOUT THE SHIT COMING DOWN ON HIM IF HE DON'T WANNA.
I RESPECT THAT.
GO GET CLEANED UP, YOU CAN HELP ME PREP.
AND FIND ME THEM SHOT GLASSES, FOR THE LOVE OF CHRIST!

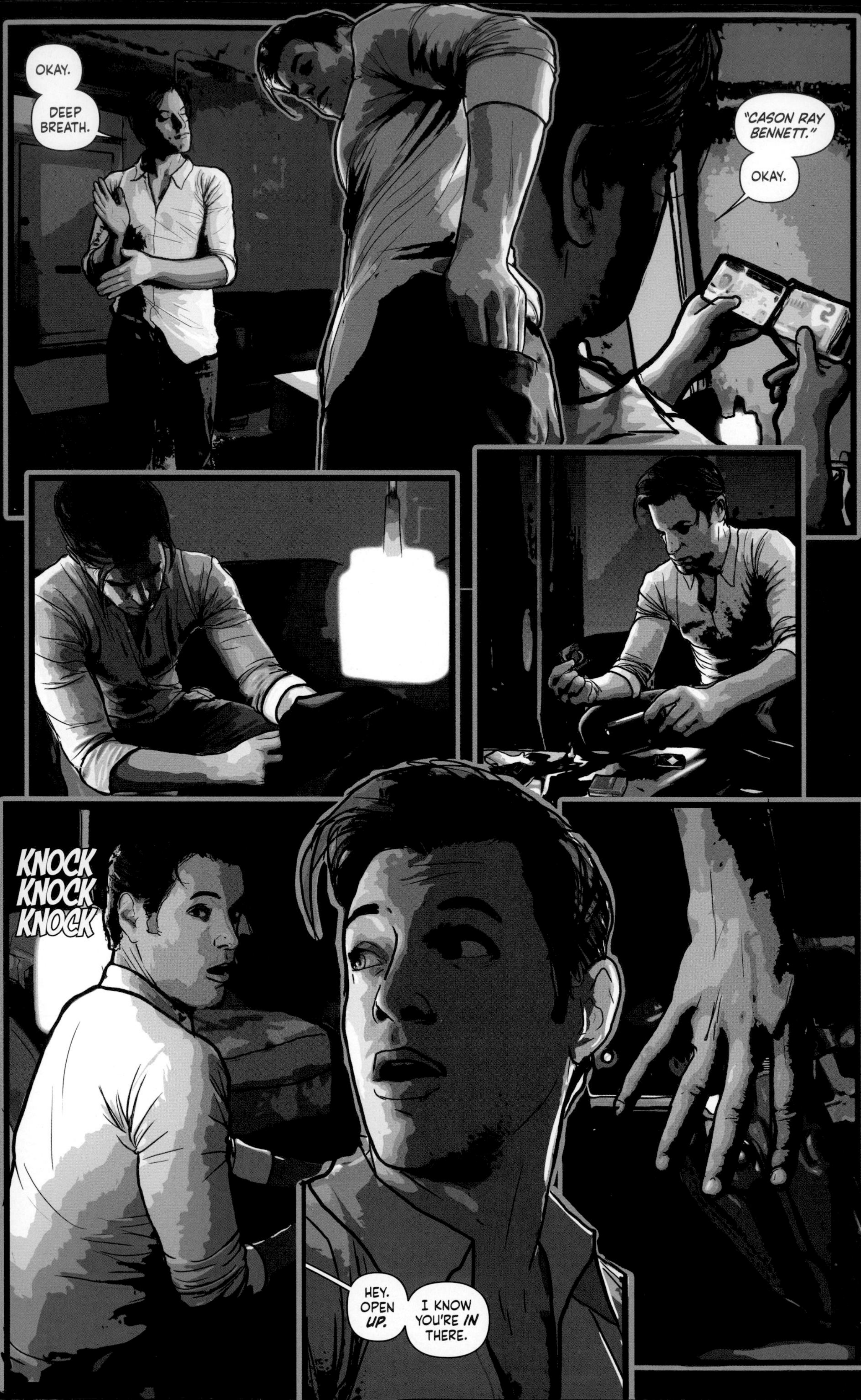
OKAY.
DEEP BREATH.
"CASON RAY BENNETT."
OKAY.
KNOCK KNOCK KNOCK
HEY. OPEN *UP.*
I KNOW YOU'RE *IN* THERE.

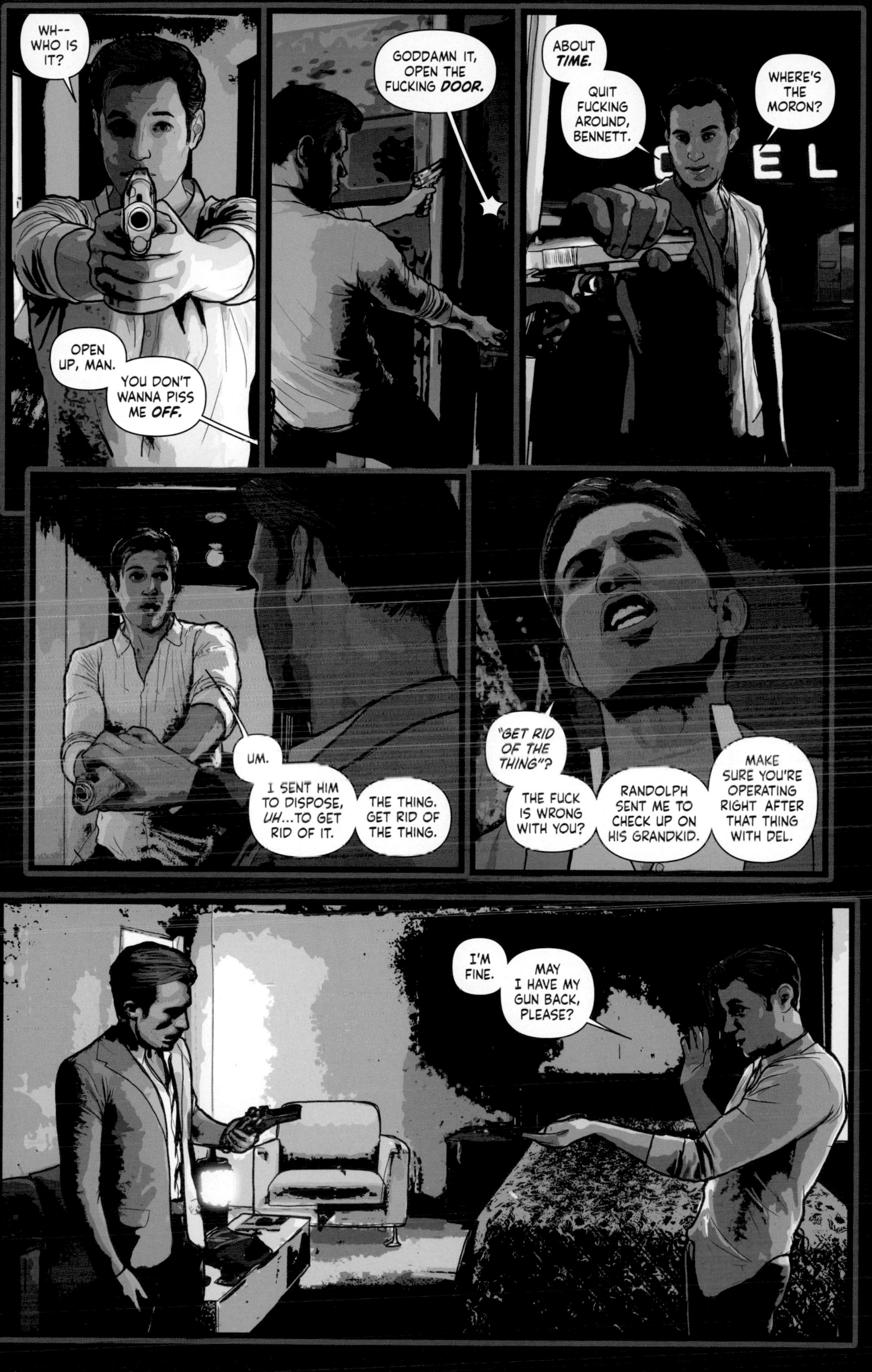
WH-- WHO IS IT?
OPEN UP, MAN.
YOU DON'T WANNA PISS ME *OFF.*
GODDAMN IT, OPEN THE FUCKING *DOOR.*
ABOUT *TIME.*
QUIT FUCKING AROUND, BENNETT.
WHERE'S THE MORON?
UM.
I SENT HIM TO DISPOSE, *UH*...TO GET RID OF IT.
THE THING. GET RID OF THE THING.
"GET RID OF THE THING"?
THE FUCK IS WRONG WITH YOU?
RANDOLPH SENT ME TO CHECK UP ON HIS GRANDKID.
MAKE SURE YOU'RE OPERATING RIGHT AFTER THAT THING WITH DEL.
I'M FINE.
MAY I HAVE MY GUN BACK, PLEASE?

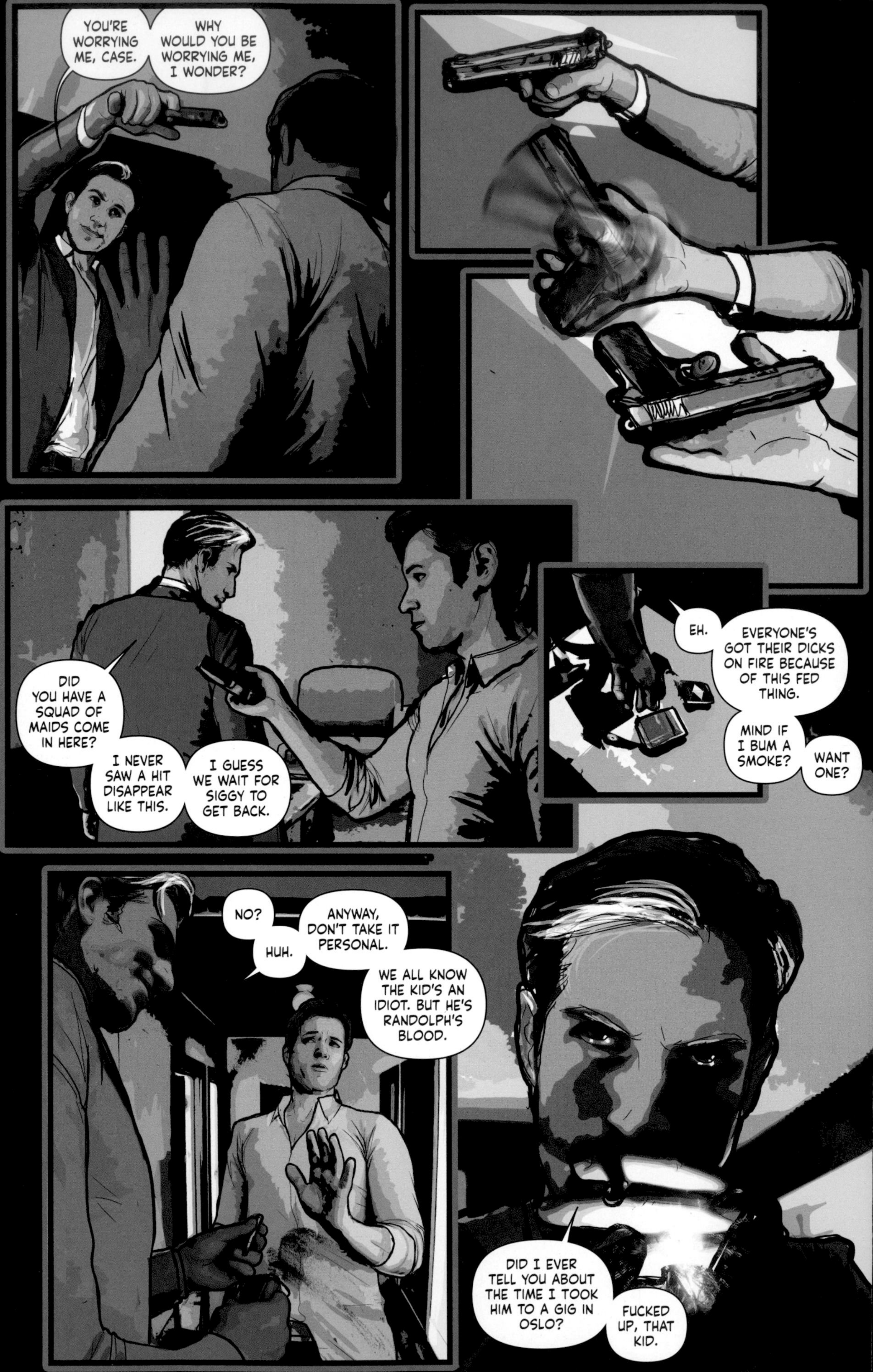
YOU'RE WORRYING ME, CASE.
WHY WOULD YOU BE WORRYING ME, I WONDER?
DID YOU HAVE A SQUAD OF MAIDS COME IN HERE?
I NEVER SAW A HIT DISAPPEAR LIKE THIS.
I GUESS WE WAIT FOR SIGGY TO GET BACK.
EH.
EVERYONE'S GOT THEIR DICKS ON FIRE BECAUSE OF THIS FED THING.
MIND IF I BUM A SMOKE?
WANT ONE?
NO?
HUH.
ANYWAY, DON'T TAKE IT PERSONAL.
WE ALL KNOW THE KID'S AN IDIOT. BUT HE'S RANDOLPH'S BLOOD.
DID I EVER TELL YOU ABOUT THE TIME I TOOK HIM TO A GIG IN OSLO?
FUCKED UP, THAT KID.

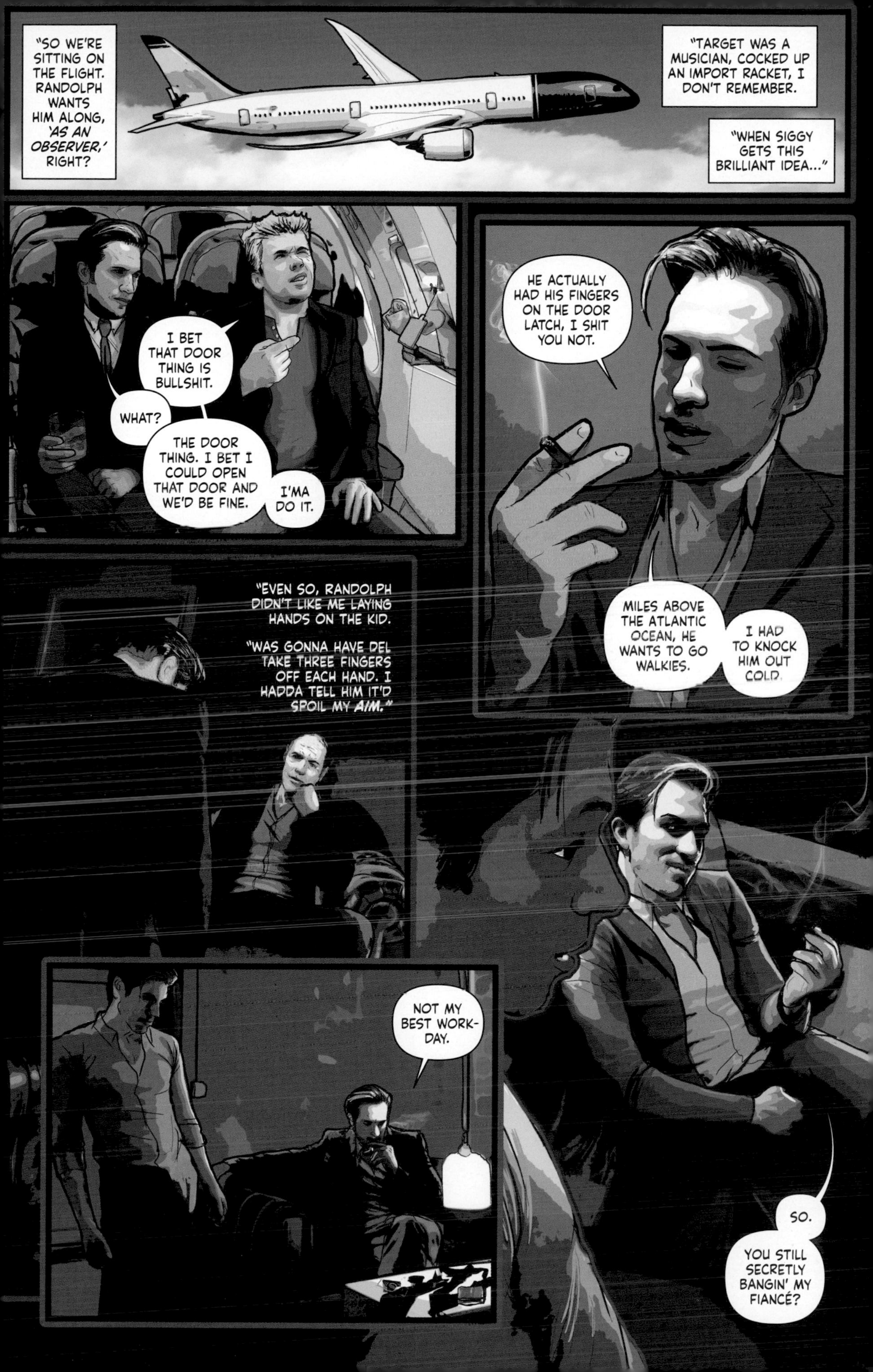
"SO WE'RE SITTING ON THE FLIGHT. RANDOLPH WANTS HIM ALONG, 'AS AN OBSERVER,' RIGHT?
"TARGET WAS A MUSICIAN, COCKED UP AN IMPORT RACKET, I DON'T REMEMBER.
"WHEN SIGGY GETS THIS BRILLIANT IDEA..."
I BET THAT DOOR THING IS BULLSHIT.
WHAT?
THE DOOR THING. I BET I COULD OPEN THAT DOOR AND WE'D BE FINE.
I'MA DO IT.
HE ACTUALLY HAD HIS FINGERS ON THE DOOR LATCH, I SHIT YOU NOT.
MILES ABOVE THE ATLANTIC OCEAN, HE WANTS TO GO WALKIES.
I HAD TO KNOCK HIM OUT COLD.
"EVEN SO, RANDOLPH DIDN'T LIKE ME LAYING HANDS ON THE KID.
"WAS GONNA HAVE DEL TAKE THREE FINGERS OFF EACH HAND. I HADDA TELL HIM IT'D SPOIL MY AIM."
NOT MY BEST WORK-DAY.
SO.
YOU STILL SECRETLY BANGIN' MY FIANCÉ?

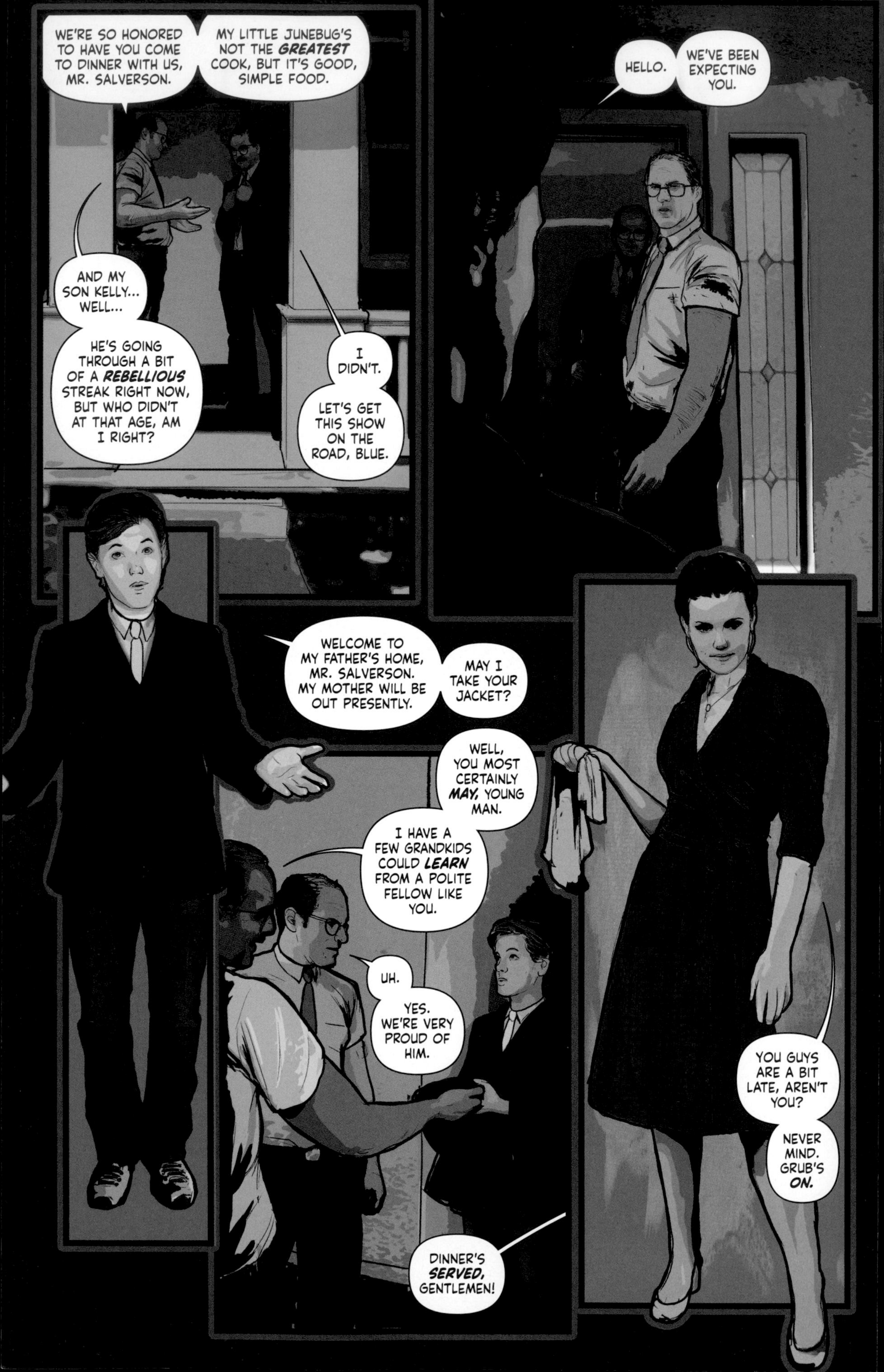
WE'RE SO HONORED TO HAVE YOU COME TO DINNER WITH US, MR. SALVERSON.
MY LITTLE JUNEBUG'S NOT THE ***GREATEST*** COOK, BUT IT'S GOOD, SIMPLE FOOD.
AND MY SON KELLY... WELL...
HE'S GOING THROUGH A BIT OF A ***REBELLIOUS*** STREAK RIGHT NOW, BUT WHO DIDN'T AT THAT AGE, AM I RIGHT?
I DIDN'T.
LET'S GET THIS SHOW ON THE ROAD, BLUE.
HELLO.
WE'VE BEEN EXPECTING YOU.
WELCOME TO MY FATHER'S HOME, MR. SALVERSON. MY MOTHER WILL BE OUT PRESENTLY.
MAY I TAKE YOUR JACKET?
WELL, YOU MOST CERTAINLY ***MAY,*** YOUNG MAN.
I HAVE A FEW GRANDKIDS COULD ***LEARN*** FROM A POLITE FELLOW LIKE YOU.
UH.
YES. WE'RE VERY PROUD OF HIM.
YOU GUYS ARE A BIT LATE, AREN'T YOU?
NEVER MIND. GRUB'S ***ON.***
DINNER'S ***SERVED,*** GENTLEMEN!

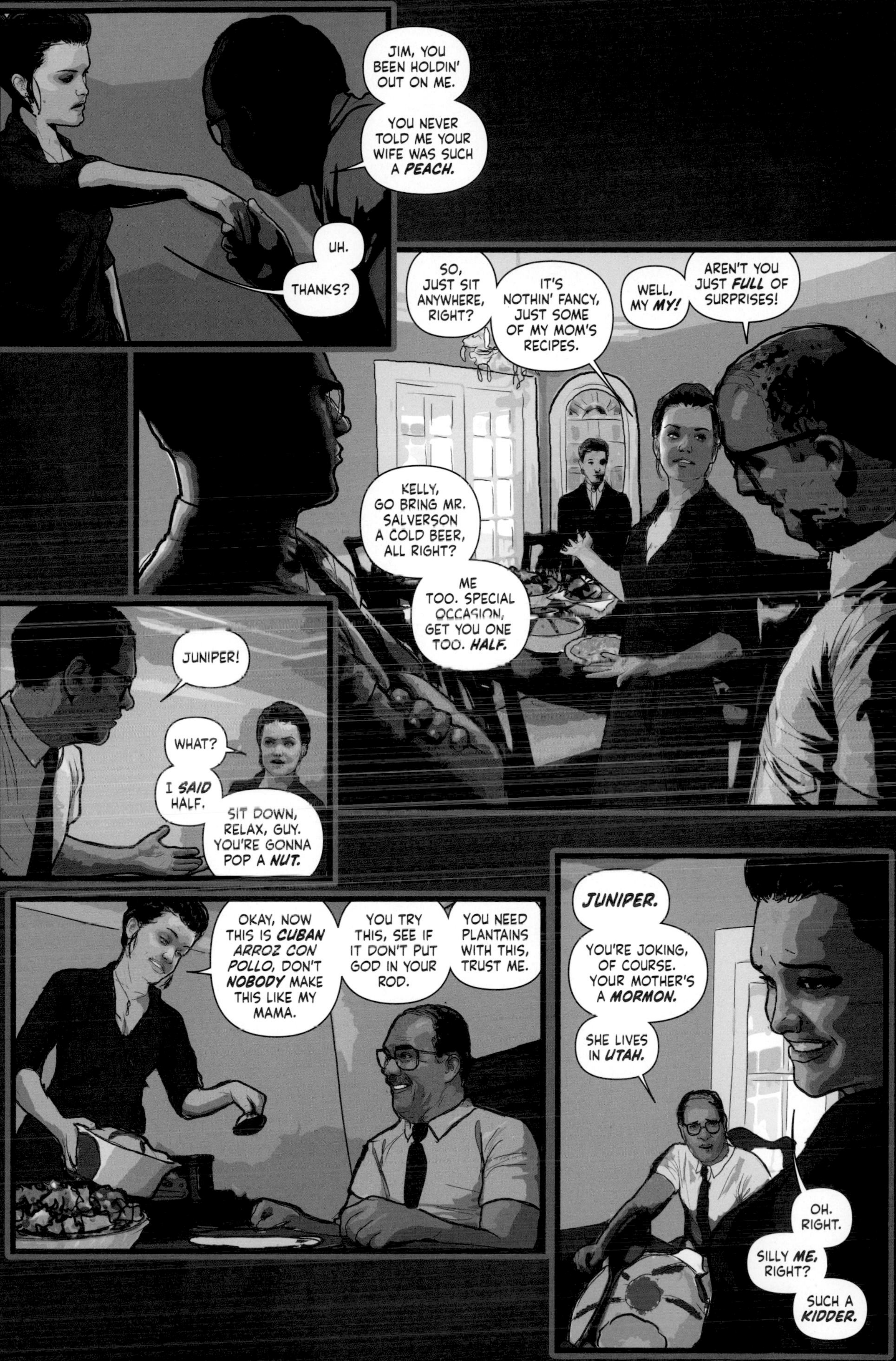

JIM, YOU BEEN HOLDIN' OUT ON ME.
YOU NEVER TOLD ME YOUR WIFE WAS SUCH A PEACH.
UH.
THANKS?
SO, JUST SIT ANYWHERE, RIGHT?
IT'S NOTHIN' FANCY, JUST SOME OF MY MOM'S RECIPES.
WELL, MY MY!
AREN'T YOU JUST FULL OF SURPRISES!
KELLY, GO BRING MR. SALVERSON A COLD BEER, ALL RIGHT?
ME TOO. SPECIAL OCCASION, GET YOU ONE TOO. HALF.
JUNIPER!
WHAT?
I SAID HALF.
SIT DOWN, RELAX, GUY. YOU'RE GONNA POP A NUT.
OKAY, NOW THIS IS CUBAN ARROZ CON POLLO, DON'T NOBODY MAKE THIS LIKE MY MAMA.
YOU TRY THIS, SEE IF IT DON'T PUT GOD IN YOUR ROD.
YOU NEED PLANTAINS WITH THIS, TRUST ME.
JUNIPER.
YOU'RE JOKING, OF COURSE. YOUR MOTHER'S A MORMON.
SHE LIVES IN UTAH.
OH. RIGHT.
SILLY ME, RIGHT?
SUCH A KIDDER.

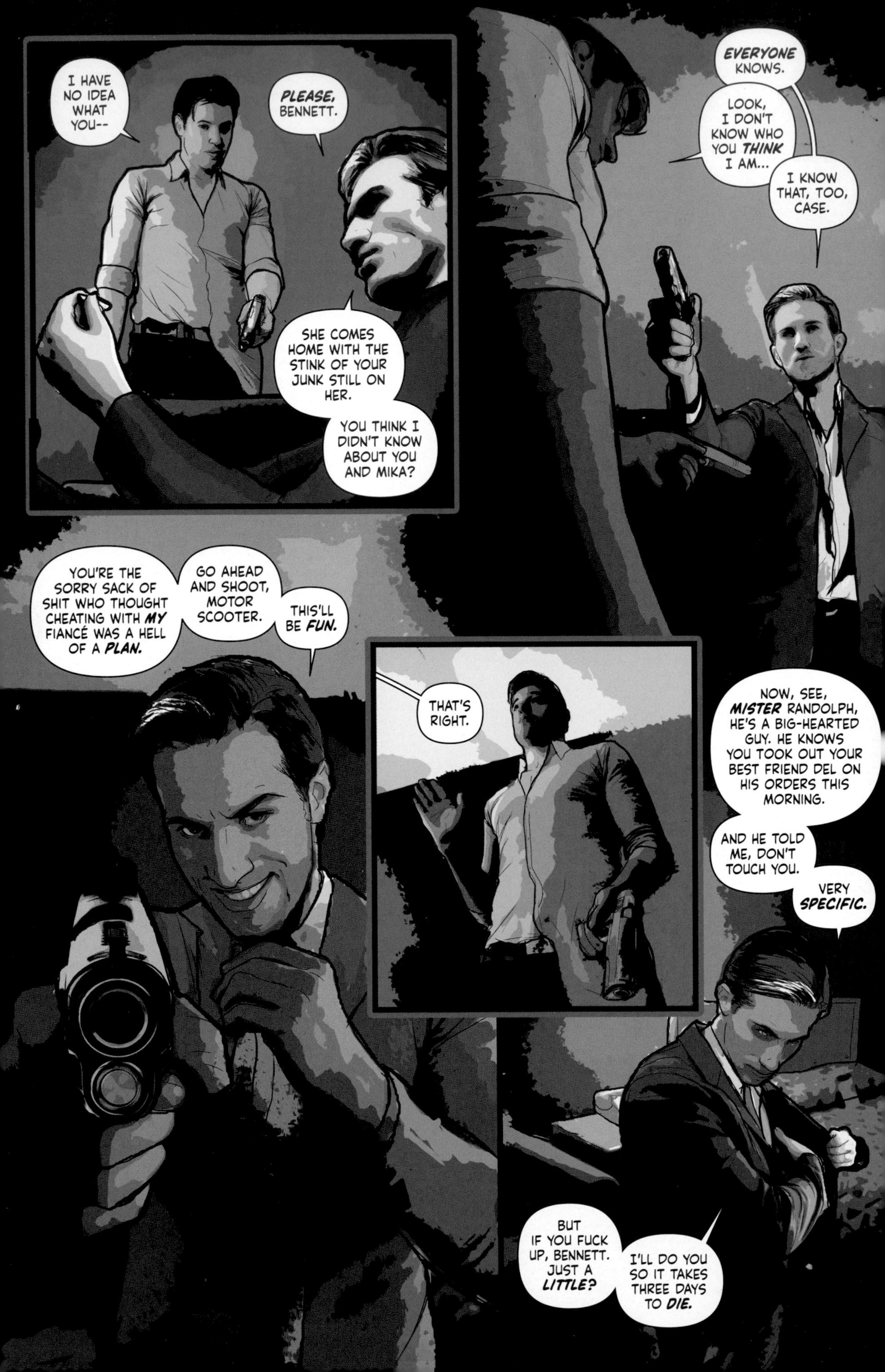
I HAVE NO IDEA WHAT YOU--
PLEASE, BENNETT.
SHE COMES HOME WITH THE STINK OF YOUR JUNK STILL ON HER.
YOU THINK I DIDN'T KNOW ABOUT YOU AND MIKA?
EVERYONE KNOWS.
LOOK, I DON'T KNOW WHO YOU THINK I AM...
I KNOW THAT, TOO, CASE.
YOU'RE THE SORRY SACK OF SHIT WHO THOUGHT CHEATING WITH MY FIANCÉ WAS A HELL OF A PLAN.
GO AHEAD AND SHOOT, MOTOR SCOOTER.
THIS'LL BE FUN.
THAT'S RIGHT.
NOW, SEE, MISTER RANDOLPH, HE'S A BIG-HEARTED GUY. HE KNOWS YOU TOOK OUT YOUR BEST FRIEND DEL ON HIS ORDERS THIS MORNING.
AND HE TOLD ME, DON'T TOUCH YOU.
VERY SPECIFIC.
BUT IF YOU FUCK UP, BENNETT. JUST A LITTLE?
I'LL DO YOU SO IT TAKES THREE DAYS TO DIE.

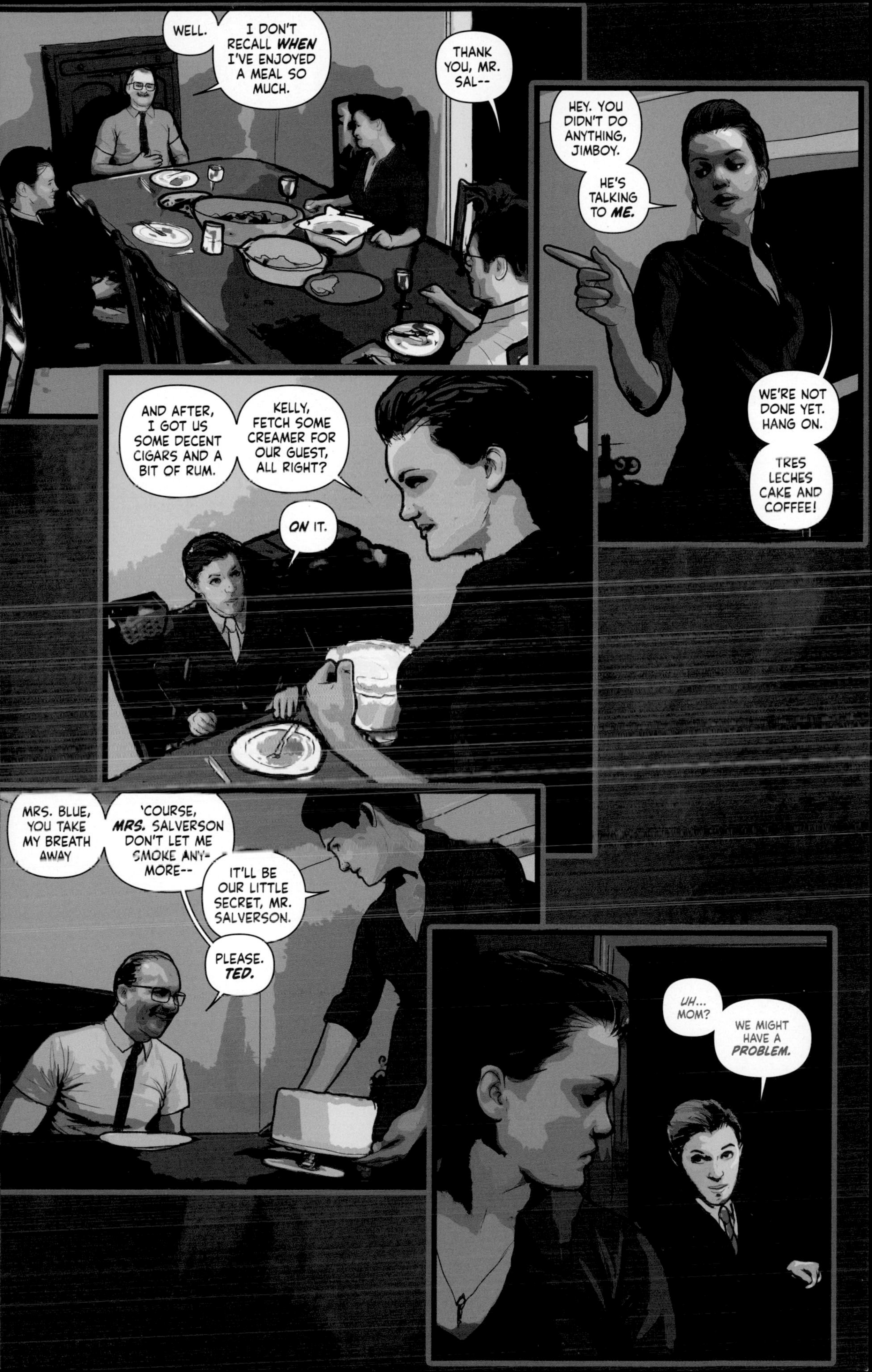
WELL.
I DON'T RECALL *WHEN* I'VE ENJOYED A MEAL SO MUCH.
THANK YOU, MR. SAL--
HEY. YOU DIDN'T DO ANYTHING, JIMBOY.
HE'S TALKING TO *ME.*
WE'RE NOT DONE YET. HANG ON.
TRES LECHES CAKE AND COFFEE!
AND AFTER, I GOT US SOME DECENT CIGARS AND A BIT OF RUM.
KELLY, FETCH SOME CREAMER FOR OUR GUEST, ALL RIGHT?
ON IT.
MRS. BLUE, YOU TAKE MY BREATH AWAY
'COURSE, *MRS.* SALVERSON DON'T LET ME SMOKE ANY-MORE--
IT'LL BE OUR LITTLE SECRET, MR. SALVERSON.
PLEASE. *TED.*
UH... MOM?
WE MIGHT HAVE A *PROBLEM.*

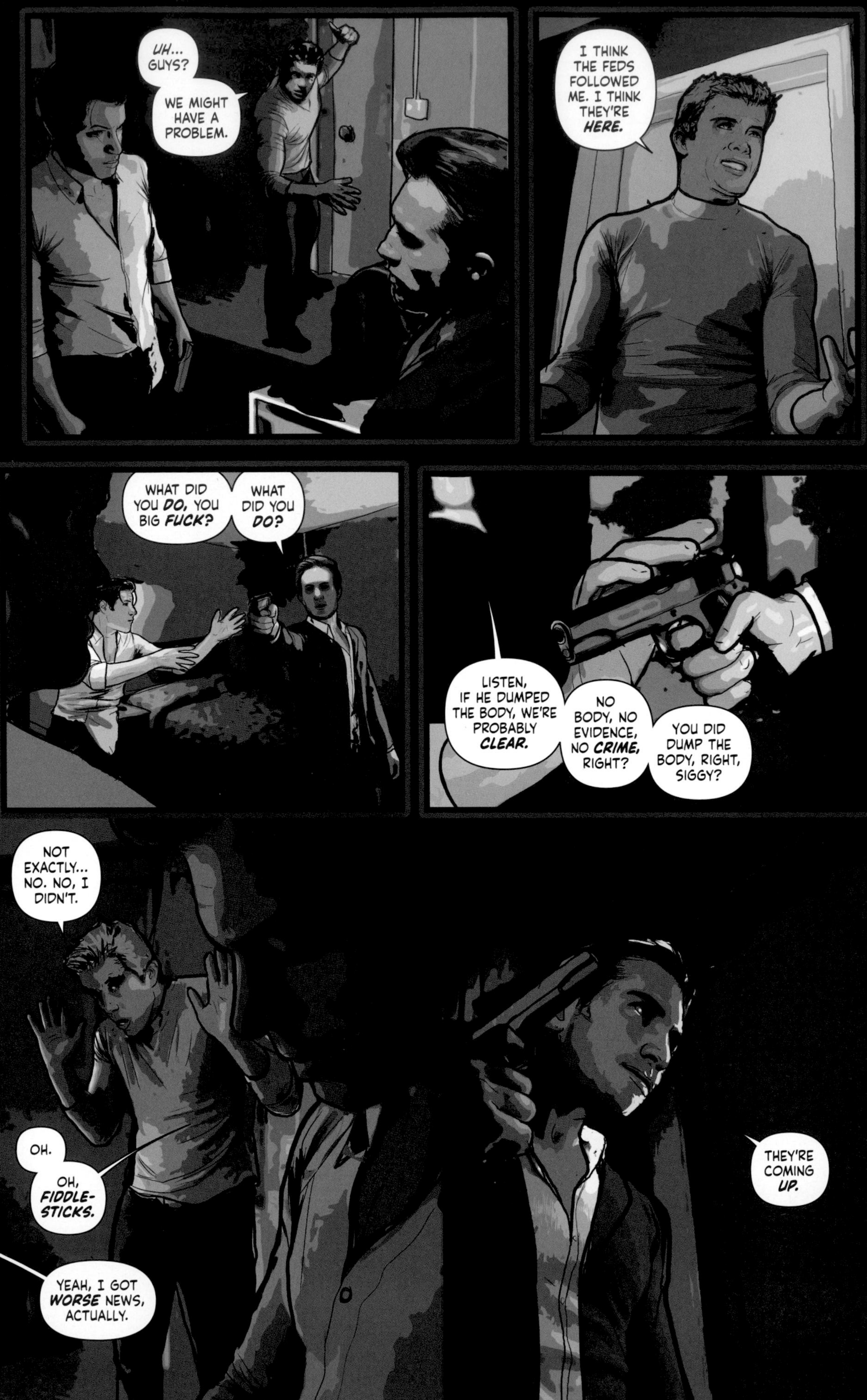
UH... GUYS?
WE MIGHT HAVE A PROBLEM.
I THINK THE FEDS FOLLOWED ME. I THINK THEY'RE HERE.
WHAT DID YOU DO, YOU BIG FUCK?
WHAT DID YOU DO?
LISTEN, IF HE DUMPED THE BODY, WE'RE PROBABLY CLEAR.
NO BODY, NO EVIDENCE, NO CRIME, RIGHT?
YOU DID DUMP THE BODY, RIGHT, SIGGY?
NOT EXACTLY... NO. NO, I DIDN'T.
OH.
OH, FIDDLE-STICKS.
YEAH, I GOT WORSE NEWS, ACTUALLY.
THEY'RE COMING UP.

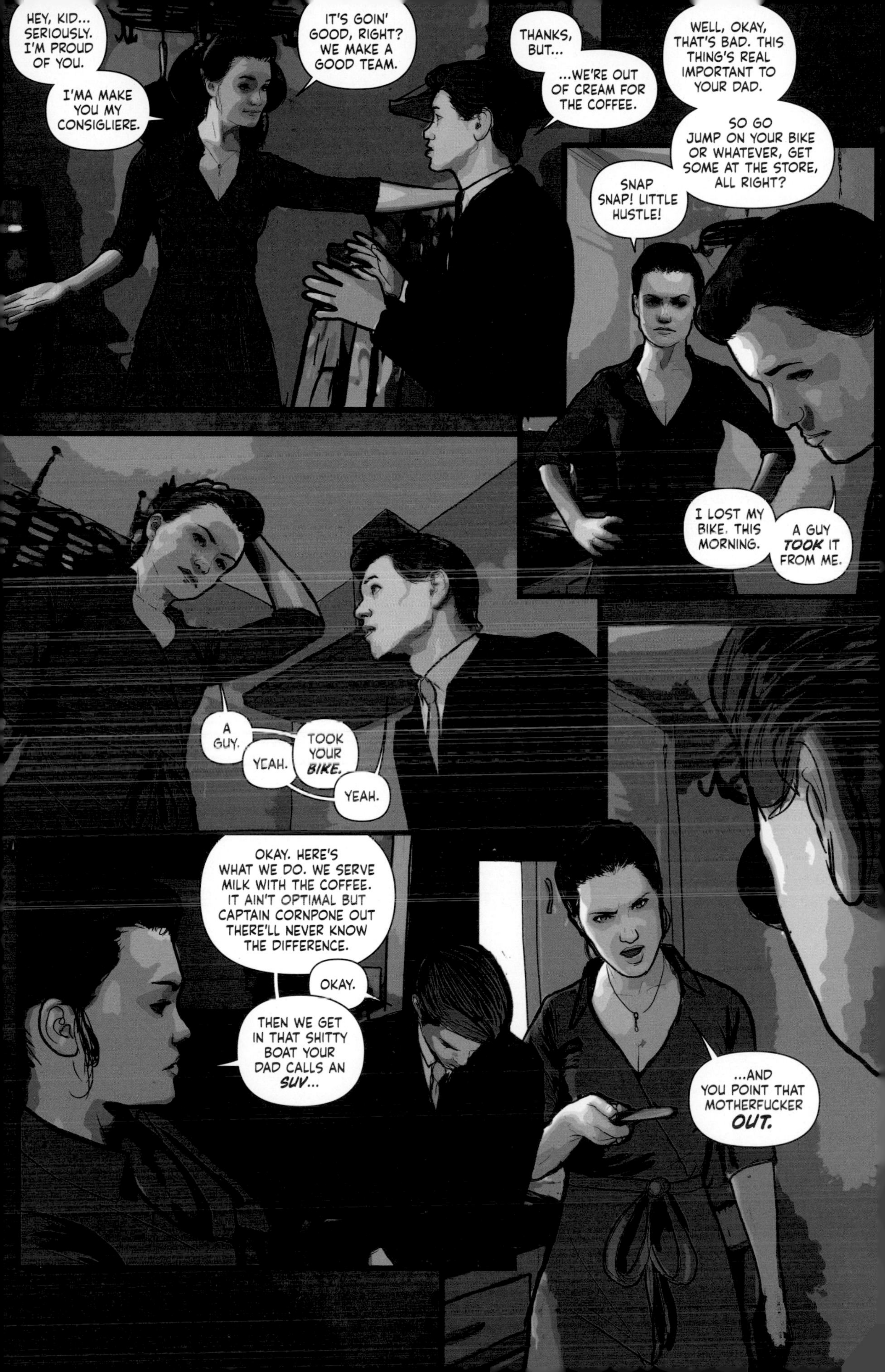
HEY, KID... SERIOUSLY. I'M PROUD OF YOU.
I'MA MAKE YOU MY CONSIGLIERE.
IT'S GOIN' GOOD, RIGHT? WE MAKE A GOOD TEAM.
THANKS, BUT...
...WE'RE OUT OF CREAM FOR THE COFFEE.
WELL, OKAY, THAT'S BAD. THIS THING'S REAL IMPORTANT TO YOUR DAD.
SO GO JUMP ON YOUR BIKE OR WHATEVER, GET SOME AT THE STORE, ALL RIGHT?
SNAP SNAP! LITTLE HUSTLE!
I LOST MY BIKE. THIS MORNING.
A GUY TOOK IT FROM ME.
A GUY.
YEAH.
TOOK YOUR BIKE.
YEAH.
OKAY. HERE'S WHAT WE DO. WE SERVE MILK WITH THE COFFEE. IT AIN'T OPTIMAL BUT CAPTAIN CORNPONE OUT THERE'LL NEVER KNOW THE DIFFERENCE.
OKAY.
THEN WE GET IN THAT SHITTY BOAT YOUR DAD CALLS AN SUV...
...AND YOU POINT THAT MOTHERFUCKER OUT.

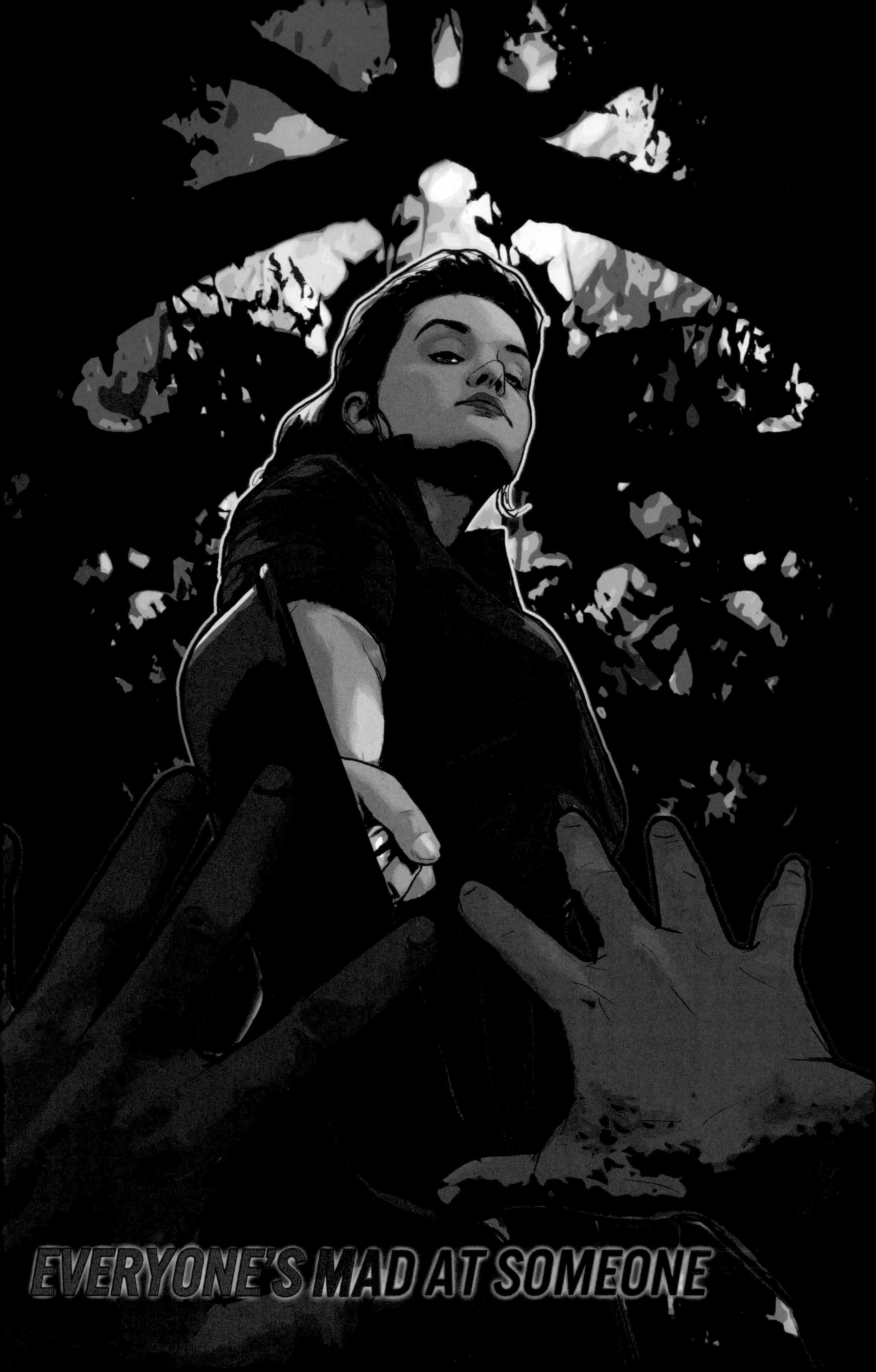
EVERYONE'S MAD AT SOMEONE

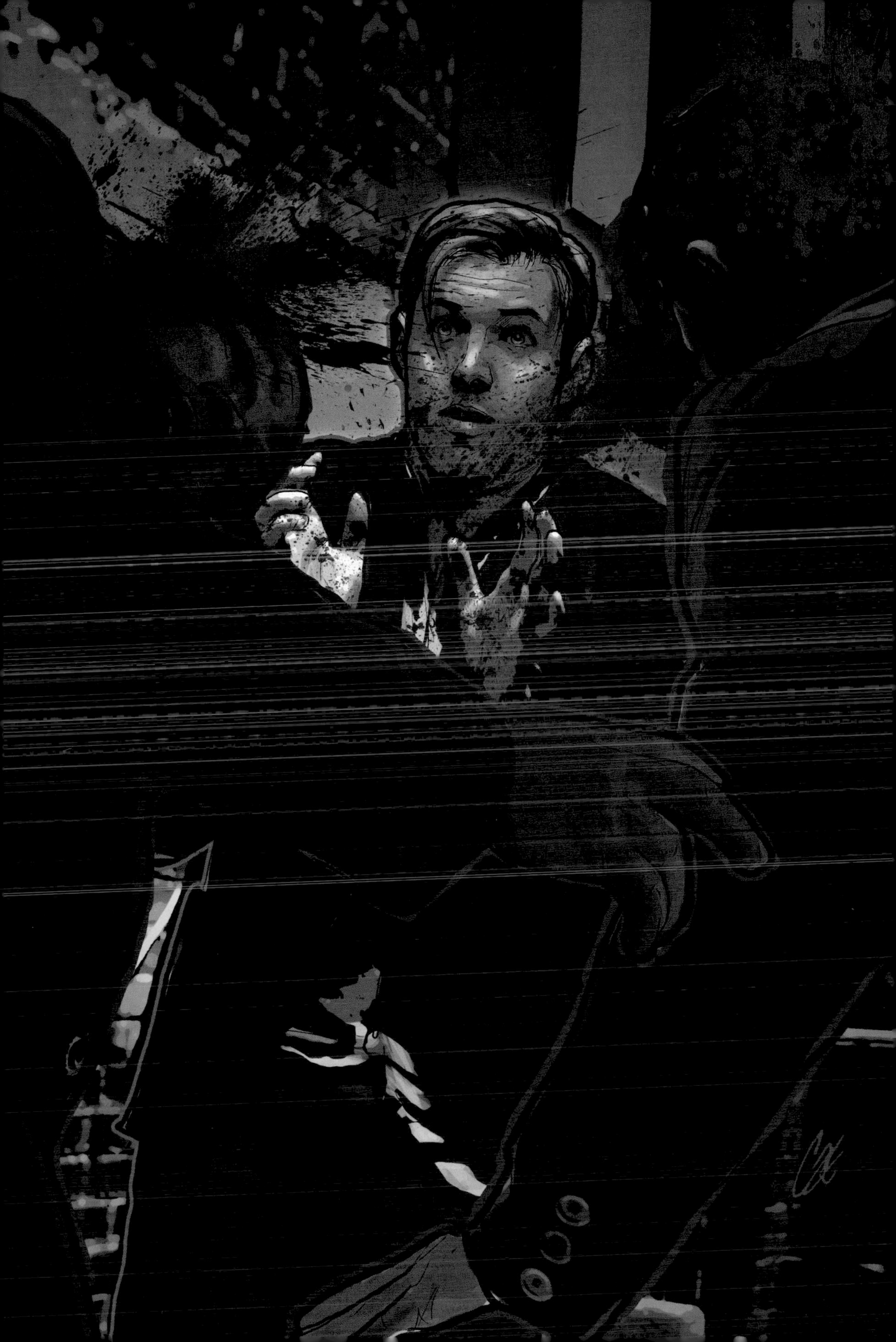

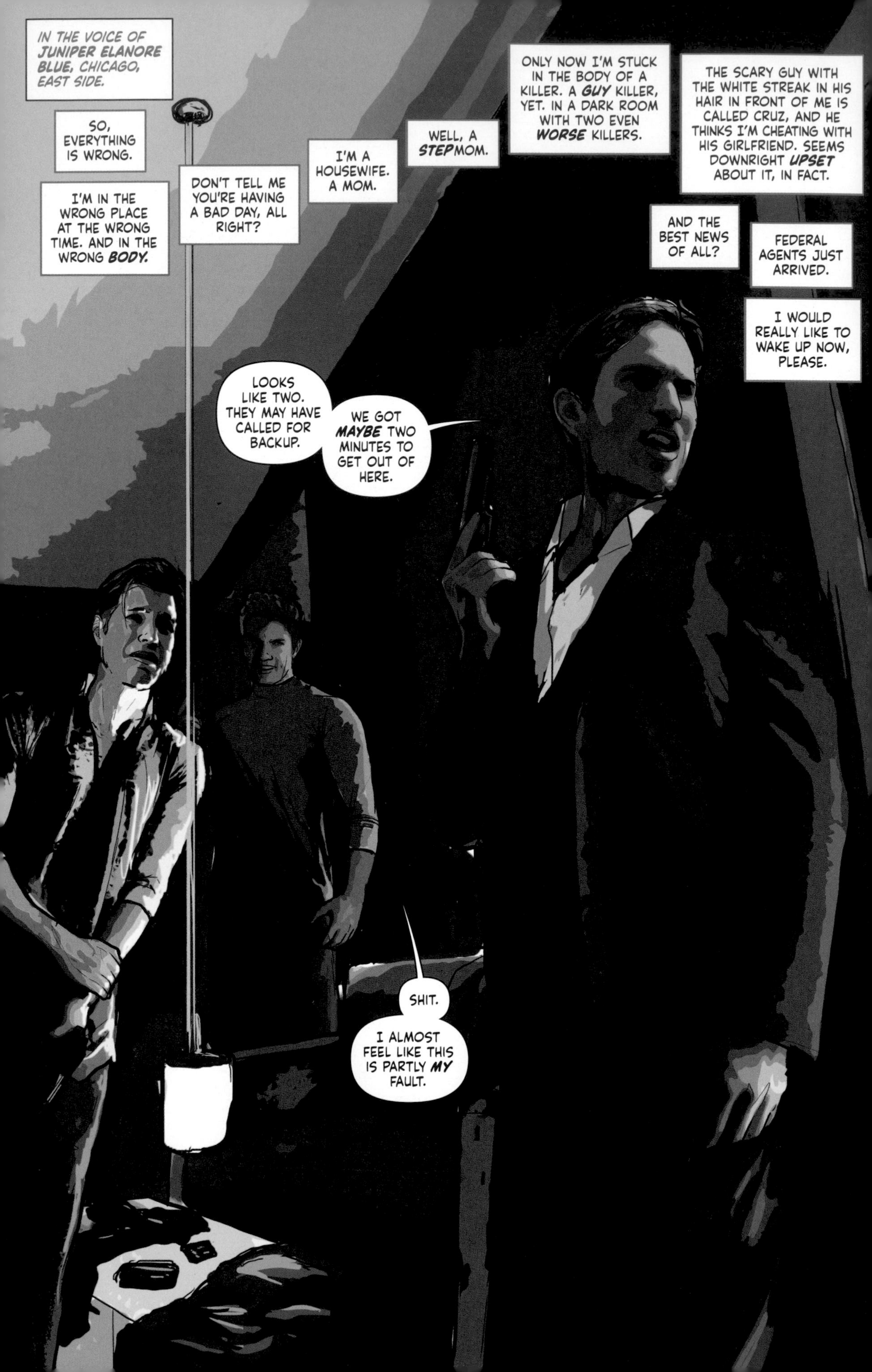
IN THE VOICE OF JUNIPER ELANORE BLUE, CHICAGO, EAST SIDE.
SO, EVERYTHING IS WRONG.
I'M IN THE WRONG PLACE AT THE WRONG TIME. AND IN THE WRONG BODY.
DON'T TELL ME YOU'RE HAVING A BAD DAY, ALL RIGHT?
I'M A HOUSEWIFE. A MOM.
WELL, A STEPMOM.
ONLY NOW I'M STUCK IN THE BODY OF A KILLER. A GUY KILLER, YET. IN A DARK ROOM WITH TWO EVEN WORSE KILLERS.
THE SCARY GUY WITH THE WHITE STREAK IN HIS HAIR IN FRONT OF ME IS CALLED CRUZ, AND HE THINKS I'M CHEATING WITH HIS GIRLFRIEND. SEEMS DOWNRIGHT UPSET ABOUT IT, IN FACT.
AND THE BEST NEWS OF ALL?
FEDERAL AGENTS JUST ARRIVED.
I WOULD REALLY LIKE TO WAKE UP NOW, PLEASE.
LOOKS LIKE TWO. THEY MAY HAVE CALLED FOR BACKUP.
WE GOT MAYBE TWO MINUTES TO GET OUT OF HERE.
SHIT.
I ALMOST FEEL LIKE THIS IS PARTLY MY FAULT.

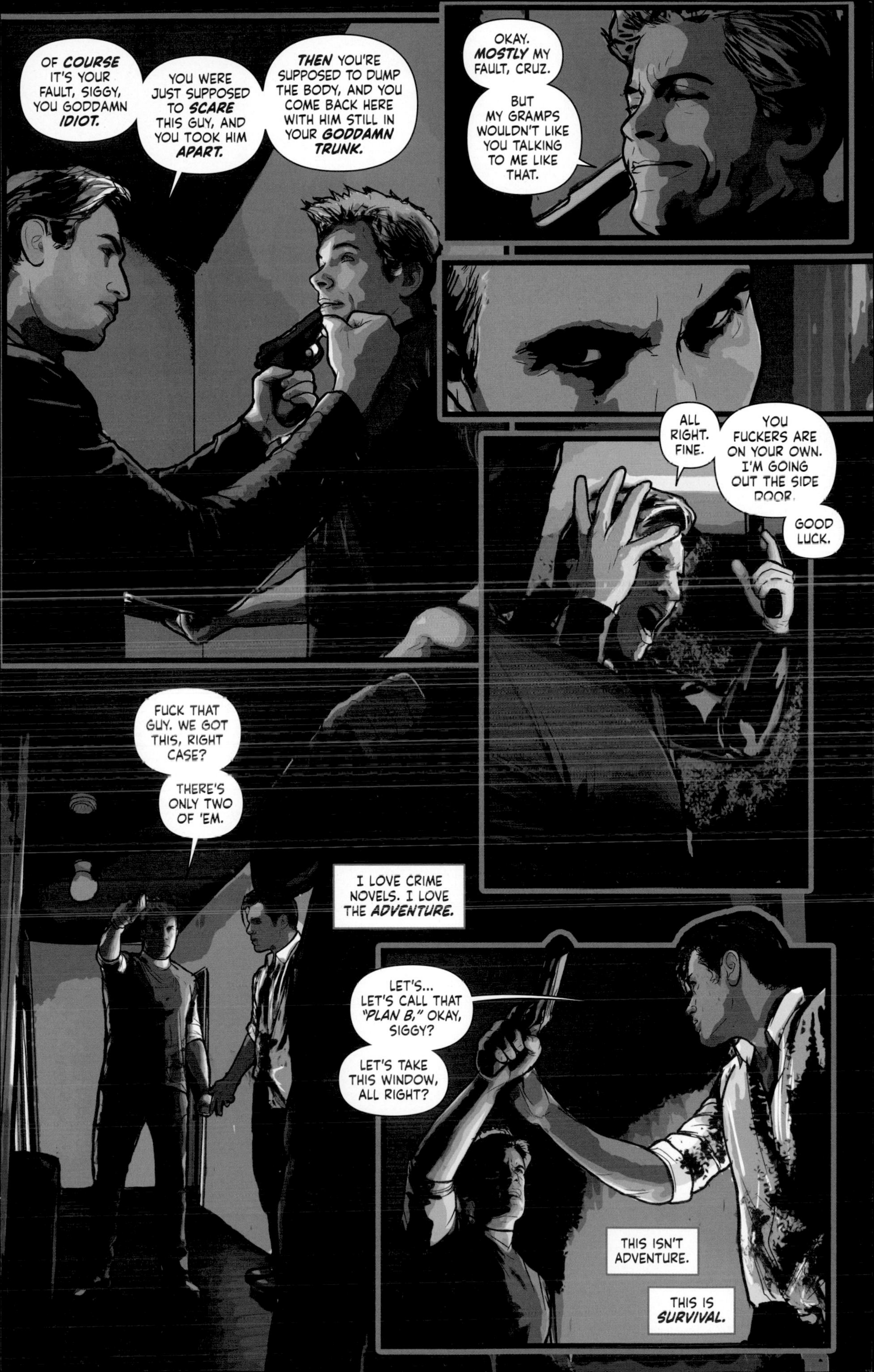

OF COURSE IT'S YOUR FAULT, SIGGY, YOU GODDAMN IDIOT.
YOU WERE JUST SUPPOSED TO SCARE THIS GUY, AND YOU TOOK HIM APART.
THEN YOU'RE SUPPOSED TO DUMP THE BODY, AND YOU COME BACK HERE WITH HIM STILL IN YOUR GODDAMN TRUNK.
OKAY. MOSTLY MY FAULT, CRUZ.
BUT MY GRAMPS WOULDN'T LIKE YOU TALKING TO ME LIKE THAT.
ALL RIGHT. FINE.
YOU FUCKERS ARE ON YOUR OWN. I'M GOING OUT THE SIDE DOOR.
GOOD LUCK.
FUCK THAT GUY. WE GOT THIS, RIGHT CASE?
THERE'S ONLY TWO OF 'EM.
I LOVE CRIME NOVELS. I LOVE THE ADVENTURE.
LET'S... LET'S CALL THAT "PLAN B," OKAY, SIGGY?
LET'S TAKE THIS WINDOW, ALL RIGHT?
THIS ISN'T ADVENTURE.
THIS IS SURVIVAL.

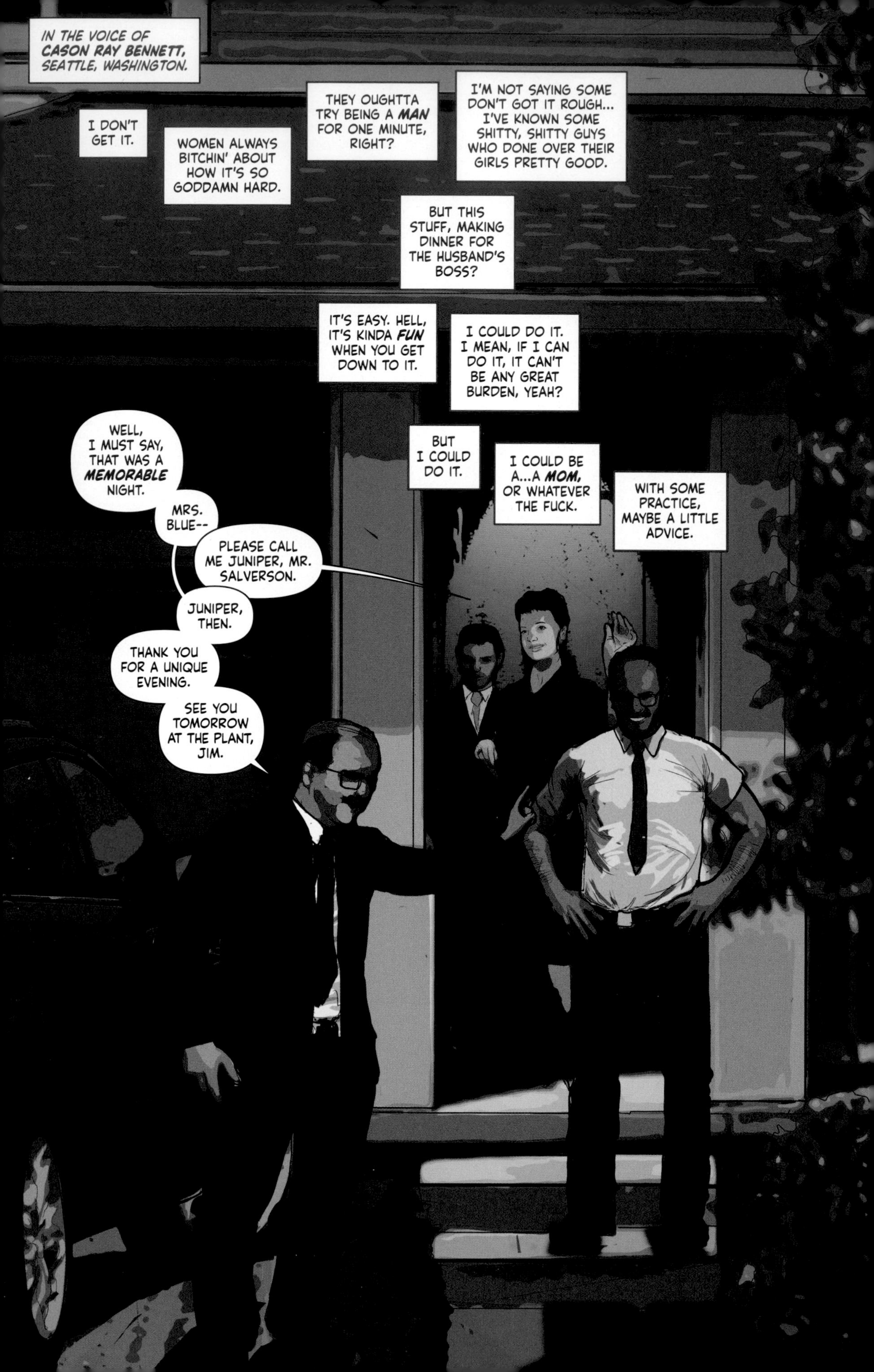
IN THE VOICE OF CASON RAY BENNETT, SEATTLE, WASHINGTON.
I DON'T GET IT.
WOMEN ALWAYS BITCHIN' ABOUT HOW IT'S SO GODDAMN HARD.
THEY OUGHTTA TRY BEING A MAN FOR ONE MINUTE, RIGHT?
I'M NOT SAYING SOME DON'T GOT IT ROUGH... I'VE KNOWN SOME SHITTY, SHITTY GUYS WHO DONE OVER THEIR GIRLS PRETTY GOOD.
BUT THIS STUFF, MAKING DINNER FOR THE HUSBAND'S BOSS?
IT'S EASY. HELL, IT'S KINDA FUN WHEN YOU GET DOWN TO IT.
I COULD DO IT. I MEAN, IF I CAN DO IT, IT CAN'T BE ANY GREAT BURDEN, YEAH?
BUT I COULD DO IT.
I COULD BE A...A MOM, OR WHATEVER THE FUCK.
WITH SOME PRACTICE, MAYBE A LITTLE ADVICE.
WELL, I MUST SAY, THAT WAS A MEMORABLE NIGHT.
MRS. BLUE--
PLEASE CALL ME JUNIPER, MR. SALVERSON.
JUNIPER, THEN.
THANK YOU FOR A UNIQUE EVENING.
SEE YOU TOMORROW AT THE PLANT, JIM.

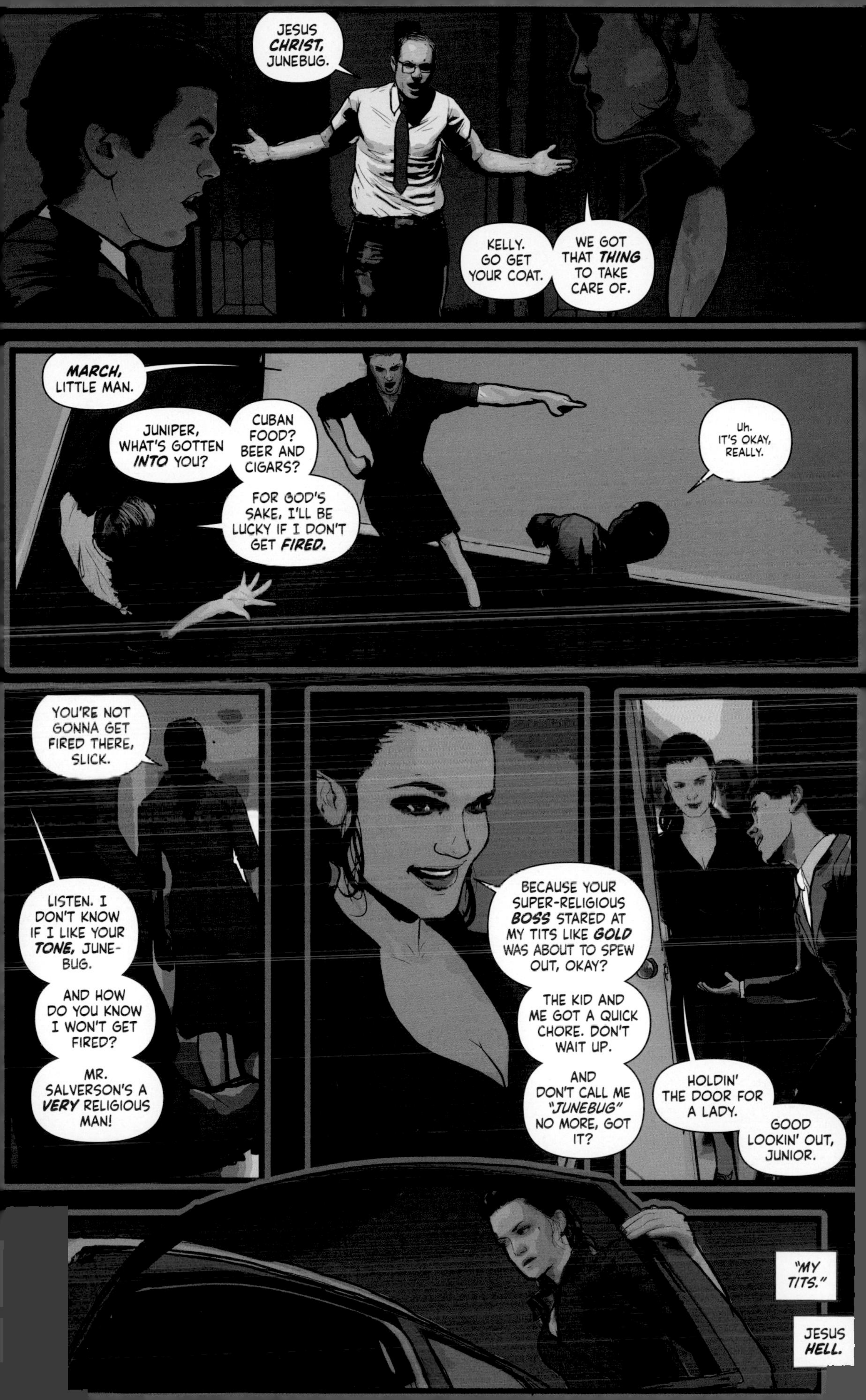
JESUS CHRIST, JUNEBUG.
KELLY. GO GET YOUR COAT.
WE GOT THAT THING TO TAKE CARE OF.
MARCH, LITTLE MAN.
JUNIPER, WHAT'S GOTTEN INTO YOU?
CUBAN FOOD? BEER AND CIGARS?
FOR GOD'S SAKE, I'LL BE LUCKY IF I DON'T GET FIRED.
Uh. IT'S OKAY, REALLY.
YOU'RE NOT GONNA GET FIRED THERE, SLICK.
LISTEN. I DON'T KNOW IF I LIKE YOUR TONE, JUNE-BUG.
AND HOW DO YOU KNOW I WON'T GET FIRED?
MR. SALVERSON'S A VERY RELIGIOUS MAN!
BECAUSE YOUR SUPER-RELIGIOUS BOSS STARED AT MY TITS LIKE GOLD WAS ABOUT TO SPEW OUT, OKAY?
THE KID AND ME GOT A QUICK CHORE. DON'T WAIT UP.
AND DON'T CALL ME "JUNEBUG" NO MORE, GOT IT?
HOLDIN' THE DOOR FOR A LADY.
GOOD LOOKIN' OUT, JUNIOR.
"MY TITS."
JESUS HELL.

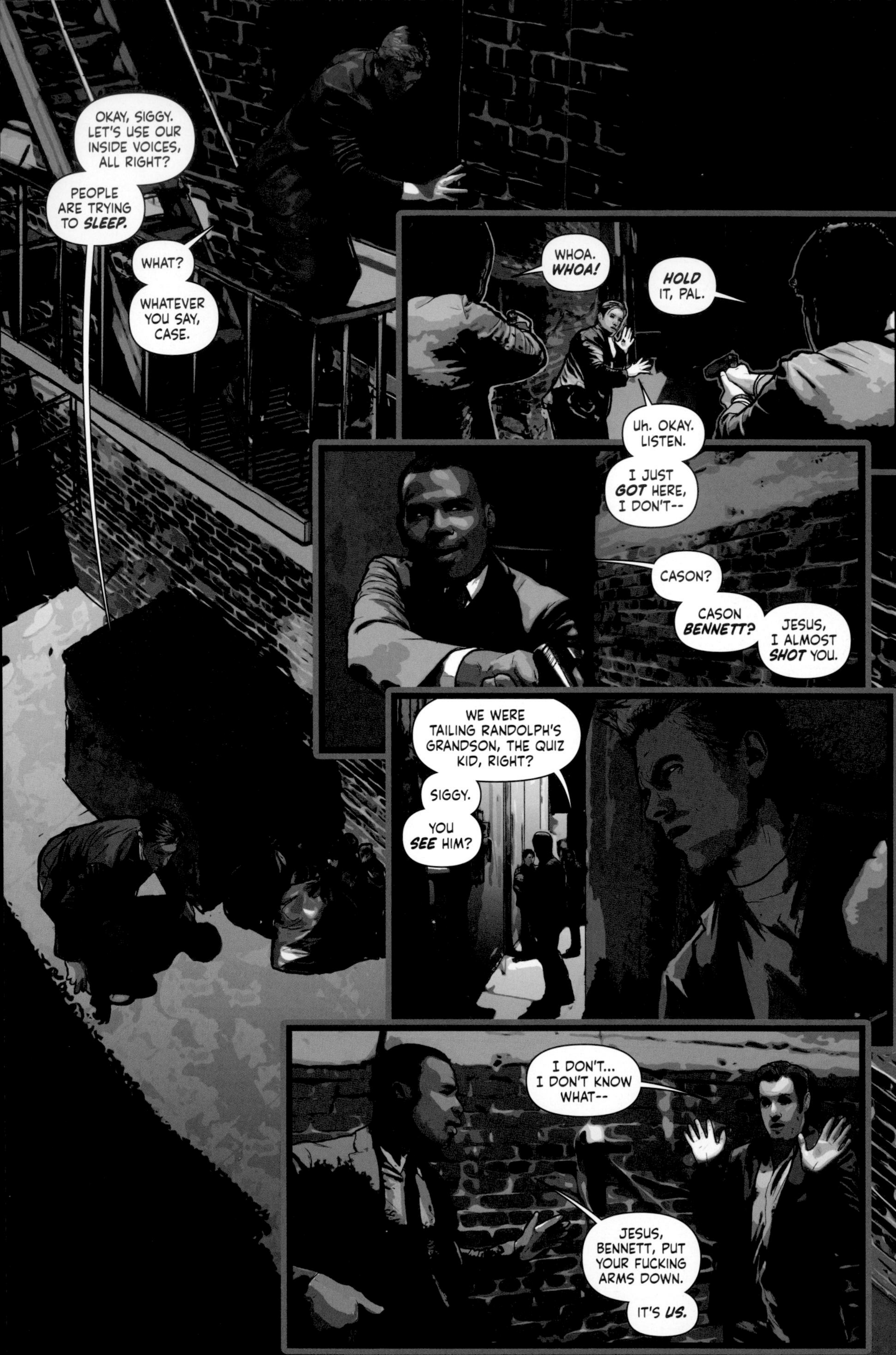
OKAY, SIGGY. LET'S USE OUR INSIDE VOICES, ALL RIGHT?
PEOPLE ARE TRYING TO **SLEEP.**
WHAT?
WHATEVER YOU SAY, CASE.
WHOA. **WHOA!**
HOLD IT, PAL.
Uh. OKAY. LISTEN.
I JUST **GOT** HERE, I DON'T--
CASON?
CASON **BENNETT?**
JESUS, I ALMOST **SHOT** YOU.
WE WERE TAILING RANDOLPH'S GRANDSON, THE QUIZ KID, RIGHT?
SIGGY.
YOU **SEE** HIM?
I DON'T... I DON'T KNOW WHAT--
JESUS, BENNETT, PUT YOUR FUCKING ARMS DOWN.
IT'S **US.**

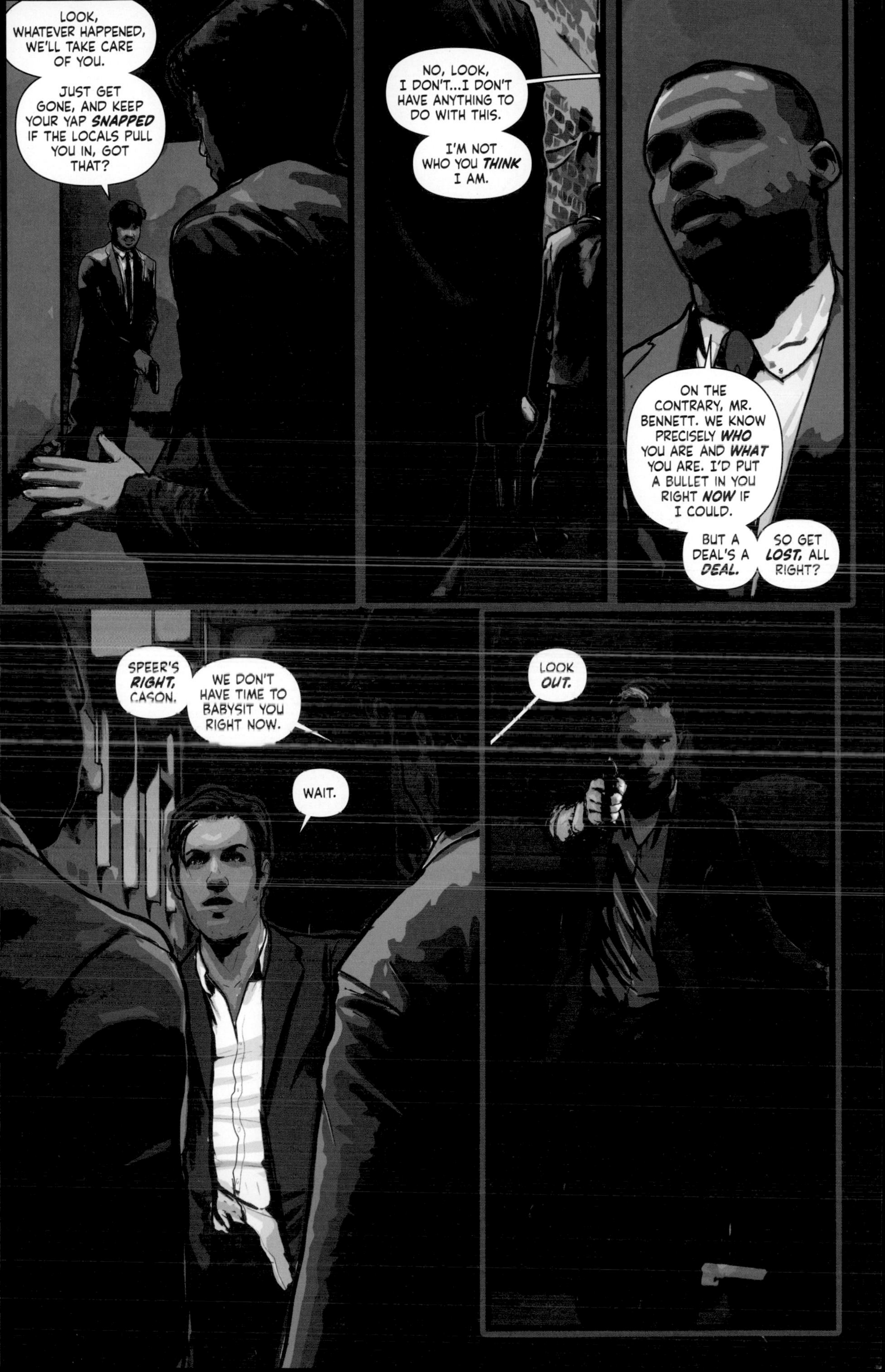
LOOK, WHATEVER HAPPENED, WE'LL TAKE CARE OF YOU.
JUST GET GONE, AND KEEP YOUR YAP SNAPPED IF THE LOCALS PULL YOU IN, GOT THAT?
NO, LOOK, I DON'T...I DON'T HAVE ANYTHING TO DO WITH THIS.
I'M NOT WHO YOU THINK I AM.
ON THE CONTRARY, MR. BENNETT. WE KNOW PRECISELY WHO YOU ARE AND WHAT YOU ARE. I'D PUT A BULLET IN YOU RIGHT NOW IF I COULD.
BUT A DEAL'S A DEAL.
SO GET LOST, ALL RIGHT?
SPEER'S RIGHT, CASON.
WE DON'T HAVE TIME TO BABYSIT YOU RIGHT NOW.
WAIT.
LOOK OUT.

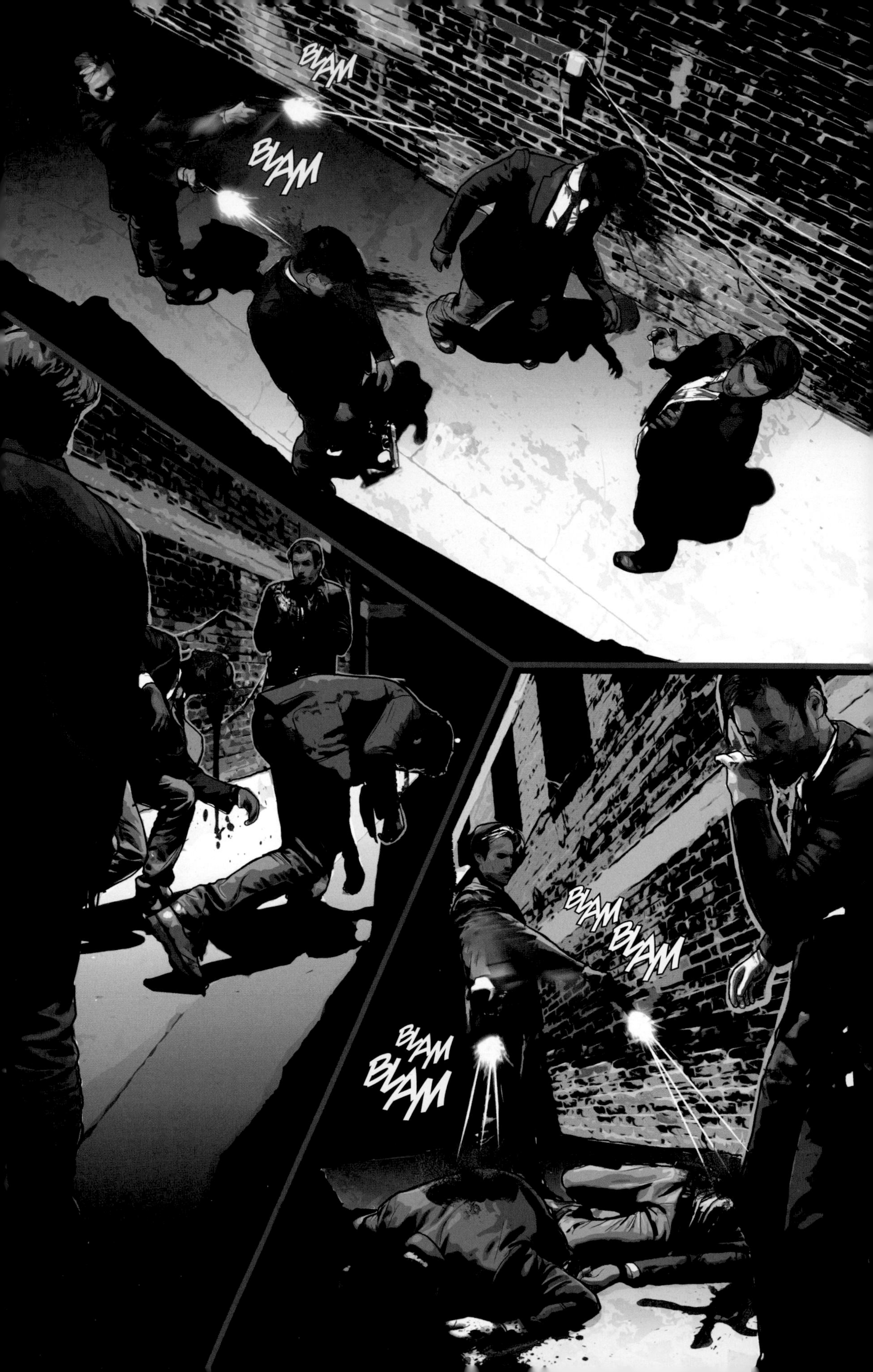
BLAM
BLAM
BLAM BLAM
BLAM BLAM

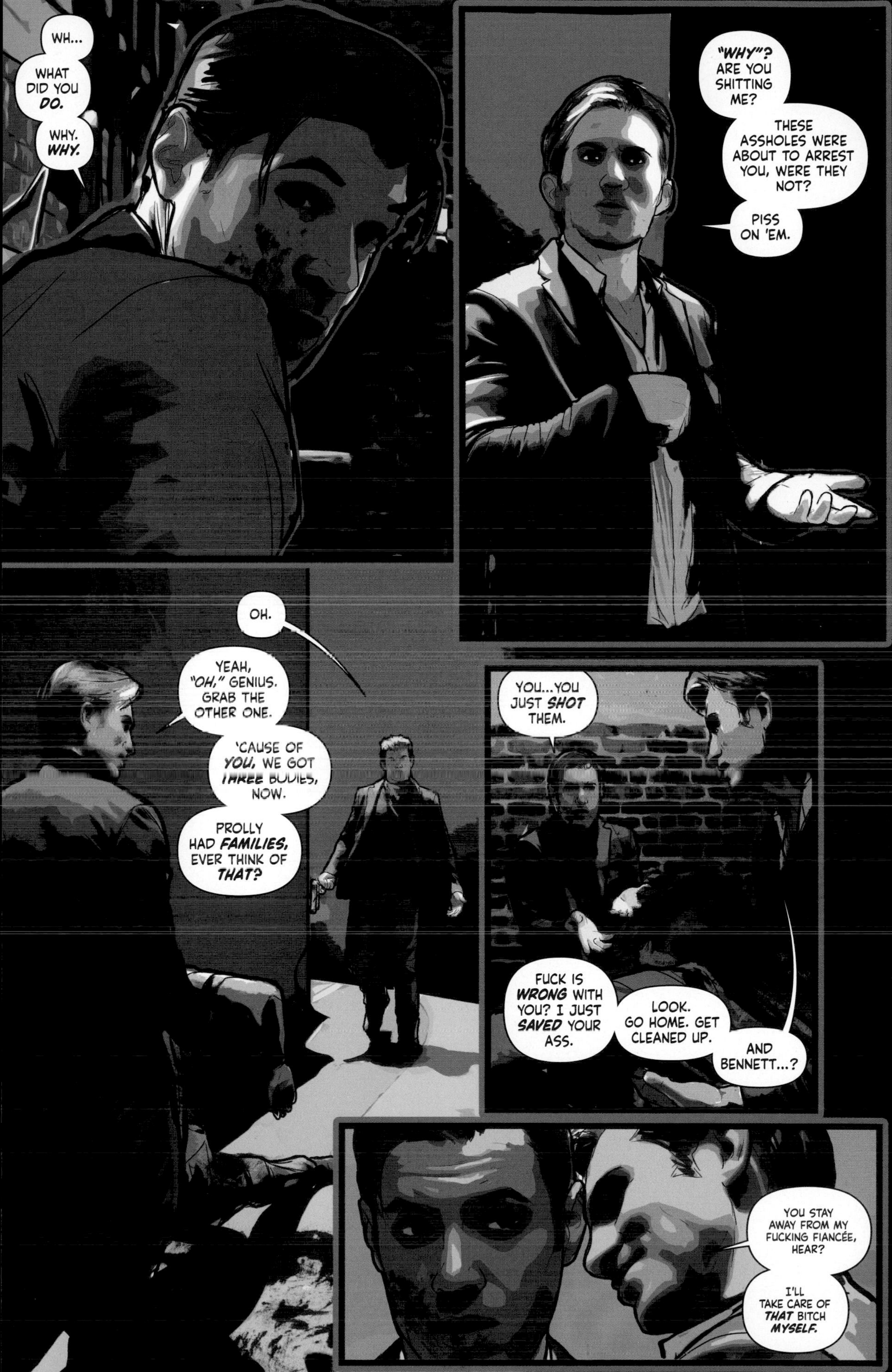
WH...
WHAT DID YOU DO.
WHY. WHY.
"WHY"? ARE YOU SHITTING ME?
THESE ASSHOLES WERE ABOUT TO ARREST YOU, WERE THEY NOT?
PISS ON 'EM.
OH.
YEAH, "OH," GENIUS. GRAB THE OTHER ONE.
'CAUSE OF YOU, WE GOT THREE BODIES, NOW.
PROLLY HAD FAMILIES, EVER THINK OF THAT?
YOU...YOU JUST SHOT THEM.
FUCK IS WRONG WITH YOU? I JUST SAVED YOUR ASS.
LOOK. GO HOME. GET CLEANED UP.
AND BENNETT...?
YOU STAY AWAY FROM MY FUCKING FIANCÉE, HEAR?
I'LL TAKE CARE OF THAT BITCH MYSELF.

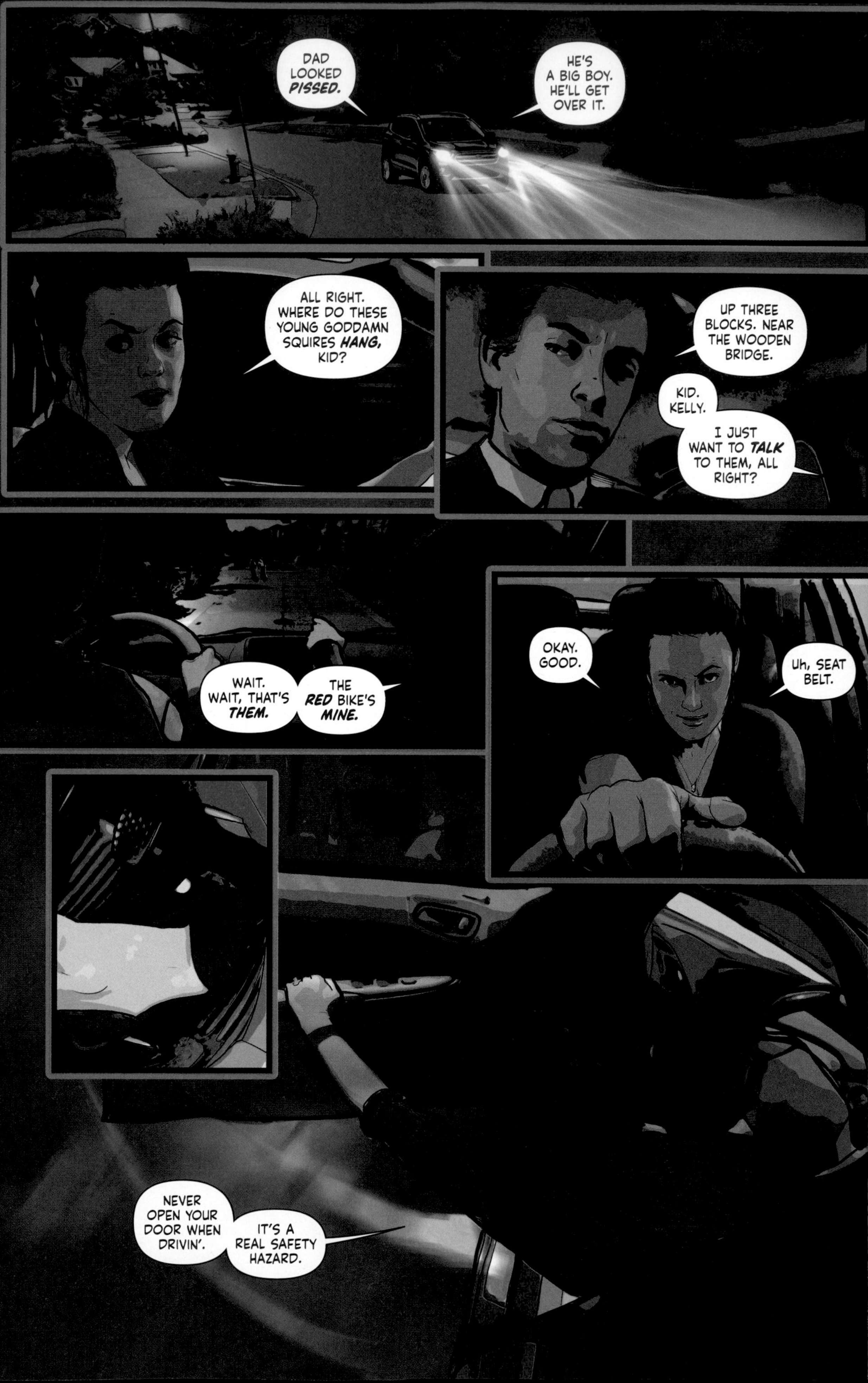
DAD LOOKED PISSED.
HE'S A BIG BOY. HE'LL GET OVER IT.
ALL RIGHT. WHERE DO THESE YOUNG GODDAMN SQUIRES HANG, KID?
UP THREE BLOCKS. NEAR THE WOODEN BRIDGE.
KID. KELLY.
I JUST WANT TO TALK TO THEM, ALL RIGHT?
WAIT. WAIT, THAT'S THEM.
THE RED BIKE'S MINE.
OKAY. GOOD.
Uh, SEAT BELT.
NEVER OPEN YOUR DOOR WHEN DRIVIN'.
IT'S A REAL SAFETY HAZARD.

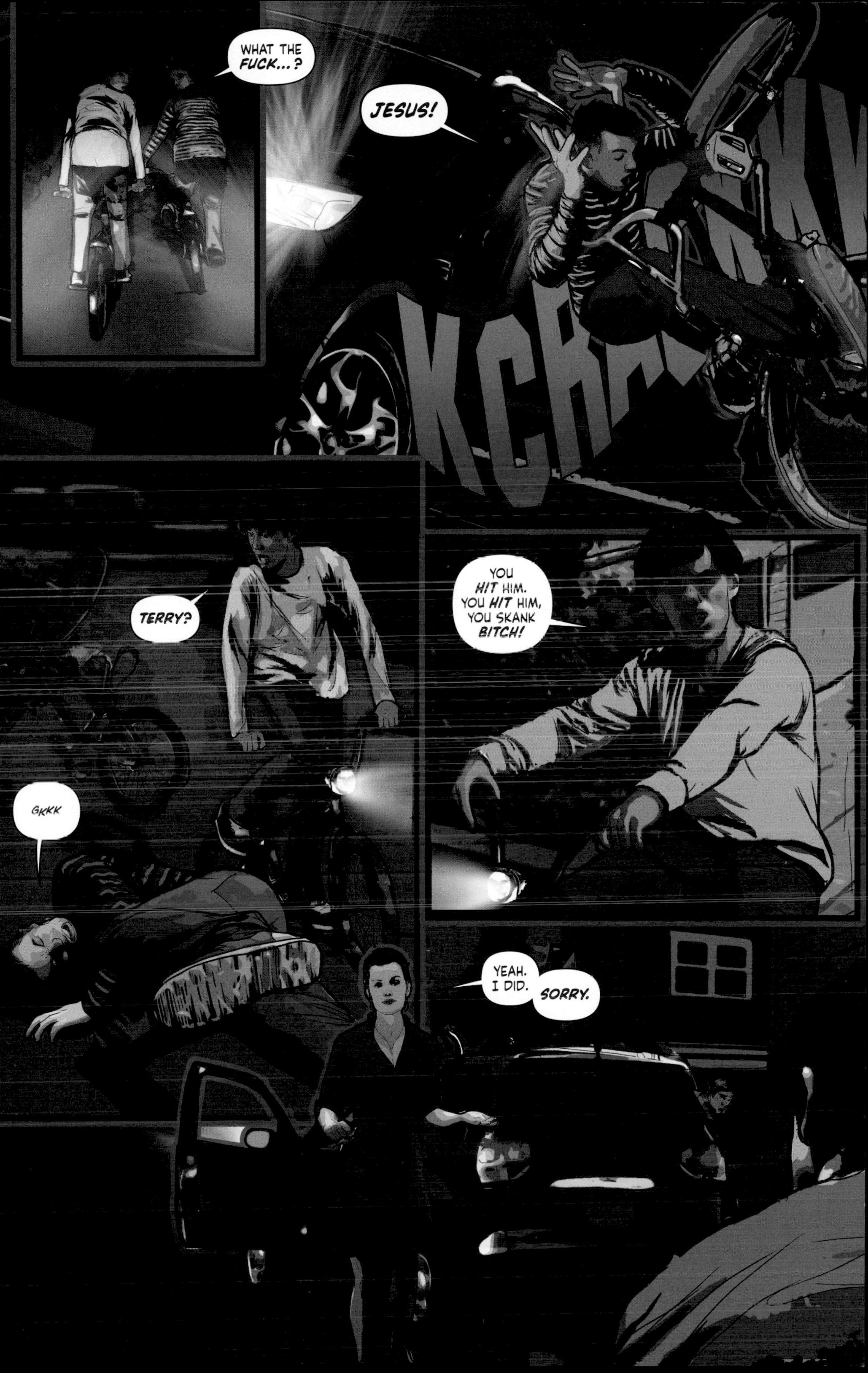
WHAT THE FUCK...?
JESUS!
KCRA
TERRY?
YOU HIT HIM. YOU HIT HIM, YOU SKANK BITCH!
GKKK
YEAH. I DID.
SORRY.

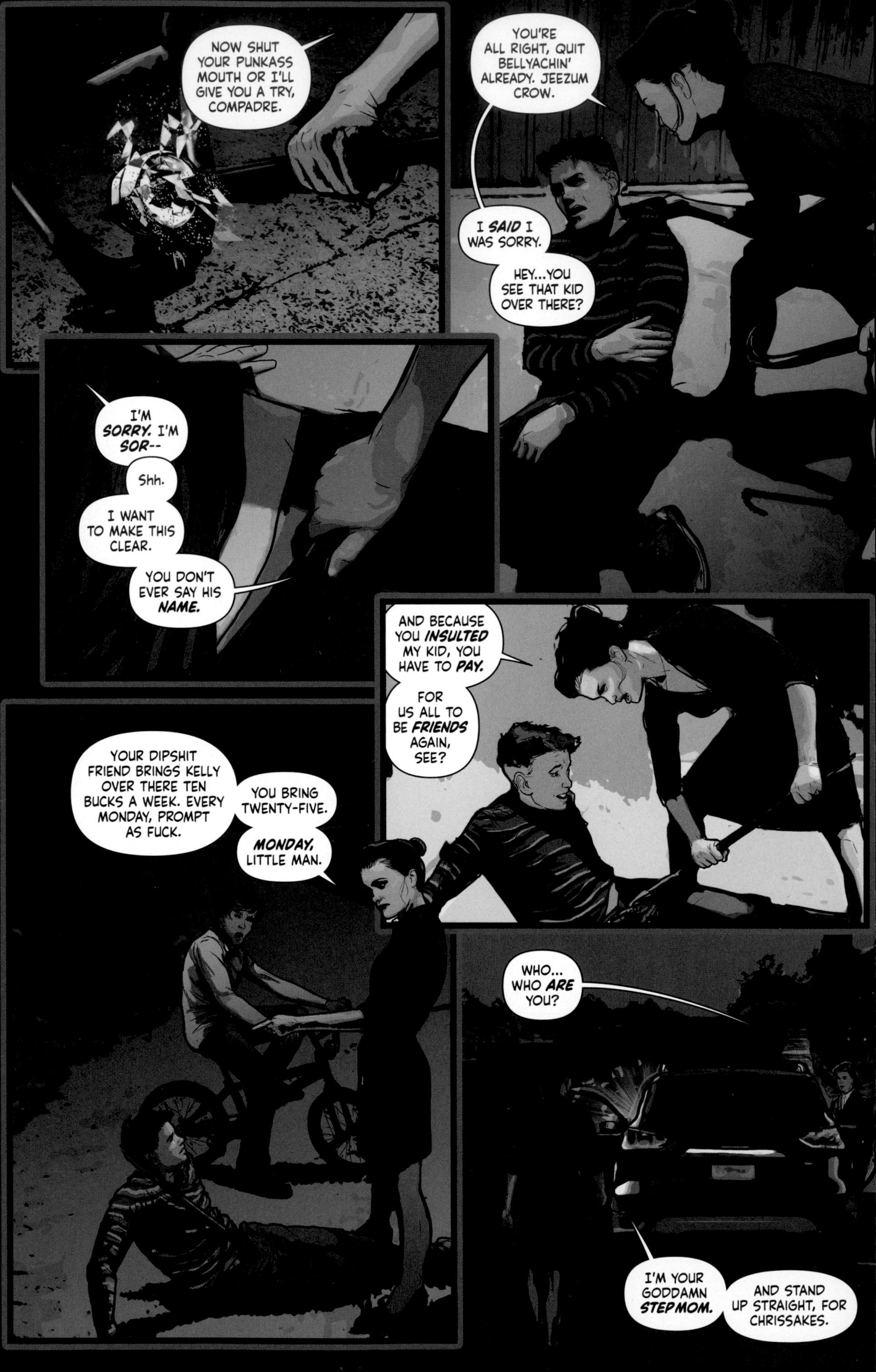
NOW SHUT YOUR PUNKASS MOUTH OR I'LL GIVE YOU A TRY, COMPADRE.
YOU'RE ALL RIGHT, QUIT BELLYACHIN' ALREADY. JEEZUM CROW.
I *SAID* I WAS SORRY.
HEY...YOU SEE THAT KID OVER THERE?
I'M *SORRY.* I'M *SOR--*
Shh.
I WANT TO MAKE THIS CLEAR.
YOU DON'T EVER SAY HIS *NAME.*
AND BECAUSE YOU *INSULTED* MY KID, YOU HAVE TO *PAY.*
FOR US ALL TO BE *FRIENDS* AGAIN, SEE?
YOUR DIPSHIT FRIEND BRINGS KELLY OVER THERE TEN BUCKS A WEEK. EVERY MONDAY, PROMPT AS FUCK.
YOU BRING TWENTY-FIVE.
MONDAY, LITTLE MAN.
WHO... WHO *ARE* YOU?
I'M YOUR GODDAMN *STEPMOM.*
AND STAND UP STRAIGHT, FOR CHRISSAKES.

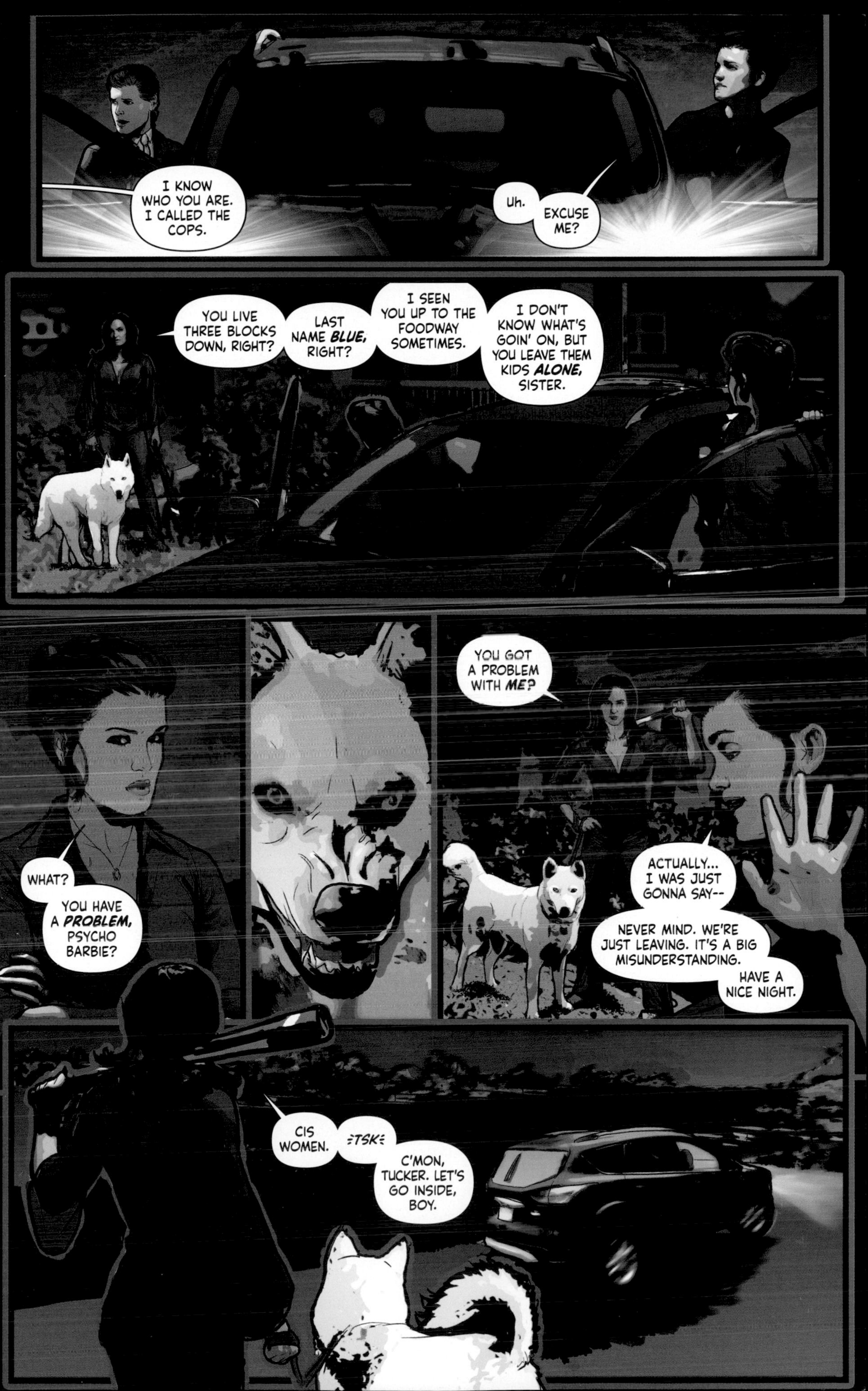
I KNOW WHO YOU ARE. I CALLED THE COPS.
Uh.
EXCUSE ME?
YOU LIVE THREE BLOCKS DOWN, RIGHT?
LAST NAME BLUE, RIGHT?
I SEEN YOU UP TO THE FOODWAY SOMETIMES.
I DON'T KNOW WHAT'S GOIN' ON, BUT YOU LEAVE THEM KIDS ALONE, SISTER.
WHAT?
YOU HAVE A PROBLEM, PSYCHO BARBIE?
YOU GOT A PROBLEM WITH ME?
ACTUALLY... I WAS JUST GONNA SAY--
NEVER MIND. WE'RE JUST LEAVING. IT'S A BIG MISUNDERSTANDING.
HAVE A NICE NIGHT.
CIS WOMEN.
TSK
C'MON, TUCKER. LET'S GO INSIDE, BOY.

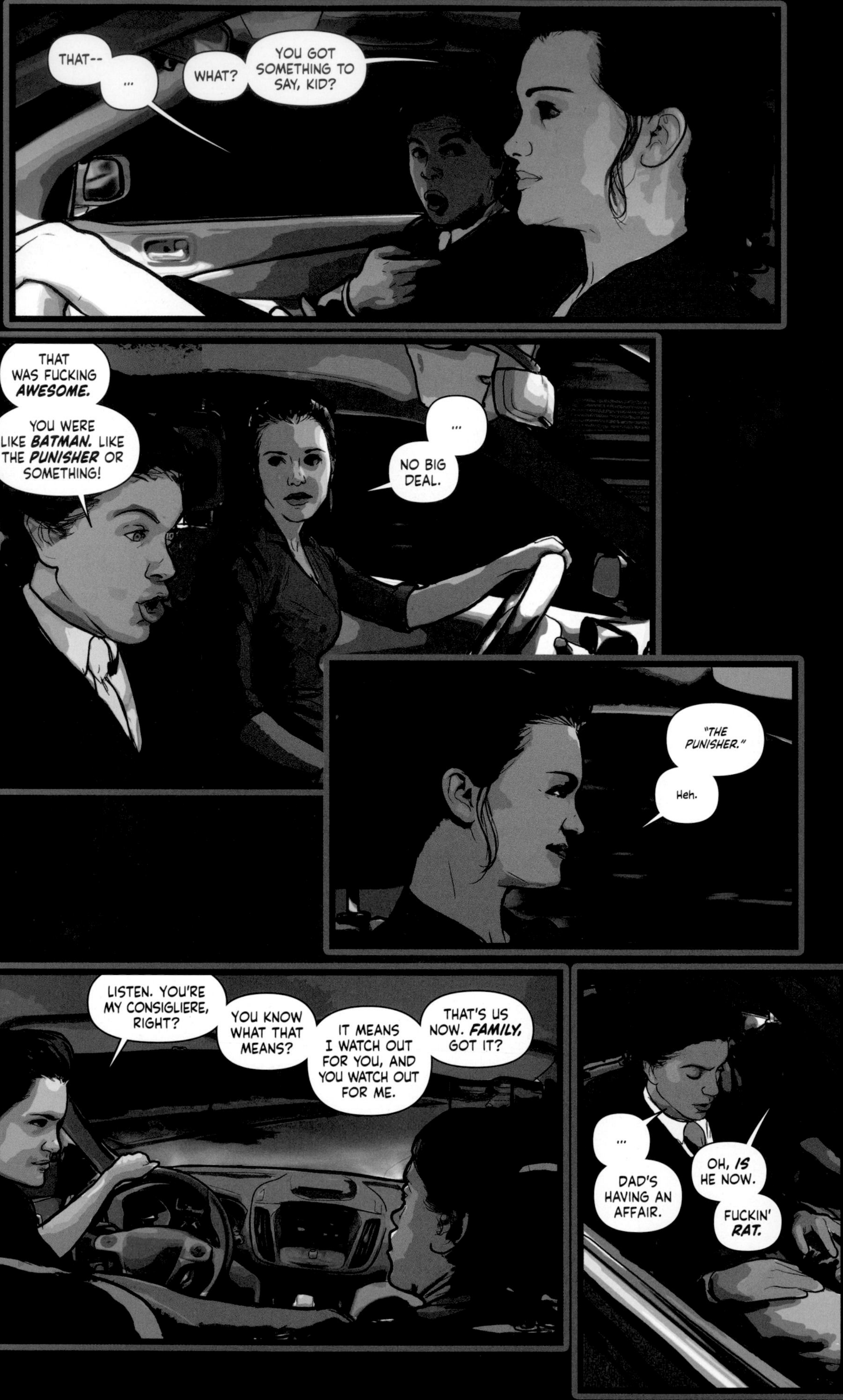
THAT--
...
WHAT?
YOU GOT SOMETHING TO SAY, KID?
THAT WAS FUCKING AWESOME.
YOU WERE LIKE BATMAN. LIKE THE PUNISHER OR SOMETHING!
...
NO BIG DEAL.
"THE PUNISHER."
Heh.
LISTEN. YOU'RE MY CONSIGLIERE, RIGHT?
YOU KNOW WHAT THAT MEANS?
IT MEANS I WATCH OUT FOR YOU, AND YOU WATCH OUT FOR ME.
THAT'S US NOW. FAMILY, GOT IT?
...
DAD'S HAVING AN AFFAIR.
OH, IS HE NOW.
FUCKIN' RAT.

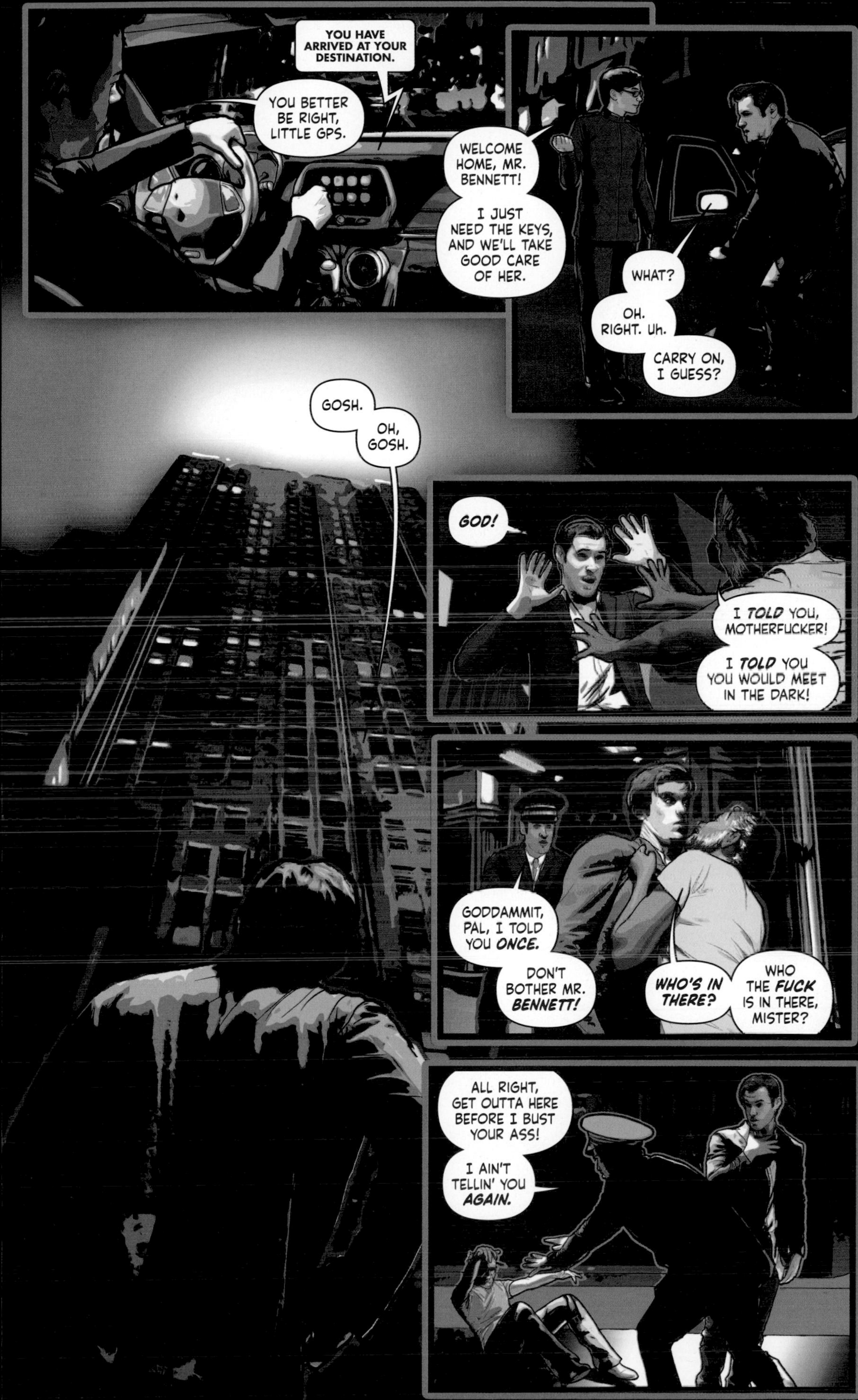
YOU HAVE ARRIVED AT YOUR DESTINATION.
YOU BETTER BE RIGHT, LITTLE GPS.
WELCOME HOME, MR. BENNETT!
I JUST NEED THE KEYS, AND WE'LL TAKE GOOD CARE OF HER.
WHAT?
OH. RIGHT. Uh.
CARRY ON, I GUESS?
GOSH.
OH, GOSH.
GOD!
I TOLD YOU, MOTHERFUCKER!
I TOLD YOU YOU WOULD MEET IN THE DARK!
GODDAMMIT, PAL, I TOLD YOU ONCE.
DON'T BOTHER MR. BENNETT!
WHO'S IN THERE?
WHO THE FUCK IS IN THERE, MISTER?
ALL RIGHT, GET OUTTA HERE BEFORE I BUST YOUR ASS!
I AIN'T TELLIN' YOU AGAIN.

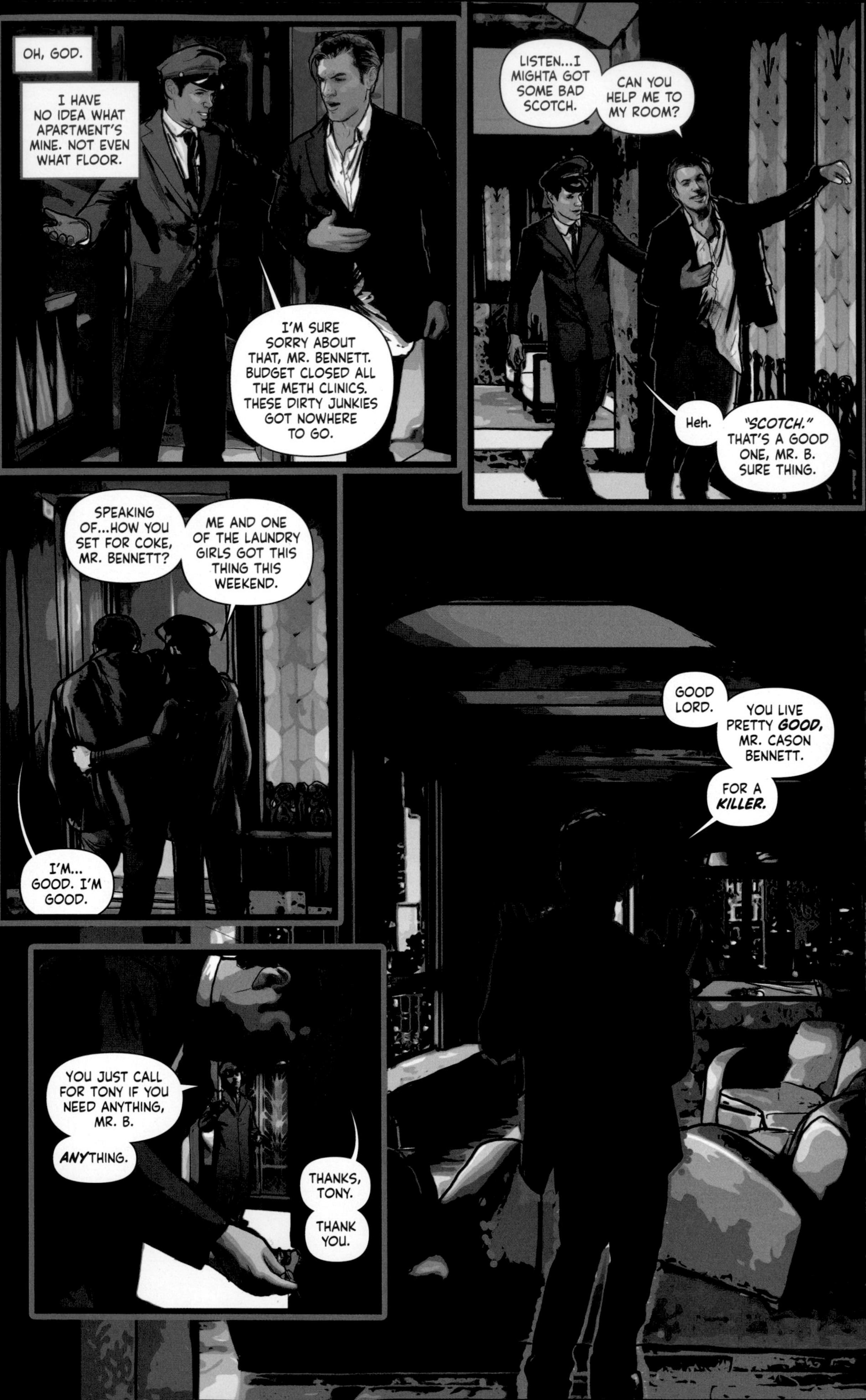
OH, GOD.
I HAVE NO IDEA WHAT APARTMENT'S MINE. NOT EVEN WHAT FLOOR.
I'M SURE SORRY ABOUT THAT, MR. BENNETT. BUDGET CLOSED ALL THE METH CLINICS. THESE DIRTY JUNKIES GOT NOWHERE TO GO.
LISTEN...I MIGHTA GOT SOME BAD SCOTCH.
CAN YOU HELP ME TO MY ROOM?
Heh.
"SCOTCH." THAT'S A GOOD ONE, MR. B. SURE THING.
SPEAKING OF...HOW YOU SET FOR COKE, MR. BENNETT?
ME AND ONE OF THE LAUNDRY GIRLS GOT THIS THING THIS WEEKEND.
I'M... GOOD. I'M GOOD.
YOU JUST CALL FOR TONY IF YOU NEED ANYTHING, MR. B.
ANYTHING.
THANKS, TONY.
THANK YOU.
GOOD LORD.
YOU LIVE PRETTY GOOD, MR. CASON BENNETT.
FOR A KILLER.

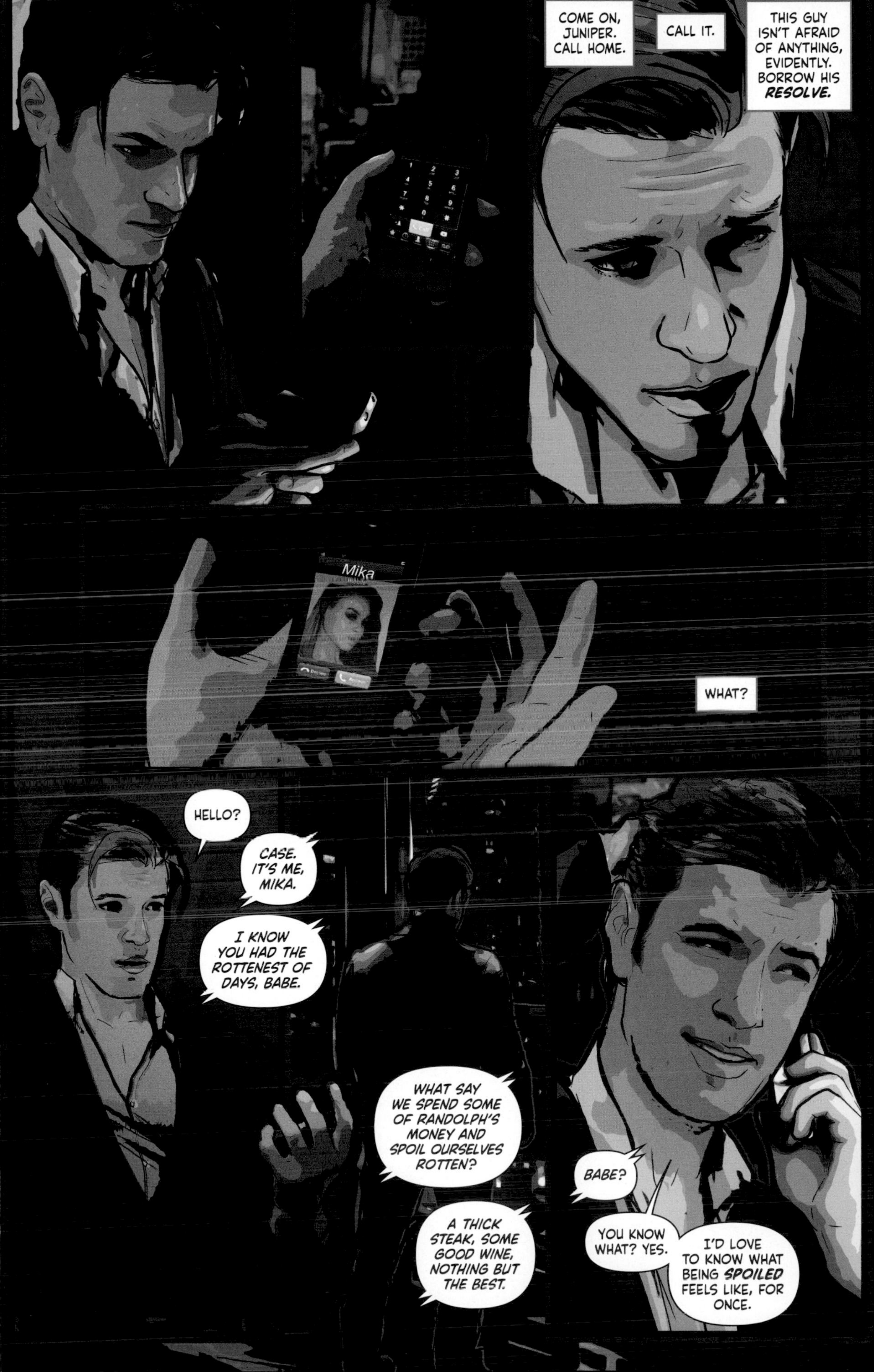
COME ON, JUNIPER. CALL HOME.
CALL IT.
THIS GUY ISN'T AFRAID OF ANYTHING, EVIDENTLY. BORROW HIS RESOLVE.
Mika
WHAT?
HELLO?
CASE. IT'S ME, MIKA.
I KNOW YOU HAD THE ROTTENEST OF DAYS, BABE.
WHAT SAY WE SPEND SOME OF RANDOLPH'S MONEY AND SPOIL OURSELVES ROTTEN?
A THICK STEAK, SOME GOOD WINE, NOTHING BUT THE BEST.
BABE?
YOU KNOW WHAT? YES.
I'D LOVE TO KNOW WHAT BEING SPOILED FEELS LIKE, FOR ONCE.

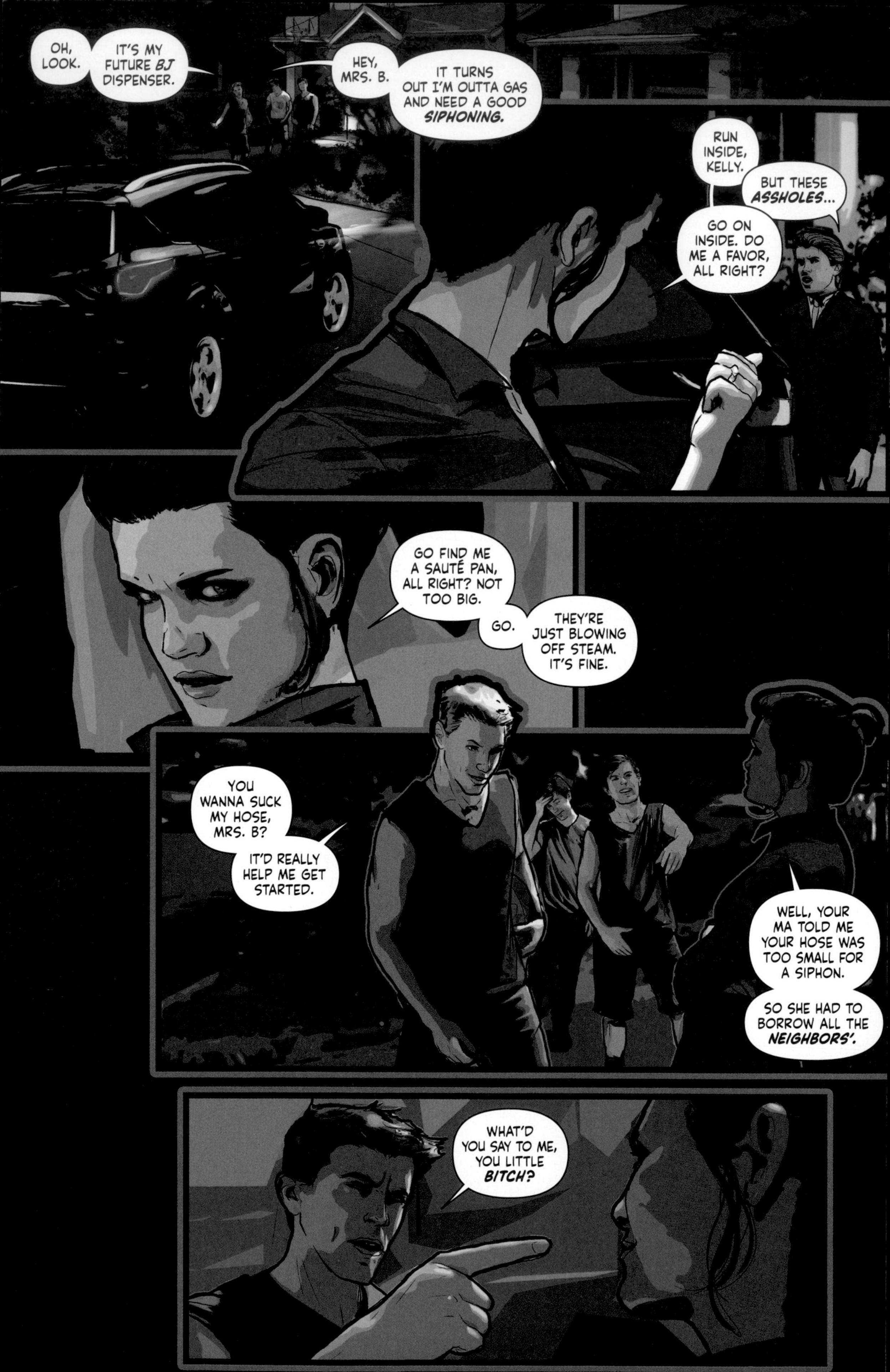
OH, LOOK.
IT'S MY FUTURE BJ DISPENSER.
HEY, MRS. B.
IT TURNS OUT I'M OUTTA GAS AND NEED A GOOD SIPHONING.
RUN INSIDE, KELLY.
BUT THESE ASSHOLES...
GO ON INSIDE. DO ME A FAVOR, ALL RIGHT?
GO FIND ME A SAUTÉ PAN, ALL RIGHT? NOT TOO BIG.
GO.
THEY'RE JUST BLOWING OFF STEAM. IT'S FINE.
YOU WANNA SUCK MY HOSE, MRS. B?
IT'D REALLY HELP ME GET STARTED.
WELL, YOUR MA TOLD ME YOUR HOSE WAS TOO SMALL FOR A SIPHON.
SO SHE HAD TO BORROW ALL THE NEIGHBORS'.
WHAT'D YOU SAY TO ME, YOU LITTLE BITCH?

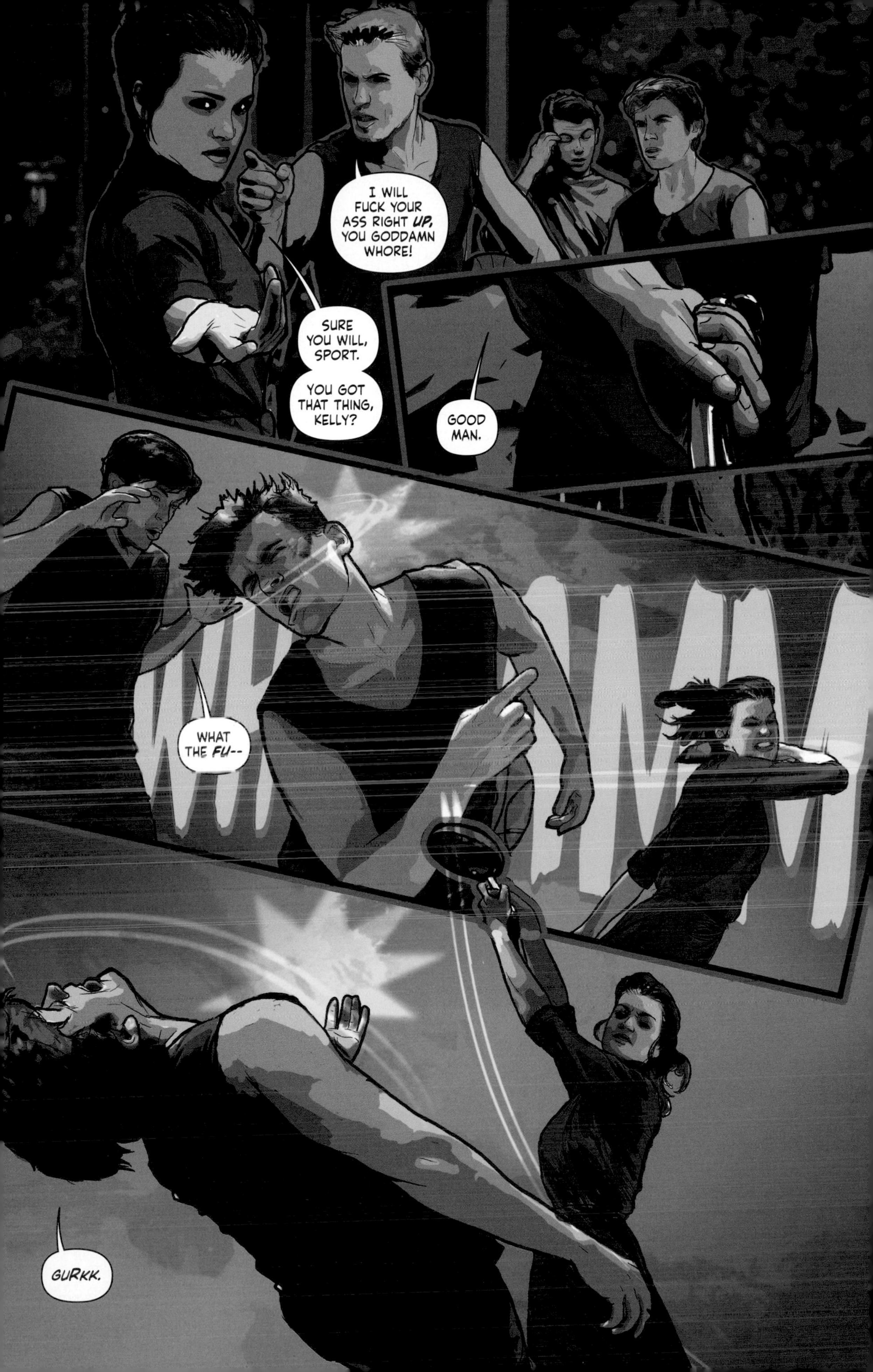
I WILL FUCK YOUR ASS RIGHT *UP*, YOU GODDAMN WHORE!
SURE YOU WILL, SPORT.
YOU GOT THAT THING, KELLY?
GOOD MAN.
WHAT THE *FU*--
GURKK.

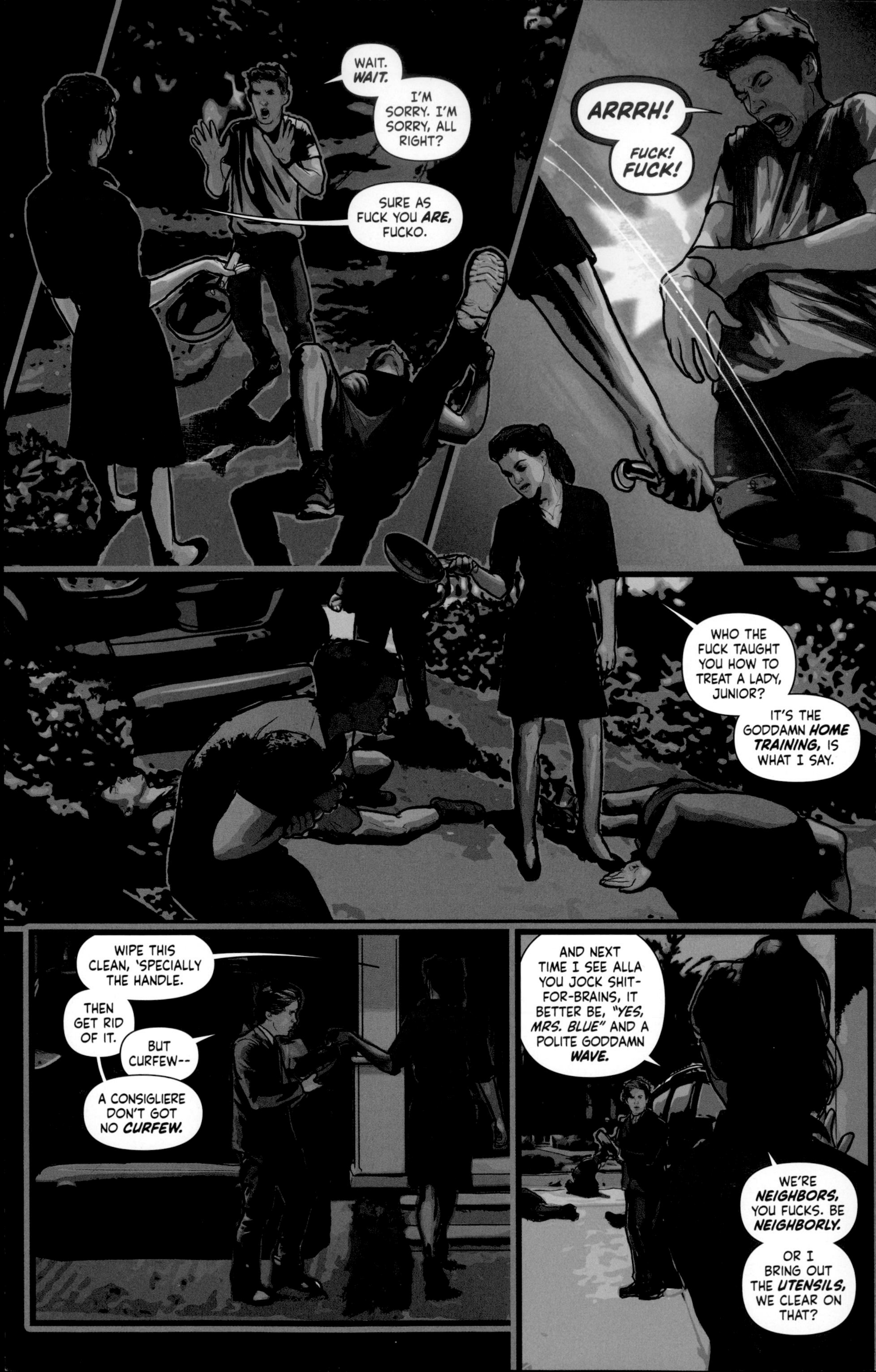
WAIT. WAIT.
I'M SORRY. I'M SORRY, ALL RIGHT?
SURE AS FUCK YOU ARE, FUCKO.
ARRRH!
FUCK! FUCK!
WHO THE FUCK TAUGHT YOU HOW TO TREAT A LADY, JUNIOR?
IT'S THE GODDAMN HOME TRAINING, IS WHAT I SAY.
WIPE THIS CLEAN, 'SPECIALLY THE HANDLE.
THEN GET RID OF IT.
BUT CURFEW--
A CONSIGLIERE DON'T GOT NO CURFEW.
AND NEXT TIME I SEE ALLA YOU JOCK SHIT-FOR-BRAINS, IT BETTER BE, "YES, MRS. BLUE" AND A POLITE GODDAMN WAVE.
WE'RE NEIGHBORS, YOU FUCKS. BE NEIGHBORLY.
OR I BRING OUT THE UTENSILS, WE CLEAR ON THAT?

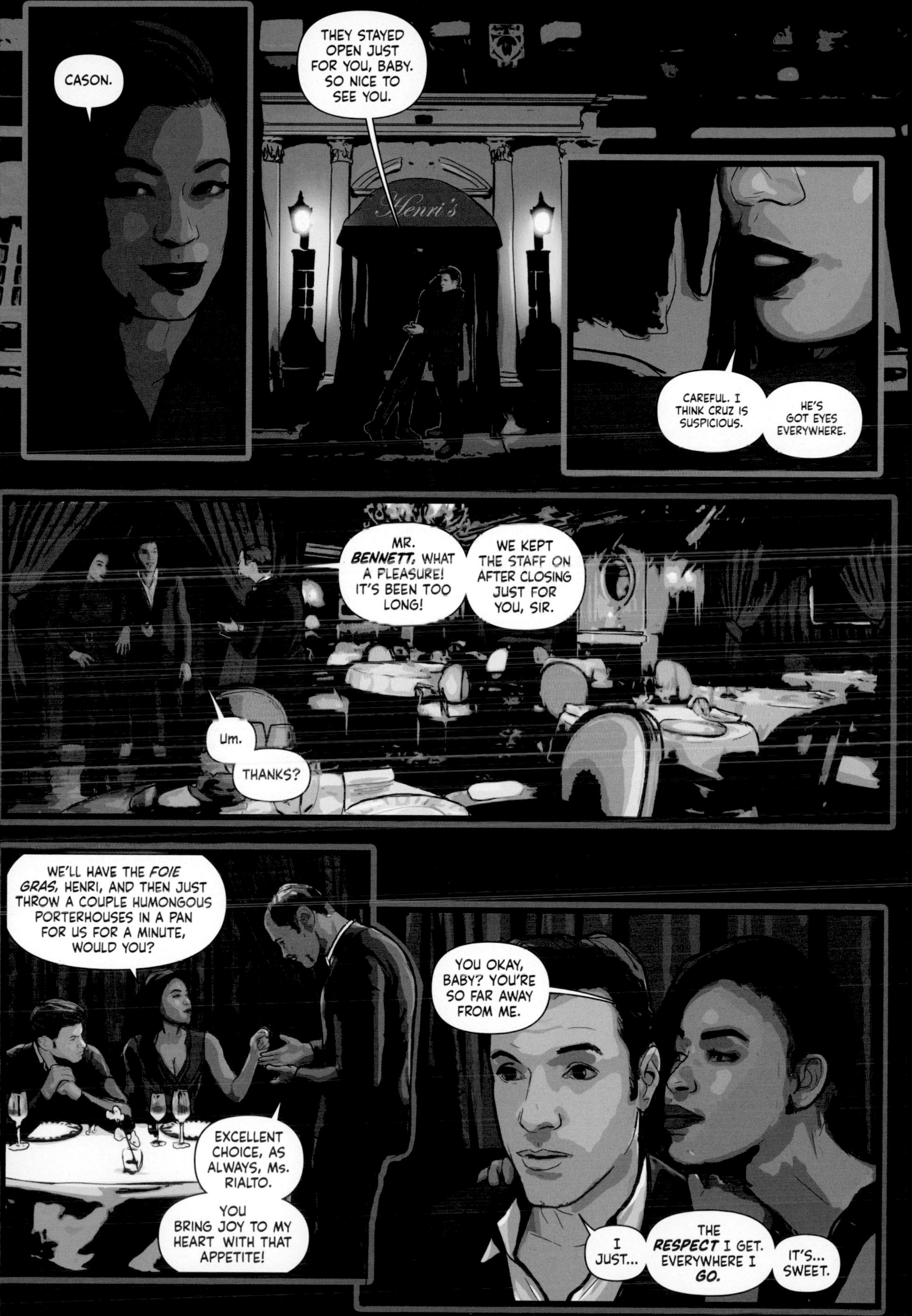
CASON.
THEY STAYED OPEN JUST FOR YOU, BABY. SO NICE TO SEE YOU.
Henri's
CAREFUL. I THINK CRUZ IS SUSPICIOUS.
HE'S GOT EYES EVERYWHERE.
MR. BENNETT, WHAT A PLEASURE! IT'S BEEN TOO LONG!
WE KEPT THE STAFF ON AFTER CLOSING JUST FOR YOU, SIR.
Um.
THANKS?
WE'LL HAVE THE FOIE GRAS, HENRI, AND THEN JUST THROW A COUPLE HUMONGOUS PORTERHOUSES IN A PAN FOR US FOR A MINUTE, WOULD YOU?
EXCELLENT CHOICE, AS ALWAYS, Ms. RIALTO.
YOU BRING JOY TO MY HEART WITH THAT APPETITE!
YOU OKAY, BABY? YOU'RE SO FAR AWAY FROM ME.
I JUST...
THE RESPECT I GET. EVERYWHERE I GO.
IT'S... SWEET.

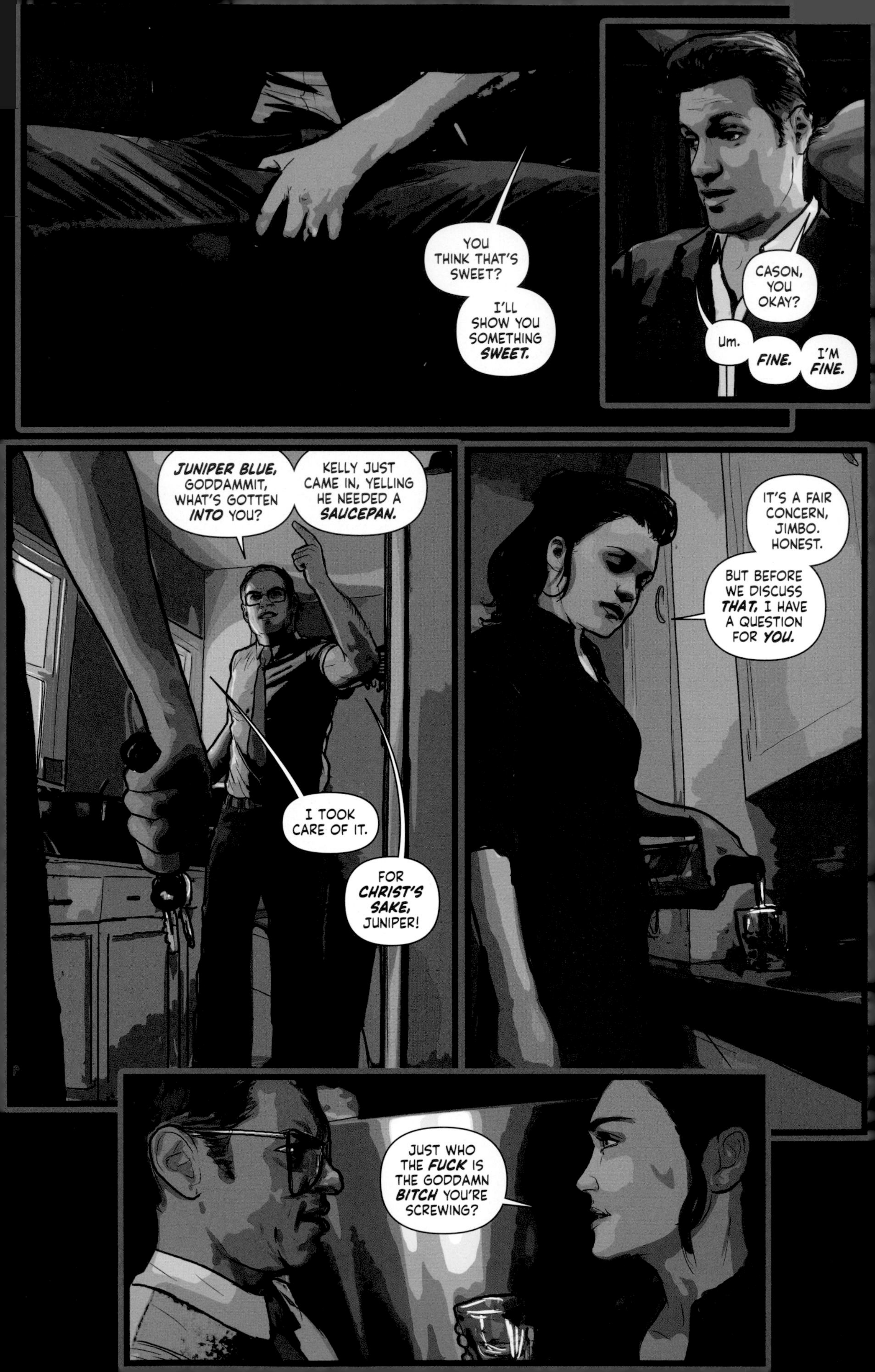

YOU THINK THAT'S SWEET?
I'LL SHOW YOU SOMETHING SWEET.
CASON, YOU OKAY?
Um.
FINE.
I'M FINE.
JUNIPER BLUE, GODDAMMIT, WHAT'S GOTTEN INTO YOU?
KELLY JUST CAME IN, YELLING HE NEEDED A SAUCEPAN.
I TOOK CARE OF IT.
FOR CHRIST'S SAKE, JUNIPER!
IT'S A FAIR CONCERN, JIMBO. HONEST.
BUT BEFORE WE DISCUSS THAT, I HAVE A QUESTION FOR YOU.
JUST WHO THE FUCK IS THE GODDAMN BITCH YOU'RE SCREWING?

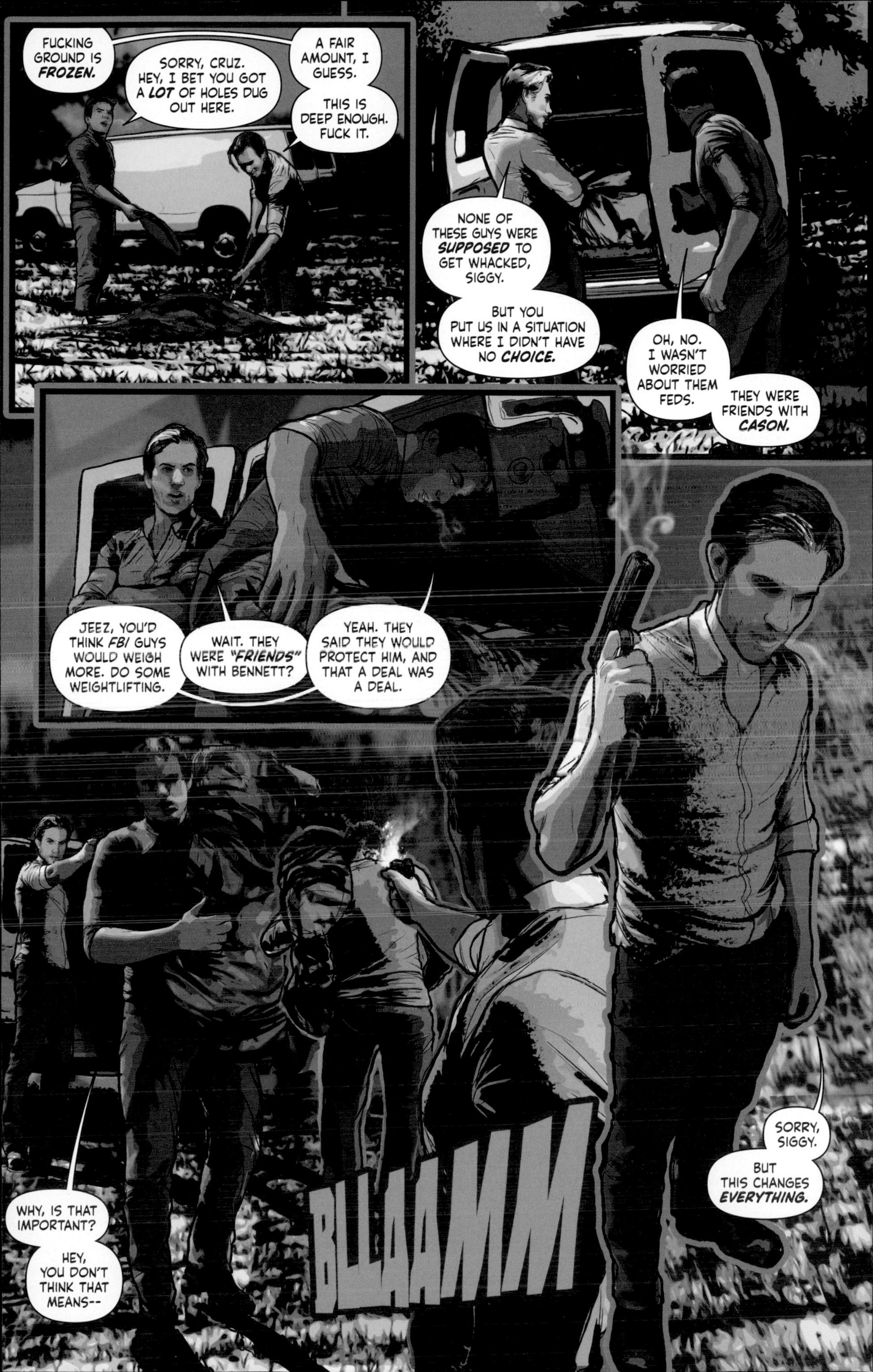
FUCKING GROUND IS ***FROZEN.***
SORRY, CRUZ. HEY, I BET YOU GOT A ***LOT*** OF HOLES DUG OUT HERE.
A FAIR AMOUNT, I GUESS.
THIS IS DEEP ENOUGH. FUCK IT.
NONE OF THESE GUYS WERE ***SUPPOSED*** TO GET WHACKED, SIGGY.
BUT YOU PUT US IN A SITUATION WHERE I DIDN'T HAVE NO ***CHOICE.***
OH, NO. I WASN'T WORRIED ABOUT THEM FEDS.
THEY WERE FRIENDS WITH ***CASON.***
JEEZ, YOU'D THINK *FBI* GUYS WOULD WEIGH MORE. DO SOME WEIGHTLIFTING.
WAIT. THEY WERE ***"FRIENDS"*** WITH BENNETT?
YEAH. THEY SAID THEY WOULD PROTECT HIM, AND THAT A DEAL WAS A DEAL.
WHY, IS THAT IMPORTANT?
HEY, YOU DON'T THINK THAT MEANS--
BLLAAMM
SORRY, SIGGY.
BUT THIS CHANGES ***EVERYTHING.***

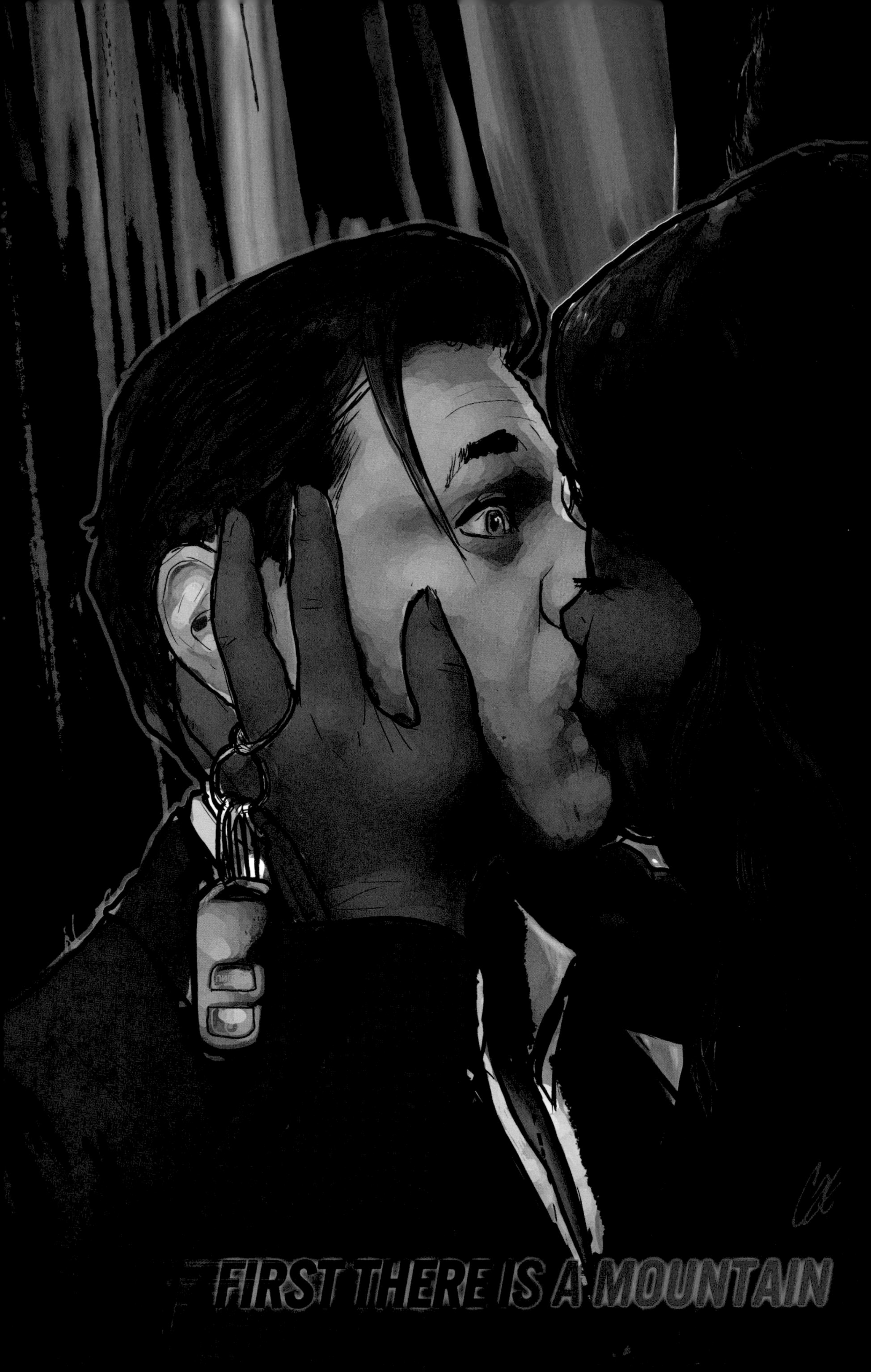
FIRST THERE IS A MOUNTAIN

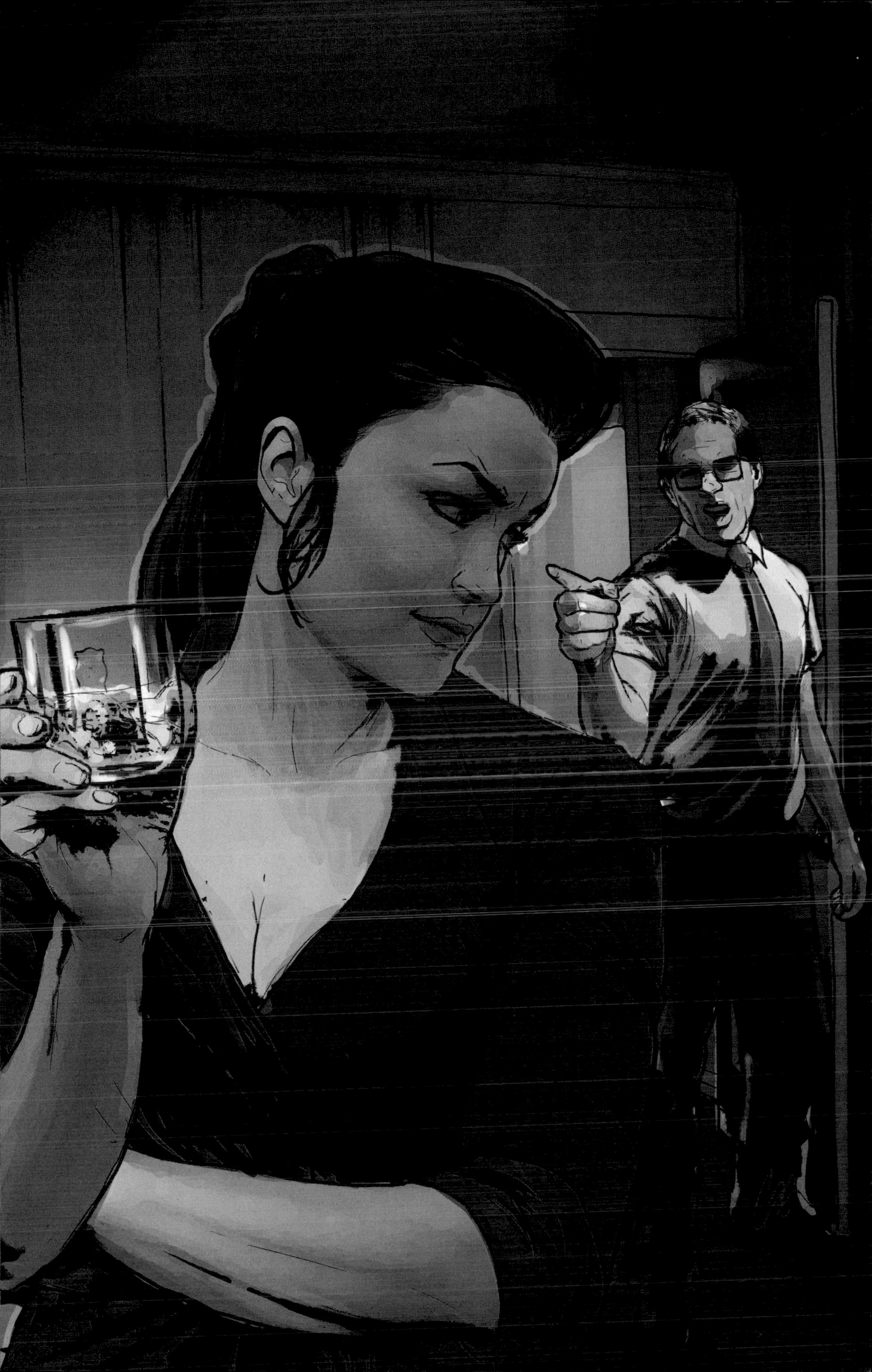

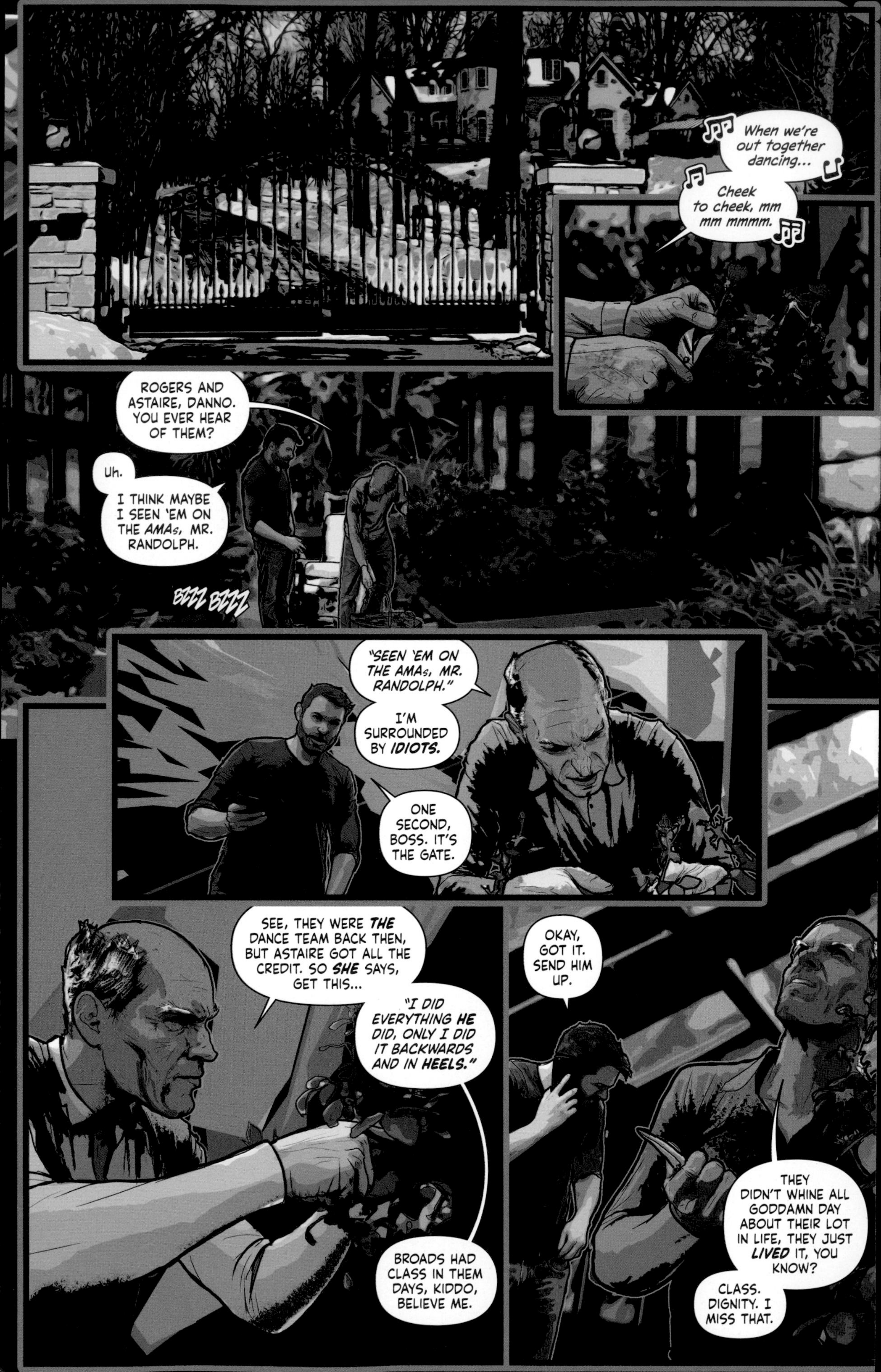
When we're out together dancing...
Cheek to cheek, mm mm mmmm.
ROGERS AND ASTAIRE, DANNO. YOU EVER HEAR OF THEM?
Uh.
I THINK MAYBE I SEEN 'EM ON THE AMAs, MR. RANDOLPH.
BZZZ BZZZ
"SEEN 'EM ON THE AMAs, MR. RANDOLPH."
I'M SURROUNDED BY IDIOTS.
ONE SECOND, BOSS. IT'S THE GATE.
SEE, THEY WERE THE DANCE TEAM BACK THEN, BUT ASTAIRE GOT ALL THE CREDIT. SO SHE SAYS, GET THIS...
"I DID EVERYTHING HE DID, ONLY I DID IT BACKWARDS AND IN HEELS."
BROADS HAD CLASS IN THEM DAYS, KIDDO, BELIEVE ME.
OKAY, GOT IT. SEND HIM UP.
THEY DIDN'T WHINE ALL GODDAMN DAY ABOUT THEIR LOT IN LIFE, THEY JUST LIVED IT, YOU KNOW?
CLASS. DIGNITY. I MISS THAT.

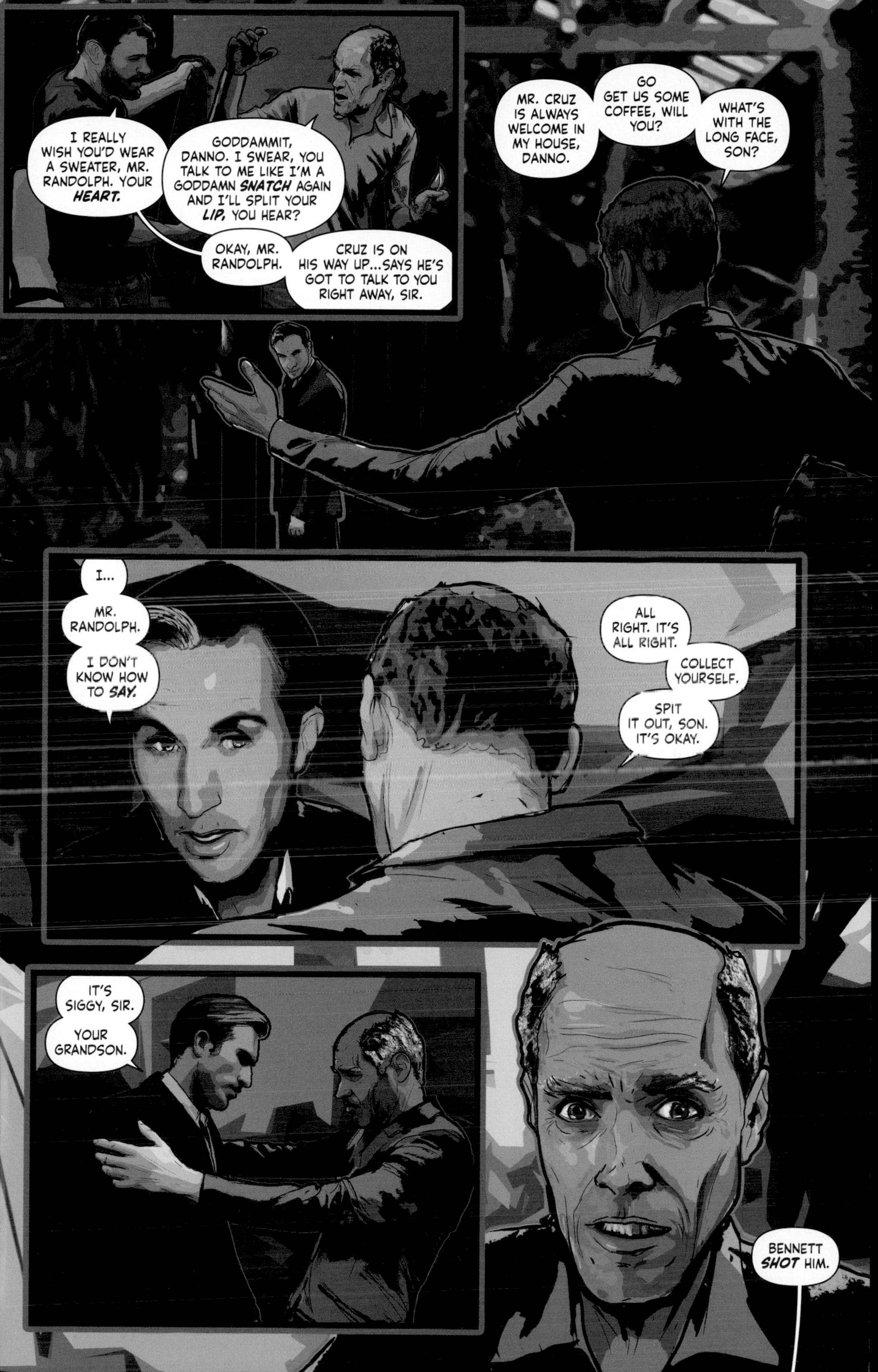
I REALLY WISH YOU'D WEAR A SWEATER, MR. RANDOLPH. YOUR **HEART.**
GODDAMMIT, DANNO. I SWEAR, YOU TALK TO ME LIKE I'M A GODDAMN **SNATCH** AGAIN AND I'LL SPLIT YOUR **LIP,** YOU HEAR?
OKAY, MR. RANDOLPH.
CRUZ IS ON HIS WAY UP...SAYS HE'S GOT TO TALK TO YOU RIGHT AWAY, SIR.
MR. CRUZ IS ALWAYS WELCOME IN MY HOUSE, DANNO.
GO GET US SOME COFFEE, WILL YOU?
WHAT'S WITH THE LONG FACE, SON?
I...
MR. RANDOLPH.
I DON'T KNOW HOW TO **SAY.**
ALL RIGHT. IT'S ALL RIGHT.
COLLECT YOURSELF.
SPIT IT OUT, SON. IT'S OKAY.
IT'S SIGGY, SIR.
YOUR GRANDSON.
BENNETT **SHOT** HIM.

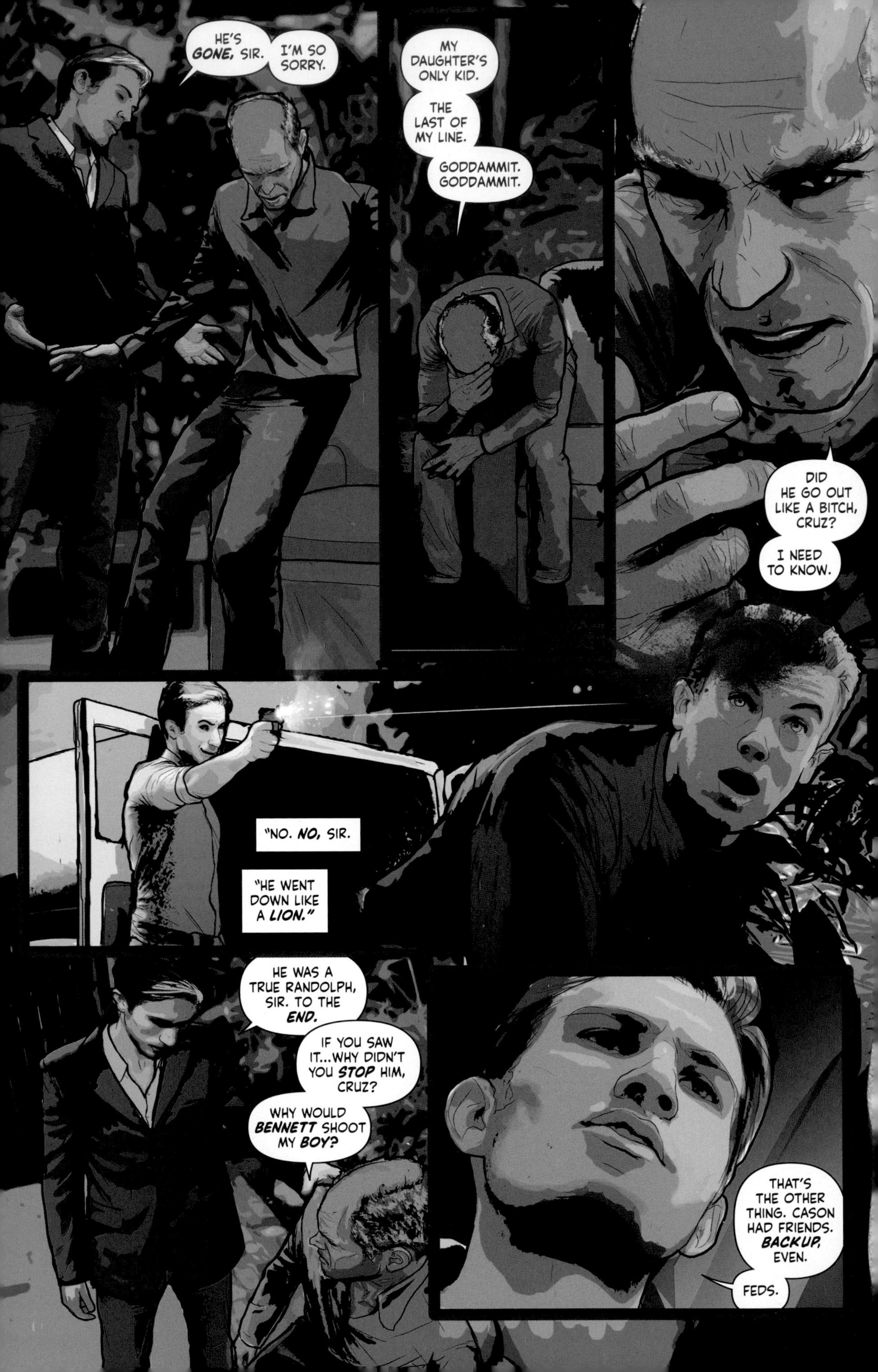
HE'S GONE, SIR.
I'M SO SORRY.
MY DAUGHTER'S ONLY KID.
THE LAST OF MY LINE.
GODDAMMIT. GODDAMMIT.
DID HE GO OUT LIKE A BITCH, CRUZ?
I NEED TO KNOW.
"NO. NO, SIR.
"HE WENT DOWN LIKE A LION."
HE WAS A TRUE RANDOLPH, SIR. TO THE END.
IF YOU SAW IT...WHY DIDN'T YOU STOP HIM, CRUZ?
WHY WOULD BENNETT SHOOT MY BOY?
THAT'S THE OTHER THING. CASON HAD FRIENDS. BACKUP, EVEN.
FEDS.

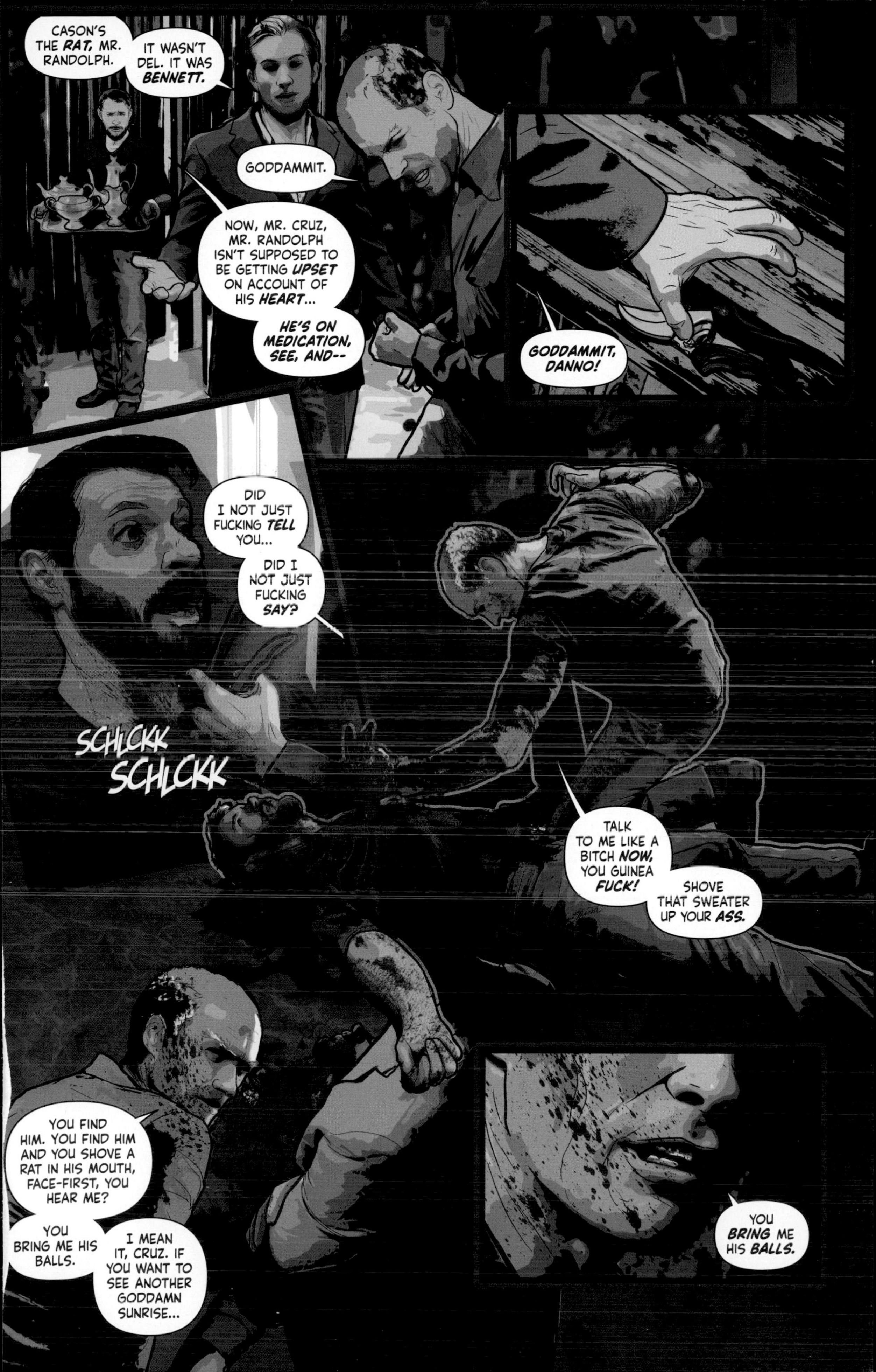
CASON'S THE RAT, MR. RANDOLPH.
IT WASN'T DEL. IT WAS BENNETT.
GODDAMMIT.
NOW, MR. CRUZ, MR. RANDOLPH ISN'T SUPPOSED TO BE GETTING UPSET ON ACCOUNT OF HIS HEART...
HE'S ON MEDICATION, SEE, AND--
GODDAMMIT, DANNO!
DID I NOT JUST FUCKING TELL YOU...
DID I NOT JUST FUCKING SAY?
SCHLCKK
SCHLCKK
TALK TO ME LIKE A BITCH NOW, YOU GUINEA FUCK!
SHOVE THAT SWEATER UP YOUR ASS.
YOU FIND HIM. YOU FIND HIM AND YOU SHOVE A RAT IN HIS MOUTH, FACE-FIRST, YOU HEAR ME?
YOU BRING ME HIS BALLS.
I MEAN IT, CRUZ. IF YOU WANT TO SEE ANOTHER GODDAMN SUNRISE...
YOU BRING ME HIS BALLS.

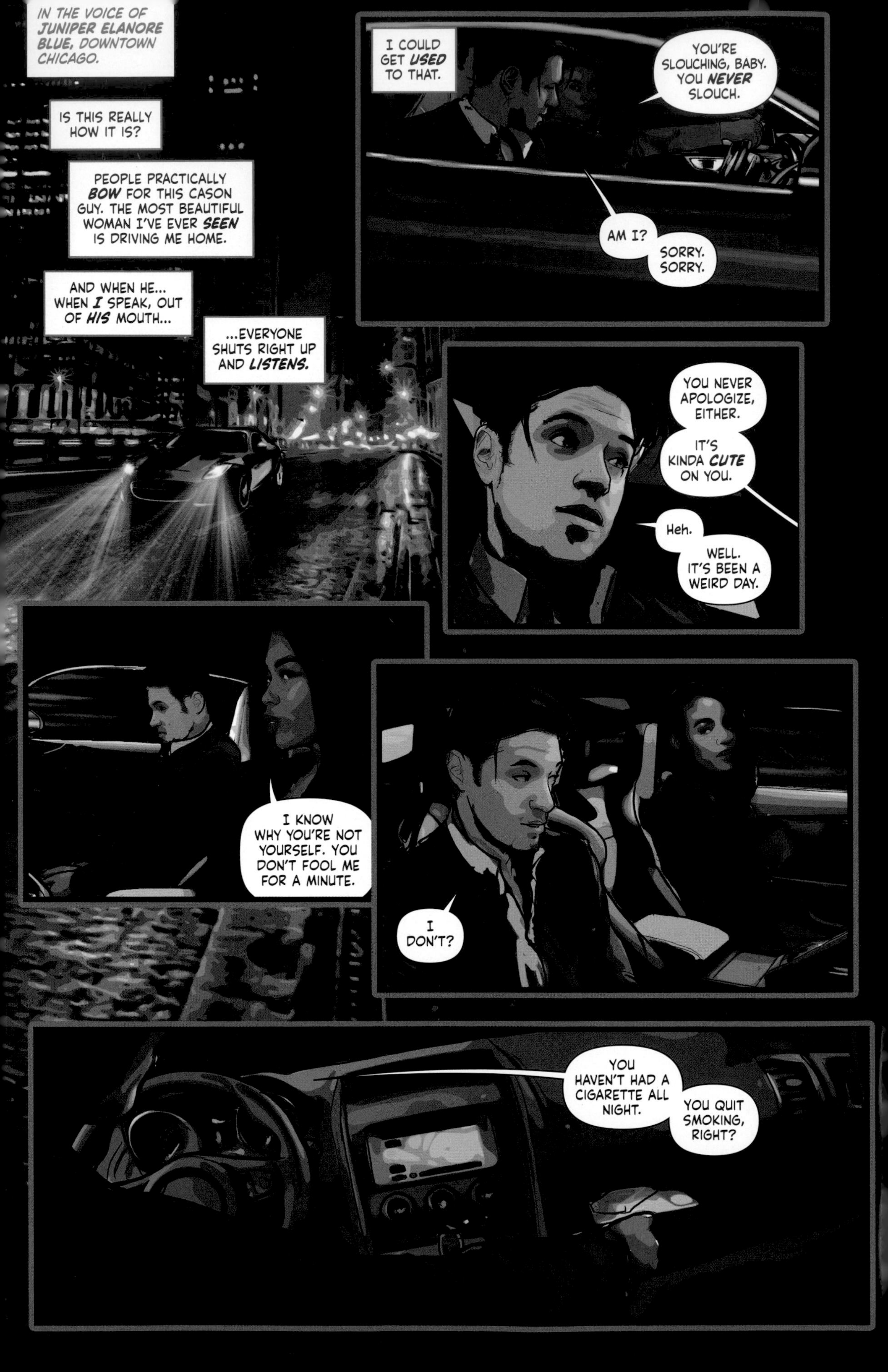

IN THE VOICE OF JUNIPER ELANORE BLUE, DOWNTOWN CHICAGO.
IS THIS REALLY HOW IT IS?
PEOPLE PRACTICALLY BOW FOR THIS CASON GUY. THE MOST BEAUTIFUL WOMAN I'VE EVER SEEN IS DRIVING ME HOME.
AND WHEN HE... WHEN I SPEAK, OUT OF HIS MOUTH...
...EVERYONE SHUTS RIGHT UP AND LISTENS.
I COULD GET USED TO THAT.
YOU'RE SLOUCHING, BABY. YOU NEVER SLOUCH.
AM I?
SORRY. SORRY.
YOU NEVER APOLOGIZE, EITHER.
IT'S KINDA CUTE ON YOU.
Heh.
WELL. IT'S BEEN A WEIRD DAY.
I KNOW WHY YOU'RE NOT YOURSELF. YOU DON'T FOOL ME FOR A MINUTE.
I DON'T?
YOU HAVEN'T HAD A CIGARETTE ALL NIGHT.
YOU QUIT SMOKING, RIGHT?

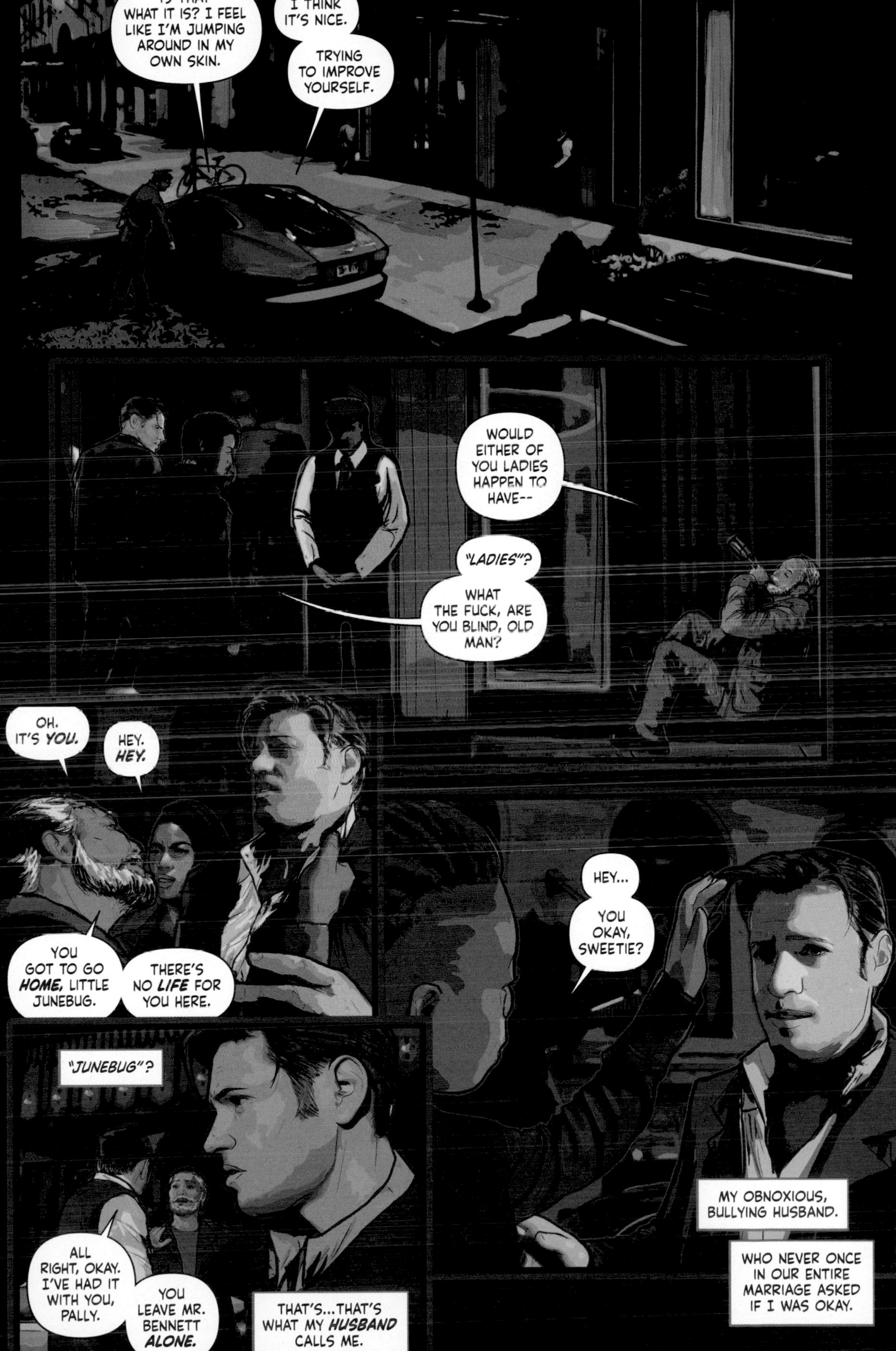

WHAT IT IS? I FEEL LIKE I'M JUMPING AROUND IN MY OWN SKIN.
I THINK IT'S NICE.
TRYING TO IMPROVE YOURSELF.
WOULD EITHER OF YOU LADIES HAPPEN TO HAVE--
"LADIES"?
WHAT THE FUCK, ARE YOU BLIND, OLD MAN?
OH. IT'S *YOU.*
HEY. ***HEY.***
YOU GOT TO GO ***HOME,*** LITTLE JUNEBUG.
THERE'S NO ***LIFE*** FOR YOU HERE.
"JUNEBUG"?
ALL RIGHT, OKAY. I'VE HAD IT WITH YOU, PALLY.
YOU LEAVE MR. BENNETT ***ALONE.***
THAT'S...THAT'S WHAT MY ***HUSBAND*** CALLS ME.
HEY...
YOU OKAY, SWEETIE?
MY OBNOXIOUS, BULLYING HUSBAND.
WHO NEVER ONCE IN OUR ENTIRE MARRIAGE ASKED IF I WAS OKAY.

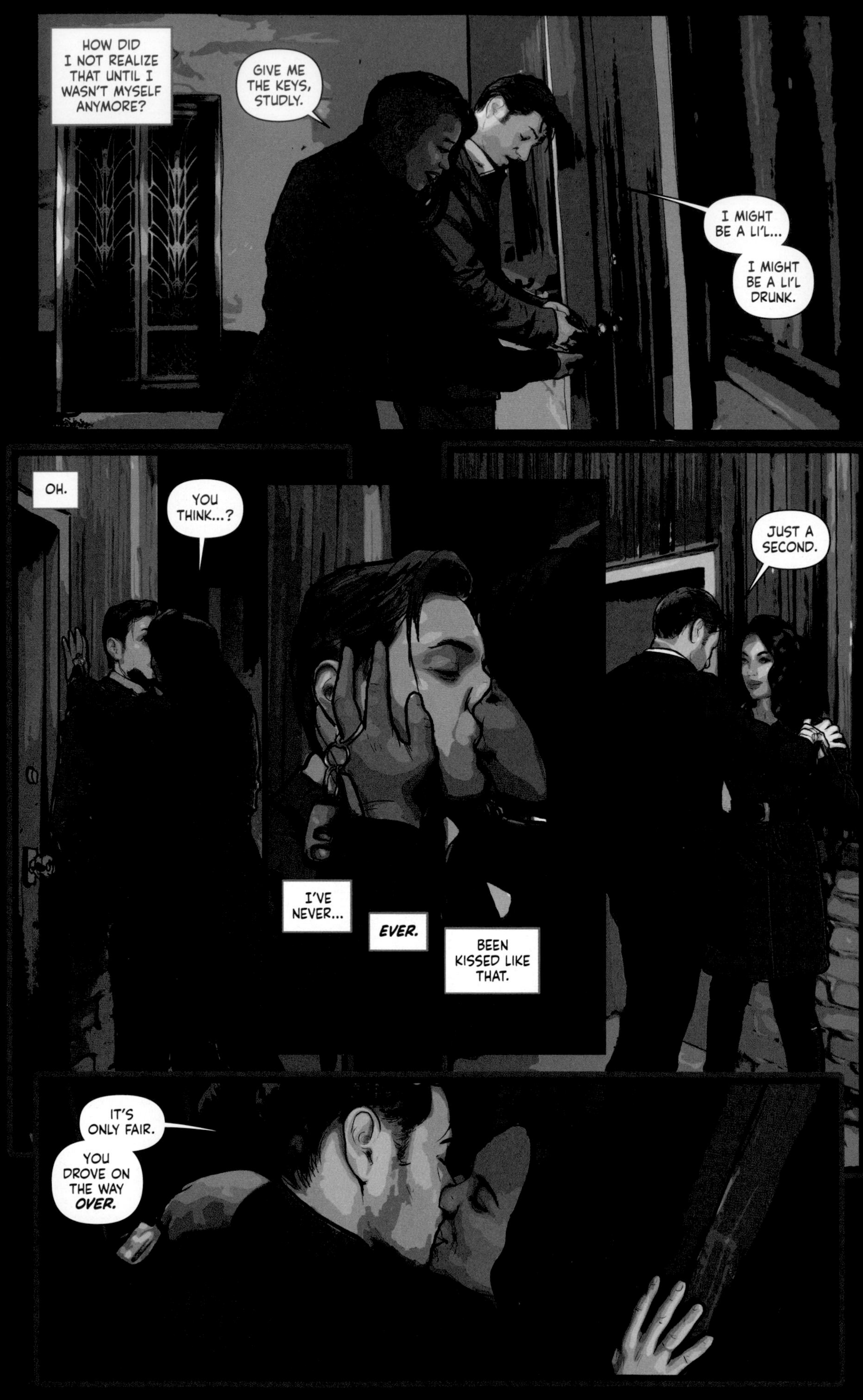

HOW DID I NOT REALIZE THAT UNTIL I WASN'T MYSELF ANYMORE?
GIVE ME THE KEYS, STUDLY.
I MIGHT BE A LI'L...
I MIGHT BE A LI'L DRUNK.
OH.
YOU THINK...?
JUST A SECOND.
I'VE NEVER...
EVER.
BEEN KISSED LIKE THAT.
IT'S ONLY FAIR.
YOU DROVE ON THE WAY OVER.

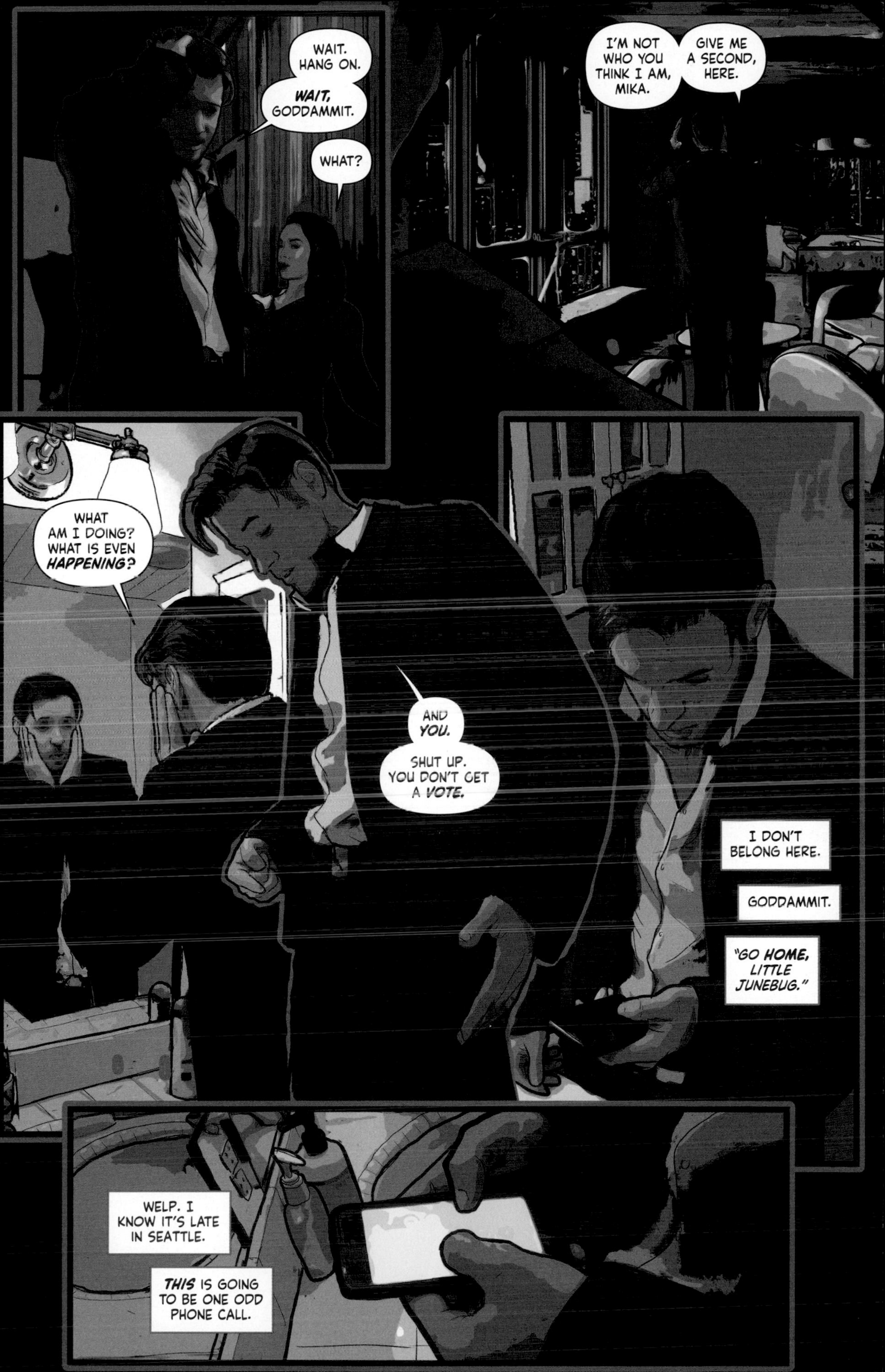
WAIT. HANG ON.
WAIT, GODDAMMIT.
WHAT?
I'M NOT WHO YOU THINK I AM, MIKA.
GIVE ME A SECOND, HERE.
WHAT AM I DOING? WHAT IS EVEN HAPPENING?
AND YOU.
SHUT UP. YOU DON'T GET A VOTE.
I DON'T BELONG HERE.
GODDAMMIT.
"GO HOME, LITTLE JUNEBUG."
WELP. I KNOW IT'S LATE IN SEATTLE.
THIS IS GOING TO BE ONE ODD PHONE CALL.

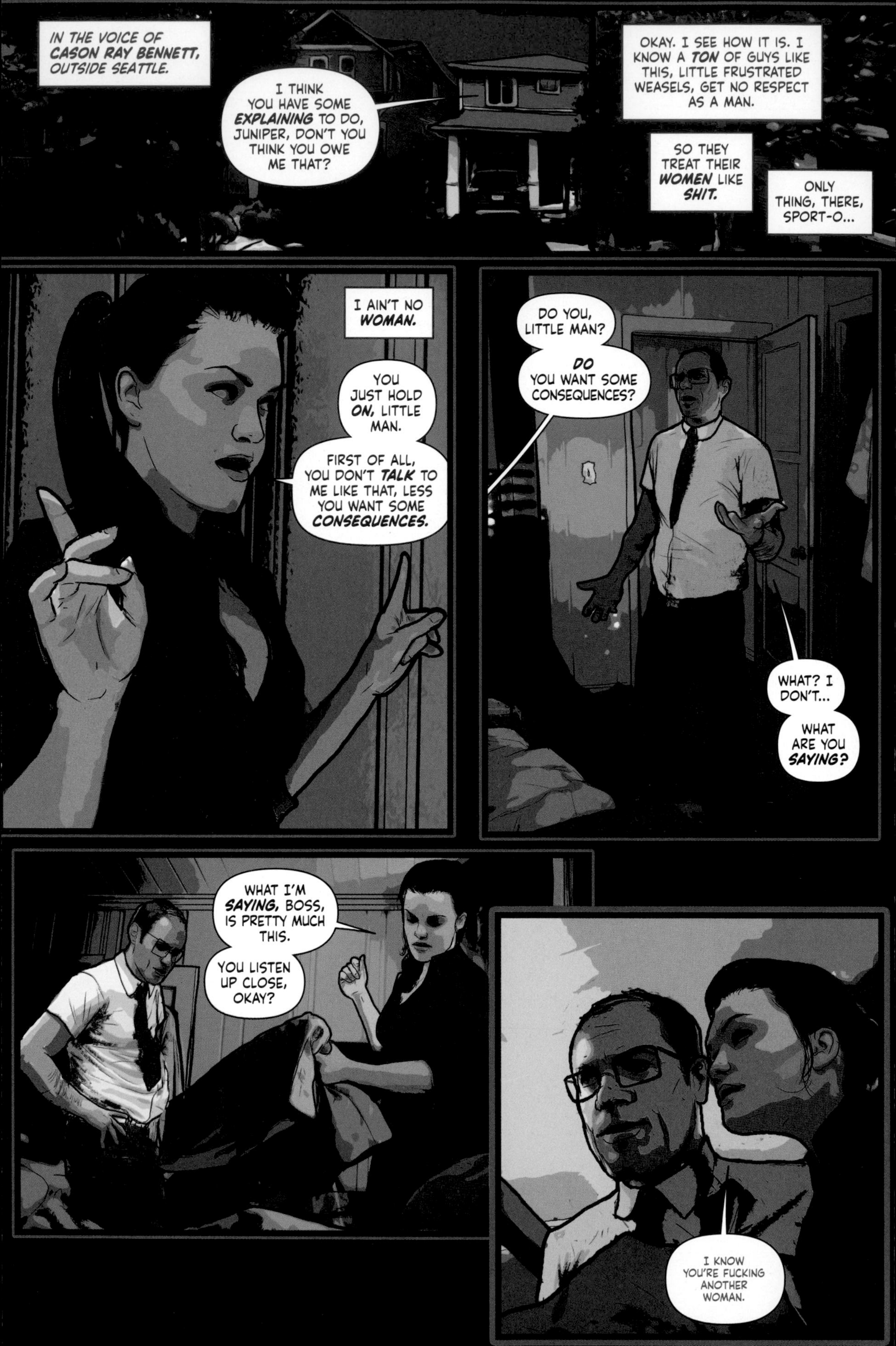
IN THE VOICE OF CASON RAY BENNETT, OUTSIDE SEATTLE.
I THINK YOU HAVE SOME EXPLAINING TO DO, JUNIPER, DON'T YOU THINK YOU OWE ME THAT?
OKAY. I SEE HOW IT IS. I KNOW A TON OF GUYS LIKE THIS, LITTLE FRUSTRATED WEASELS, GET NO RESPECT AS A MAN.
SO THEY TREAT THEIR WOMEN LIKE SHIT.
ONLY THING, THERE, SPORT-O...
I AIN'T NO WOMAN.
YOU JUST HOLD ON, LITTLE MAN.
FIRST OF ALL, YOU DON'T TALK TO ME LIKE THAT, LESS YOU WANT SOME CONSEQUENCES.
DO YOU, LITTLE MAN?
DO YOU WANT SOME CONSEQUENCES?
WHAT? I DON'T...
WHAT ARE YOU SAYING?
WHAT I'M SAYING, BOSS, IS PRETTY MUCH THIS.
YOU LISTEN UP CLOSE, OKAY?
I KNOW YOU'RE FUCKING ANOTHER WOMAN.

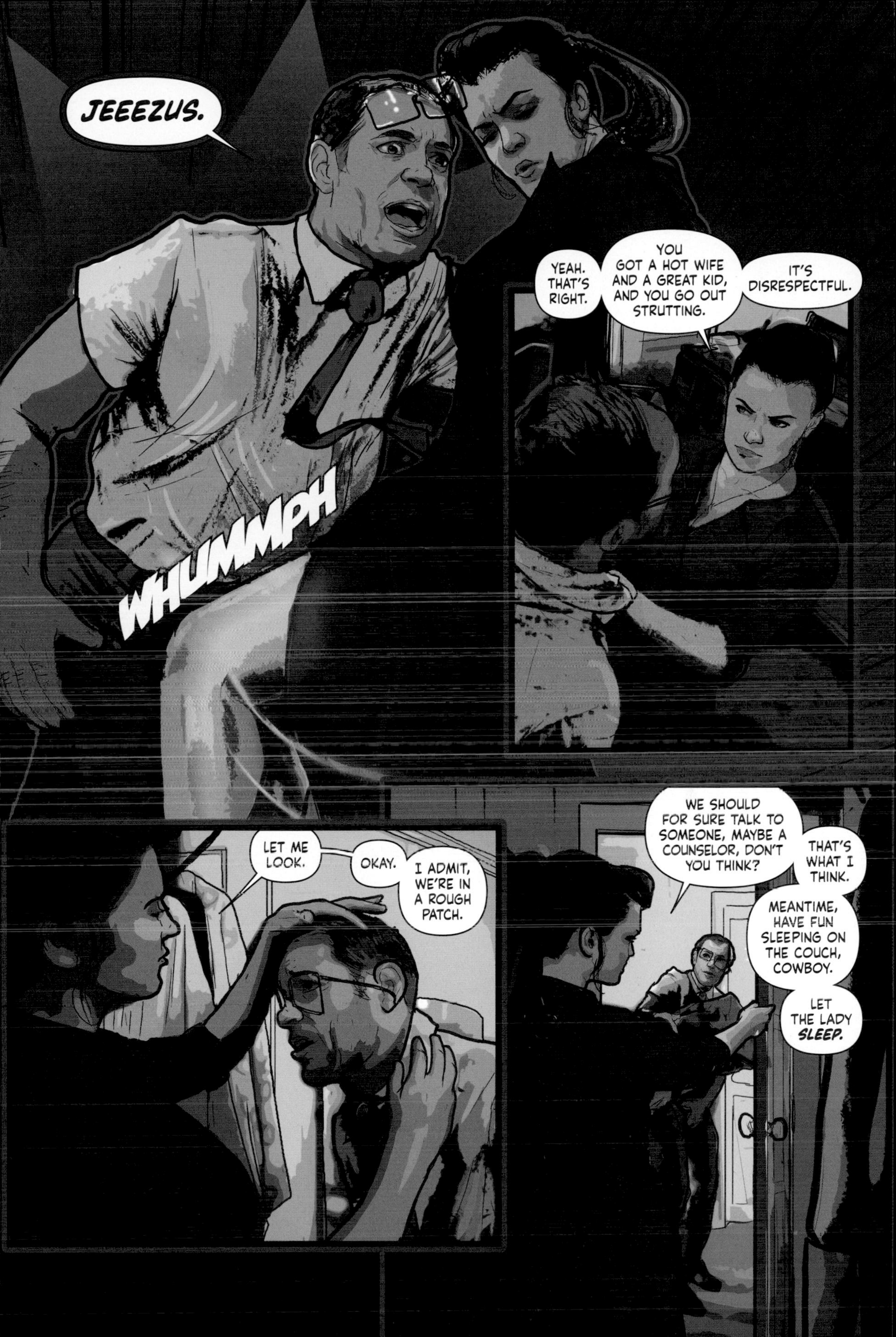
JEEEZUS.
WHUMMPH
YEAH. THAT'S RIGHT.
YOU GOT A HOT WIFE AND A GREAT KID, AND YOU GO OUT STRUTTING.
IT'S DISRESPECTFUL.
LET ME LOOK.
OKAY.
I ADMIT, WE'RE IN A ROUGH PATCH.
WE SHOULD FOR SURE TALK TO SOMEONE, MAYBE A COUNSELOR, DON'T YOU THINK?
THAT'S WHAT I THINK.
MEANTIME, HAVE FUN SLEEPING ON THE COUCH, COWBOY.
LET THE LADY *SLEEP.*

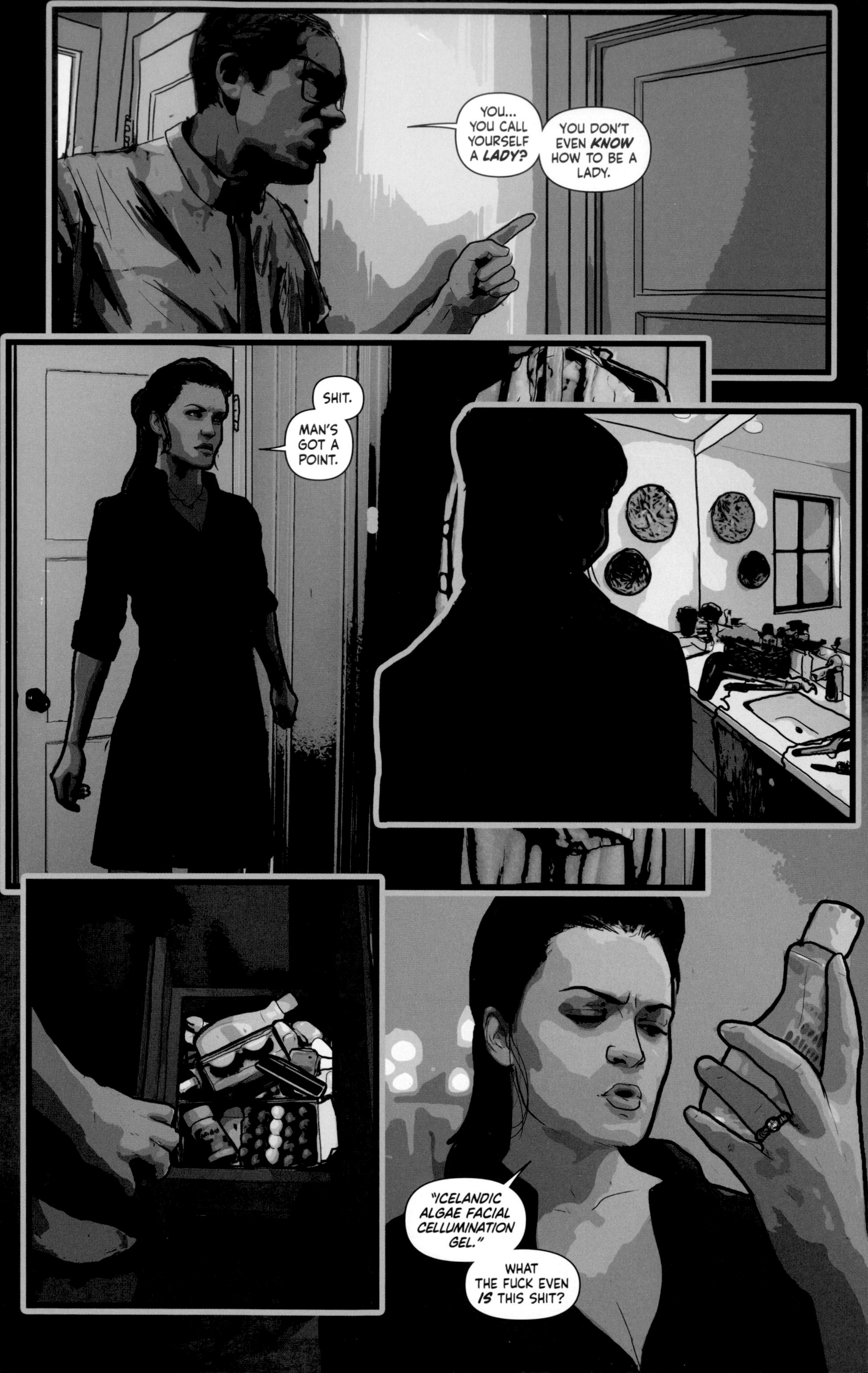
YOU... YOU CALL YOURSELF A *LADY?*
YOU DON'T EVEN *KNOW* HOW TO BE A LADY.
SHIT.
MAN'S GOT A POINT.
"ICELANDIC ALGAE FACIAL CELLUMINATION GEL."
WHAT THE FUCK EVEN *IS* THIS SHIT?

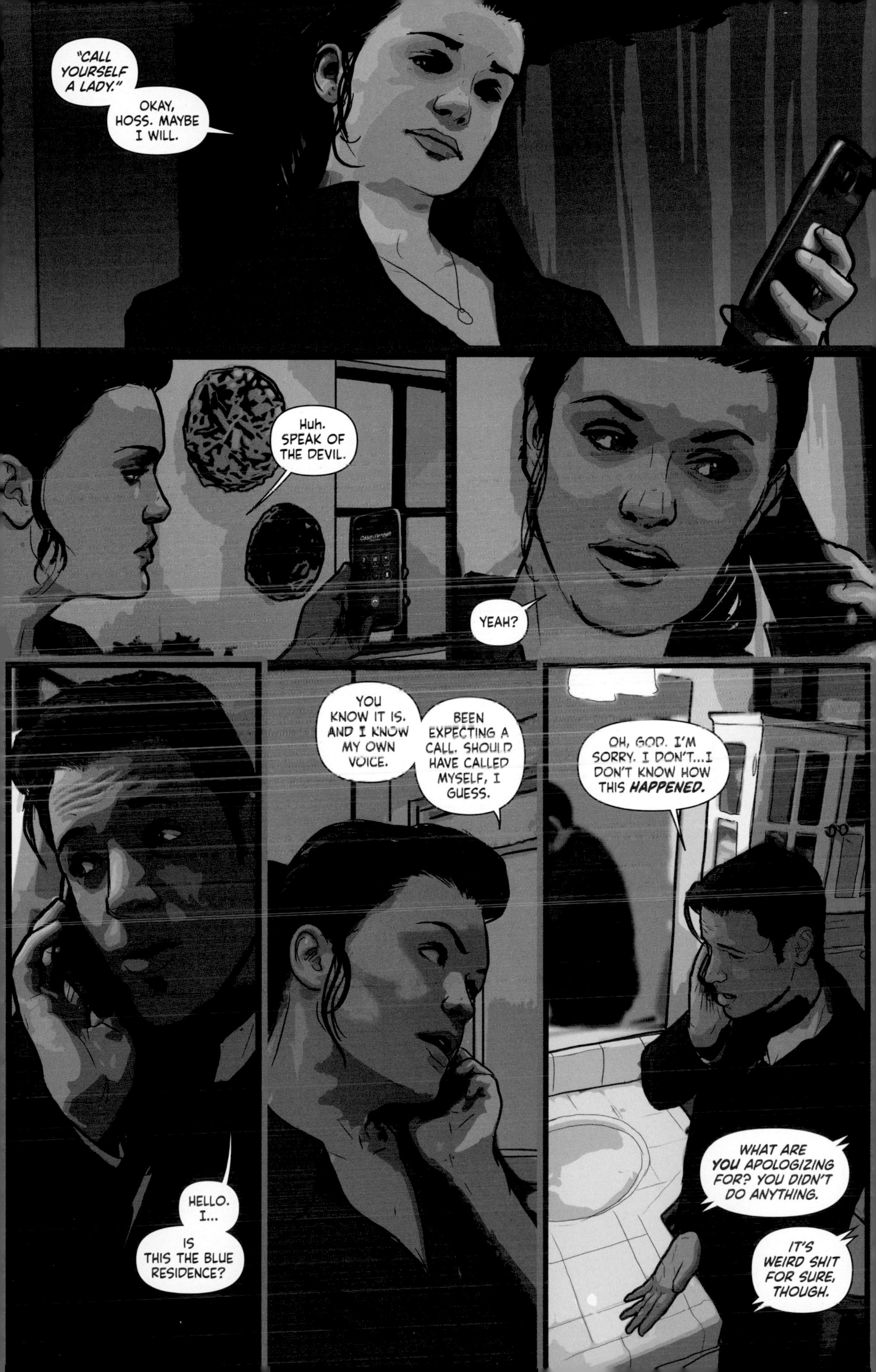
"CALL YOURSELF A LADY."
OKAY, HOSS. MAYBE I WILL.
Huh. SPEAK OF THE DEVIL.
YEAH?
HELLO. I...
IS THIS THE BLUE RESIDENCE?
YOU KNOW IT IS. AND I KNOW MY OWN VOICE.
BEEN EXPECTING A CALL. SHOULD HAVE CALLED MYSELF, I GUESS.
OH, GOD. I'M SORRY. I DON'T...I DON'T KNOW HOW THIS *HAPPENED.*
WHAT ARE *YOU* APOLOGIZING FOR? YOU DIDN'T DO ANYTHING.
IT'S WEIRD SHIT FOR SURE, THOUGH.

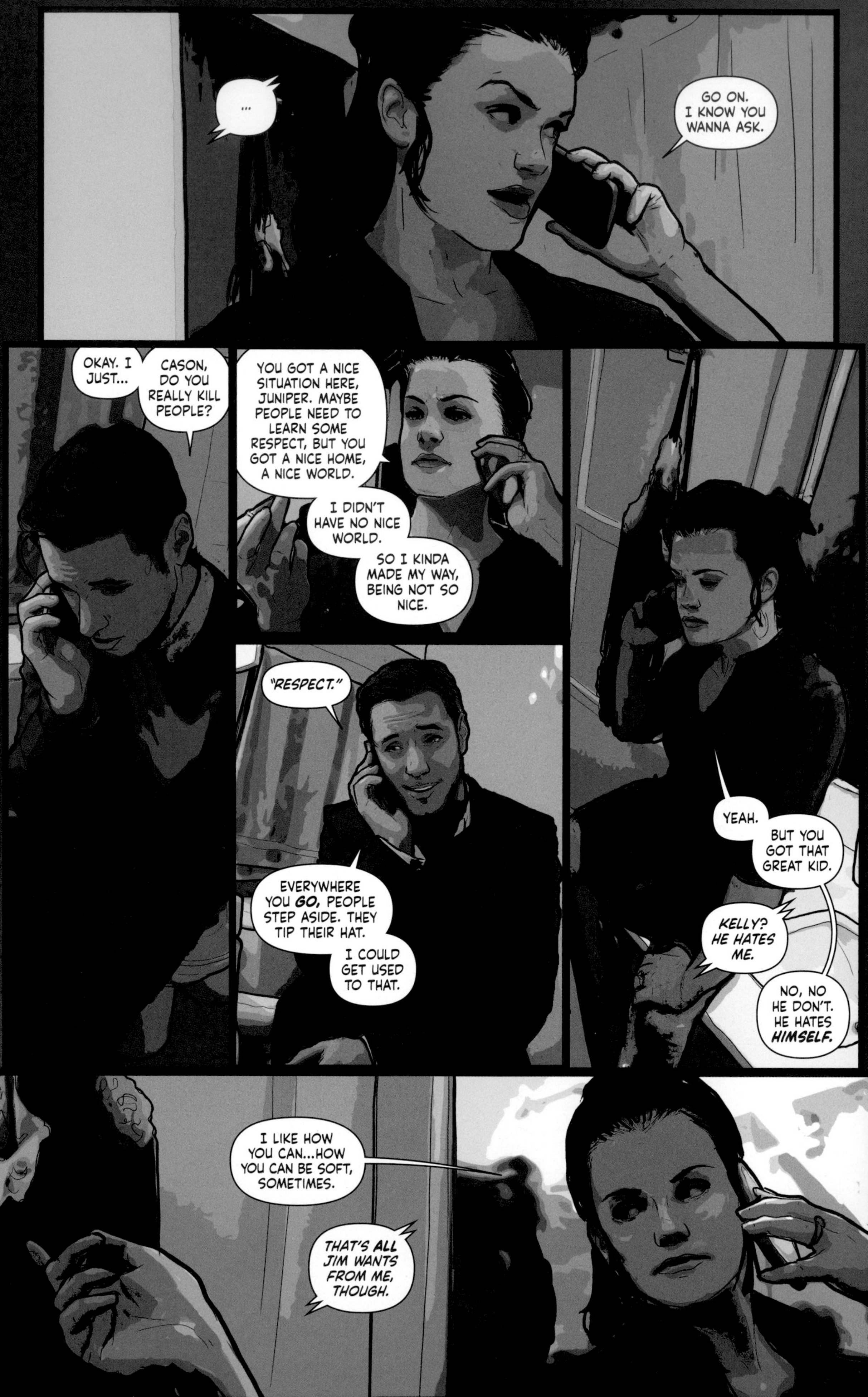
...
GO ON. I KNOW YOU WANNA ASK.
OKAY. I JUST...
CASON, DO YOU REALLY KILL PEOPLE?
YOU GOT A NICE SITUATION HERE, JUNIPER. MAYBE PEOPLE NEED TO LEARN SOME RESPECT, BUT YOU GOT A NICE HOME, A NICE WORLD.
I DIDN'T HAVE NO NICE WORLD.
SO I KINDA MADE MY WAY, BEING NOT SO NICE.
"RESPECT."
EVERYWHERE YOU **GO,** PEOPLE STEP ASIDE. THEY TIP THEIR HAT.
I COULD GET USED TO THAT.
YEAH.
BUT YOU GOT THAT GREAT KID.
KELLY? HE HATES ME.
NO, NO HE DON'T. HE HATES ***HIMSELF.***
I LIKE HOW YOU CAN...HOW YOU CAN BE SOFT, SOMETIMES.
*THAT'S **ALL** JIM WANTS FROM ME, THOUGH.*

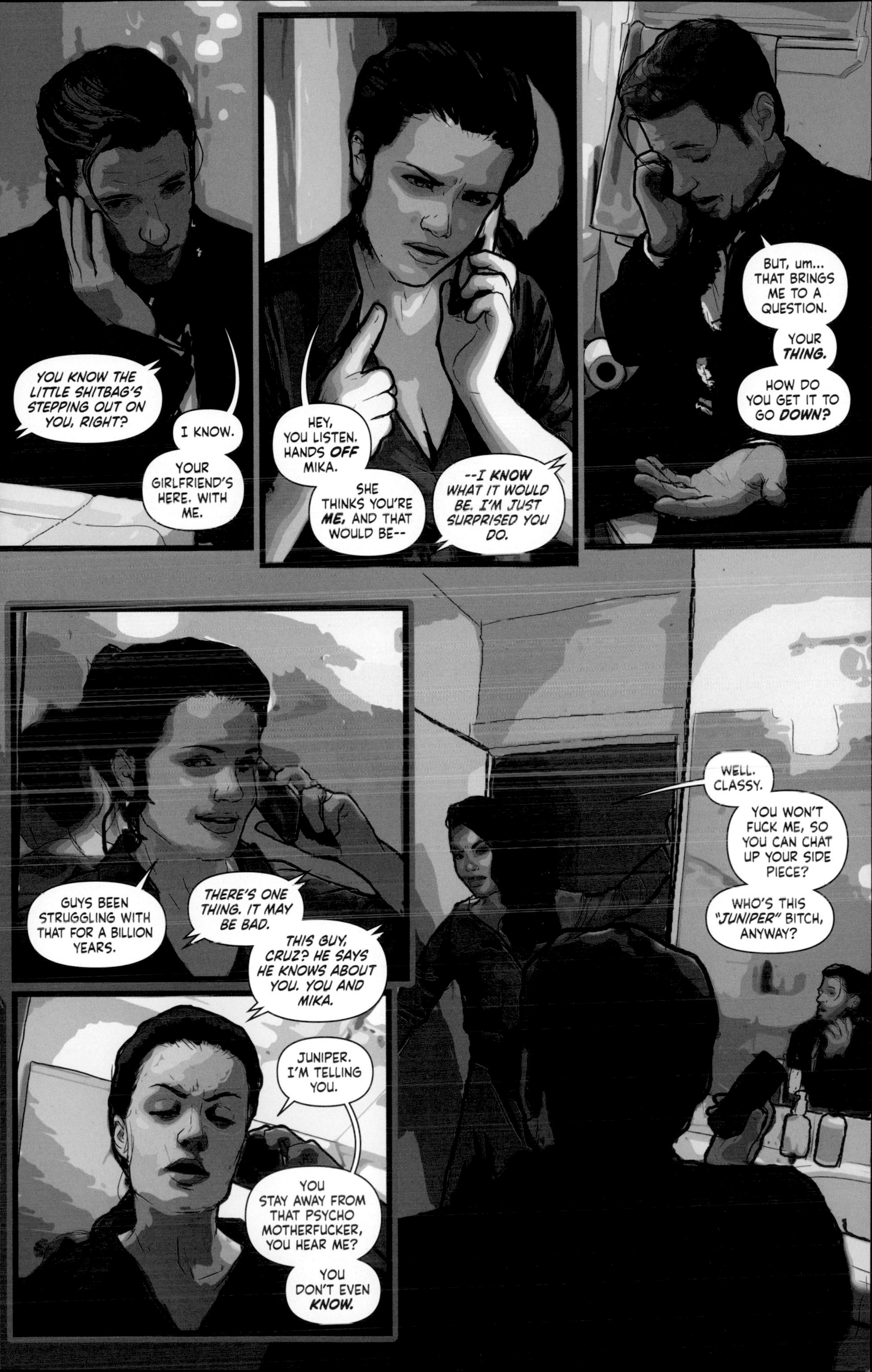
YOU KNOW THE LITTLE SHITBAG'S STEPPING OUT ON YOU, RIGHT?
I KNOW.
YOUR GIRLFRIEND'S HERE. WITH ME.
HEY, YOU LISTEN. HANDS OFF MIKA.
SHE THINKS YOU'RE ME, AND THAT WOULD BE--
--I KNOW WHAT IT WOULD BE. I'M JUST SURPRISED YOU DO.
BUT, UM... THAT BRINGS ME TO A QUESTION.
YOUR THING.
HOW DO YOU GET IT TO GO DOWN?
GUYS BEEN STRUGGLING WITH THAT FOR A BILLION YEARS.
THERE'S ONE THING. IT MAY BE BAD.
THIS GUY, CRUZ? HE SAYS HE KNOWS ABOUT YOU. YOU AND MIKA.
JUNIPER. I'M TELLING YOU.
YOU STAY AWAY FROM THAT PSYCHO MOTHERFUCKER, YOU HEAR ME?
YOU DON'T EVEN KNOW.
WELL. CLASSY.
YOU WON'T FUCK ME, SO YOU CAN CHAT UP YOUR SIDE PIECE?
WHO'S THIS "JUNIPER" BITCH, ANYWAY?

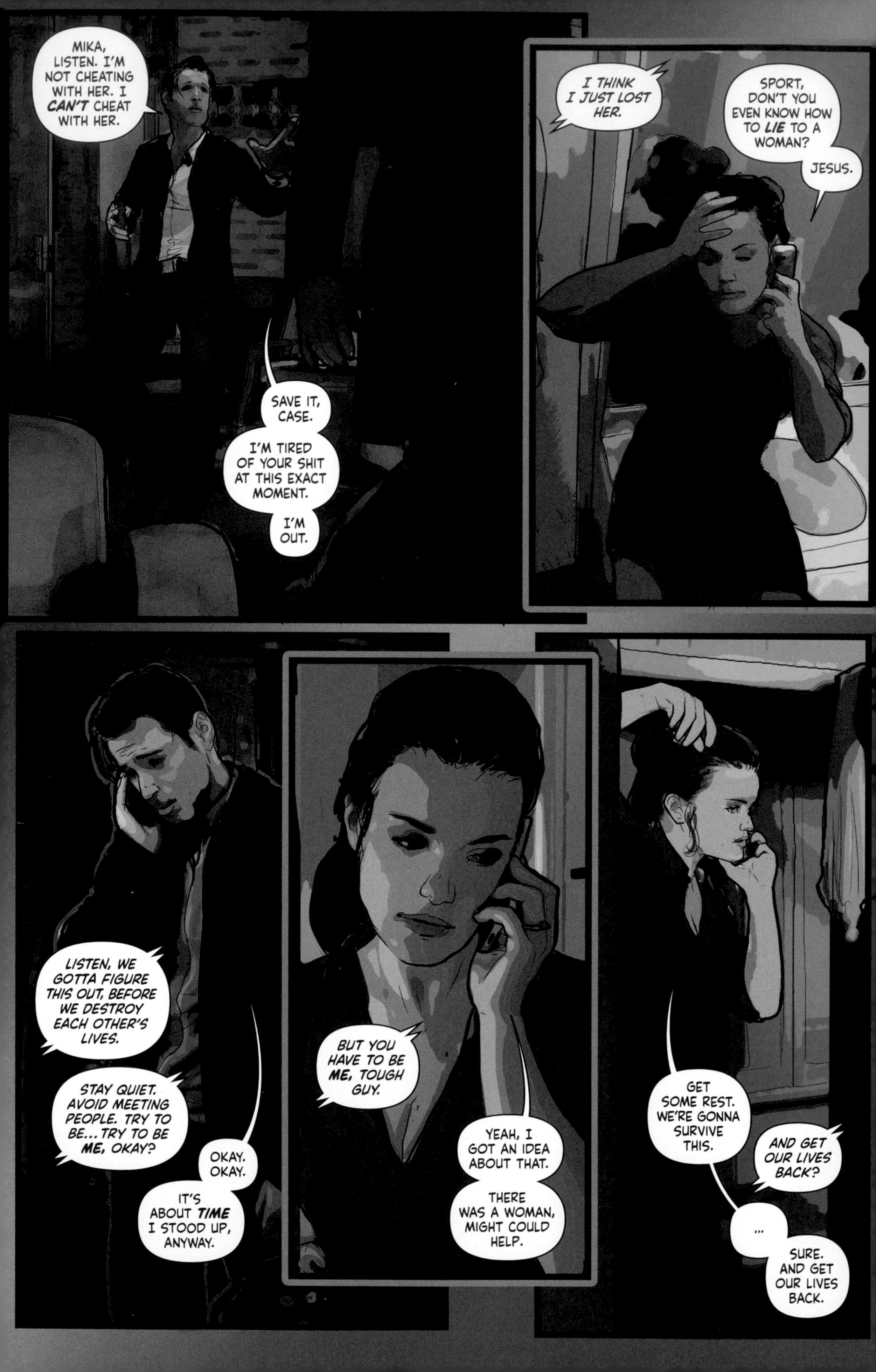
MIKA, LISTEN. I'M NOT CHEATING WITH HER. I *CAN'T* CHEAT WITH HER.
SAVE IT, CASE.
I'M TIRED OF YOUR SHIT AT THIS EXACT MOMENT.
I'M OUT.
I THINK I JUST LOST HER.
SPORT, DON'T YOU EVEN KNOW HOW TO *LIE* TO A WOMAN?
JESUS.
LISTEN, WE GOTTA FIGURE THIS OUT, BEFORE WE DESTROY EACH OTHER'S LIVES.
STAY QUIET. AVOID MEETING PEOPLE. TRY TO BE... TRY TO BE ME, OKAY?
OKAY. OKAY.
IT'S ABOUT *TIME* I STOOD UP, ANYWAY.
BUT YOU HAVE TO BE ME, TOUGH GUY.
YEAH, I GOT AN IDEA ABOUT THAT.
THERE WAS A WOMAN, MIGHT COULD HELP.
GET SOME REST. WE'RE GONNA SURVIVE THIS.
AND GET OUR LIVES BACK?
...
SURE. AND GET OUR LIVES BACK.

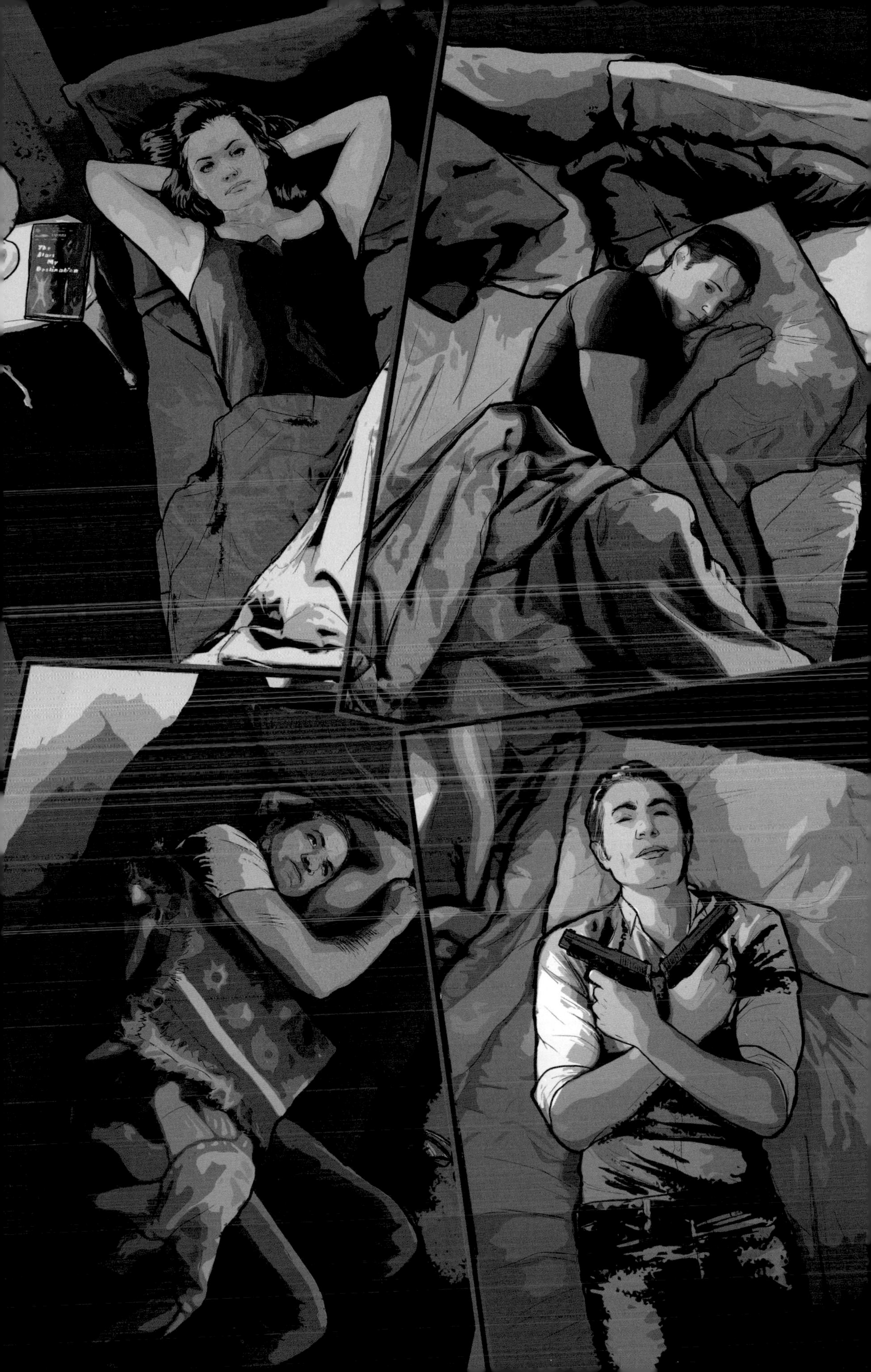

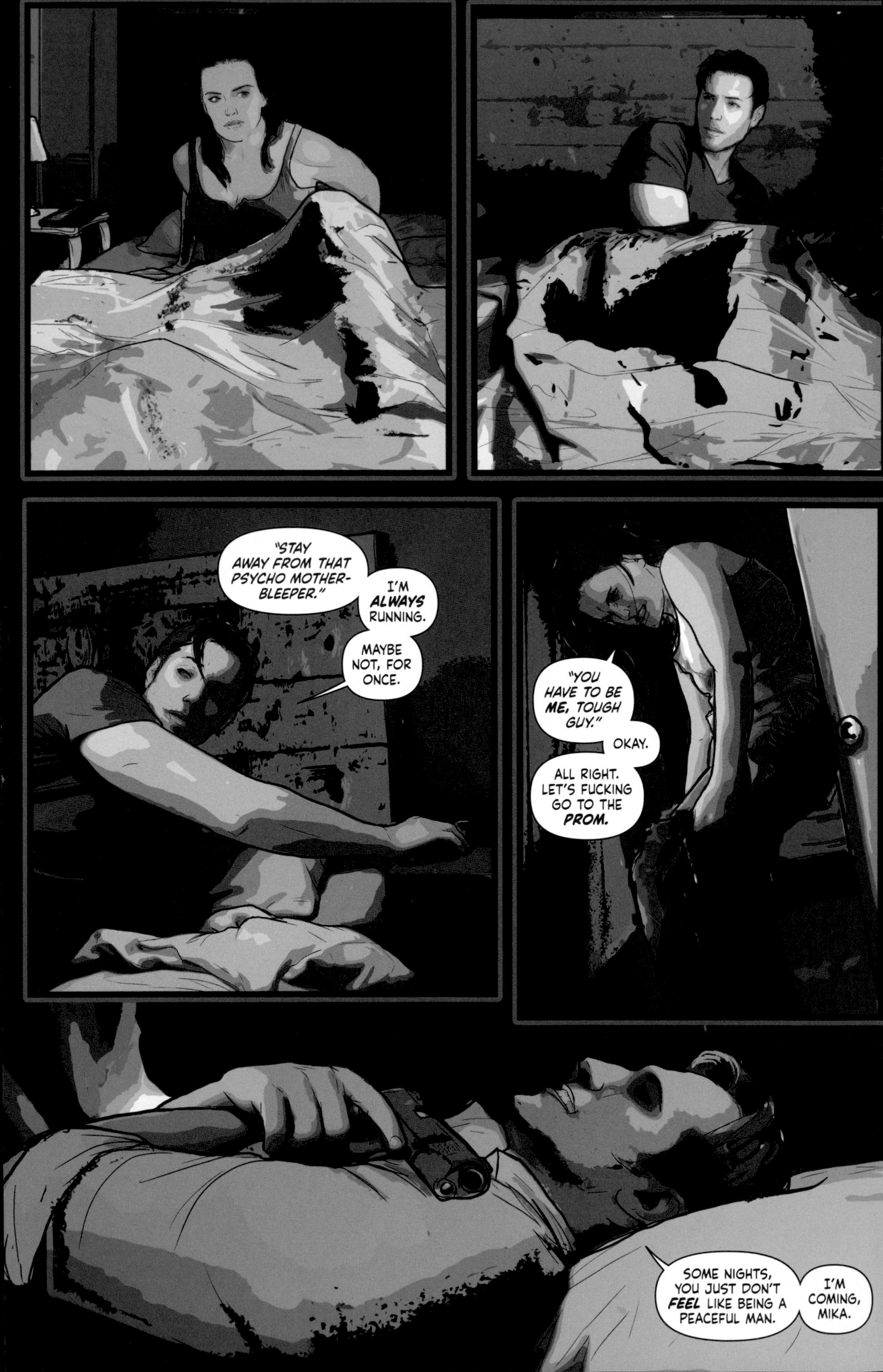
"STAY AWAY FROM THAT PSYCHO MOTHER-BLEEPER."
I'M ***ALWAYS*** RUNNING.
MAYBE NOT, FOR ONCE.
"YOU HAVE TO BE ***ME,*** TOUGH GUY."
OKAY.
ALL RIGHT. LET'S FUCKING GO TO THE ***PROM.***
SOME NIGHTS, YOU JUST DON'T ***FEEL*** LIKE BEING A PEACEFUL MAN.
I'M COMING, MIKA.

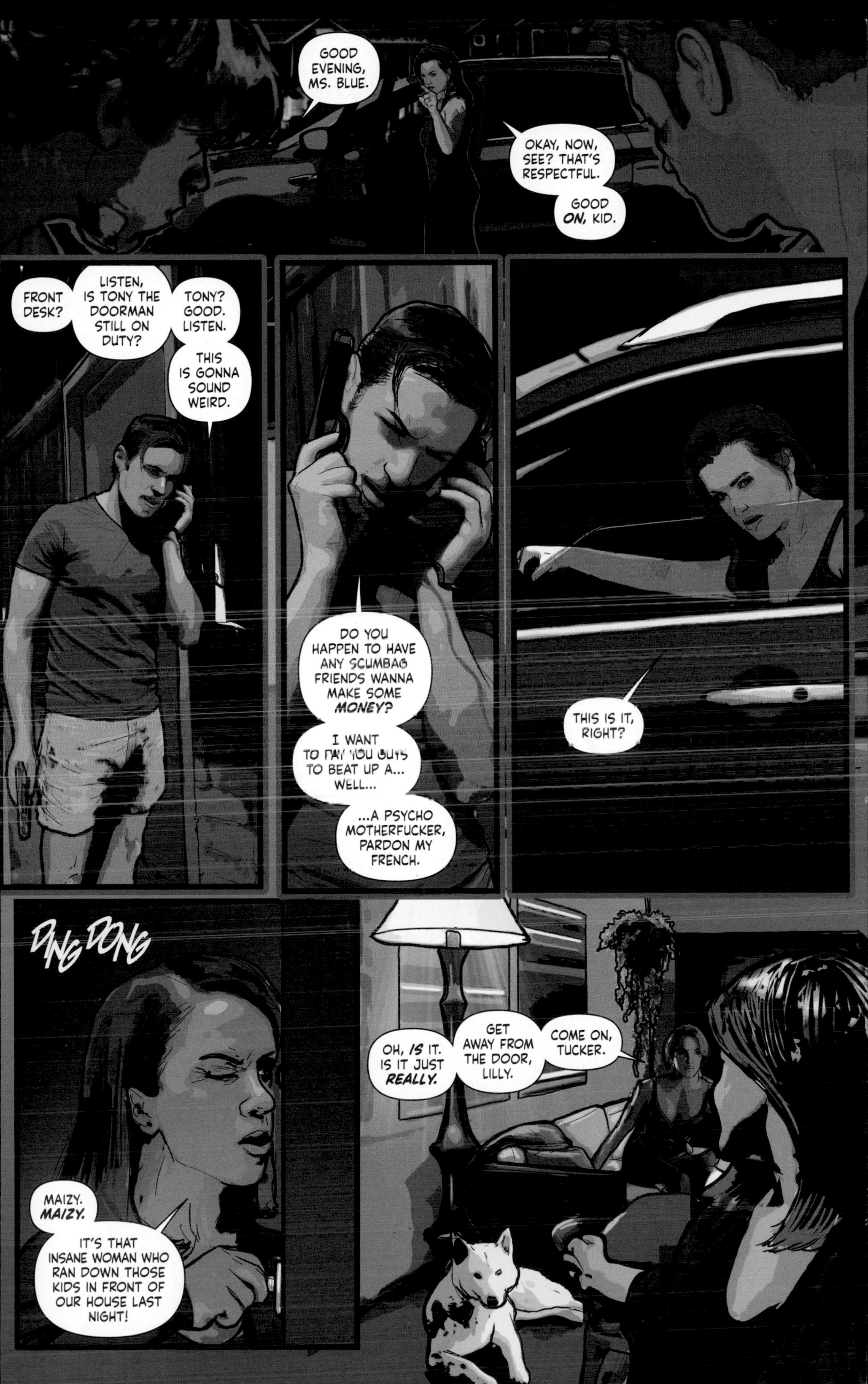
GOOD EVENING, MS. BLUE.
OKAY, NOW, SEE? THAT'S RESPECTFUL.
GOOD *ON*, KID.
FRONT DESK?
LISTEN, IS TONY THE DOORMAN STILL ON DUTY?
TONY? GOOD. LISTEN.
THIS IS GONNA SOUND WEIRD.
DO YOU HAPPEN TO HAVE ANY SCUMBAG FRIENDS WANNA MAKE SOME *MONEY?*
I WANT TO PAY YOU GUYS TO BEAT UP A... WELL...
...A PSYCHO MOTHERFUCKER, PARDON MY FRENCH.
THIS IS IT, RIGHT?
DING DONG
MAIZY. *MAIZY.*
IT'S THAT INSANE WOMAN WHO RAN DOWN THOSE KIDS IN FRONT OF OUR HOUSE LAST NIGHT!
OH, *IS* IT. IS IT JUST *REALLY.*
GET AWAY FROM THE DOOR, LILLY.
COME ON, TUCKER.

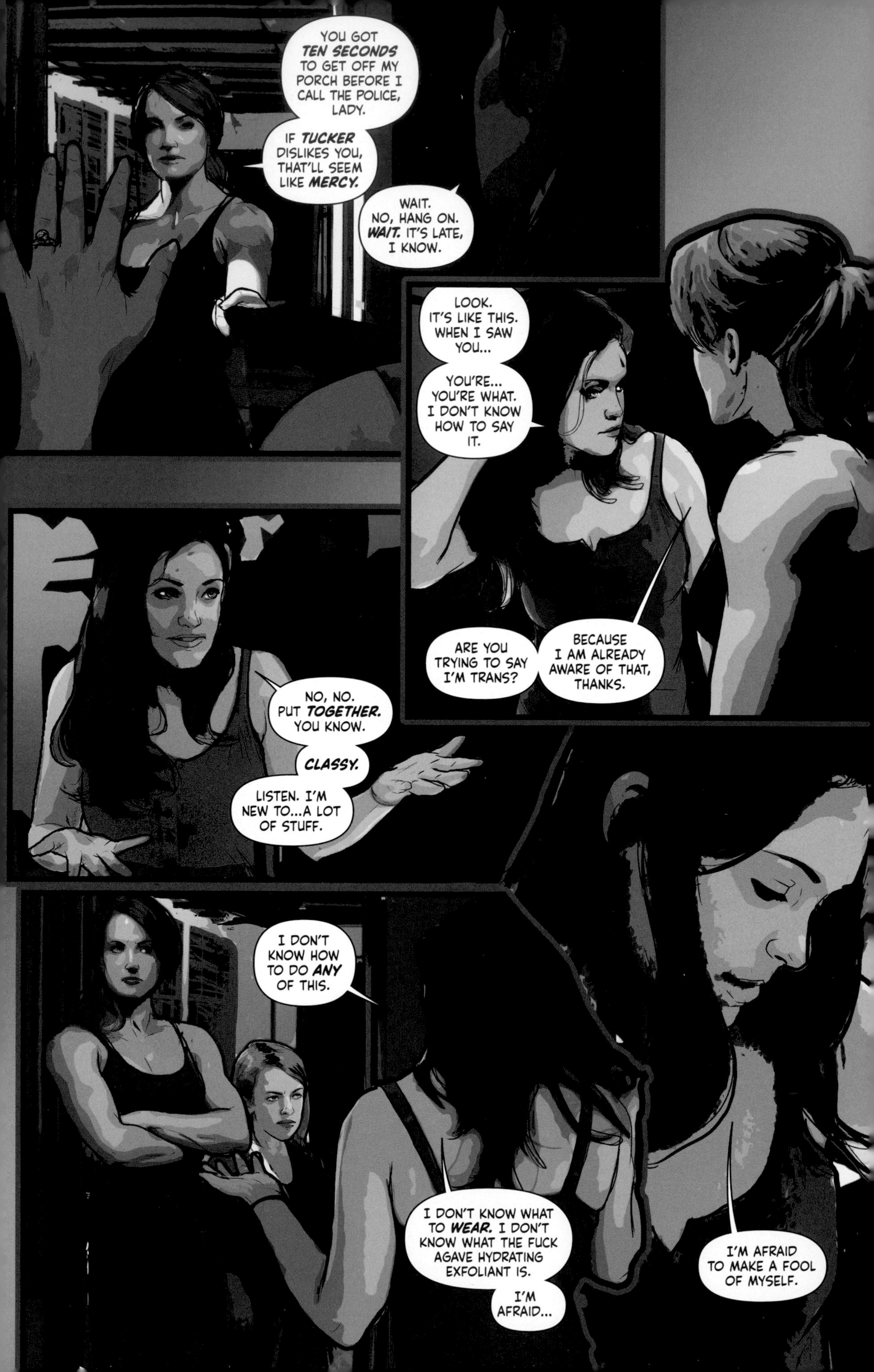
YOU GOT *TEN SECONDS* TO GET OFF MY PORCH BEFORE I CALL THE POLICE, LADY.
IF *TUCKER* DISLIKES YOU, THAT'LL SEEM LIKE *MERCY.*
WAIT. NO, HANG ON. *WAIT.* IT'S LATE, I KNOW.
LOOK. IT'S LIKE THIS. WHEN I SAW YOU...
YOU'RE... YOU'RE WHAT. I DON'T KNOW HOW TO SAY IT.
ARE YOU TRYING TO SAY I'M TRANS?
BECAUSE I AM ALREADY AWARE OF THAT, THANKS.
NO, NO. PUT *TOGETHER.* YOU KNOW.
CLASSY.
LISTEN. I'M NEW TO...A LOT OF STUFF.
I DON'T KNOW HOW TO DO *ANY* OF THIS.
I DON'T KNOW WHAT TO *WEAR.* I DON'T KNOW WHAT THE FUCK AGAVE HYDRATING EXFOLIANT IS.
I'M AFRAID...
I'M AFRAID TO MAKE A FOOL OF MYSELF.

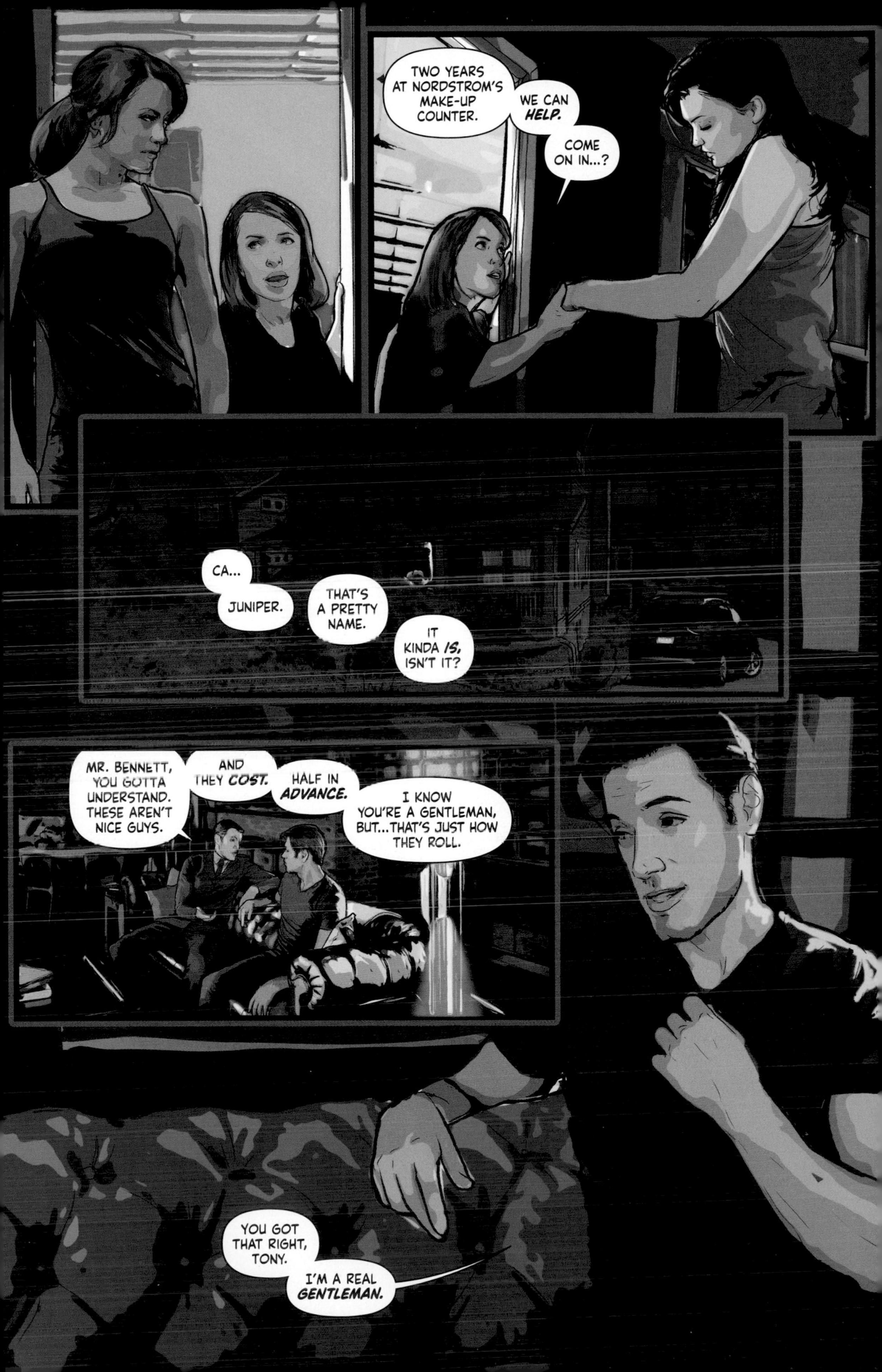
TWO YEARS AT NORDSTROM'S MAKE-UP COUNTER.
WE CAN *HELP.*
COME ON IN...?
CA...
JUNIPER.
THAT'S A PRETTY NAME.
IT KINDA *IS,* ISN'T IT?
MR. BENNETT, YOU GOTTA UNDERSTAND. THESE AREN'T NICE GUYS.
AND THEY *COST.*
HALF IN *ADVANCE.*
I KNOW YOU'RE A GENTLEMAN, BUT...THAT'S JUST HOW THEY ROLL.
YOU GOT THAT RIGHT, TONY.
I'M A REAL *GENTLEMAN.*

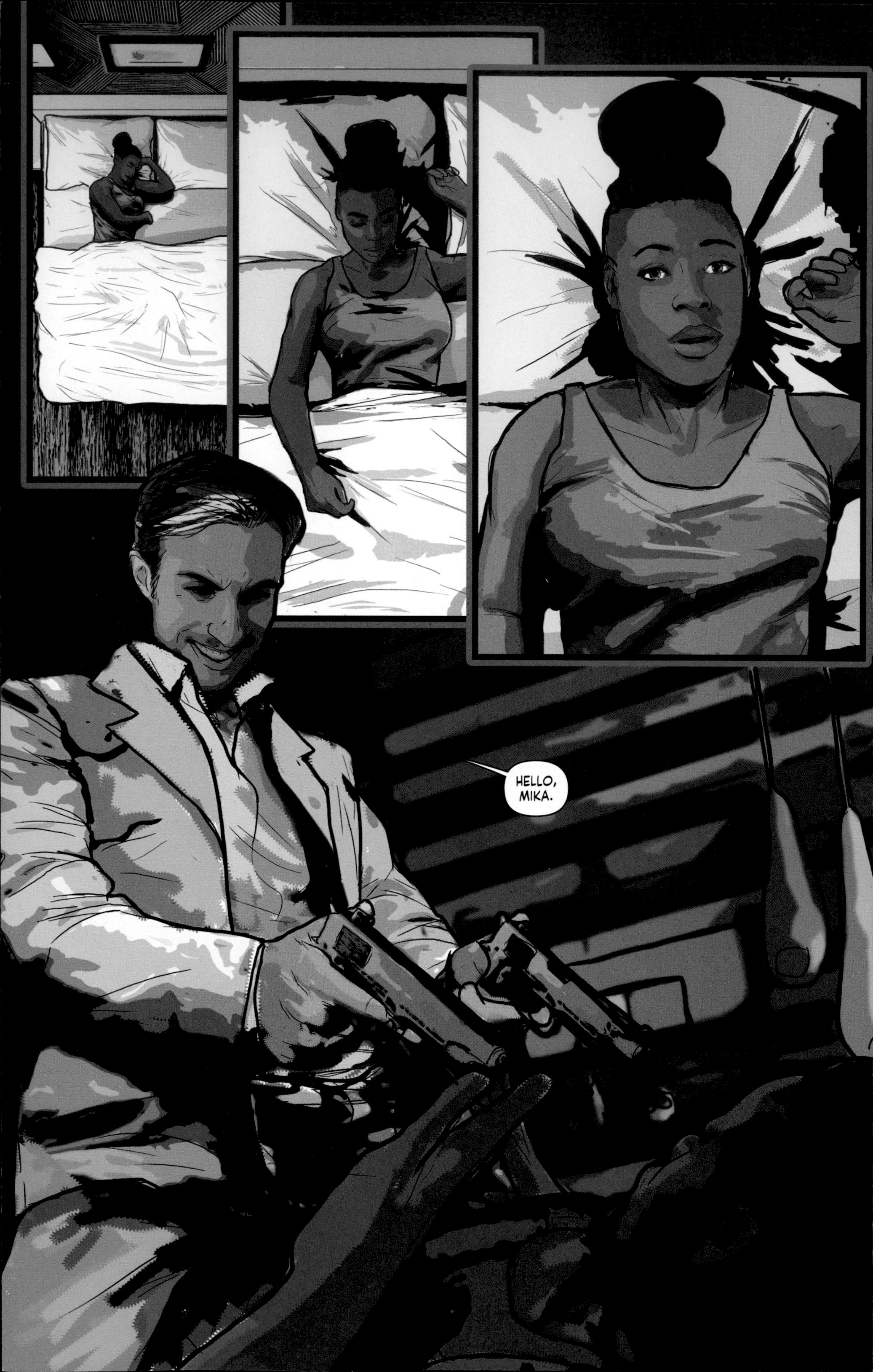
HELLO, MIKA.

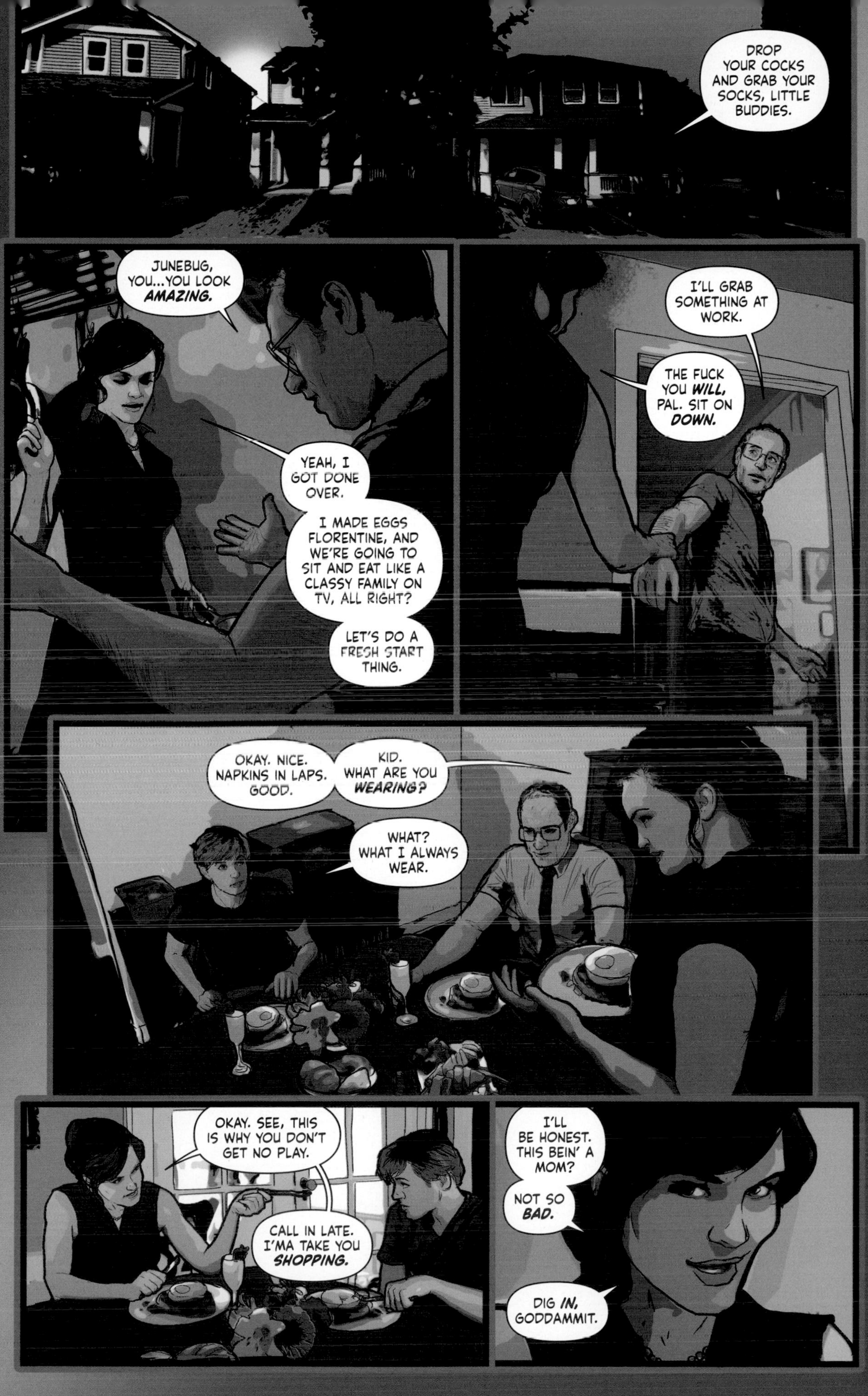
DROP YOUR COCKS AND GRAB YOUR SOCKS, LITTLE BUDDIES.
JUNEBUG, YOU...YOU LOOK AMAZING.
YEAH, I GOT DONE OVER.
I MADE EGGS FLORENTINE, AND WE'RE GOING TO SIT AND EAT LIKE A CLASSY FAMILY ON TV, ALL RIGHT?
LET'S DO A FRESH START THING.
I'LL GRAB SOMETHING AT WORK.
THE FUCK YOU WILL, PAL. SIT ON DOWN.
OKAY. NICE. NAPKINS IN LAPS. GOOD.
KID. WHAT ARE YOU WEARING?
WHAT? WHAT I ALWAYS WEAR.
OKAY. SEE, THIS IS WHY YOU DON'T GET NO PLAY.
CALL IN LATE. I'MA TAKE YOU SHOPPING.
I'LL BE HONEST. THIS BEIN' A MOM?
NOT SO BAD.
DIG IN, GODDAMMIT.

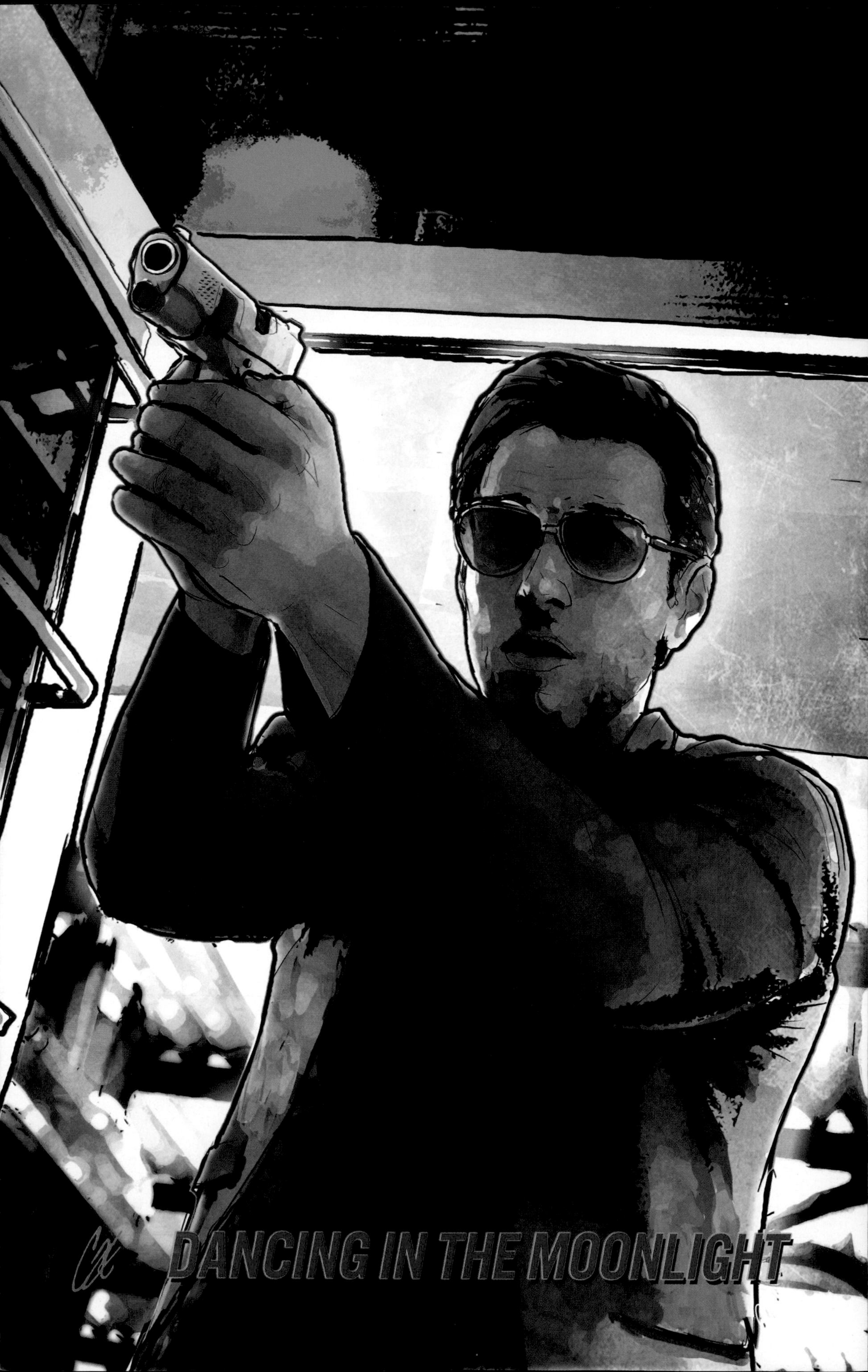
DANCING IN THE MOONLIGHT

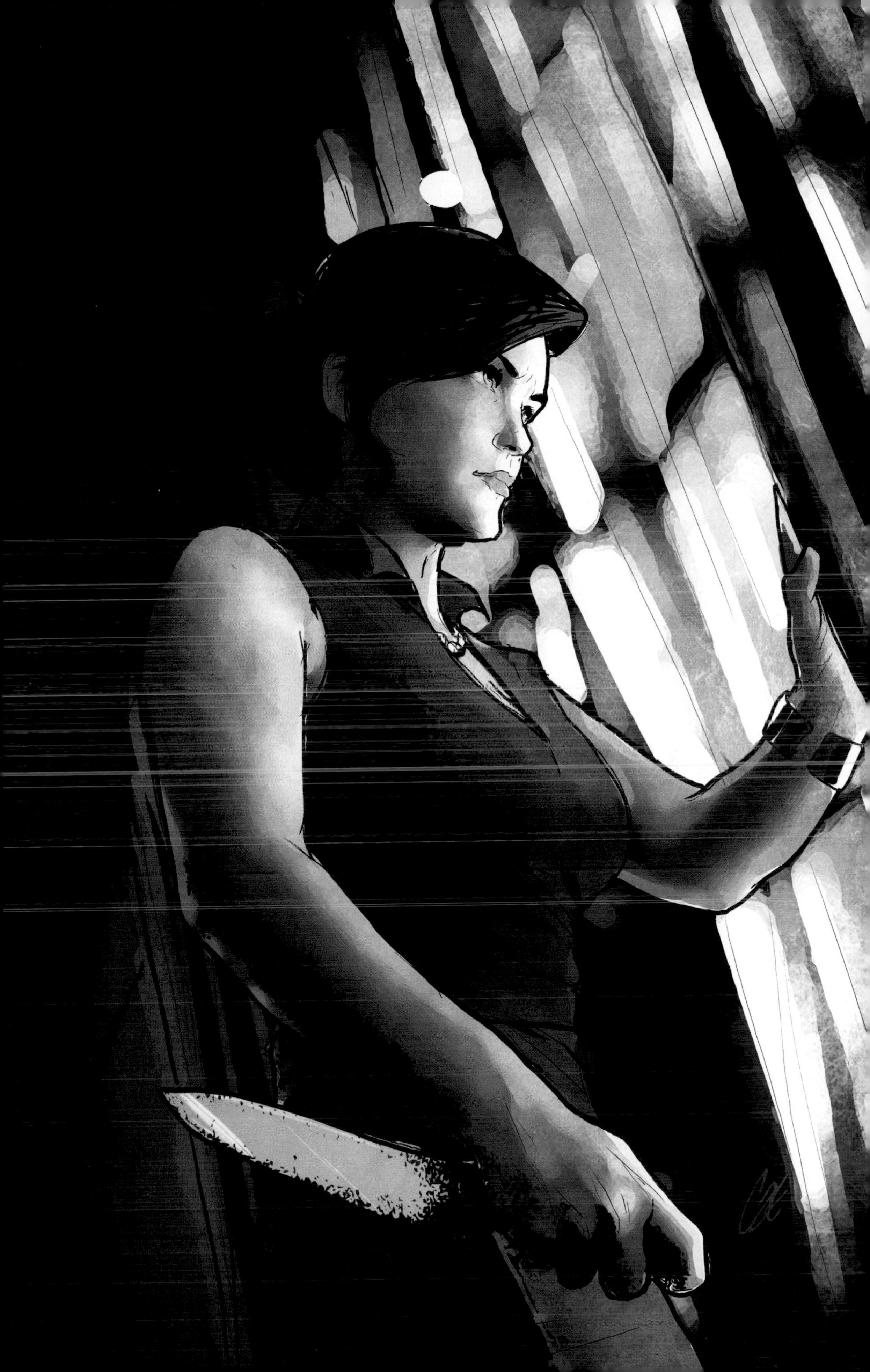

AND ONE SAID,
"OH, MY GOD."

AND THE OTHER SAID,
"OH, THANK GOD."

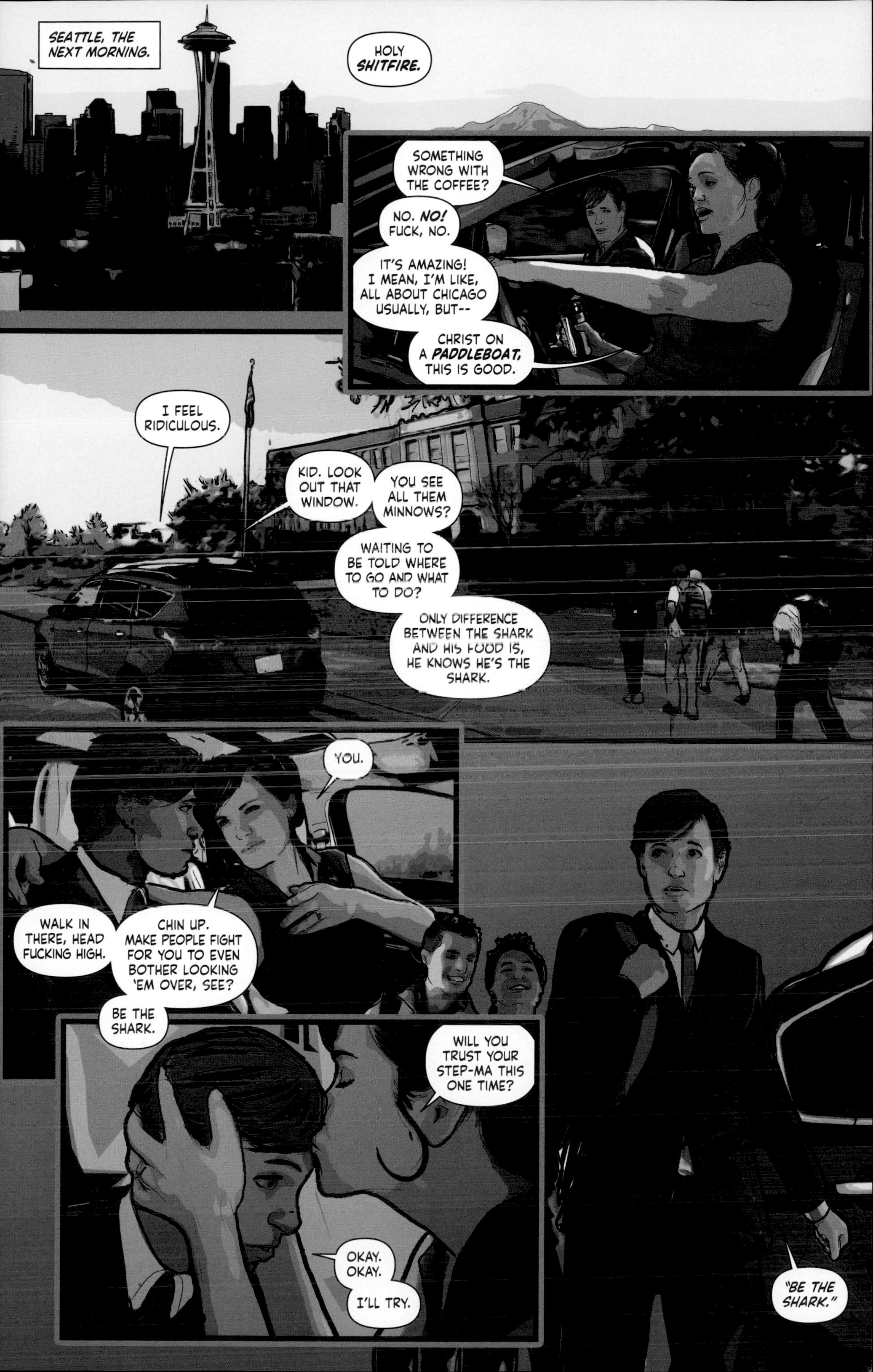
SEATTLE, THE NEXT MORNING.
HOLY SHITFIRE.
SOMETHING WRONG WITH THE COFFEE?
NO. NO! FUCK, NO.
IT'S AMAZING! I MEAN, I'M LIKE, ALL ABOUT CHICAGO USUALLY, BUT--
CHRIST ON A PADDLEBOAT, THIS IS GOOD.
I FEEL RIDICULOUS.
KID. LOOK OUT THAT WINDOW.
YOU SEE ALL THEM MINNOWS?
WAITING TO BE TOLD WHERE TO GO AND WHAT TO DO?
ONLY DIFFERENCE BETWEEN THE SHARK AND HIS FOOD IS, HE KNOWS HE'S THE SHARK.
YOU.
WALK IN THERE, HEAD FUCKING HIGH.
CHIN UP. MAKE PEOPLE FIGHT FOR YOU TO EVEN BOTHER LOOKING 'EM OVER, SEE?
BE THE SHARK.
WILL YOU TRUST YOUR STEP-MA THIS ONE TIME?
OKAY. OKAY.
I'LL TRY.
"BE THE SHARK."

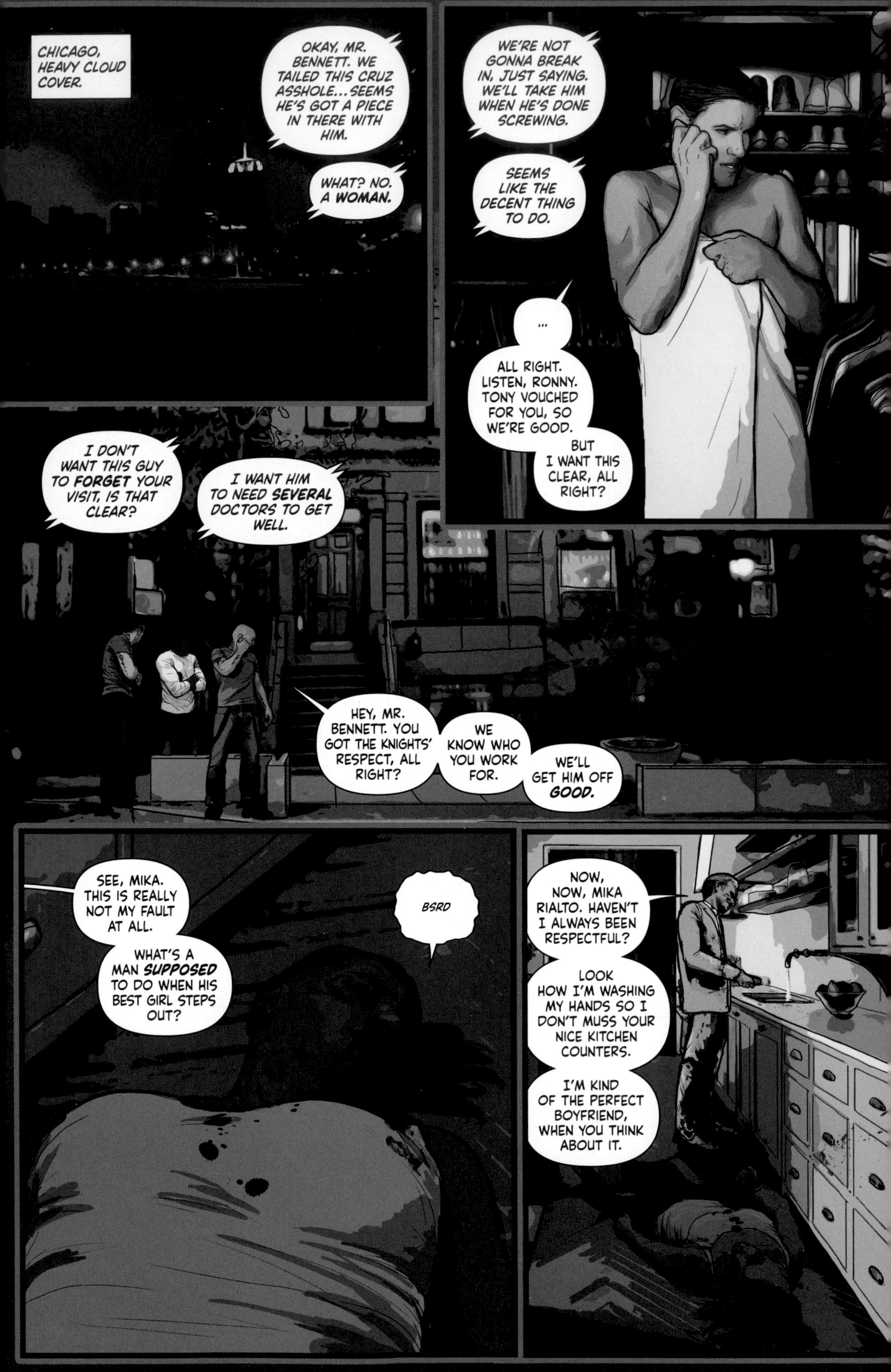
CHICAGO, HEAVY CLOUD COVER.
OKAY, MR. BENNETT. WE TAILED THIS CRUZ ASSHOLE...SEEMS HE'S GOT A PIECE IN THERE WITH HIM.
WHAT? NO. A WOMAN.
WE'RE NOT GONNA BREAK IN, JUST SAYING. WE'LL TAKE HIM WHEN HE'S DONE SCREWING.
SEEMS LIKE THE DECENT THING TO DO.
...
ALL RIGHT. LISTEN, RONNY. TONY VOUCHED FOR YOU, SO WE'RE GOOD.
BUT I WANT THIS CLEAR, ALL RIGHT?
I DON'T WANT THIS GUY TO FORGET YOUR VISIT, IS THAT CLEAR?
I WANT HIM TO NEED SEVERAL DOCTORS TO GET WELL.
HEY, MR. BENNETT. YOU GOT THE KNIGHTS' RESPECT, ALL RIGHT?
WE KNOW WHO YOU WORK FOR.
WE'LL GET HIM OFF GOOD.
SEE, MIKA. THIS IS REALLY NOT MY FAULT AT ALL.
WHAT'S A MAN SUPPOSED TO DO WHEN HIS BEST GIRL STEPS OUT?
BSRD
NOW, NOW, MIKA RIALTO. HAVEN'T I ALWAYS BEEN RESPECTFUL?
LOOK HOW I'M WASHING MY HANDS SO I DON'T MUSS YOUR NICE KITCHEN COUNTERS.
I'M KIND OF THE PERFECT BOYFRIEND, WHEN YOU THINK ABOUT IT.

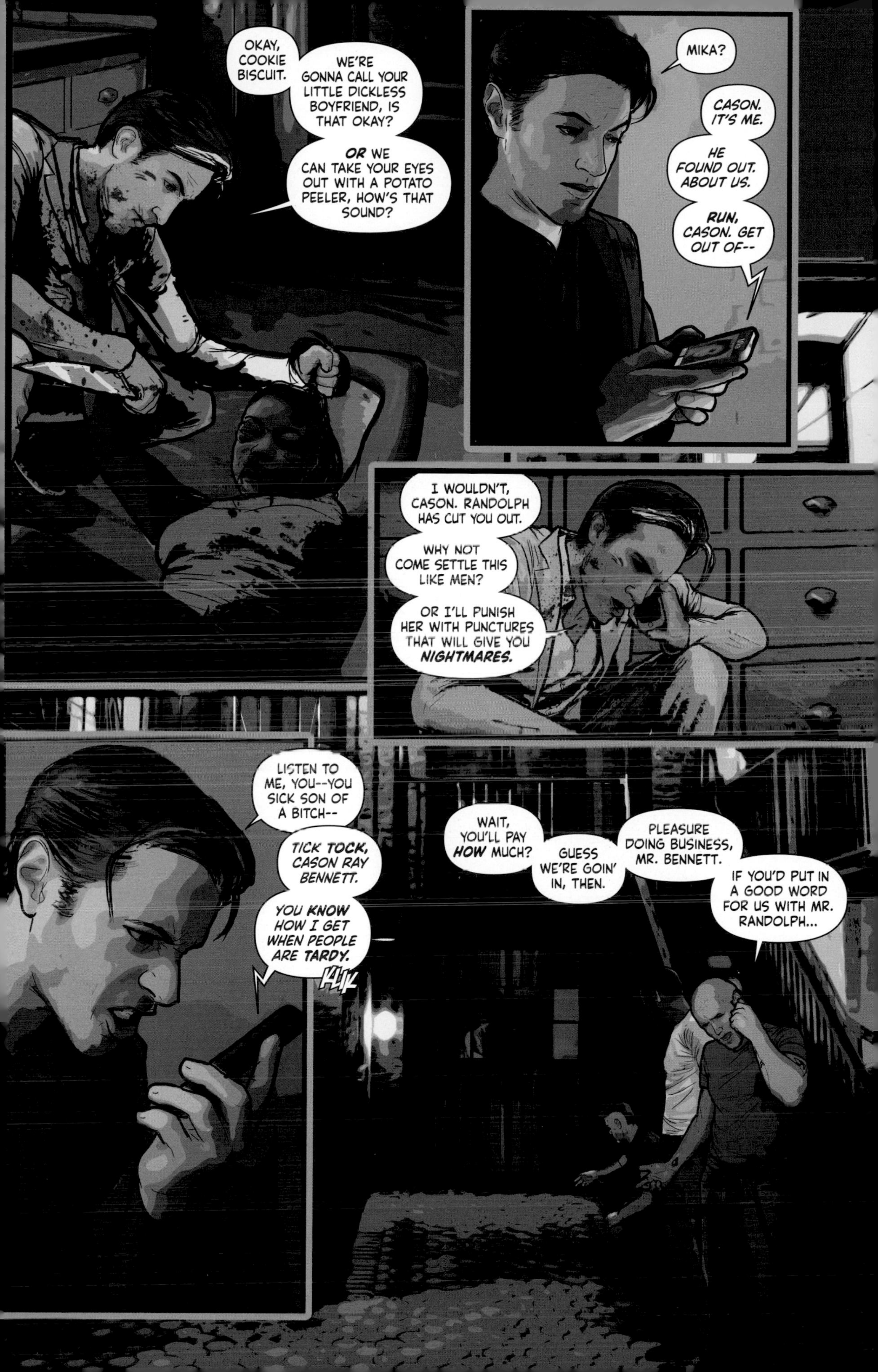
OKAY, COOKIE BISCUIT.
WE'RE GONNA CALL YOUR LITTLE DICKLESS BOYFRIEND, IS THAT OKAY?
OR WE CAN TAKE YOUR EYES OUT WITH A POTATO PEELER, HOW'S THAT SOUND?
MIKA?
CASON. IT'S ME.
HE FOUND OUT. ABOUT US.
RUN, CASON. GET OUT OF--
I WOULDN'T, CASON. RANDOLPH HAS CUT YOU OUT.
WHY NOT COME SETTLE THIS LIKE MEN?
OR I'LL PUNISH HER WITH PUNCTURES THAT WILL GIVE YOU NIGHTMARES.
LISTEN TO ME, YOU--YOU SICK SON OF A BITCH--
TICK TOCK, CASON RAY BENNETT.
YOU KNOW HOW I GET WHEN PEOPLE ARE TARDY.
KLIK
WAIT, YOU'LL PAY HOW MUCH?
GUESS WE'RE GOIN' IN, THEN.
PLEASURE DOING BUSINESS, MR. BENNETT.
IF YOU'D PUT IN A GOOD WORD FOR US WITH MR. RANDOLPH...

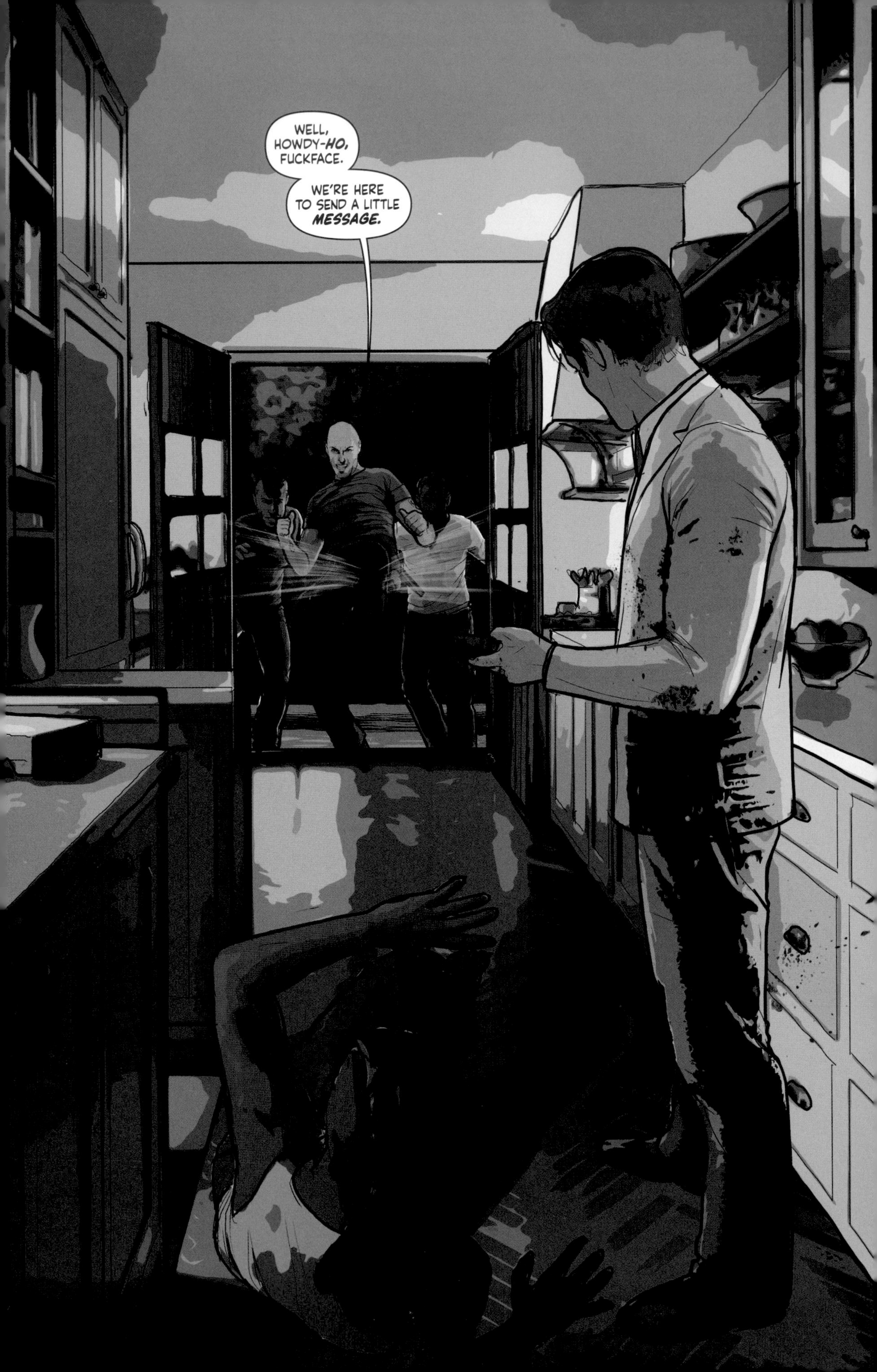
WELL, HOWDY-*HO,* FUCKFACE.
WE'RE HERE TO SEND A LITTLE *MESSAGE.*

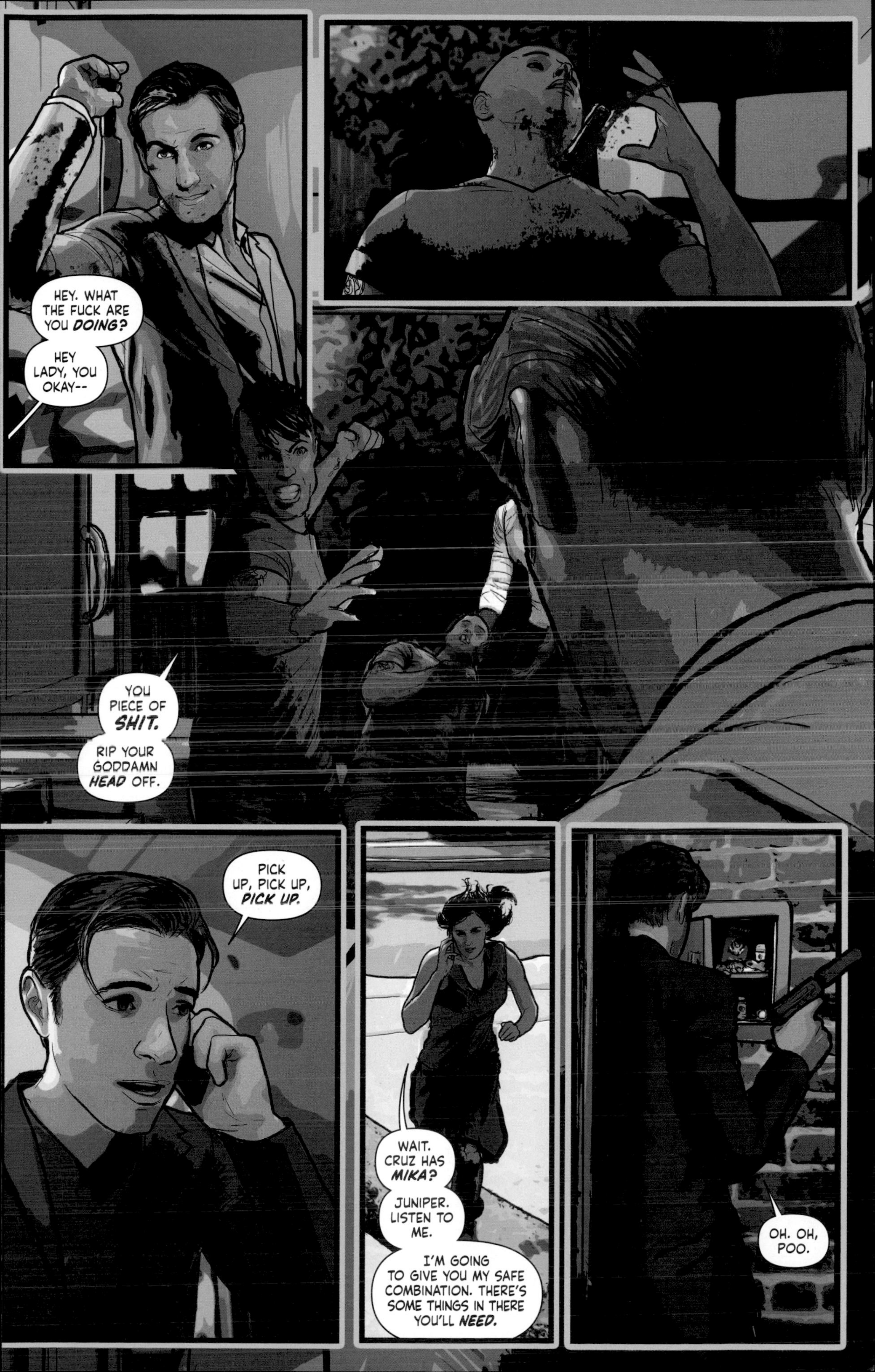
HEY. WHAT THE FUCK ARE YOU DOING?
HEY LADY, YOU OKAY--
YOU PIECE OF SHIT.
RIP YOUR GODDAMN HEAD OFF.
PICK UP, PICK UP, PICK UP.
WAIT. CRUZ HAS MIKA?
JUNIPER. LISTEN TO ME.
I'M GOING TO GIVE YOU MY SAFE COMBINATION. THERE'S SOME THINGS IN THERE YOU'LL NEED.
OH. OH, POO.

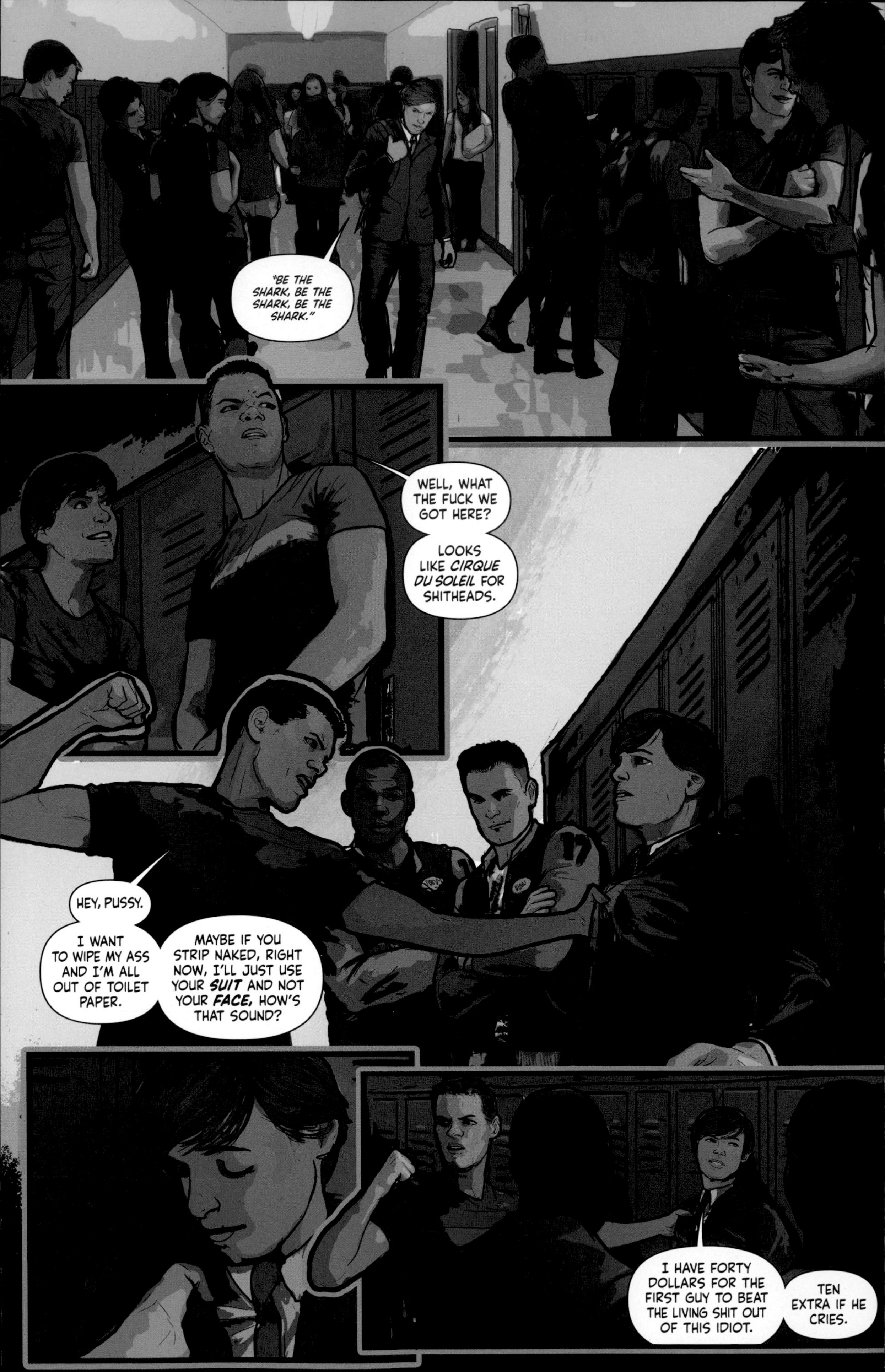
"BE THE SHARK, BE THE SHARK, BE THE SHARK."
WELL, WHAT THE FUCK WE GOT HERE?
LOOKS LIKE *CIRQUE DU SOLEIL* FOR SHITHEADS.
HEY, PUSSY.
I WANT TO WIPE MY ASS AND I'M ALL OUT OF TOILET PAPER.
MAYBE IF YOU STRIP NAKED, RIGHT NOW, I'LL JUST USE YOUR **SUIT** AND NOT YOUR **FACE,** HOW'S THAT SOUND?
I HAVE FORTY DOLLARS FOR THE FIRST GUY TO BEAT THE LIVING SHIT OUT OF THIS IDIOT.
TEN EXTRA IF HE CRIES.

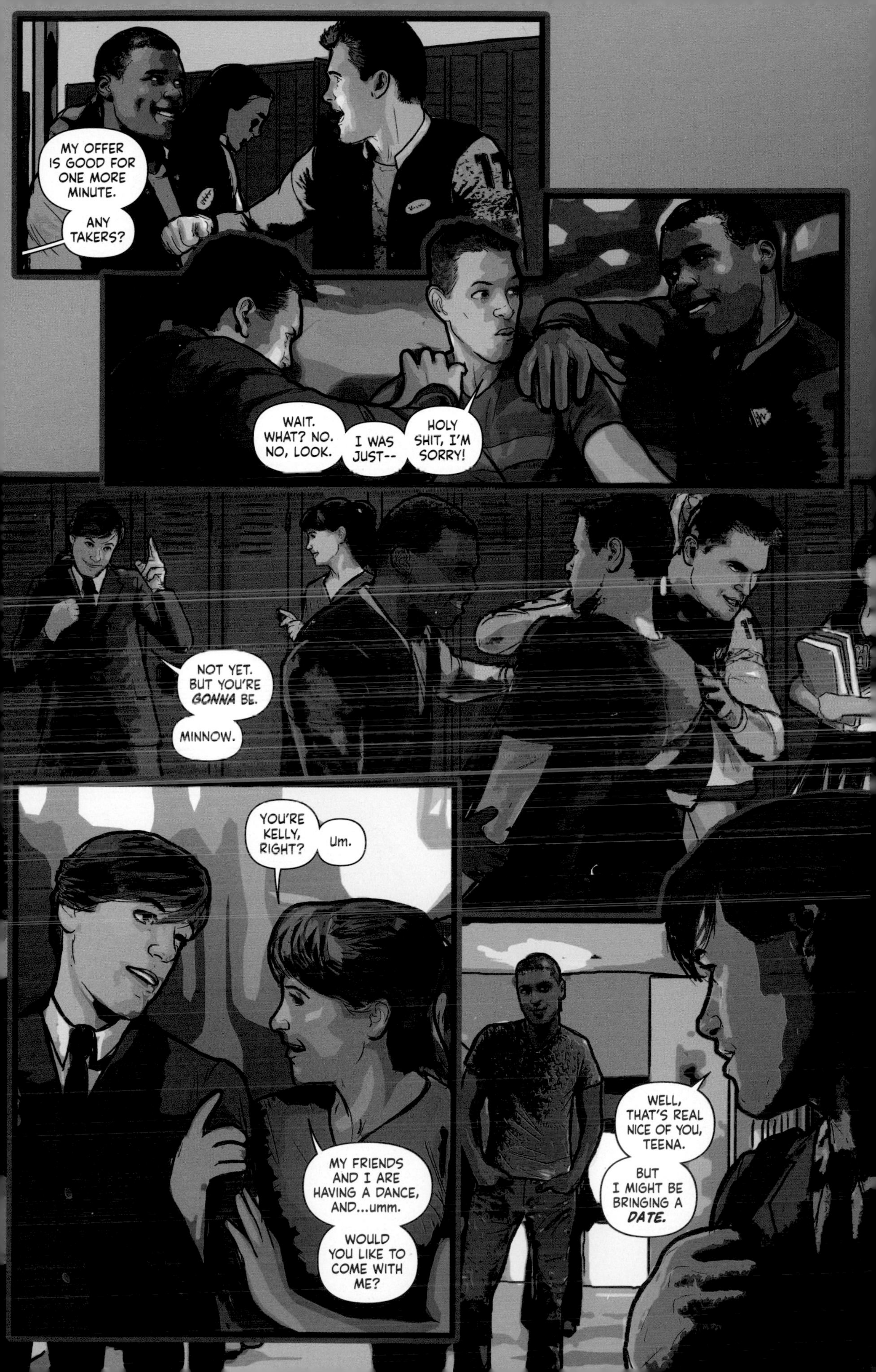
MY OFFER IS GOOD FOR ONE MORE MINUTE.
ANY TAKERS?
WAIT. WHAT? NO. NO, LOOK.
I WAS JUST--
HOLY SHIT, I'M SORRY!
NOT YET. BUT YOU'RE *GONNA* BE.
MINNOW.
YOU'RE KELLY, RIGHT?
Um.
MY FRIENDS AND I ARE HAVING A DANCE, AND...umm.
WOULD YOU LIKE TO COME WITH ME?
WELL, THAT'S REAL NICE OF YOU, TEENA.
BUT I MIGHT BE BRINGING A ***DATE.***

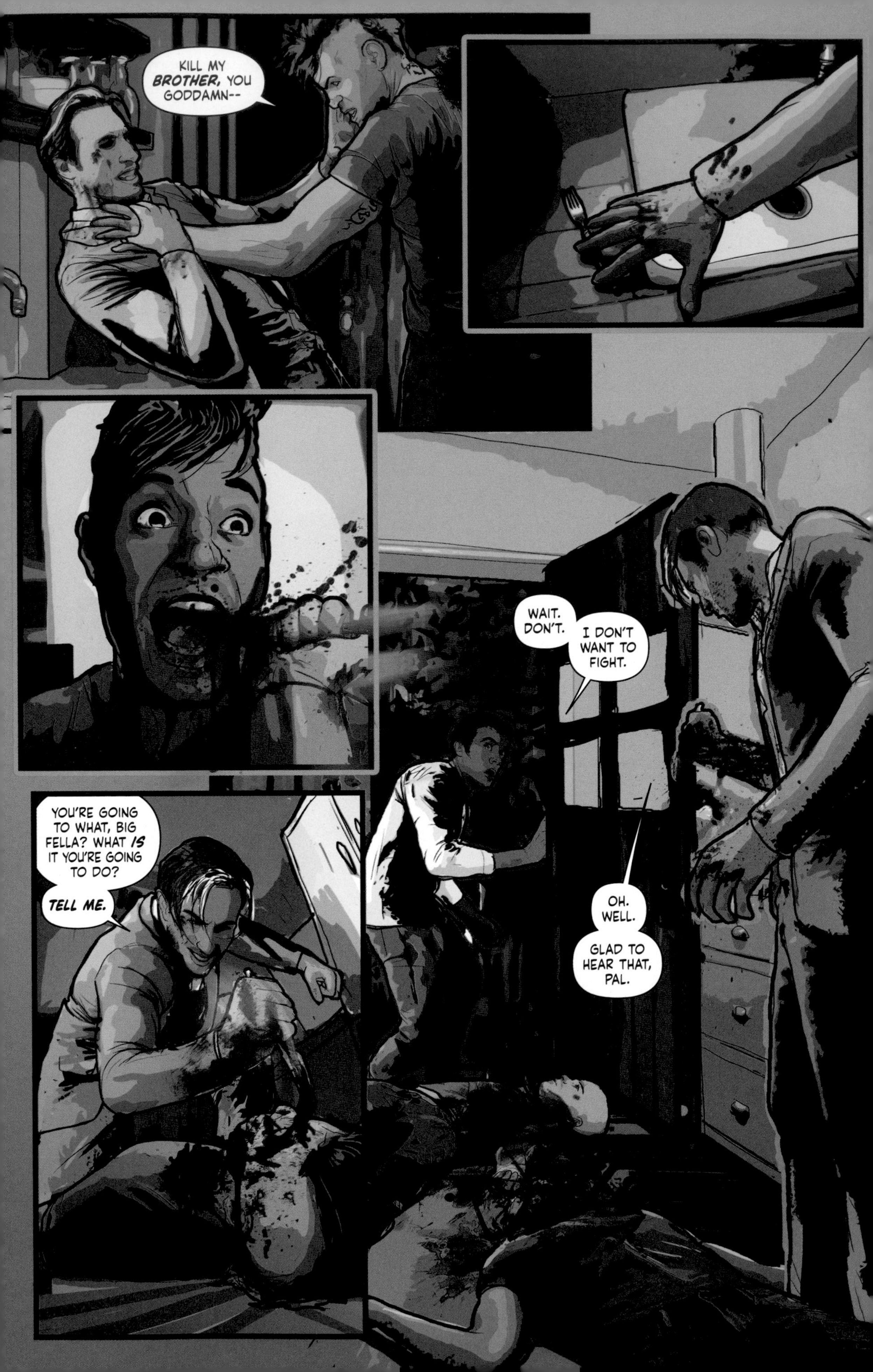
KILL MY BROTHER, YOU GODDAMN--
YOU'RE GOING TO WHAT, BIG FELLA? WHAT IS IT YOU'RE GOING TO DO?
TELL ME.
WAIT. DON'T.
I DON'T WANT TO FIGHT.
OH. WELL.
GLAD TO HEAR THAT, PAL.

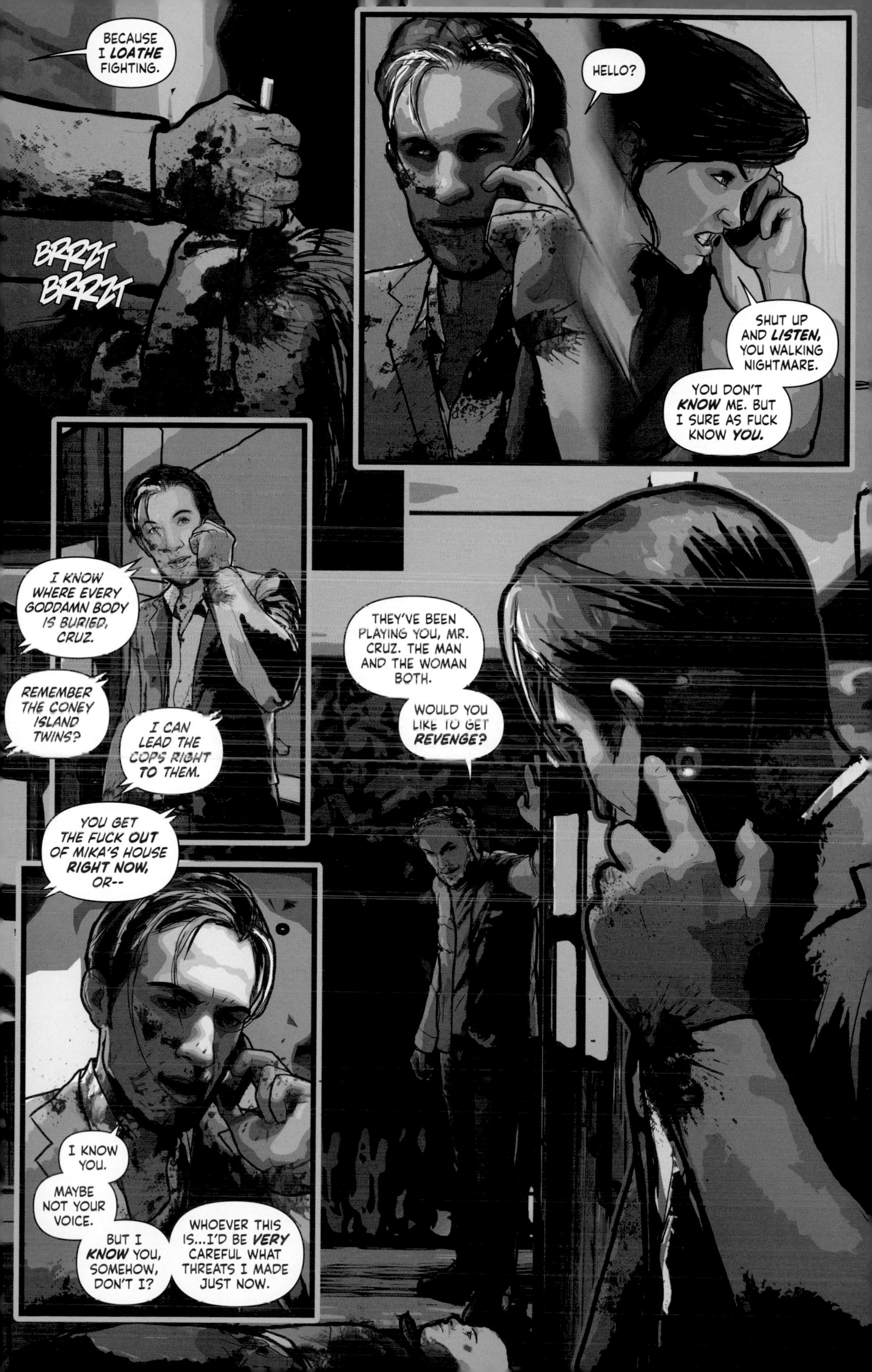
BECAUSE I LOATHE FIGHTING.
BRRZT BRRZT
HELLO?
SHUT UP AND LISTEN, YOU WALKING NIGHTMARE.
YOU DON'T KNOW ME. BUT I SURE AS FUCK KNOW YOU.
I KNOW WHERE EVERY GODDAMN BODY IS BURIED, CRUZ.
REMEMBER THE CONEY ISLAND TWINS?
I CAN LEAD THE COPS RIGHT TO THEM.
YOU GET THE FUCK OUT OF MIKA'S HOUSE RIGHT NOW, OR--
I KNOW YOU.
MAYBE NOT YOUR VOICE.
BUT I KNOW YOU, SOMEHOW, DON'T I?
WHOEVER THIS IS...I'D BE VERY CAREFUL WHAT THREATS I MADE JUST NOW.
THEY'VE BEEN PLAYING YOU, MR. CRUZ. THE MAN AND THE WOMAN BOTH.
WOULD YOU LIKE TO GET REVENGE?

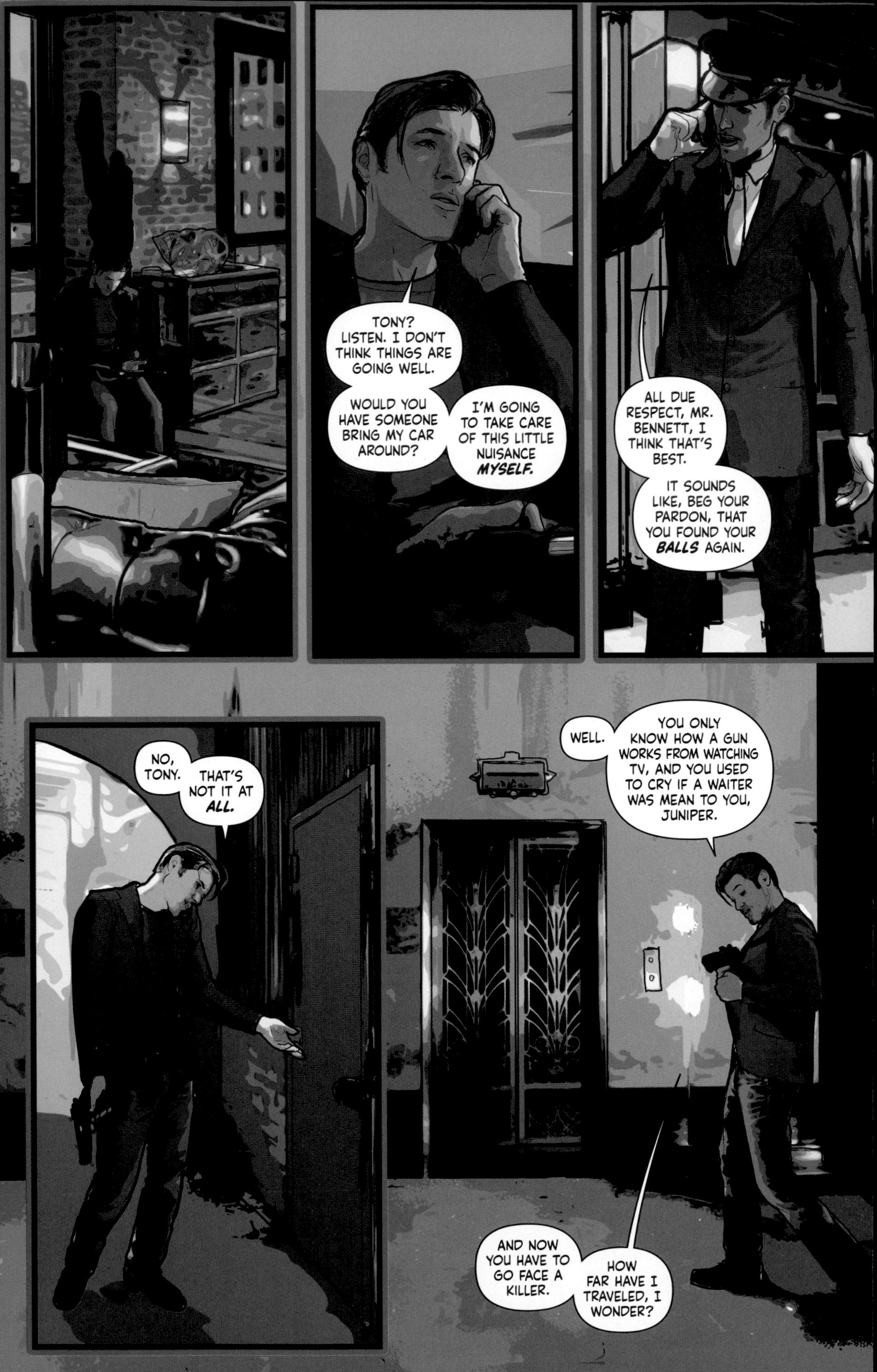
TONY? LISTEN. I DON'T THINK THINGS ARE GOING WELL.
WOULD YOU HAVE SOMEONE BRING MY CAR AROUND?
I'M GOING TO TAKE CARE OF THIS LITTLE NUISANCE *MYSELF.*
ALL DUE RESPECT, MR. BENNETT, I THINK THAT'S BEST.
IT SOUNDS LIKE, BEG YOUR PARDON, THAT YOU FOUND YOUR *BALLS* AGAIN.
NO, TONY.
THAT'S NOT IT AT *ALL.*
WELL.
YOU ONLY KNOW HOW A GUN WORKS FROM WATCHING TV, AND YOU USED TO CRY IF A WAITER WAS MEAN TO YOU, JUNIPER.
AND NOW YOU HAVE TO GO FACE A KILLER.
HOW FAR HAVE I TRAVELED, I WONDER?

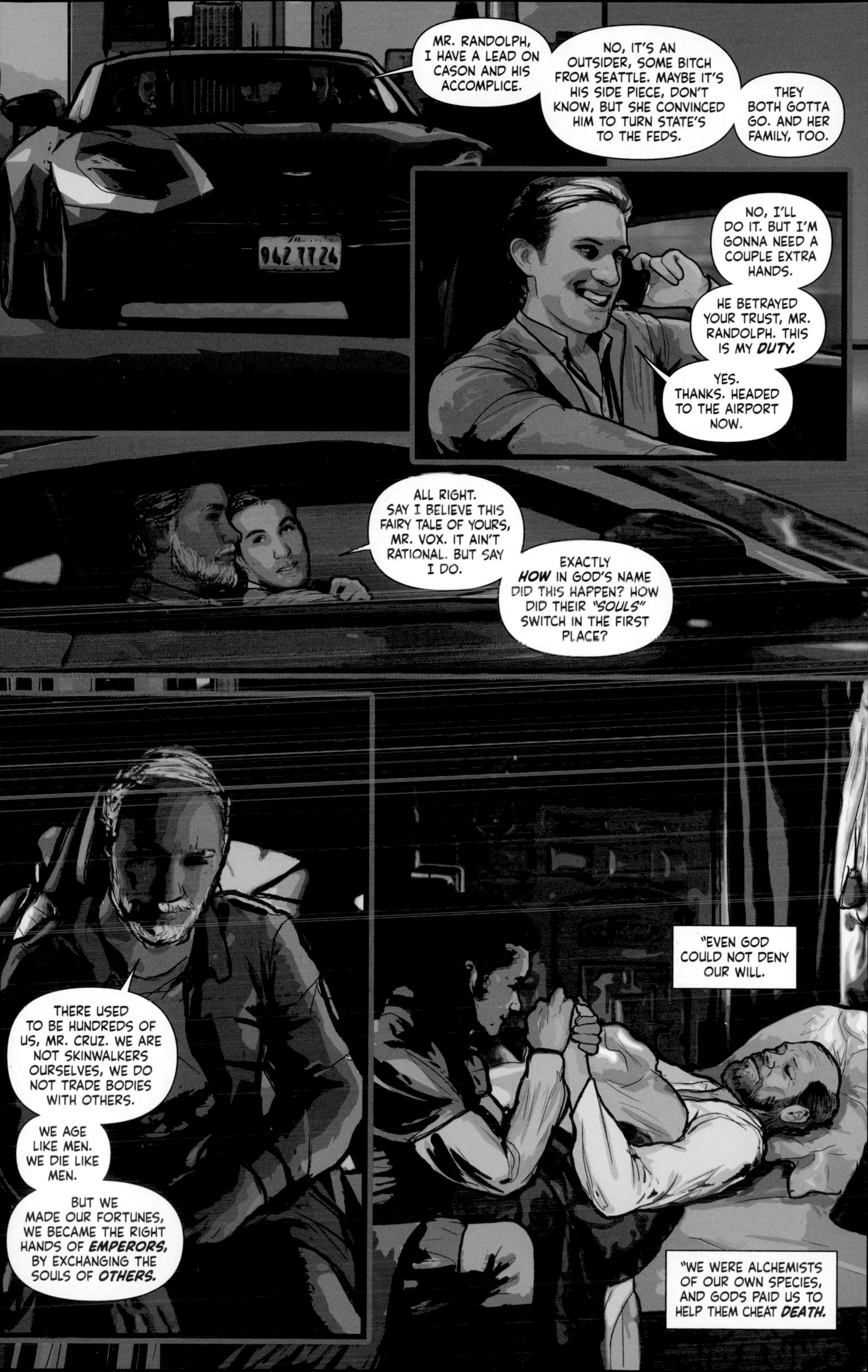
MR. RANDOLPH, I HAVE A LEAD ON CASON AND HIS ACCOMPLICE.
NO, IT'S AN OUTSIDER, SOME BITCH FROM SEATTLE. MAYBE IT'S HIS SIDE PIECE, DON'T KNOW, BUT SHE CONVINCED HIM TO TURN STATE'S TO THE FEDS.
THEY BOTH GOTTA GO. AND HER FAMILY, TOO.
NO, I'LL DO IT. BUT I'M GONNA NEED A COUPLE EXTRA HANDS.
HE BETRAYED YOUR TRUST, MR. RANDOLPH. THIS IS MY ***DUTY.***
YES. THANKS. HEADED TO THE AIRPORT NOW.
ALL RIGHT. SAY I BELIEVE THIS FAIRY TALE OF YOURS, MR. VOX. IT AIN'T RATIONAL. BUT SAY I DO.
EXACTLY ***HOW*** IN GOD'S NAME DID THIS HAPPEN? HOW DID THEIR *"SOULS"* SWITCH IN THE FIRST PLACE?
THERE USED TO BE HUNDREDS OF US, MR. CRUZ. WE ARE NOT SKINWALKERS OURSELVES, WE DO NOT TRADE BODIES WITH OTHERS.
WE AGE LIKE MEN. WE DIE LIKE MEN.
BUT WE MADE OUR FORTUNES, WE BECAME THE RIGHT HANDS OF ***EMPERORS,*** BY EXCHANGING THE SOULS OF ***OTHERS.***
"EVEN GOD COULD NOT DENY OUR WILL.
"WE WERE ALCHEMISTS OF OUR OWN SPECIES, AND GODS PAID US TO HELP THEM CHEAT ***DEATH.***

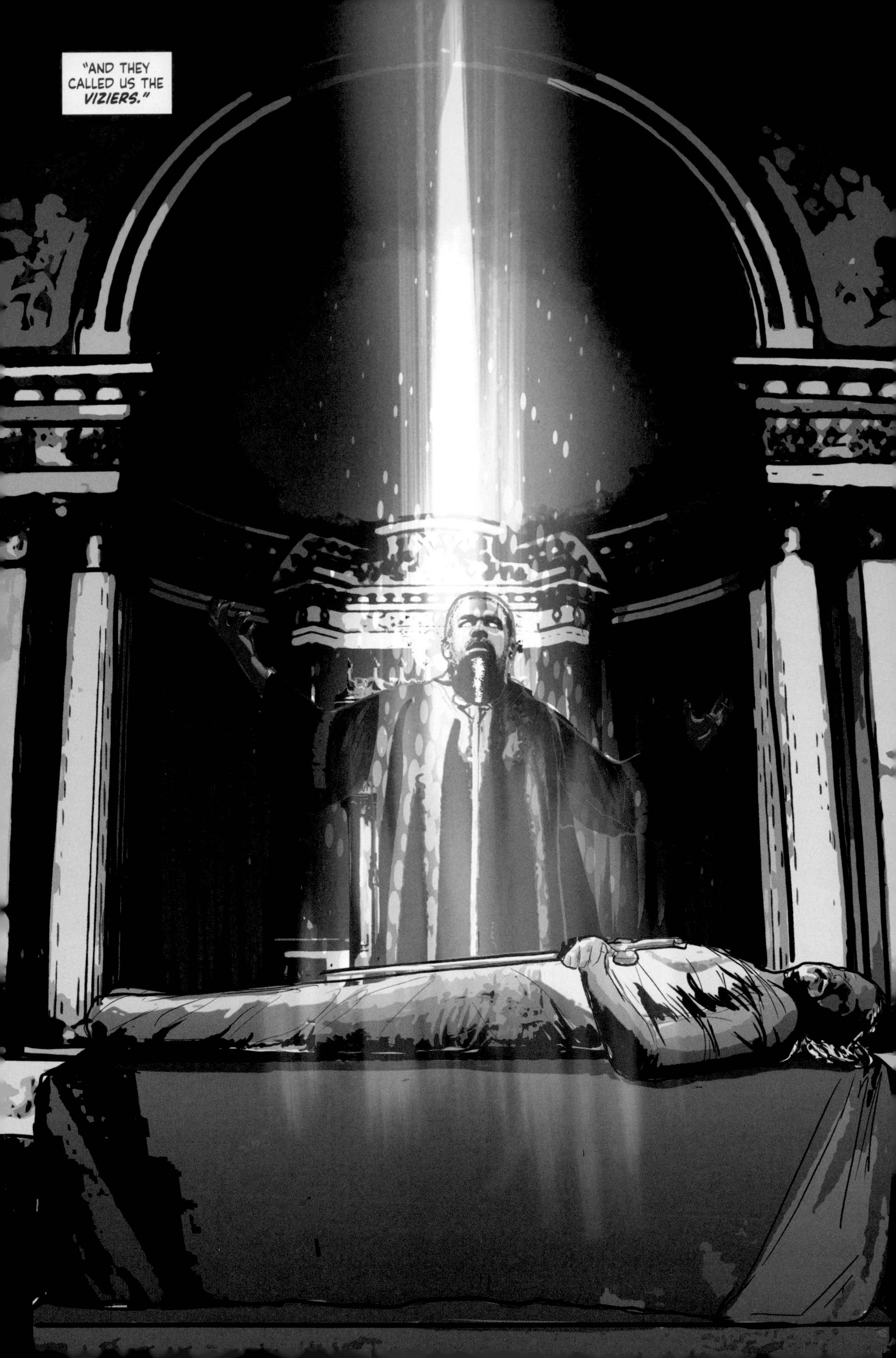
"AND THEY CALLED US THE *VIZIERS.*"

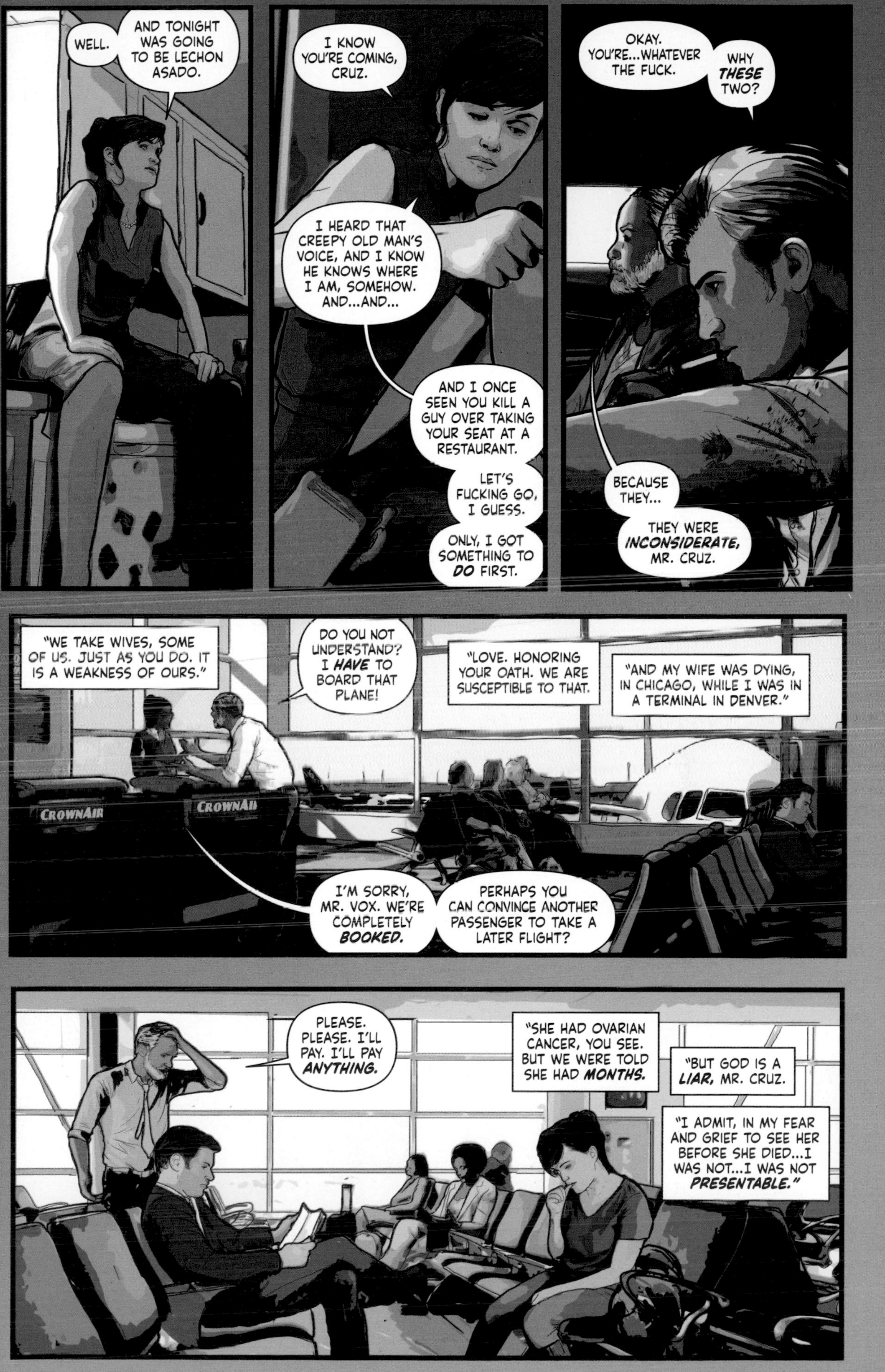
WELL.
AND TONIGHT WAS GOING TO BE LECHON ASADO.
I KNOW YOU'RE COMING, CRUZ.
I HEARD THAT CREEPY OLD MAN'S VOICE, AND I KNOW HE KNOWS WHERE I AM, SOMEHOW. AND...AND...
AND I ONCE SEEN YOU KILL A GUY OVER TAKING YOUR SEAT AT A RESTAURANT.
LET'S FUCKING GO, I GUESS.
ONLY, I GOT SOMETHING TO DO FIRST.
OKAY. YOU'RE...WHATEVER THE FUCK.
WHY THESE TWO?
BECAUSE THEY...
THEY WERE INCONSIDERATE, MR. CRUZ.
"WE TAKE WIVES, SOME OF US. JUST AS YOU DO. IT IS A WEAKNESS OF OURS."
DO YOU NOT UNDERSTAND? I HAVE TO BOARD THAT PLANE!
"LOVE. HONORING YOUR OATH. WE ARE SUSCEPTIBLE TO THAT.
"AND MY WIFE WAS DYING, IN CHICAGO, WHILE I WAS IN A TERMINAL IN DENVER."
CROWNAIR
CROWNAIR
I'M SORRY, MR. VOX. WE'RE COMPLETELY BOOKED.
PERHAPS YOU CAN CONVINCE ANOTHER PASSENGER TO TAKE A LATER FLIGHT?
PLEASE. PLEASE. I'LL PAY. I'LL PAY ANYTHING.
"SHE HAD OVARIAN CANCER, YOU SEE. BUT WE WERE TOLD SHE HAD MONTHS.
"BUT GOD IS A LIAR, MR. CRUZ.
"I ADMIT, IN MY FEAR AND GRIEF TO SEE HER BEFORE SHE DIED...I WAS NOT...I WAS NOT PRESENTABLE."

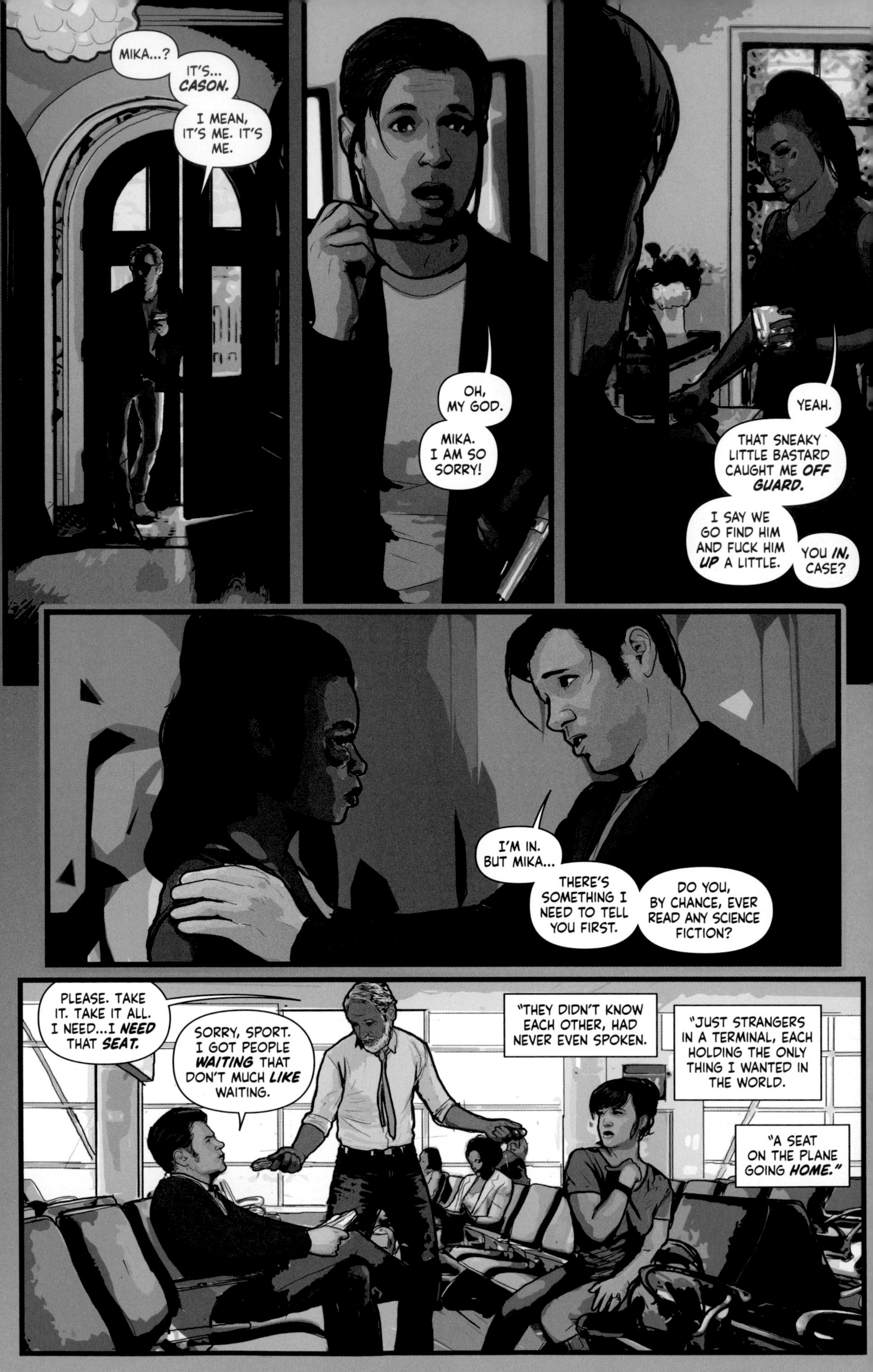
MIKA...?
IT'S... CASON.
I MEAN, IT'S ME. IT'S ME.
OH, MY GOD.
MIKA. I AM SO SORRY!
YEAH.
THAT SNEAKY LITTLE BASTARD CAUGHT ME OFF GUARD.
I SAY WE GO FIND HIM AND FUCK HIM UP A LITTLE.
YOU IN, CASE?
I'M IN. BUT MIKA...
THERE'S SOMETHING I NEED TO TELL YOU FIRST.
DO YOU, BY CHANCE, EVER READ ANY SCIENCE FICTION?
PLEASE. TAKE IT. TAKE IT ALL. I NEED...I NEED THAT SEAT.
SORRY, SPORT. I GOT PEOPLE WAITING THAT DON'T MUCH LIKE WAITING.
"THEY DIDN'T KNOW EACH OTHER, HAD NEVER EVEN SPOKEN.
"JUST STRANGERS IN A TERMINAL, EACH HOLDING THE ONLY THING I WANTED IN THE WORLD.
"A SEAT ON THE PLANE GOING HOME."

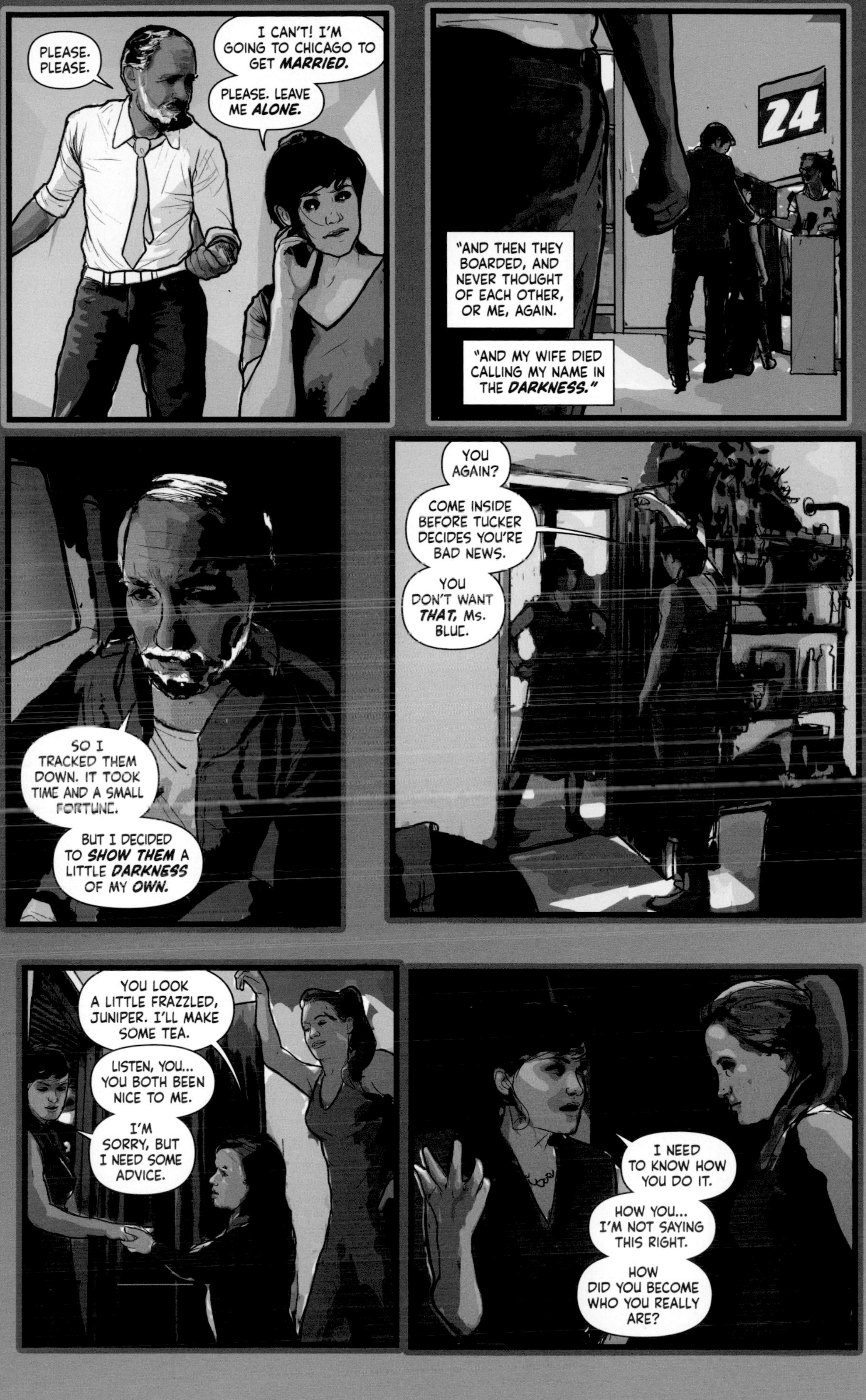
PLEASE. PLEASE.
I CAN'T! I'M GOING TO CHICAGO TO GET MARRIED.
PLEASE. LEAVE ME ALONE.
24
"AND THEN THEY BOARDED, AND NEVER THOUGHT OF EACH OTHER, OR ME, AGAIN.
"AND MY WIFE DIED CALLING MY NAME IN THE DARKNESS."
SO I TRACKED THEM DOWN. IT TOOK TIME AND A SMALL FORTUNE.
BUT I DECIDED TO SHOW THEM A LITTLE DARKNESS OF MY OWN.
YOU AGAIN?
COME INSIDE BEFORE TUCKER DECIDES YOU'RE BAD NEWS.
YOU DON'T WANT THAT, Ms. BLUE.
YOU LOOK A LITTLE FRAZZLED, JUNIPER. I'LL MAKE SOME TEA.
LISTEN, YOU... YOU BOTH BEEN NICE TO ME.
I'M SORRY, BUT I NEED SOME ADVICE.
I NEED TO KNOW HOW YOU DO IT.
HOW YOU... I'M NOT SAYING THIS RIGHT.
HOW DID YOU BECOME WHO YOU REALLY ARE?

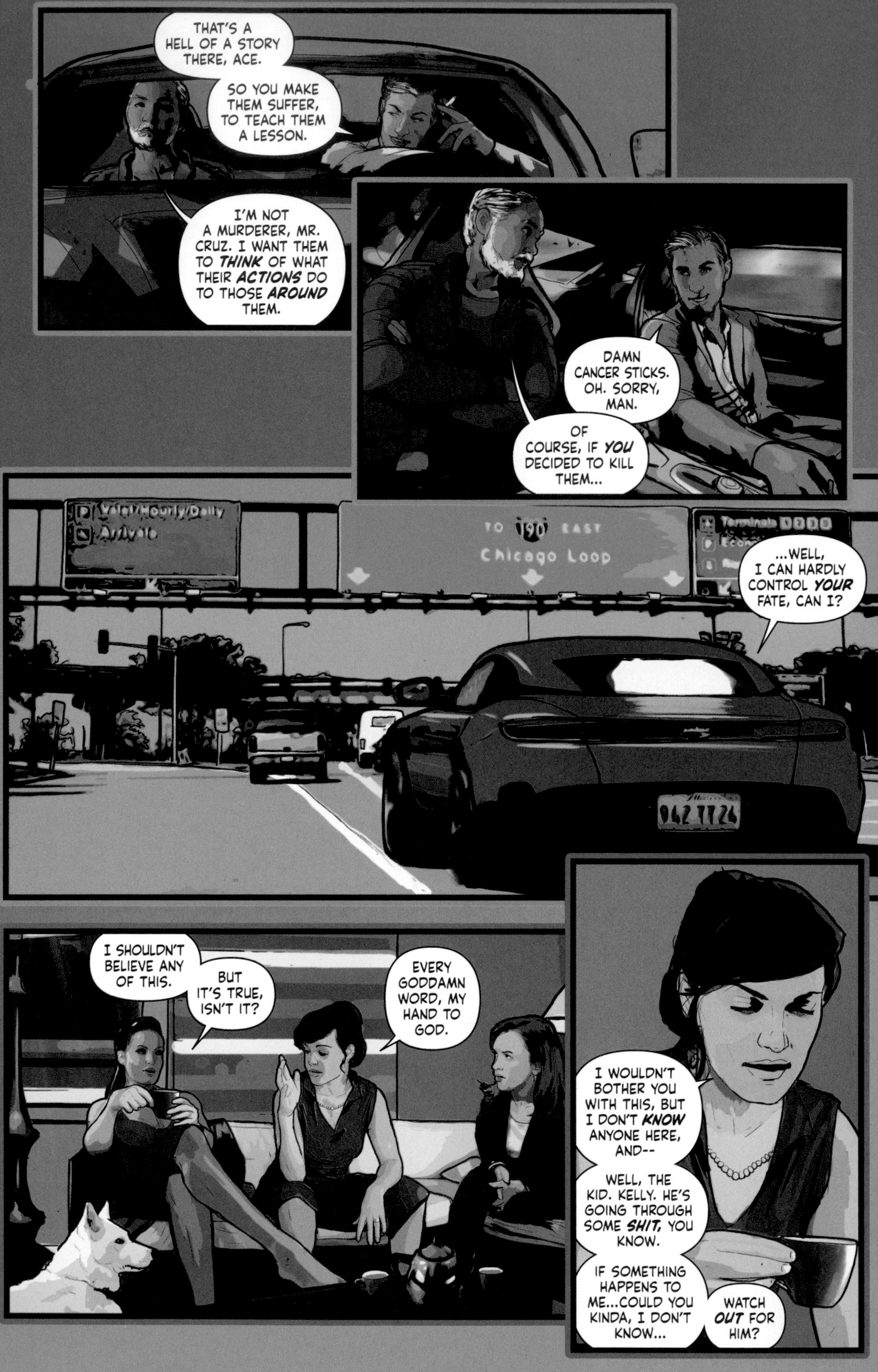
THAT'S A HELL OF A STORY THERE, ACE.
SO YOU MAKE THEM SUFFER, TO TEACH THEM A LESSON.
I'M NOT A MURDERER, MR. CRUZ. I WANT THEM TO THINK OF WHAT THEIR ACTIONS DO TO THOSE AROUND THEM.
DAMN CANCER STICKS. OH. SORRY, MAN.
OF COURSE, IF YOU DECIDED TO KILL THEM...
TO 190 EAST
Chicago Loop
...WELL, I CAN HARDLY CONTROL YOUR FATE, CAN I?
I SHOULDN'T BELIEVE ANY OF THIS.
BUT IT'S TRUE, ISN'T IT?
EVERY GODDAMN WORD, MY HAND TO GOD.
I WOULDN'T BOTHER YOU WITH THIS, BUT I DON'T KNOW ANYONE HERE, AND--
WELL, THE KID. KELLY. HE'S GOING THROUGH SOME SHIT, YOU KNOW.
IF SOMETHING HAPPENS TO ME...COULD YOU KINDA, I DON'T KNOW...
WATCH OUT FOR HIM?

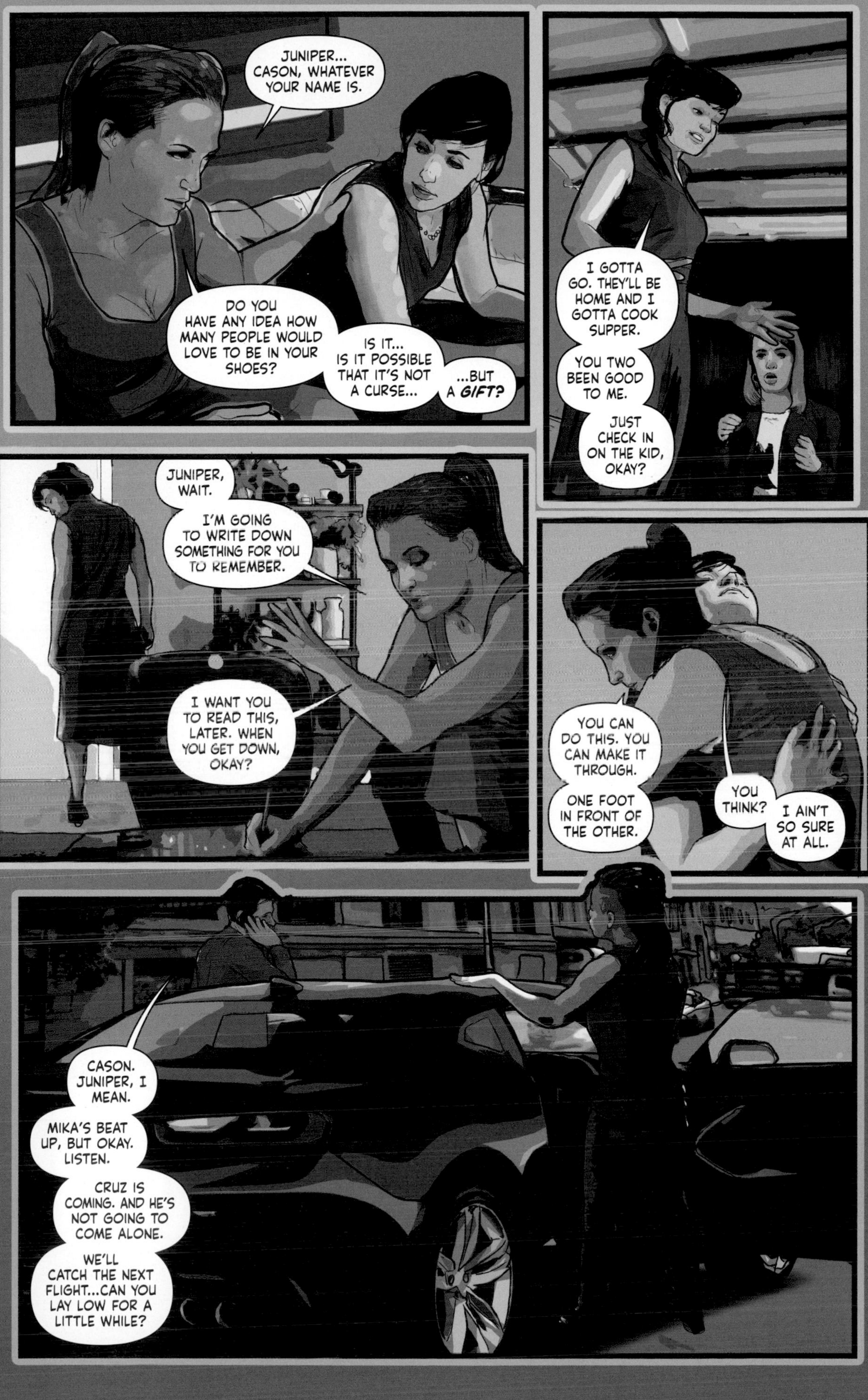
JUNIPER... CASON, WHATEVER YOUR NAME IS.
DO YOU HAVE ANY IDEA HOW MANY PEOPLE WOULD LOVE TO BE IN YOUR SHOES?
IS IT... IS IT POSSIBLE THAT IT'S NOT A CURSE...
...BUT A *GIFT?*
I GOTTA GO. THEY'LL BE HOME AND I GOTTA COOK SUPPER.
YOU TWO BEEN GOOD TO ME.
JUST CHECK IN ON THE KID, OKAY?
JUNIPER, WAIT.
I'M GOING TO WRITE DOWN SOMETHING FOR YOU TO REMEMBER.
I WANT YOU TO READ THIS, LATER. WHEN YOU GET DOWN, OKAY?
YOU CAN DO THIS. YOU CAN MAKE IT THROUGH.
ONE FOOT IN FRONT OF THE OTHER.
YOU THINK?
I AIN'T SO SURE AT ALL.
CASON. JUNIPER, I MEAN.
MIKA'S BEAT UP, BUT OKAY. LISTEN.
CRUZ IS COMING. AND HE'S NOT GOING TO COME ALONE.
WE'LL CATCH THE NEXT FLIGHT...CAN YOU LAY LOW FOR A LITTLE WHILE?

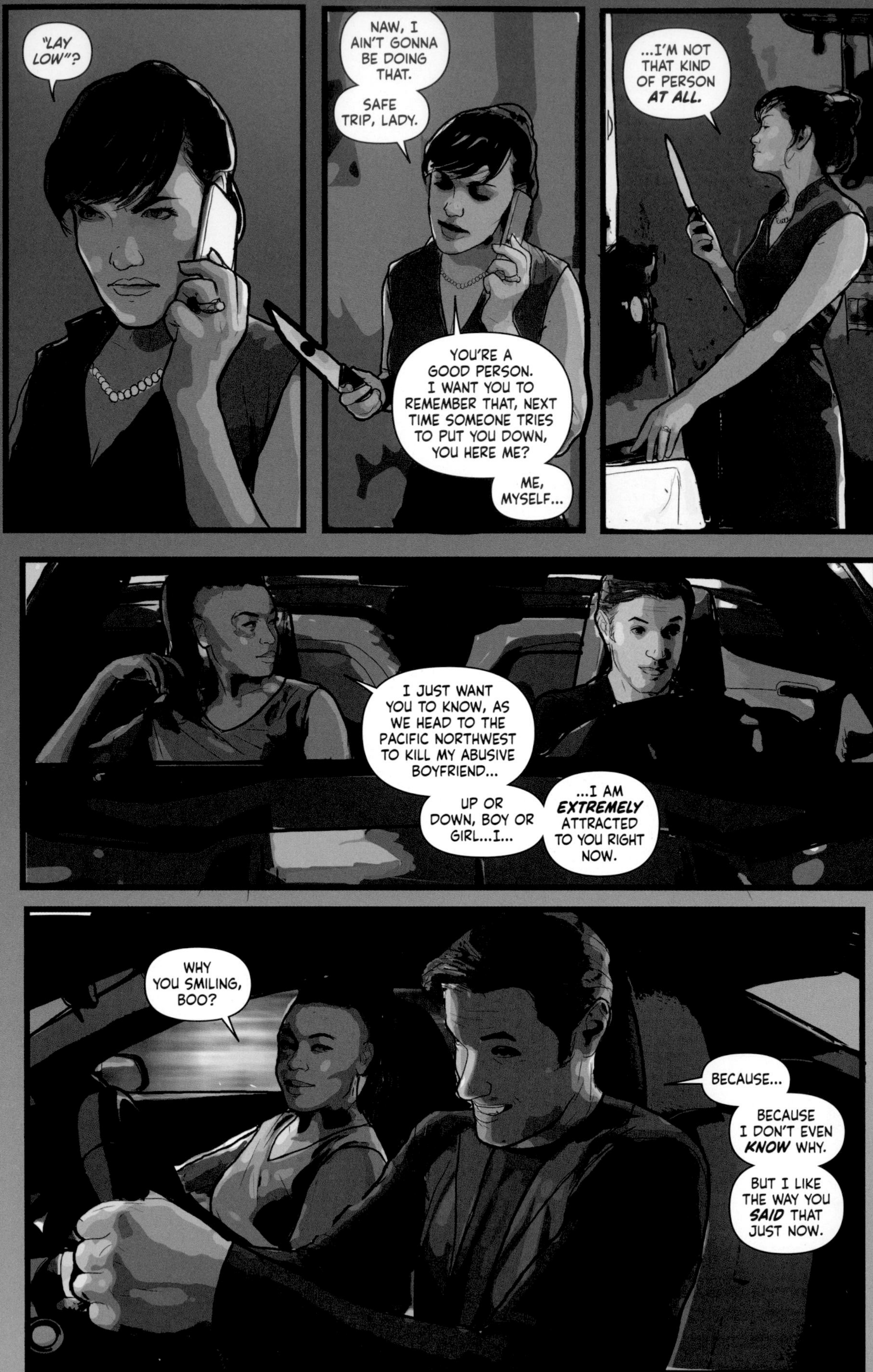
"LAY LOW"?
NAW, I AIN'T GONNA BE DOING THAT.
SAFE TRIP, LADY.
YOU'RE A GOOD PERSON. I WANT YOU TO REMEMBER THAT, NEXT TIME SOMEONE TRIES TO PUT YOU DOWN, YOU HERE ME?
ME, MYSELF...
...I'M NOT THAT KIND OF PERSON ***AT ALL.***
I JUST WANT YOU TO KNOW, AS WE HEAD TO THE PACIFIC NORTHWEST TO KILL MY ABUSIVE BOYFRIEND...
UP OR DOWN, BOY OR GIRL...I...
...I AM ***EXTREMELY*** ATTRACTED TO YOU RIGHT NOW.
WHY YOU SMILING, BOO?
BECAUSE...
BECAUSE I DON'T EVEN ***KNOW*** WHY.
BUT I LIKE THE WAY YOU ***SAID*** THAT JUST NOW.

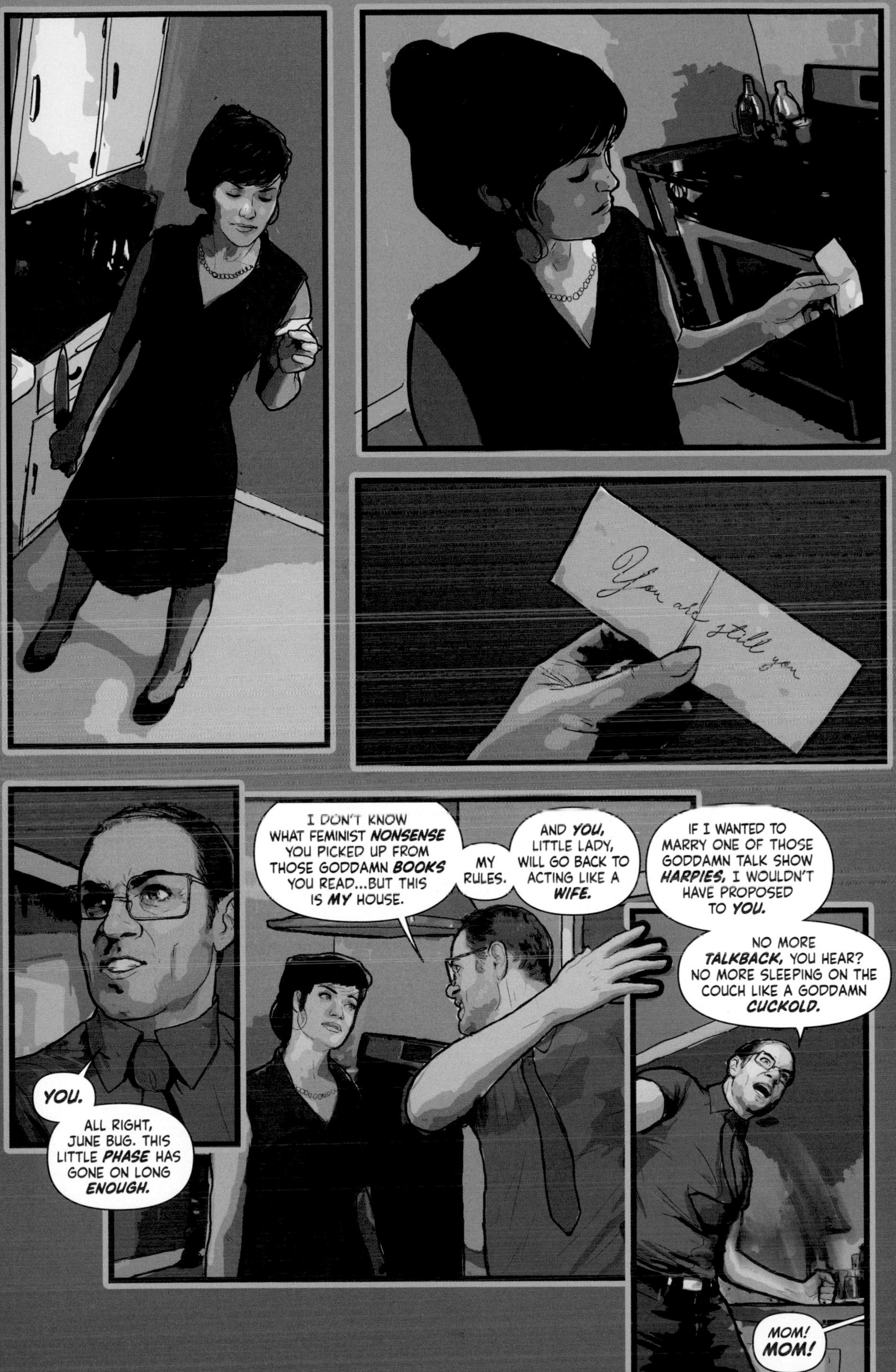
You are still you
YOU.
ALL RIGHT, JUNE BUG. THIS LITTLE PHASE HAS GONE ON LONG ENOUGH.
I DON'T KNOW WHAT FEMINIST NONSENSE YOU PICKED UP FROM THOSE GODDAMN BOOKS YOU READ...BUT THIS IS MY HOUSE.
MY RULES.
AND YOU, LITTLE LADY, WILL GO BACK TO ACTING LIKE A WIFE.
IF I WANTED TO MARRY ONE OF THOSE GODDAMN TALK SHOW HARPIES, I WOULDN'T HAVE PROPOSED TO YOU.
NO MORE TALKBACK, YOU HEAR? NO MORE SLEEPING ON THE COUCH LIKE A GODDAMN CUCKOLD.
MOM! MOM!

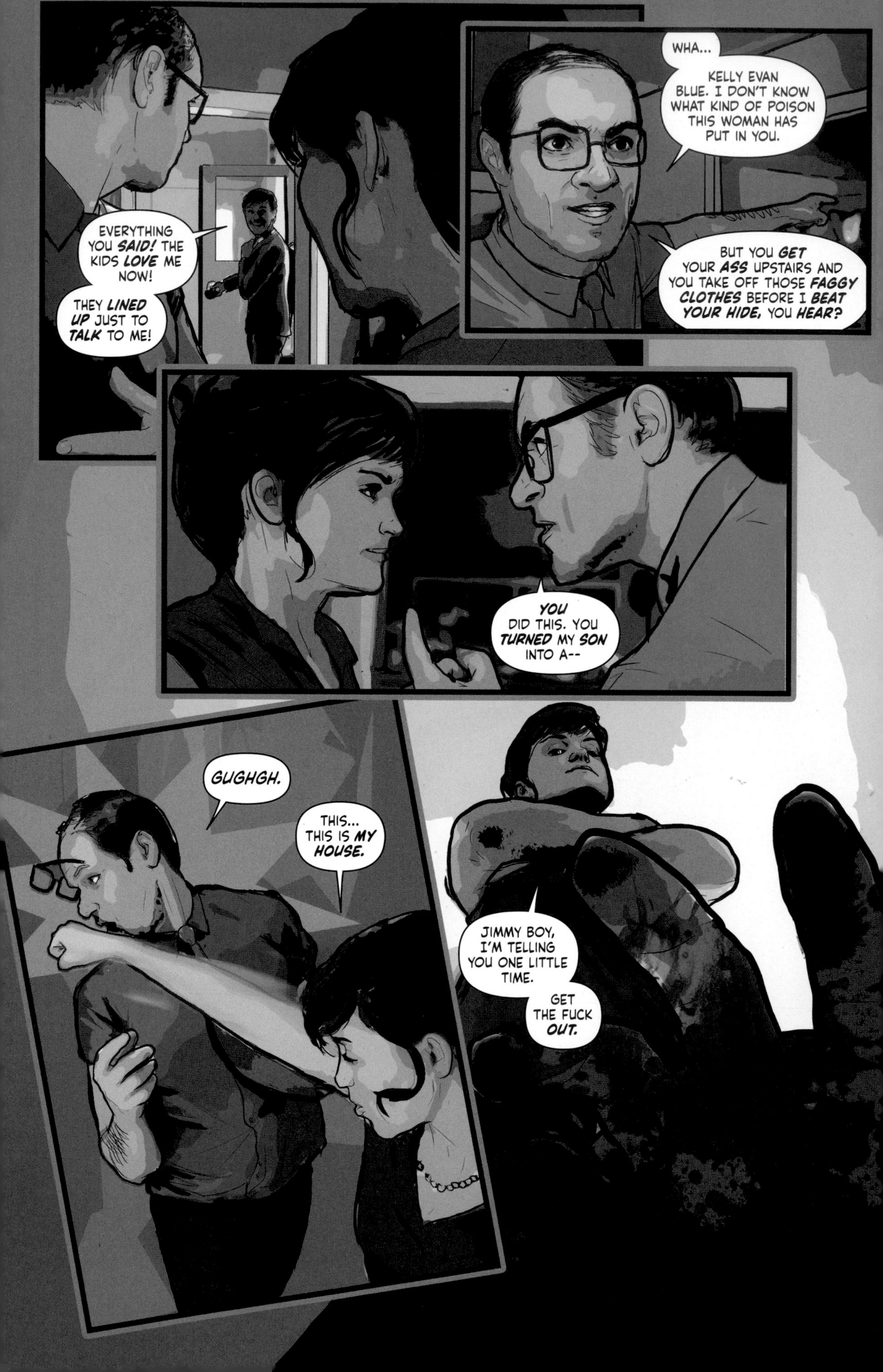
EVERYTHING YOU SAID! THE KIDS LOVE ME NOW!
THEY LINED UP JUST TO TALK TO ME!
WHA...
KELLY EVAN BLUE. I DON'T KNOW WHAT KIND OF POISON THIS WOMAN HAS PUT IN YOU.
BUT YOU GET YOUR ASS UPSTAIRS AND YOU TAKE OFF THOSE FAGGY CLOTHES BEFORE I BEAT YOUR HIDE, YOU HEAR?
YOU DID THIS. YOU TURNED MY SON INTO A--
GUGHGH.
THIS... THIS IS MY HOUSE.
JIMMY BOY, I'M TELLING YOU ONE LITTLE TIME.
GET THE FUCK OUT.

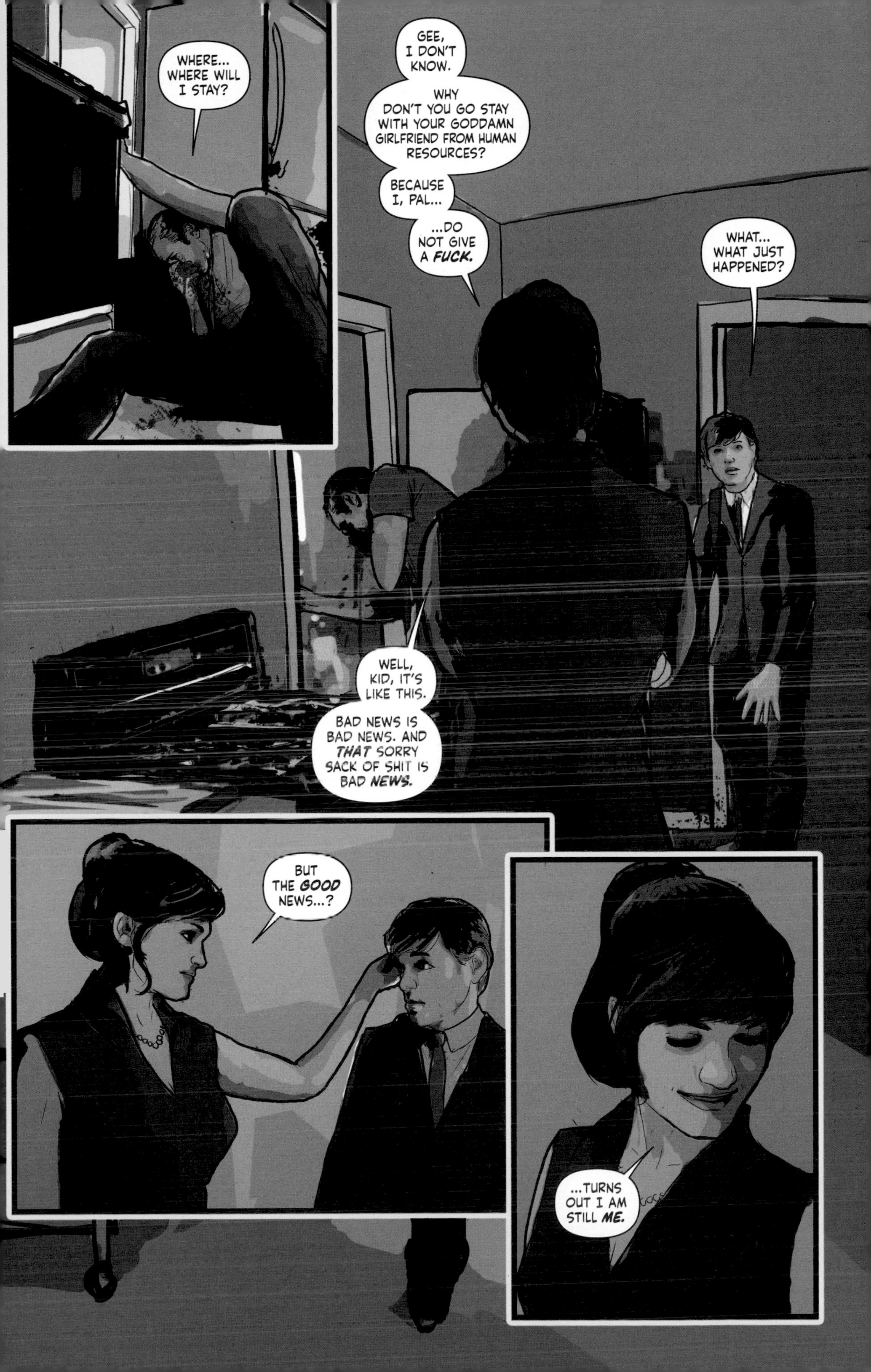
WHERE... WHERE WILL I STAY?
GEE, I DON'T KNOW.
WHY DON'T YOU GO STAY WITH YOUR GODDAMN GIRLFRIEND FROM HUMAN RESOURCES?
BECAUSE I, PAL...
...DO NOT GIVE A FUCK.
WHAT... WHAT JUST HAPPENED?
WELL, KID, IT'S LIKE THIS.
BAD NEWS IS BAD NEWS. AND THAT SORRY SACK OF SHIT IS BAD NEWS.
BUT THE GOOD NEWS...?
...TURNS OUT I AM STILL ME.

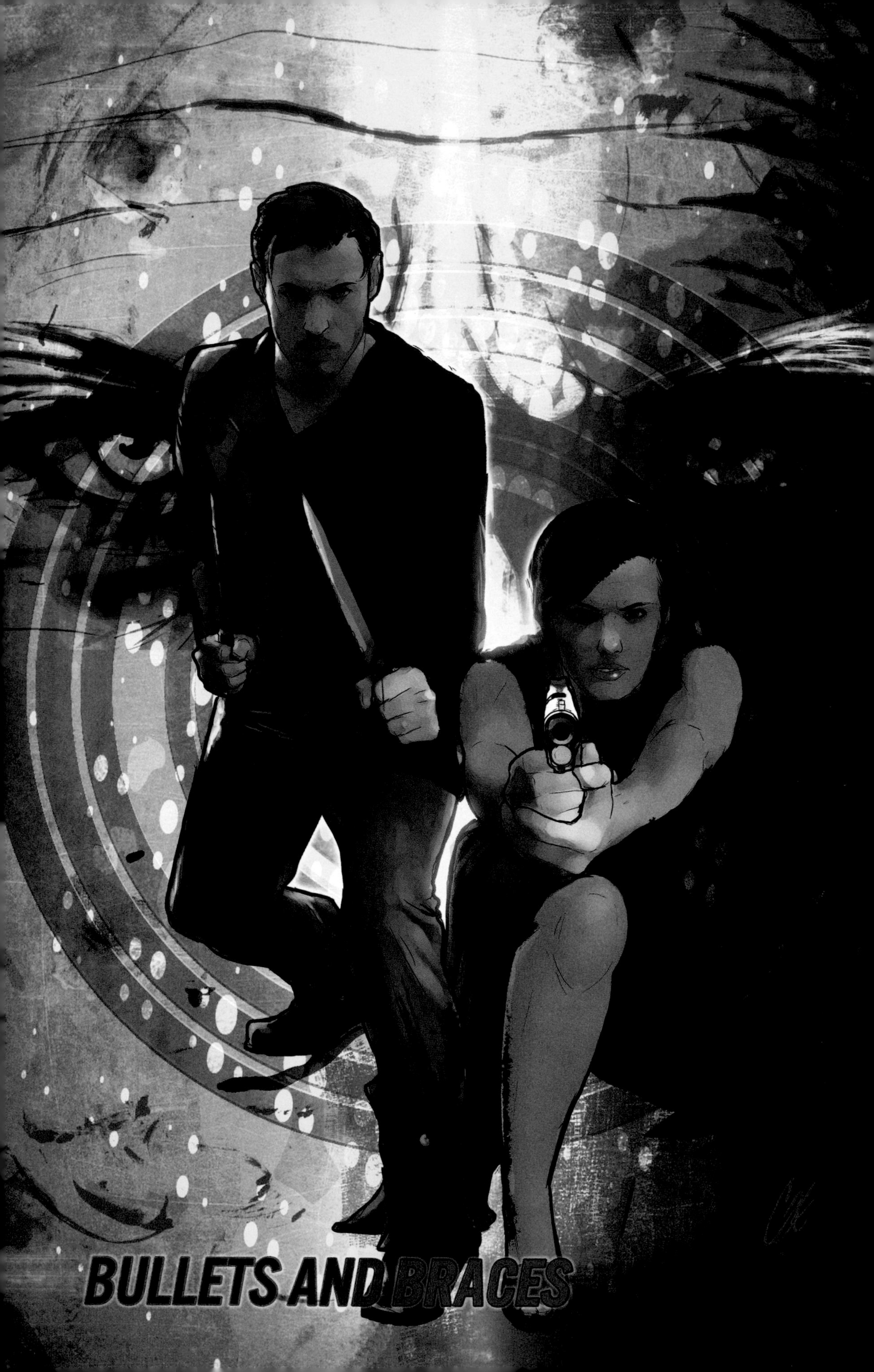
BULLETS AND BRACES

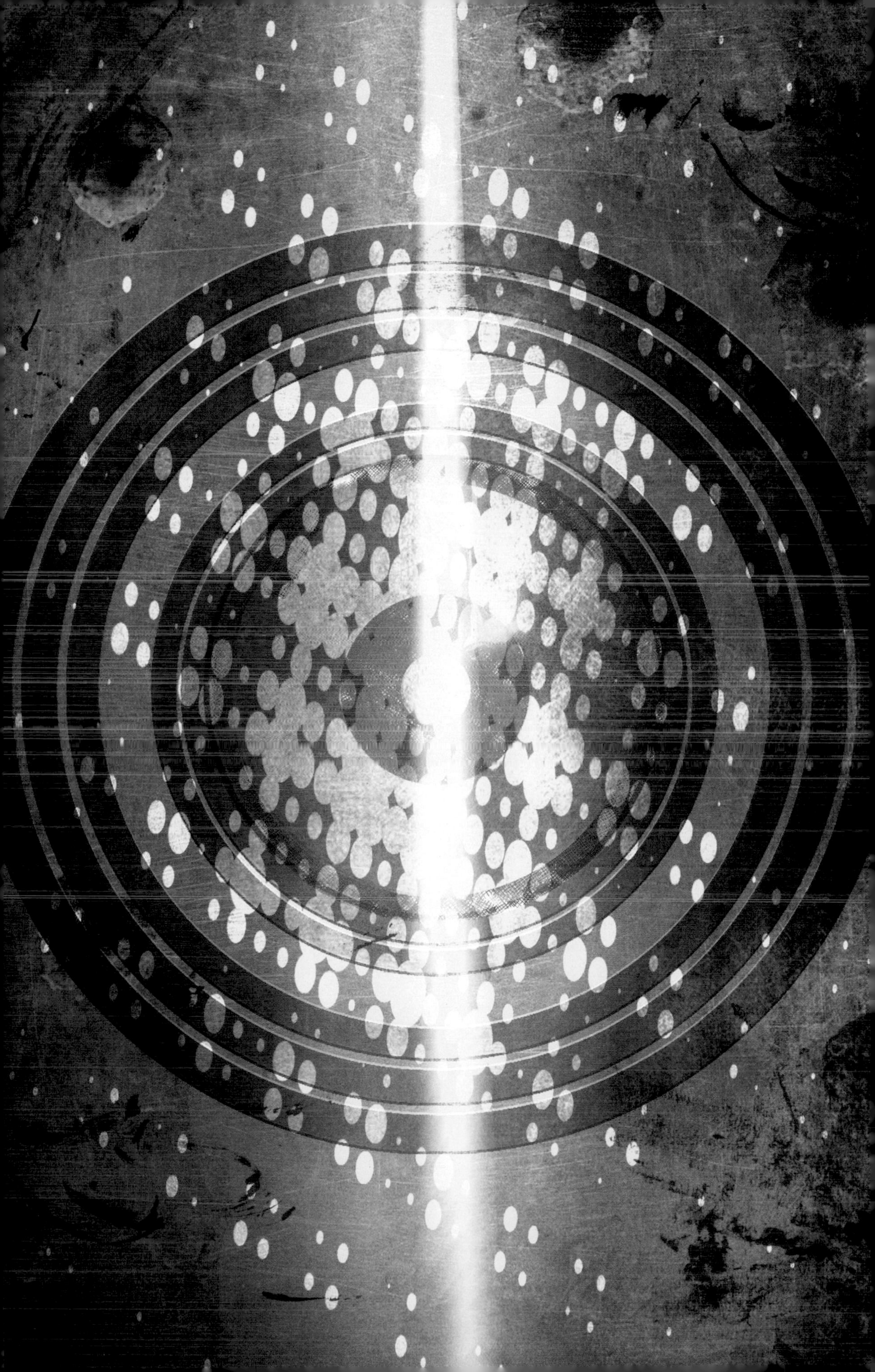

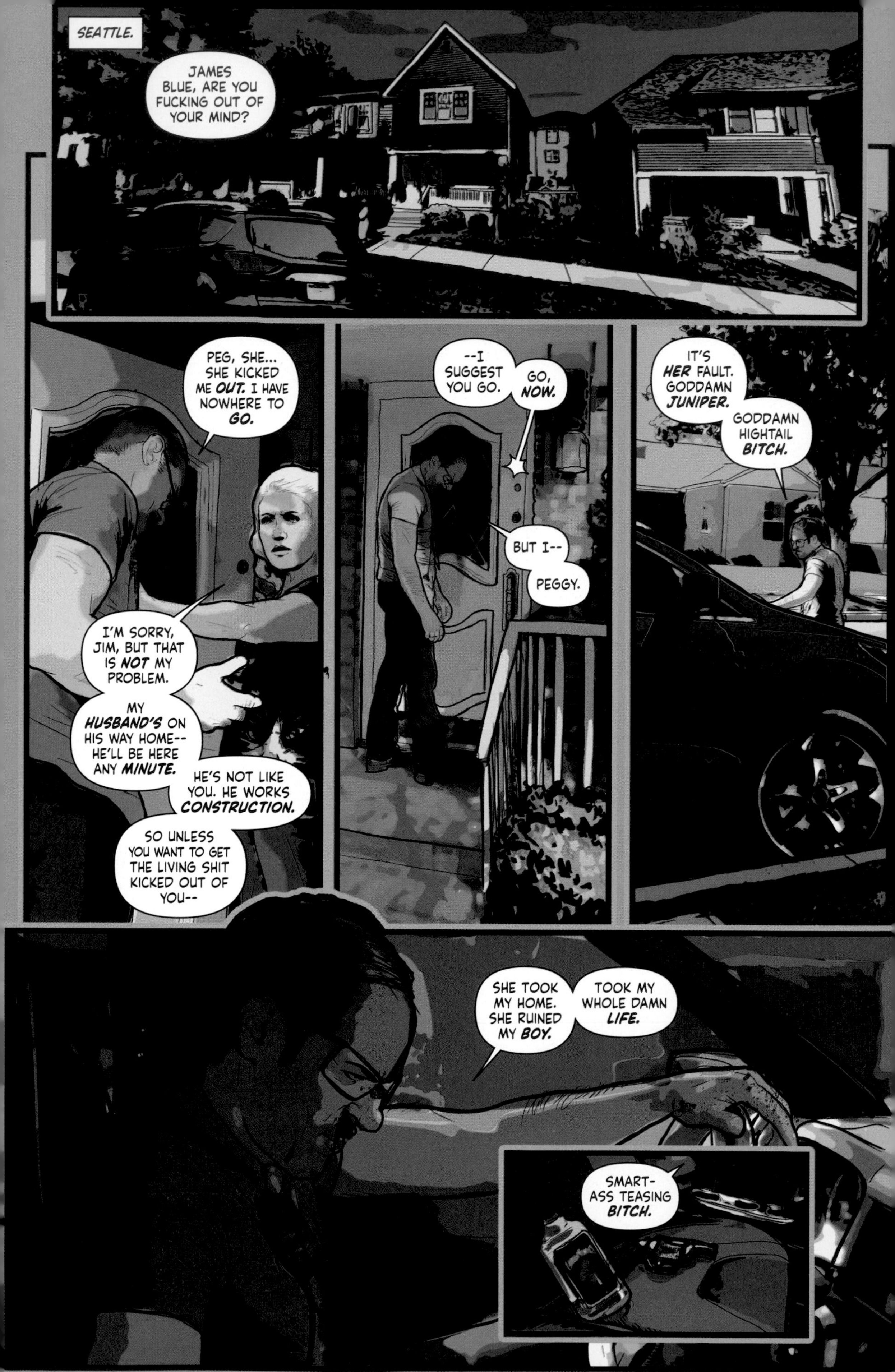
SEATTLE.
JAMES BLUE, ARE YOU FUCKING OUT OF YOUR MIND?
PEG, SHE... SHE KICKED ME OUT. I HAVE NOWHERE TO GO.
I'M SORRY, JIM, BUT THAT IS NOT MY PROBLEM.
MY HUSBAND'S ON HIS WAY HOME--HE'LL BE HERE ANY MINUTE.
HE'S NOT LIKE YOU. HE WORKS CONSTRUCTION.
SO UNLESS YOU WANT TO GET THE LIVING SHIT KICKED OUT OF YOU--
--I SUGGEST YOU GO.
GO, NOW.
BUT I--
PEGGY.
IT'S HER FAULT. GODDAMN JUNIPER.
GODDAMN HIGHTAIL BITCH.
SHE TOOK MY HOME. SHE RUINED MY BOY.
TOOK MY WHOLE DAMN LIFE.
SMART-ASS TEASING BITCH.

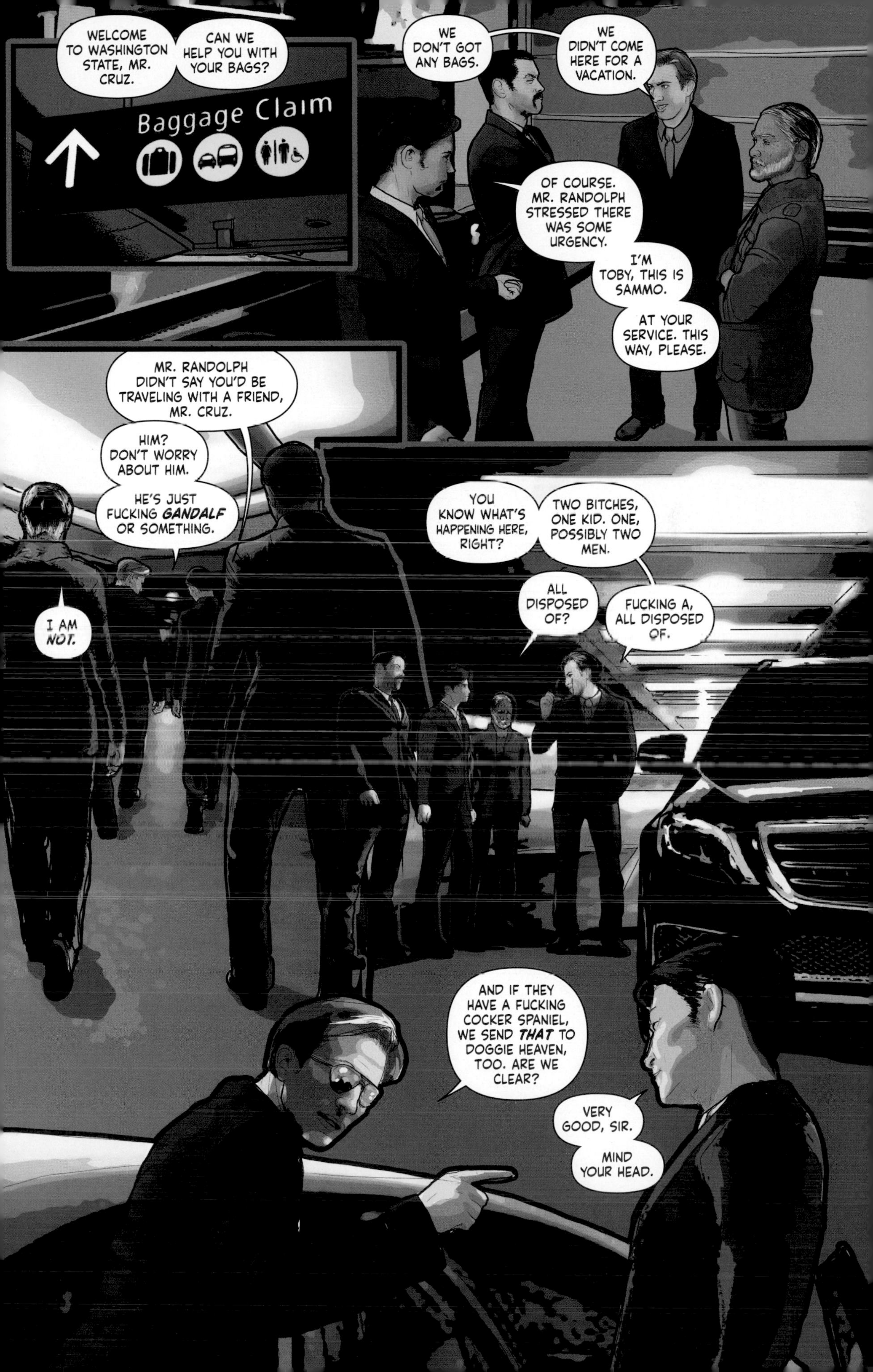
Baggage Claim
WELCOME TO WASHINGTON STATE, MR. CRUZ.
CAN WE HELP YOU WITH YOUR BAGS?
WE DON'T GOT ANY BAGS.
WE DIDN'T COME HERE FOR A VACATION.
OF COURSE. MR. RANDOLPH STRESSED THERE WAS SOME URGENCY.
I'M TOBY, THIS IS SAMMO.
AT YOUR SERVICE. THIS WAY, PLEASE.
MR. RANDOLPH DIDN'T SAY YOU'D BE TRAVELING WITH A FRIEND, MR. CRUZ.
HIM? DON'T WORRY ABOUT HIM.
HE'S JUST FUCKING GANDALF OR SOMETHING.
I AM NOT.
YOU KNOW WHAT'S HAPPENING HERE, RIGHT?
TWO BITCHES, ONE KID. ONE, POSSIBLY TWO MEN.
ALL DISPOSED OF?
FUCKING A, ALL DISPOSED OF.
AND IF THEY HAVE A FUCKING COCKER SPANIEL, WE SEND THAT TO DOGGIE HEAVEN, TOO. ARE WE CLEAR?
VERY GOOD, SIR.
MIND YOUR HEAD.

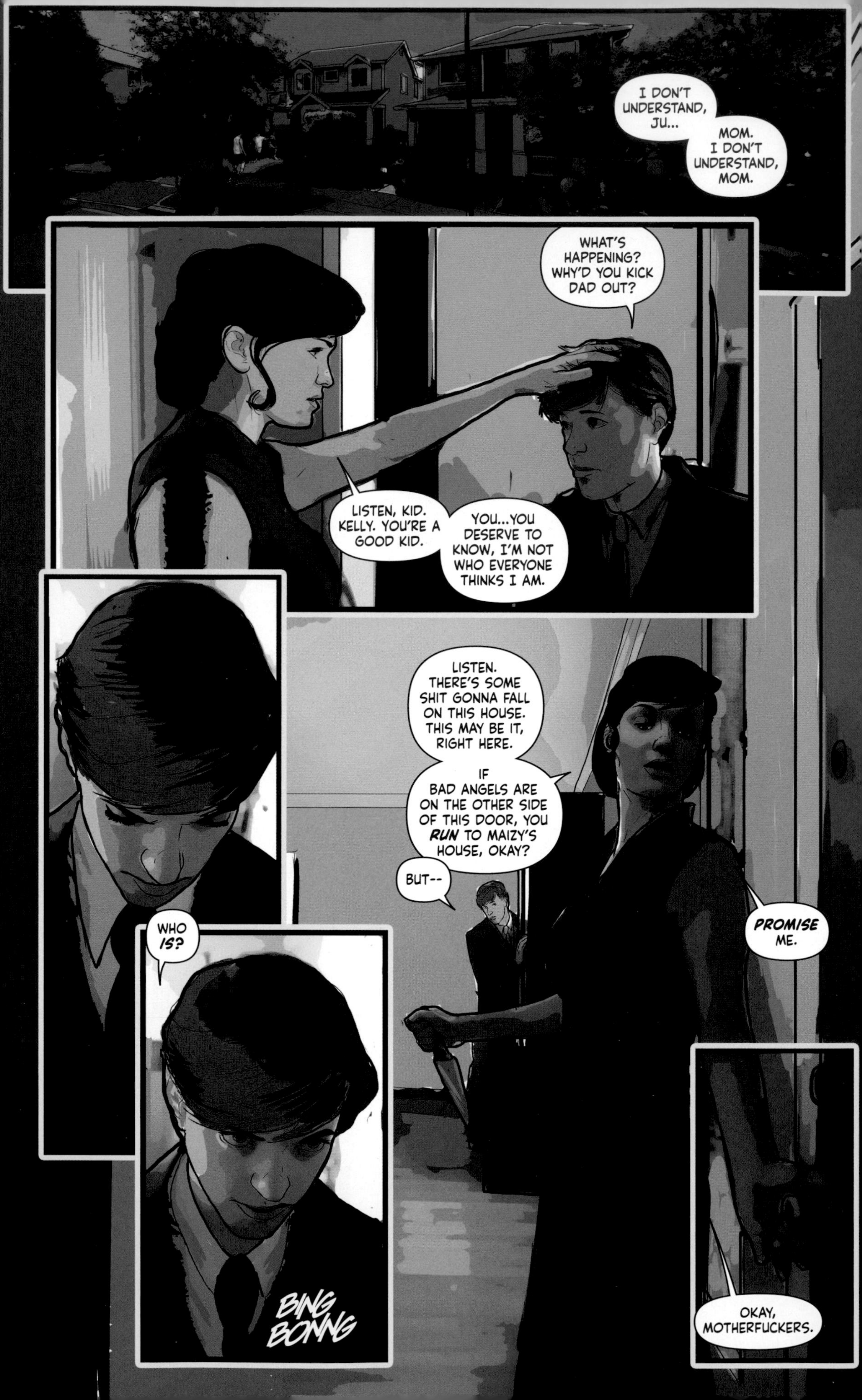
I DON'T UNDERSTAND, JU...
MOM. I DON'T UNDERSTAND, MOM.
WHAT'S HAPPENING? WHY'D YOU KICK DAD OUT?
LISTEN, KID. KELLY. YOU'RE A GOOD KID.
YOU...YOU DESERVE TO KNOW, I'M NOT WHO EVERYONE THINKS I AM.
LISTEN. THERE'S SOME SHIT GONNA FALL ON THIS HOUSE. THIS MAY BE IT, RIGHT HERE.
IF BAD ANGELS ARE ON THE OTHER SIDE OF THIS DOOR, YOU ***RUN*** TO MAIZY'S HOUSE, OKAY?
BUT--
PROMISE ME.
WHO ***IS?***
BING BONNG
OKAY, MOTHERFUCKERS.

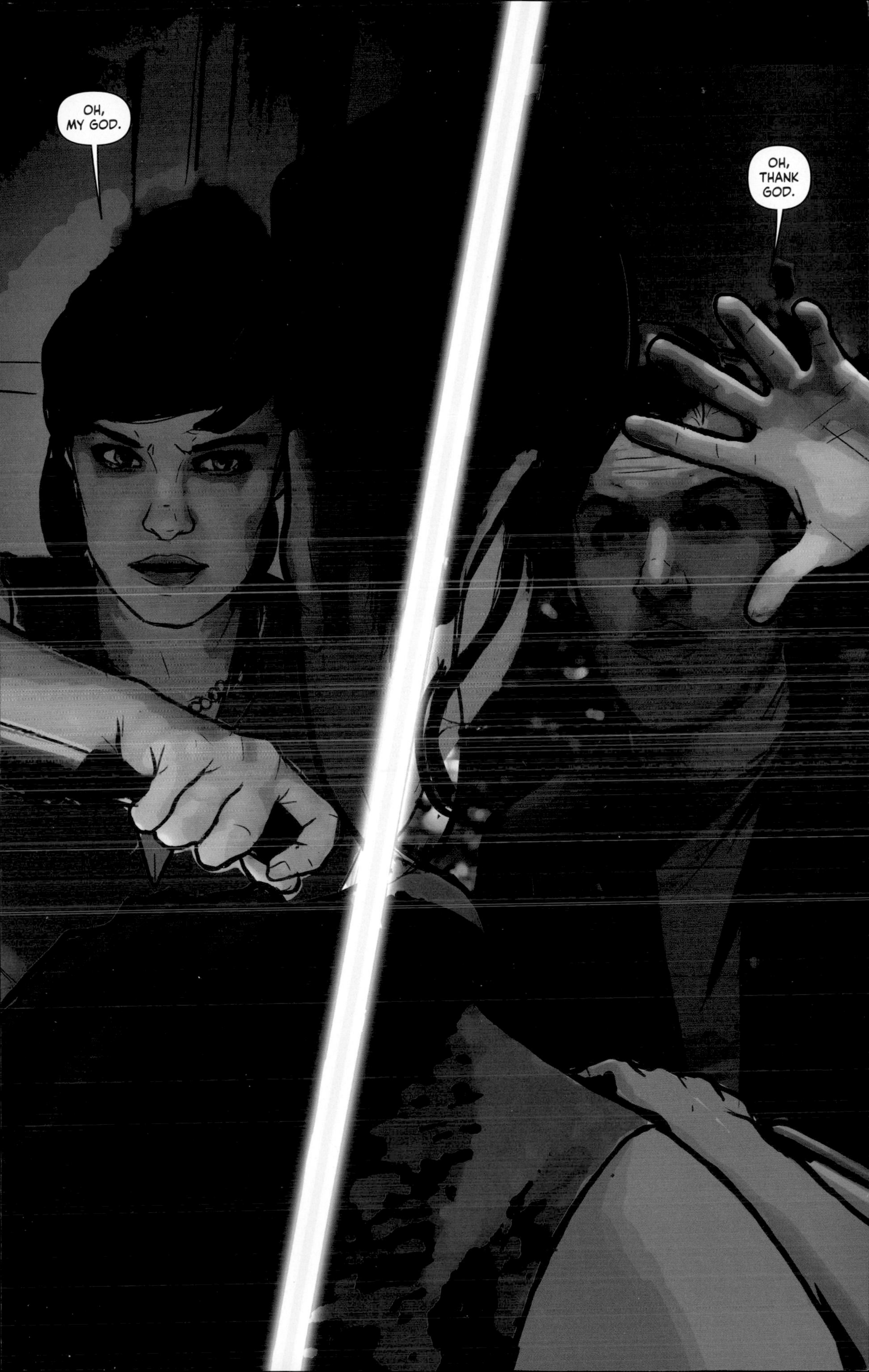
OH, MY GOD.
OH, THANK GOD.

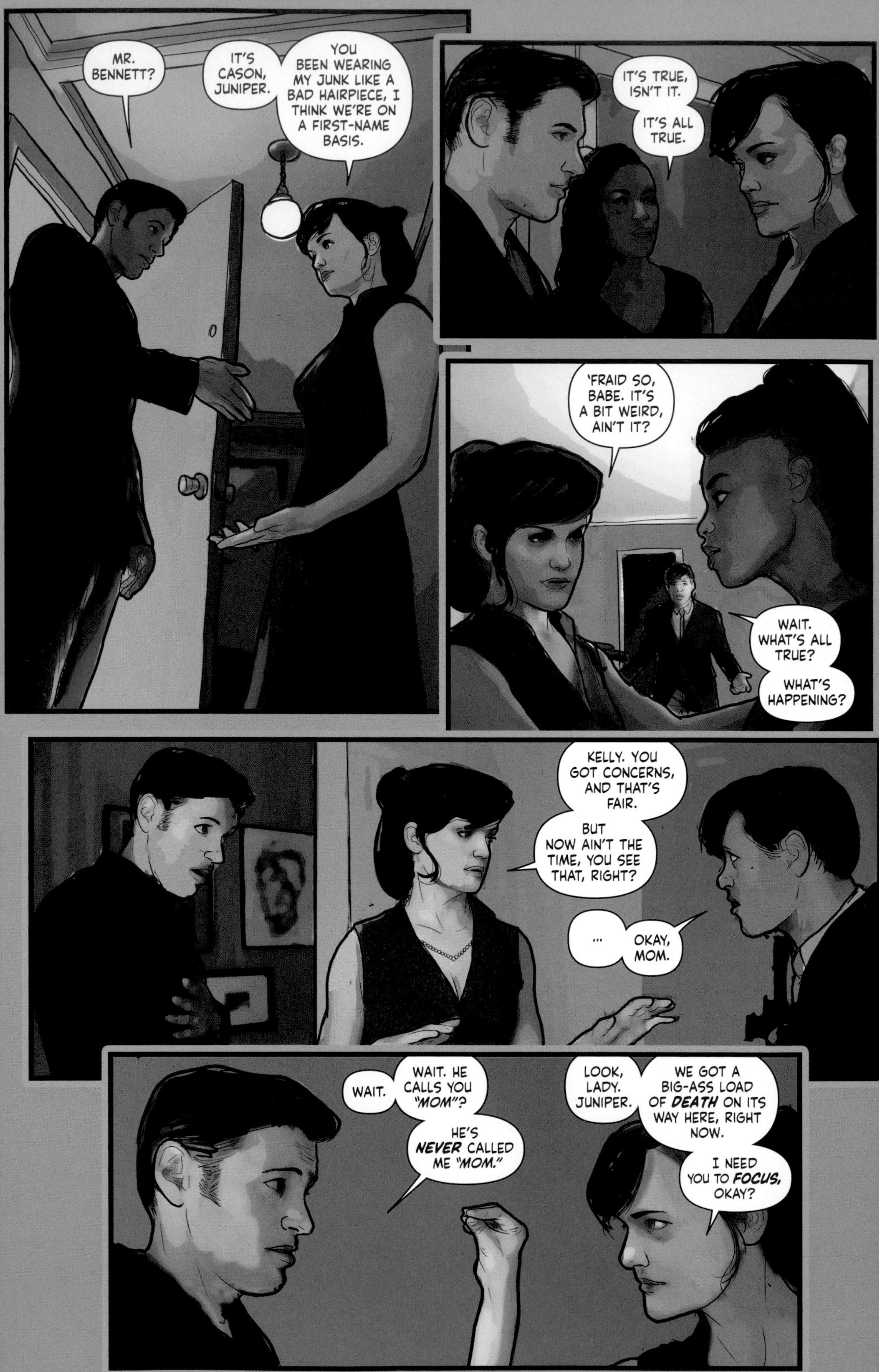
MR. BENNETT?
IT'S CASON, JUNIPER.
YOU BEEN WEARING MY JUNK LIKE A BAD HAIRPIECE, I THINK WE'RE ON A FIRST-NAME BASIS.
IT'S TRUE, ISN'T IT.
IT'S ALL TRUE.
'FRAID SO, BABE. IT'S A BIT WEIRD, AIN'T IT?
WAIT. WHAT'S ALL TRUE?
WHAT'S HAPPENING?
KELLY. YOU GOT CONCERNS, AND THAT'S FAIR.
BUT NOW AIN'T THE TIME, YOU SEE THAT, RIGHT?
...
OKAY, MOM.
WAIT.
WAIT. HE CALLS YOU "MOM"?
HE'S NEVER CALLED ME "MOM."
LOOK, LADY. JUNIPER.
WE GOT A BIG-ASS LOAD OF DEATH ON ITS WAY HERE, RIGHT NOW.
I NEED YOU TO FOCUS, OKAY?

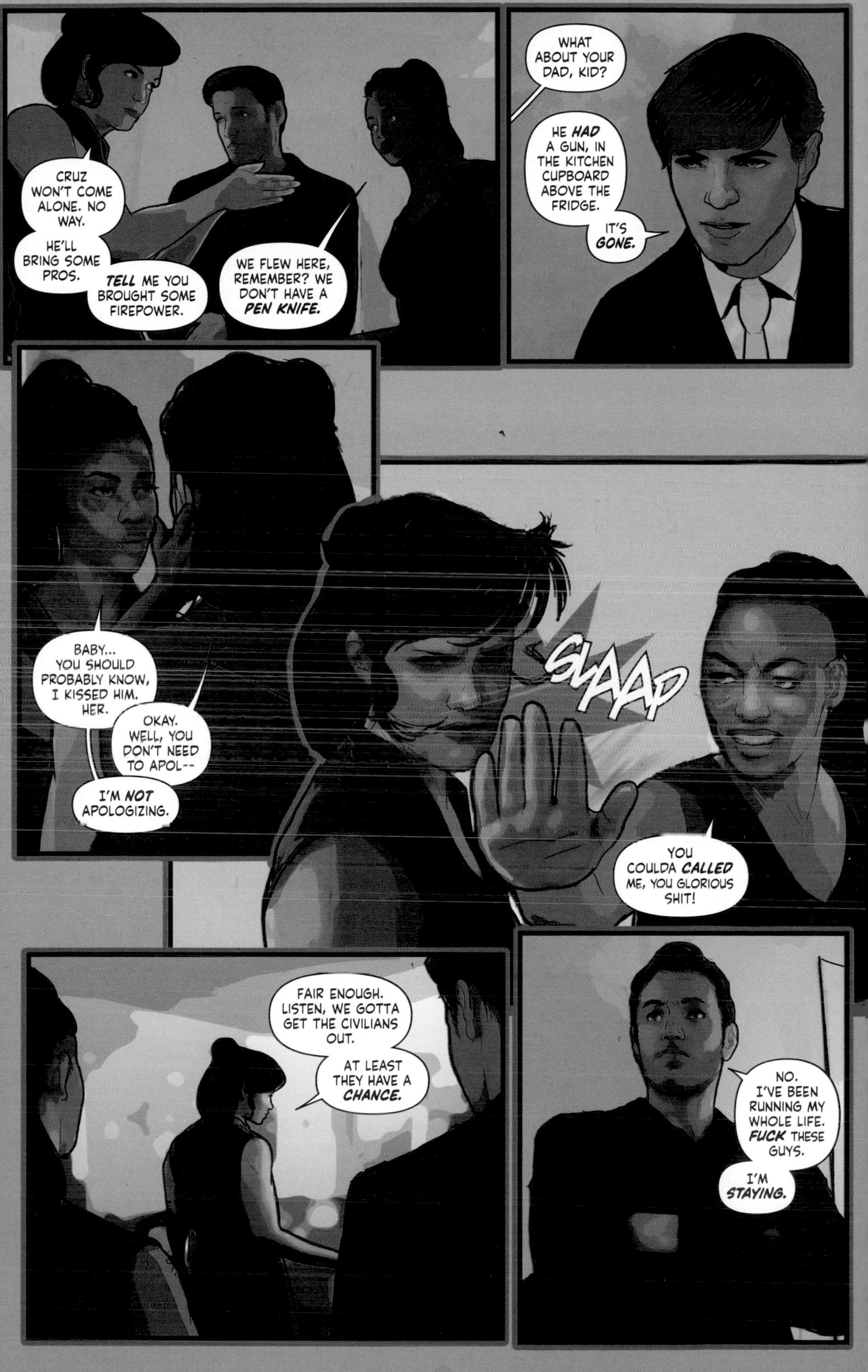
CRUZ WON'T COME ALONE. NO WAY.
HE'LL BRING SOME PROS.
TELL ME YOU BROUGHT SOME FIREPOWER.
WE FLEW HERE, REMEMBER? WE DON'T HAVE A PEN KNIFE.
WHAT ABOUT YOUR DAD, KID?
HE HAD A GUN, IN THE KITCHEN CUPBOARD ABOVE THE FRIDGE.
IT'S GONE.
BABY... YOU SHOULD PROBABLY KNOW, I KISSED HIM. HER.
OKAY. WELL, YOU DON'T NEED TO APOL--
I'M NOT APOLOGIZING.
SLAAAP
YOU COULDA CALLED ME, YOU GLORIOUS SHIT!
FAIR ENOUGH. LISTEN, WE GOTTA GET THE CIVILIANS OUT.
AT LEAST THEY HAVE A CHANCE.
NO. I'VE BEEN RUNNING MY WHOLE LIFE. FUCK THESE GUYS.
I'M STAYING.

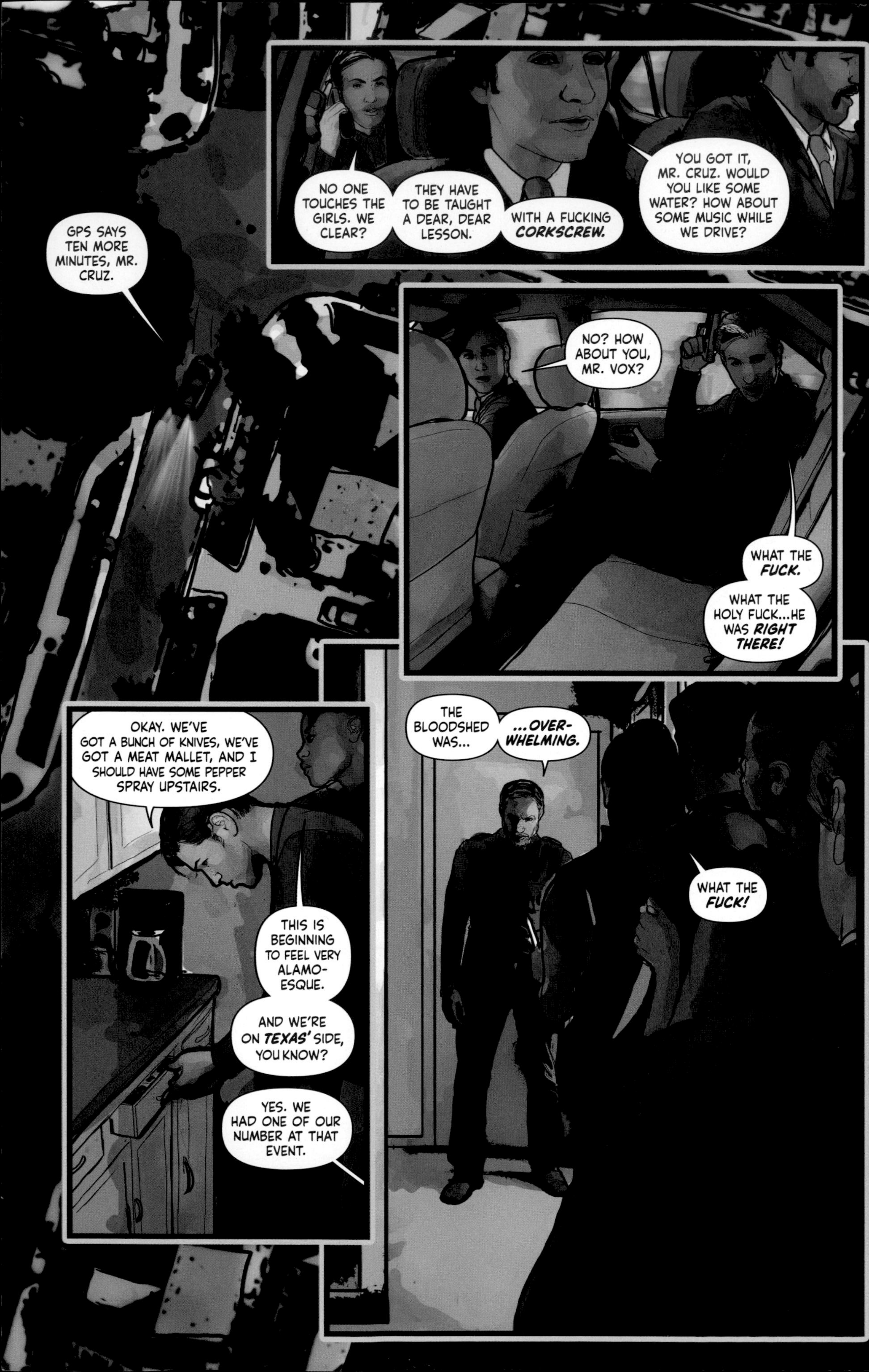
NO ONE TOUCHES THE GIRLS. WE CLEAR?
THEY HAVE TO BE TAUGHT A DEAR, DEAR LESSON.
WITH A FUCKING CORKSCREW.
YOU GOT IT, MR. CRUZ. WOULD YOU LIKE SOME WATER? HOW ABOUT SOME MUSIC WHILE WE DRIVE?
GPS SAYS TEN MORE MINUTES, MR. CRUZ.
NO? HOW ABOUT YOU, MR. VOX?
WHAT THE FUCK.
WHAT THE HOLY FUCK...HE WAS RIGHT THERE!
OKAY. WE'VE GOT A BUNCH OF KNIVES, WE'VE GOT A MEAT MALLET, AND I SHOULD HAVE SOME PEPPER SPRAY UPSTAIRS.
THIS IS BEGINNING TO FEEL VERY ALAMO-ESQUE.
AND WE'RE ON TEXAS' SIDE, YOU KNOW?
YES. WE HAD ONE OF OUR NUMBER AT THAT EVENT.
THE BLOODSHED WAS...
...OVER-WHELMING.
WHAT THE FUCK!

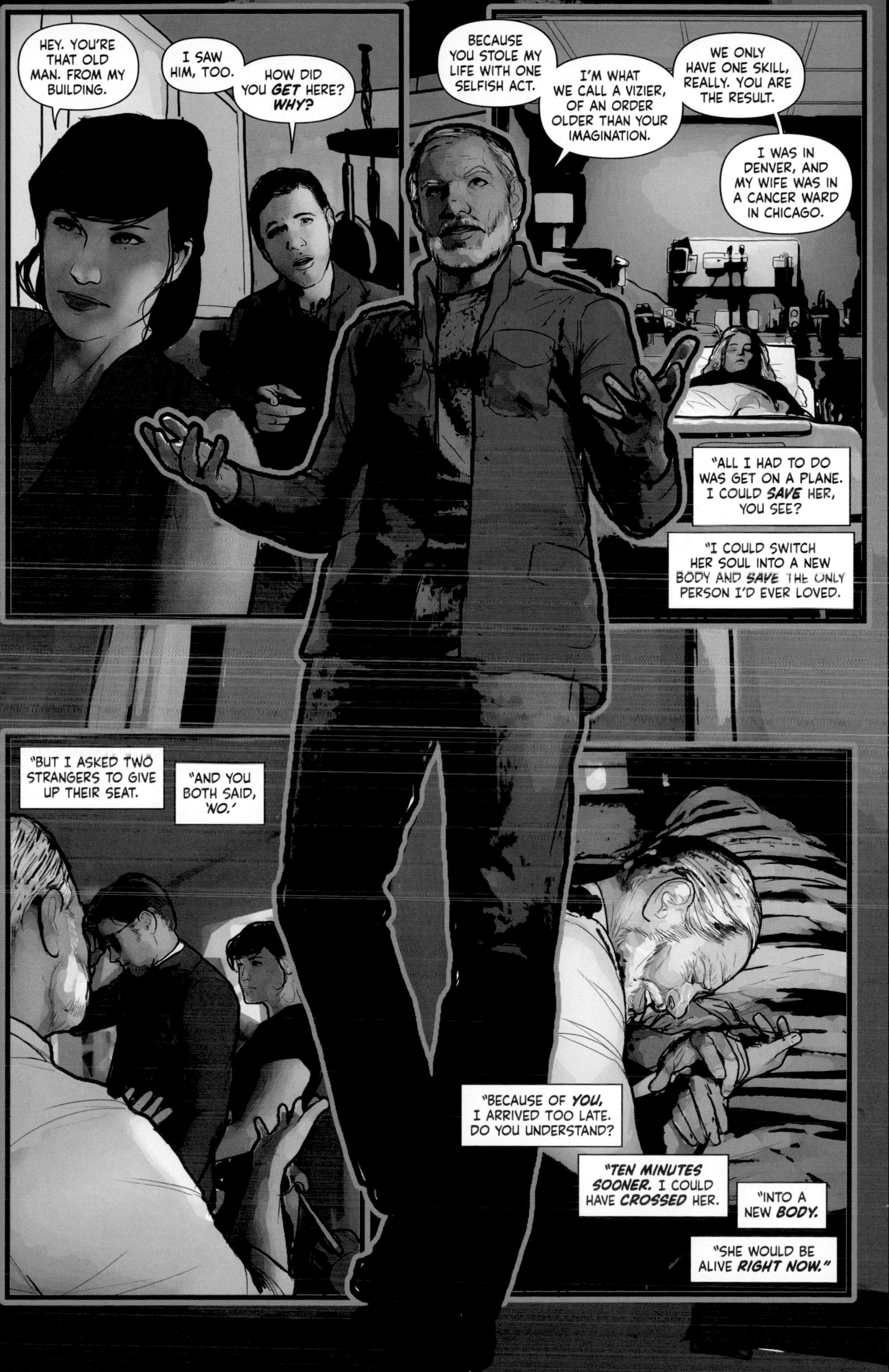
HEY. YOU'RE THAT OLD MAN. FROM MY BUILDING.
I SAW HIM, TOO.
HOW DID YOU GET HERE? WHY?
BECAUSE YOU STOLE MY LIFE WITH ONE SELFISH ACT.
I'M WHAT WE CALL A VIZIER, OF AN ORDER OLDER THAN YOUR IMAGINATION.
WE ONLY HAVE ONE SKILL, REALLY. YOU ARE THE RESULT.
I WAS IN DENVER, AND MY WIFE WAS IN A CANCER WARD IN CHICAGO.
"ALL I HAD TO DO WAS GET ON A PLANE. I COULD SAVE HER, YOU SEE?
"I COULD SWITCH HER SOUL INTO A NEW BODY AND SAVE THE ONLY PERSON I'D EVER LOVED.
"BUT I ASKED TWO STRANGERS TO GIVE UP THEIR SEAT.
"AND YOU BOTH SAID, 'NO.'
"BECAUSE OF YOU, I ARRIVED TOO LATE. DO YOU UNDERSTAND?
"TEN MINUTES SOONER. I COULD HAVE CROSSED HER.
"INTO A NEW BODY.
"SHE WOULD BE ALIVE RIGHT NOW."

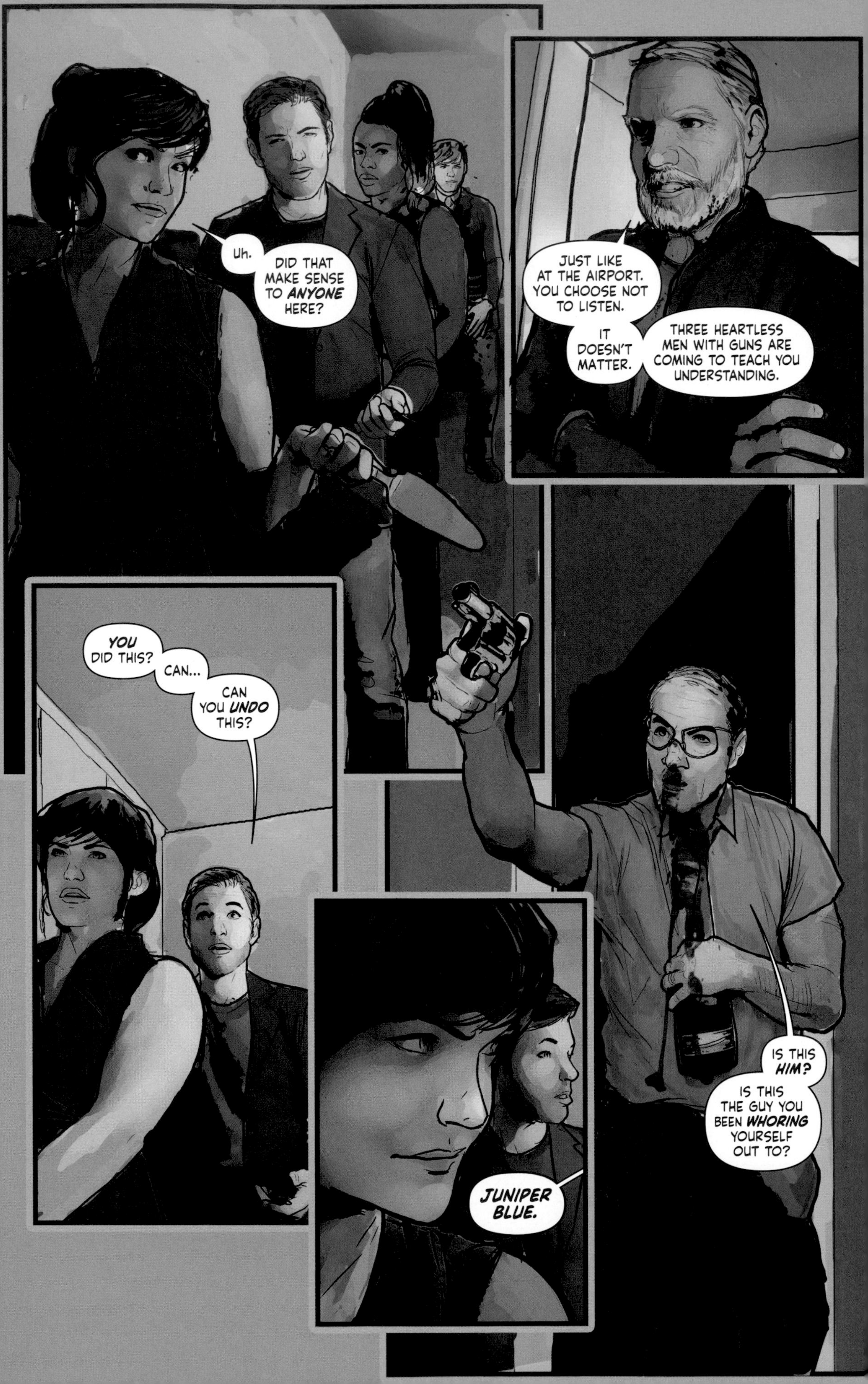
Uh.
DID THAT MAKE SENSE TO ANYONE HERE?
JUST LIKE AT THE AIRPORT. YOU CHOOSE NOT TO LISTEN.
IT DOESN'T MATTER.
THREE HEARTLESS MEN WITH GUNS ARE COMING TO TEACH YOU UNDERSTANDING.
YOU DID THIS?
CAN...
CAN YOU UNDO THIS?
JUNIPER BLUE.
IS THIS HIM?
IS THIS THE GUY YOU BEEN WHORING YOURSELF OUT TO?

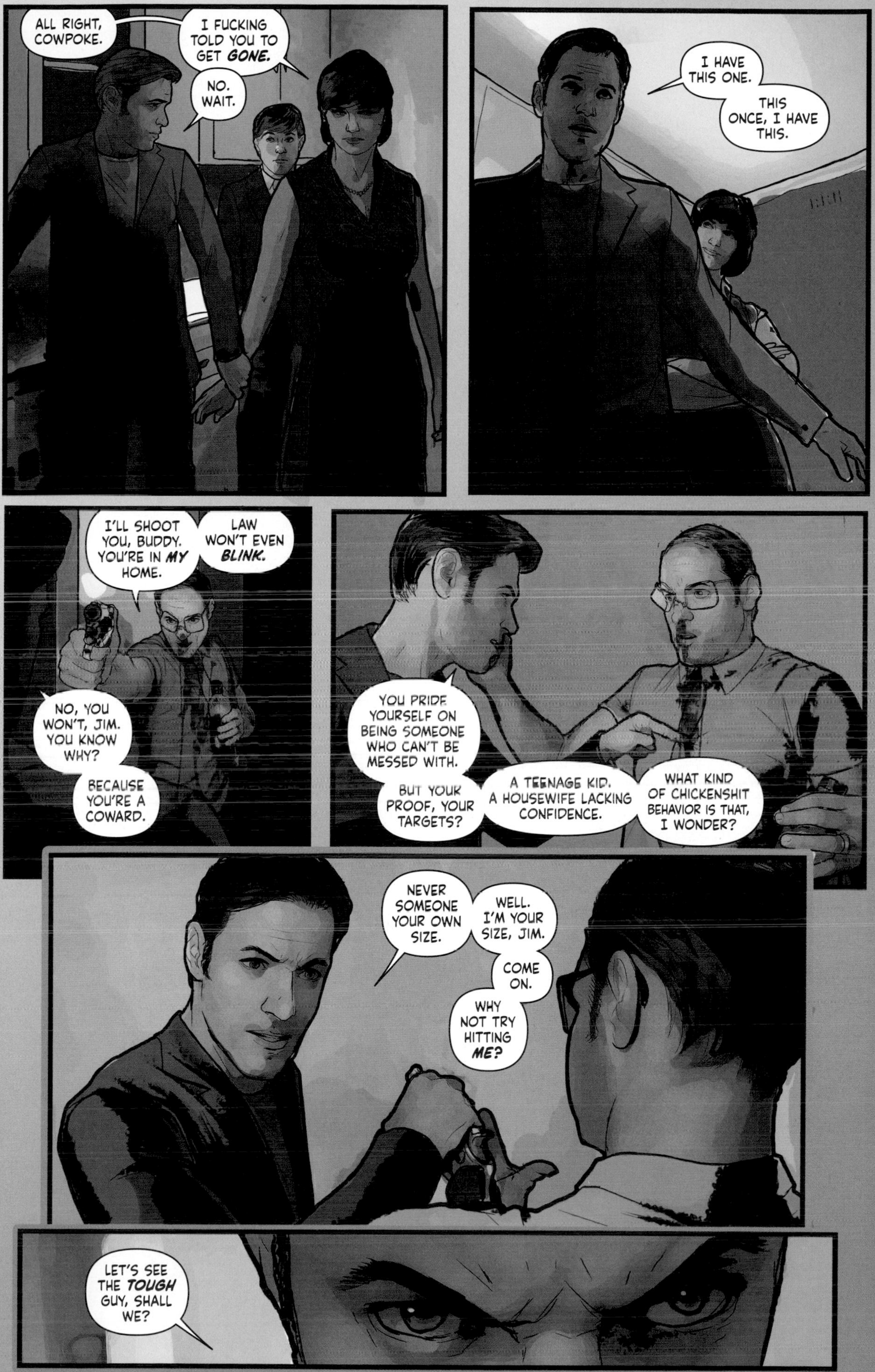
ALL RIGHT, COWPOKE.
I FUCKING TOLD YOU TO GET GONE.
NO. WAIT.
I HAVE THIS ONE.
THIS ONCE, I HAVE THIS.
I'LL SHOOT YOU, BUDDY. YOU'RE IN MY HOME.
LAW WON'T EVEN BLINK.
NO, YOU WON'T, JIM. YOU KNOW WHY?
BECAUSE YOU'RE A COWARD.
YOU PRIDE YOURSELF ON BEING SOMEONE WHO CAN'T BE MESSED WITH.
BUT YOUR PROOF, YOUR TARGETS?
A TEENAGE KID. A HOUSEWIFE LACKING CONFIDENCE.
WHAT KIND OF CHICKENSHIT BEHAVIOR IS THAT, I WONDER?
NEVER SOMEONE YOUR OWN SIZE.
WELL. I'M YOUR SIZE, JIM.
COME ON.
WHY NOT TRY HITTING ME?
LET'S SEE THE TOUGH GUY, SHALL WE?

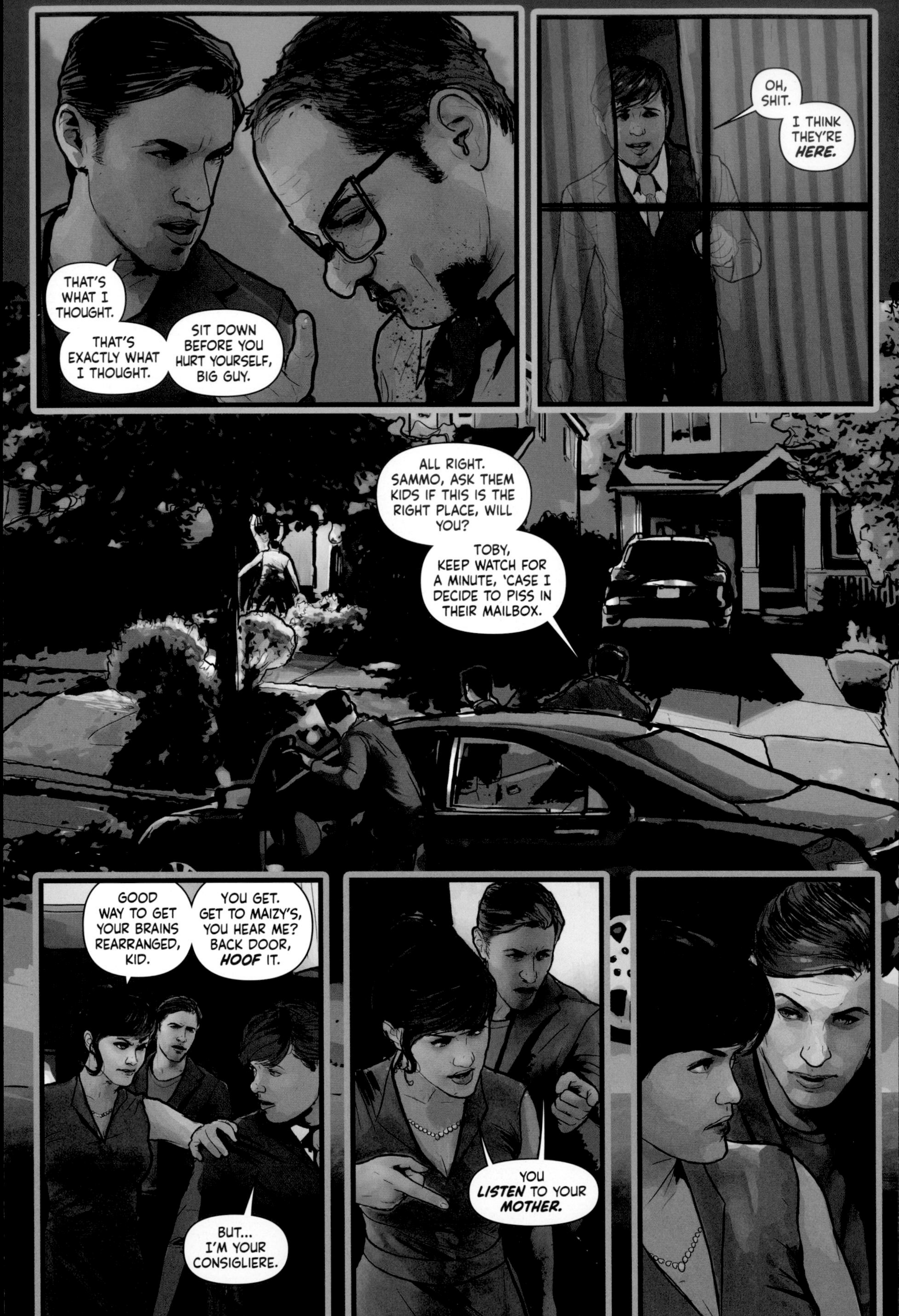
THAT'S WHAT I THOUGHT.
THAT'S EXACTLY WHAT I THOUGHT.
SIT DOWN BEFORE YOU HURT YOURSELF, BIG GUY.
OH, SHIT.
I THINK THEY'RE ***HERE.***
ALL RIGHT. SAMMO, ASK THEM KIDS IF THIS IS THE RIGHT PLACE, WILL YOU?
TOBY, KEEP WATCH FOR A MINUTE, 'CASE I DECIDE TO PISS IN THEIR MAILBOX.
GOOD WAY TO GET YOUR BRAINS REARRANGED, KID.
YOU GET. GET TO MAIZY'S, YOU HEAR ME? BACK DOOR, ***HOOF*** IT.
BUT... I'M YOUR CONSIGLIERE.
YOU ***LISTEN*** TO YOUR ***MOTHER.***

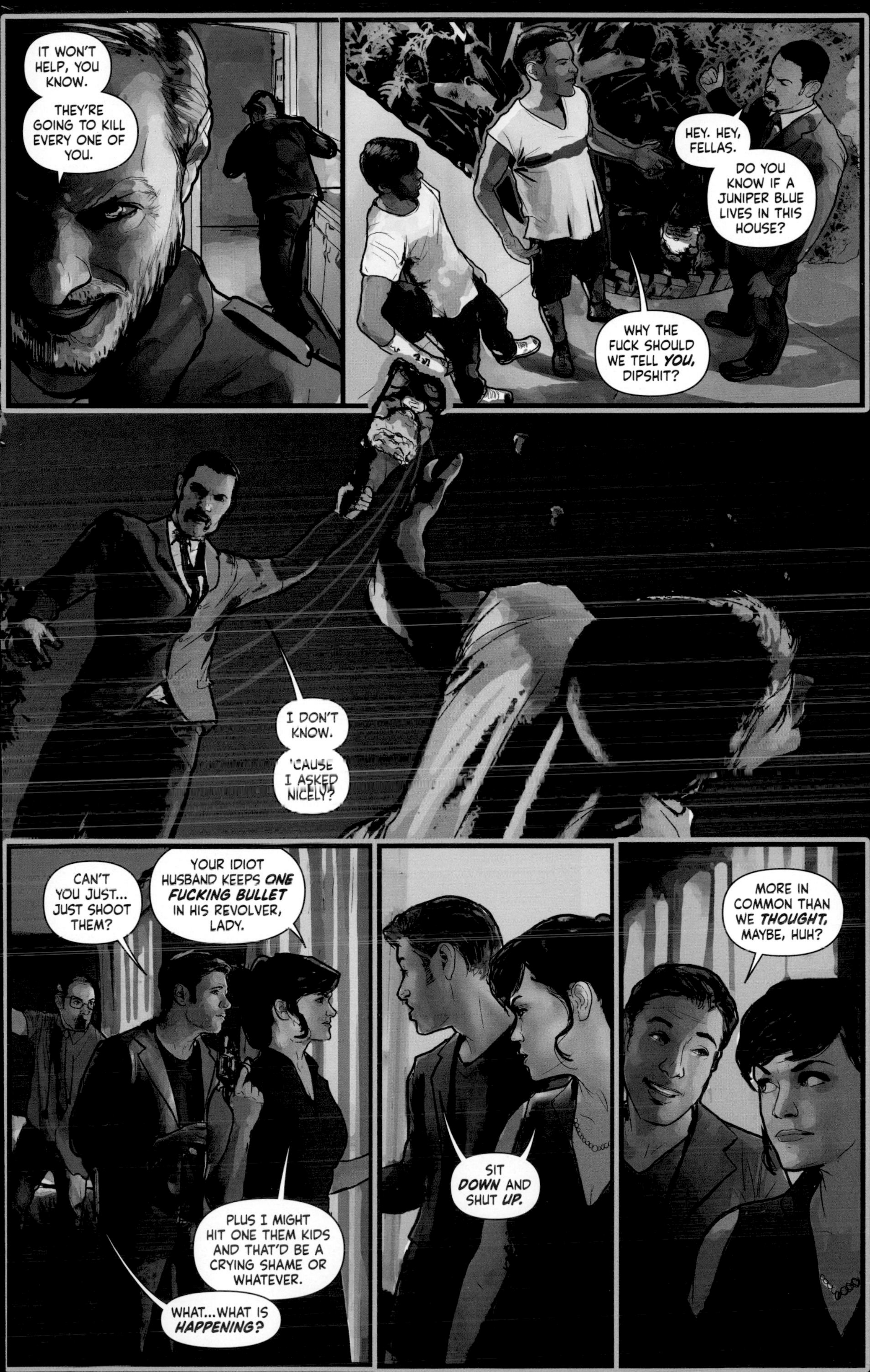
IT WON'T HELP, YOU KNOW.
THEY'RE GOING TO KILL EVERY ONE OF YOU.
HEY. HEY, FELLAS.
DO YOU KNOW IF A JUNIPER BLUE LIVES IN THIS HOUSE?
WHY THE FUCK SHOULD WE TELL *YOU*, DIPSHIT?
I DON'T KNOW.
'CAUSE I ASKED NICELY?
CAN'T YOU JUST... JUST SHOOT THEM?
YOUR IDIOT HUSBAND KEEPS *ONE FUCKING BULLET* IN HIS REVOLVER, LADY.
PLUS I MIGHT HIT ONE THEM KIDS AND THAT'D BE A CRYING SHAME OR WHATEVER.
WHAT...WHAT IS *HAPPENING?*
SIT *DOWN* AND SHUT *UP*.
MORE IN COMMON THAN WE *THOUGHT*, MAYBE, HUH?

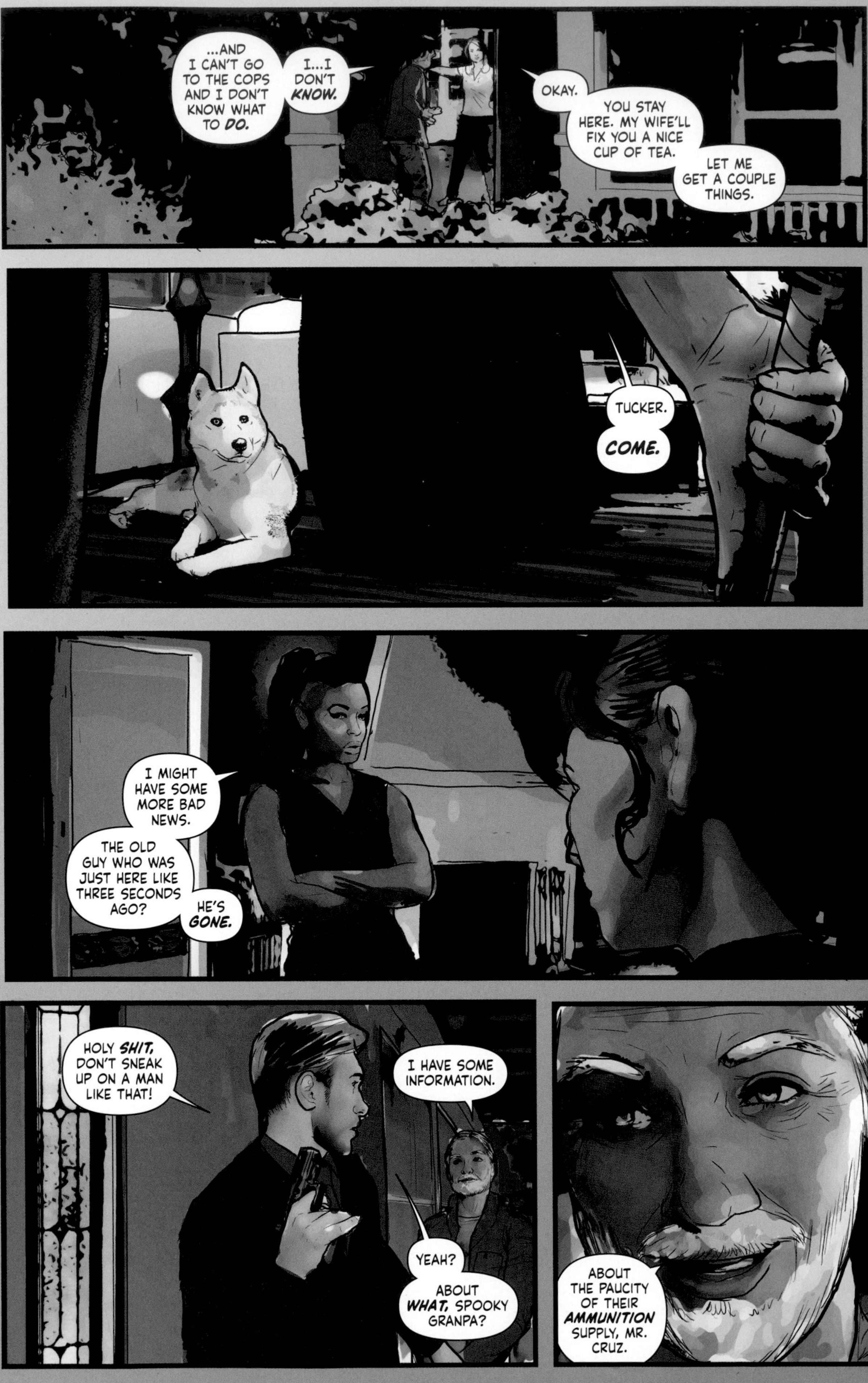

...AND I CAN'T GO TO THE COPS AND I DON'T KNOW WHAT TO *DO.*
I...I DON'T *KNOW.*
OKAY.
YOU STAY HERE. MY WIFE'LL FIX YOU A NICE CUP OF TEA.
LET ME GET A COUPLE THINGS.
TUCKER.
COME.
I MIGHT HAVE SOME MORE BAD NEWS.
THE OLD GUY WHO WAS JUST HERE LIKE THREE SECONDS AGO?
HE'S *GONE.*
HOLY *SHIT,* DON'T SNEAK UP ON A MAN LIKE THAT!
I HAVE SOME INFORMATION.
YEAH?
ABOUT *WHAT,* SPOOKY GRANPA?
ABOUT THE PAUCITY OF THEIR *AMMUNITION* SUPPLY, MR. CRUZ.

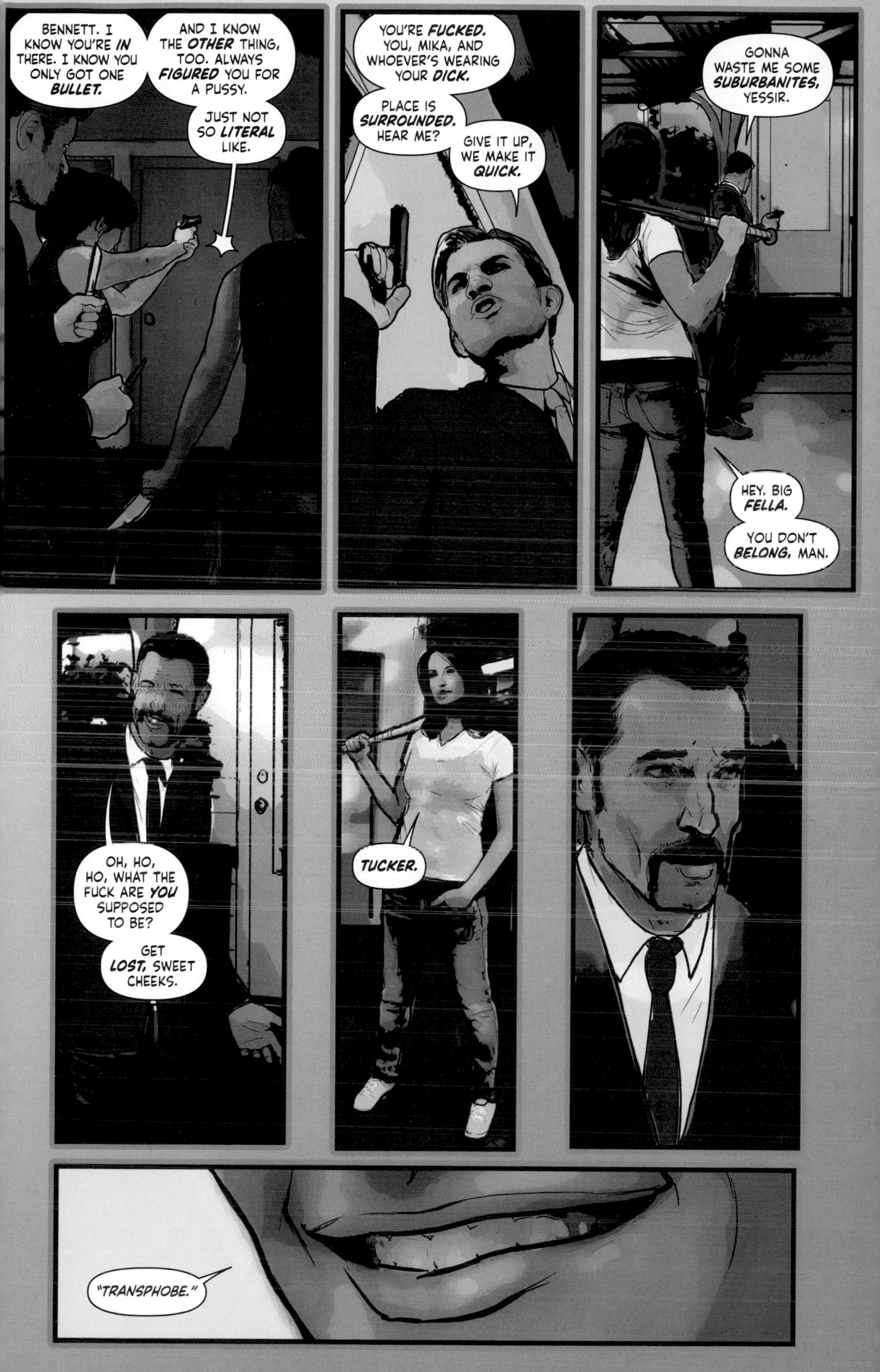
BENNETT. I KNOW YOU'RE *IN* THERE. I KNOW YOU ONLY GOT ONE *BULLET.*
AND I KNOW THE *OTHER* THING, TOO. ALWAYS *FIGURED* YOU FOR A PUSSY.
JUST NOT SO *LITERAL* LIKE.
YOU'RE *FUCKED.* YOU, MIKA, AND WHOEVER'S WEARING YOUR *DICK.*
PLACE IS *SURROUNDED.* HEAR ME?
GIVE IT UP, WE MAKE IT *QUICK.*
GONNA WASTE ME SOME *SUBURBANITES,* YESSIR.
HEY. BIG *FELLA.*
YOU DON'T *BELONG,* MAN.
OH, HO, HO, WHAT THE FUCK ARE *YOU* SUPPOSED TO BE?
GET *LOST,* SWEET CHEEKS.
TUCKER.
"TRANSPHOBE."

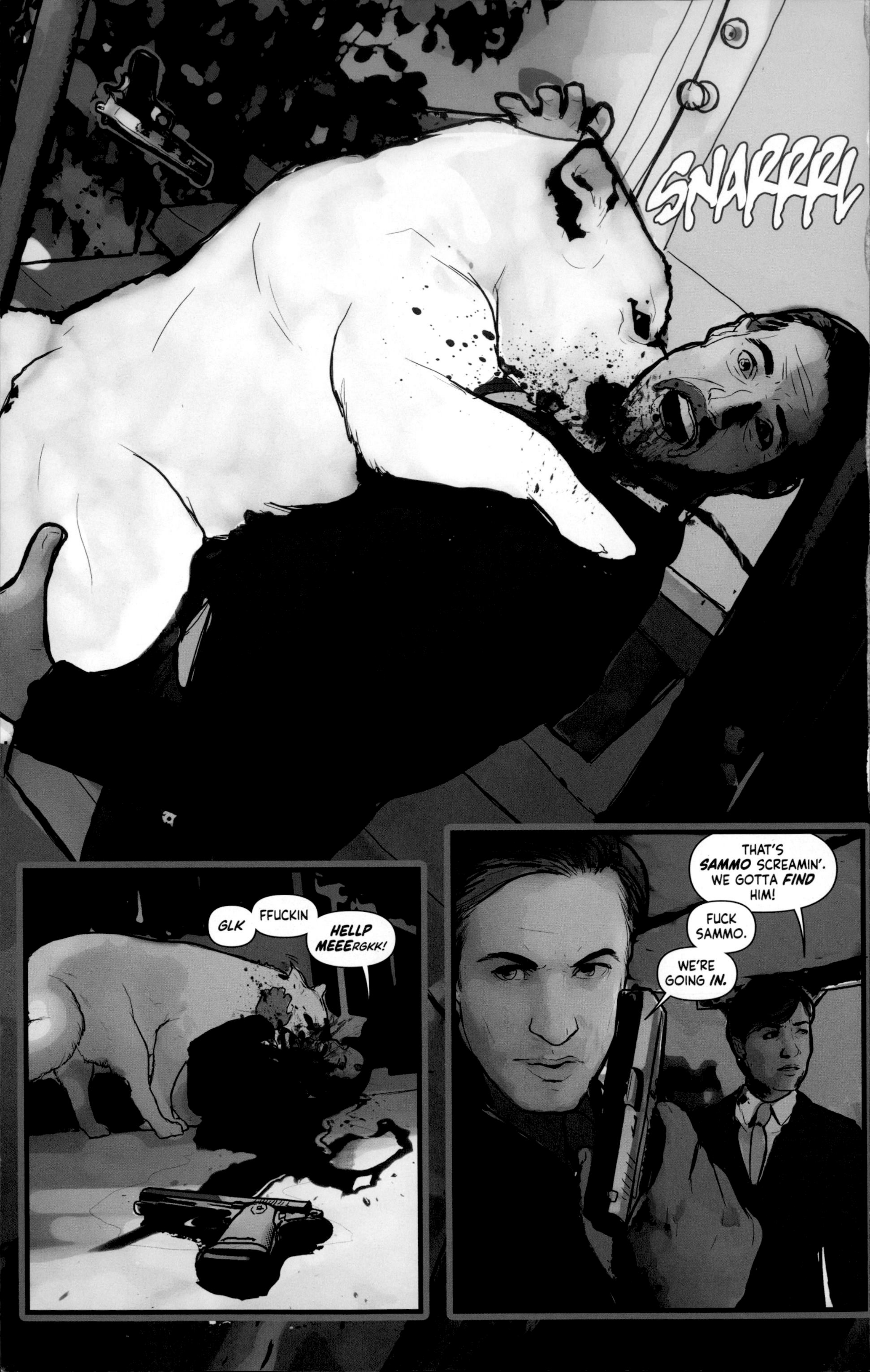
SNARRRL
GLK
FFUCKIN
HELLP MEEERGKK!
THAT'S SAMMO SCREAMIN'. WE GOTTA FIND HIM!
FUCK SAMMO.
WE'RE GOING IN.

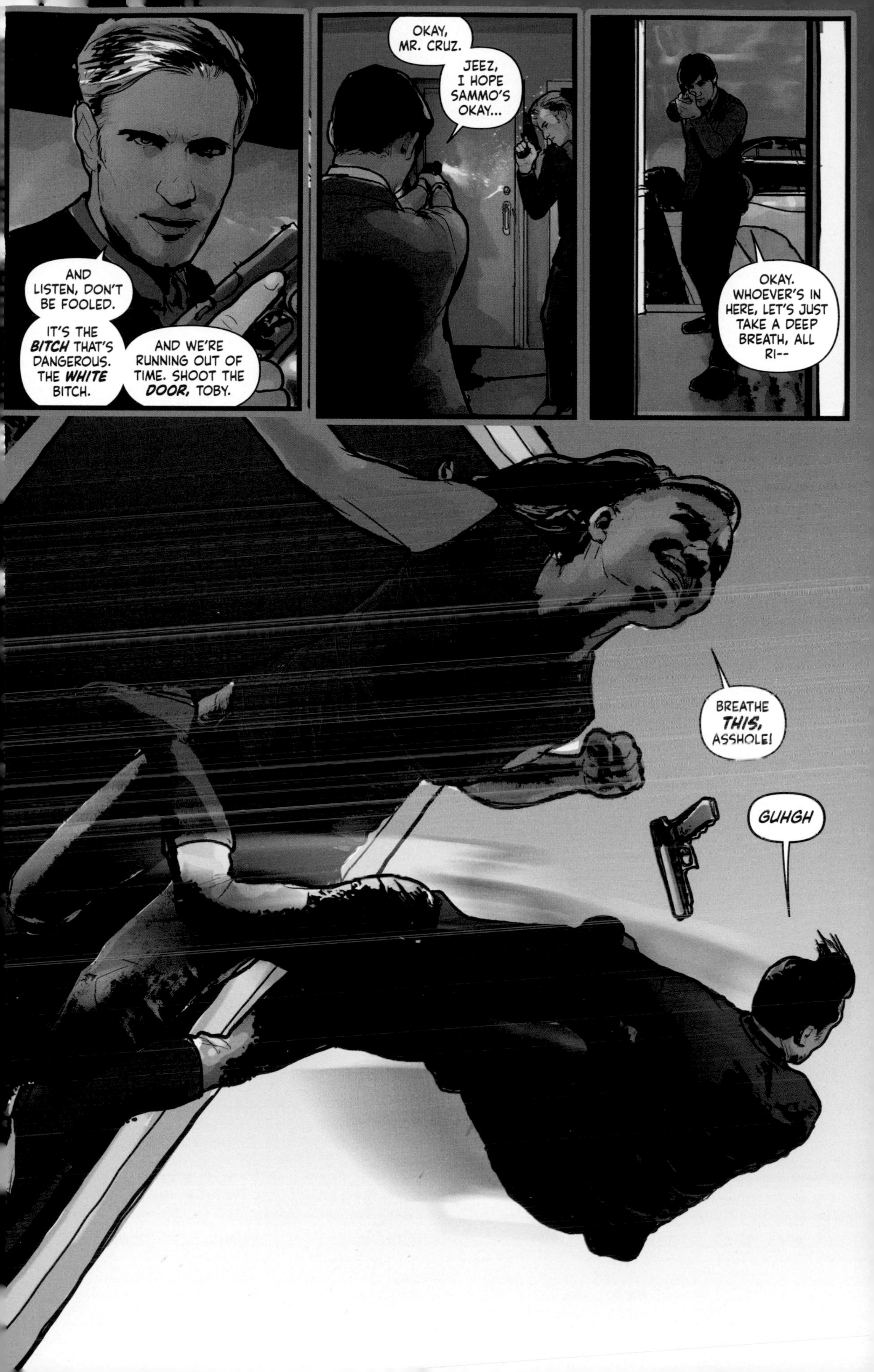
AND LISTEN, DON'T BE FOOLED.
IT'S THE *BITCH* THAT'S DANGEROUS. THE *WHITE* BITCH.
AND WE'RE RUNNING OUT OF TIME. SHOOT THE *DOOR,* TOBY.
OKAY, MR. CRUZ.
JEEZ, I HOPE SAMMO'S OKAY...
OKAY. WHOEVER'S IN HERE, LET'S JUST TAKE A DEEP BREATH, ALL RI--
BREATHE *THIS,* ASSHOLE!
GUHGH

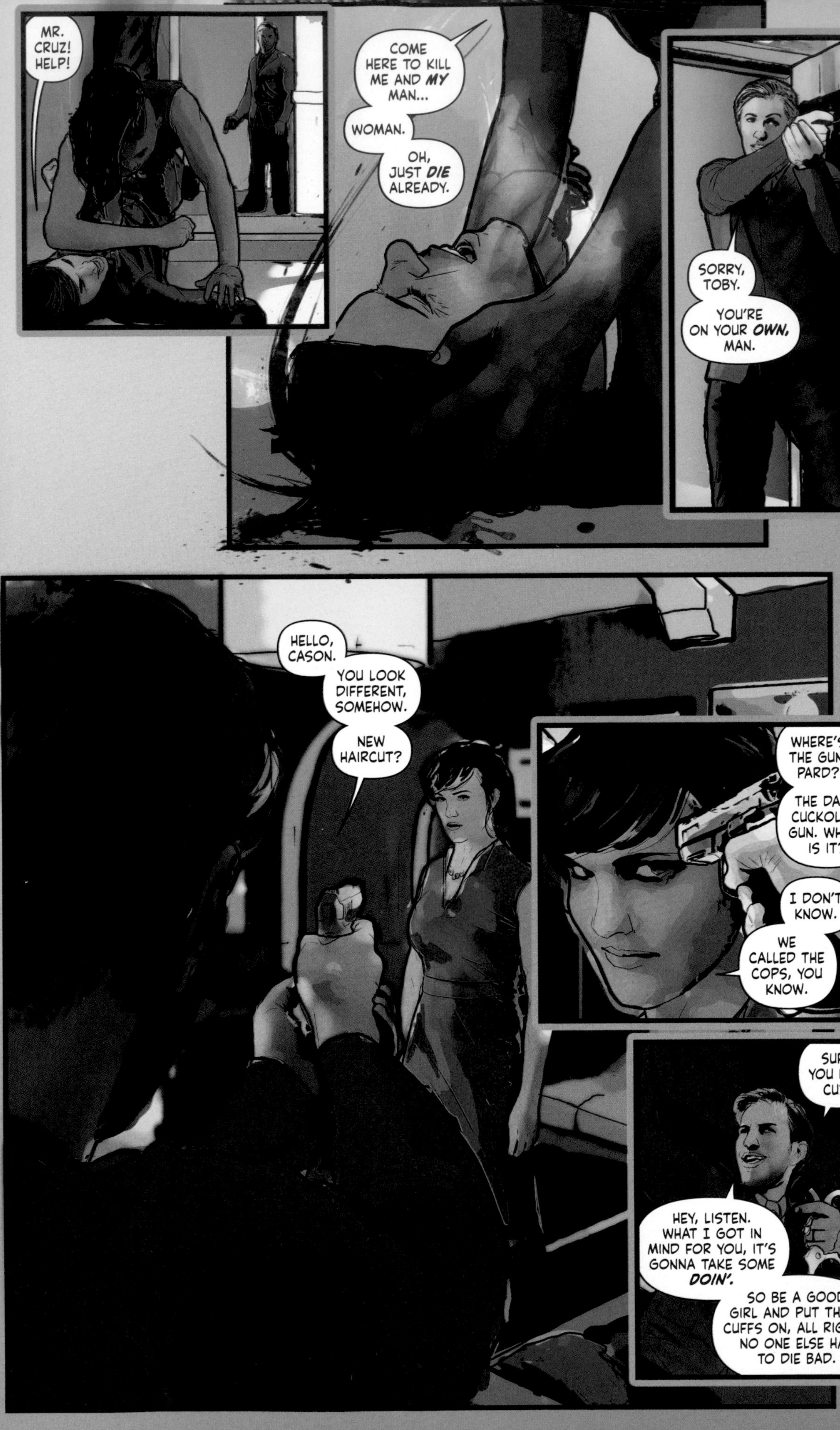
MR. CRUZ! HELP!
COME HERE TO KILL ME AND MY MAN...
WOMAN.
OH, JUST DIE ALREADY.
SORRY, TOBY.
YOU'RE ON YOUR OWN, MAN.
HELLO, CASON.
YOU LOOK DIFFERENT, SOMEHOW.
NEW HAIRCUT?
WHERE'S THE GUN, PARD?
THE DAMN CUCKOLD'S GUN. WHERE IS IT?
I DON'T KNOW.
WE CALLED THE COPS, YOU KNOW.
SURE YOU DID, CUZ.
HEY, LISTEN. WHAT I GOT IN MIND FOR YOU, IT'S GONNA TAKE SOME DOIN'.
SO BE A GOOD GIRL AND PUT THESE CUFFS ON, ALL RIGHT? NO ONE ELSE HAS TO DIE BAD.

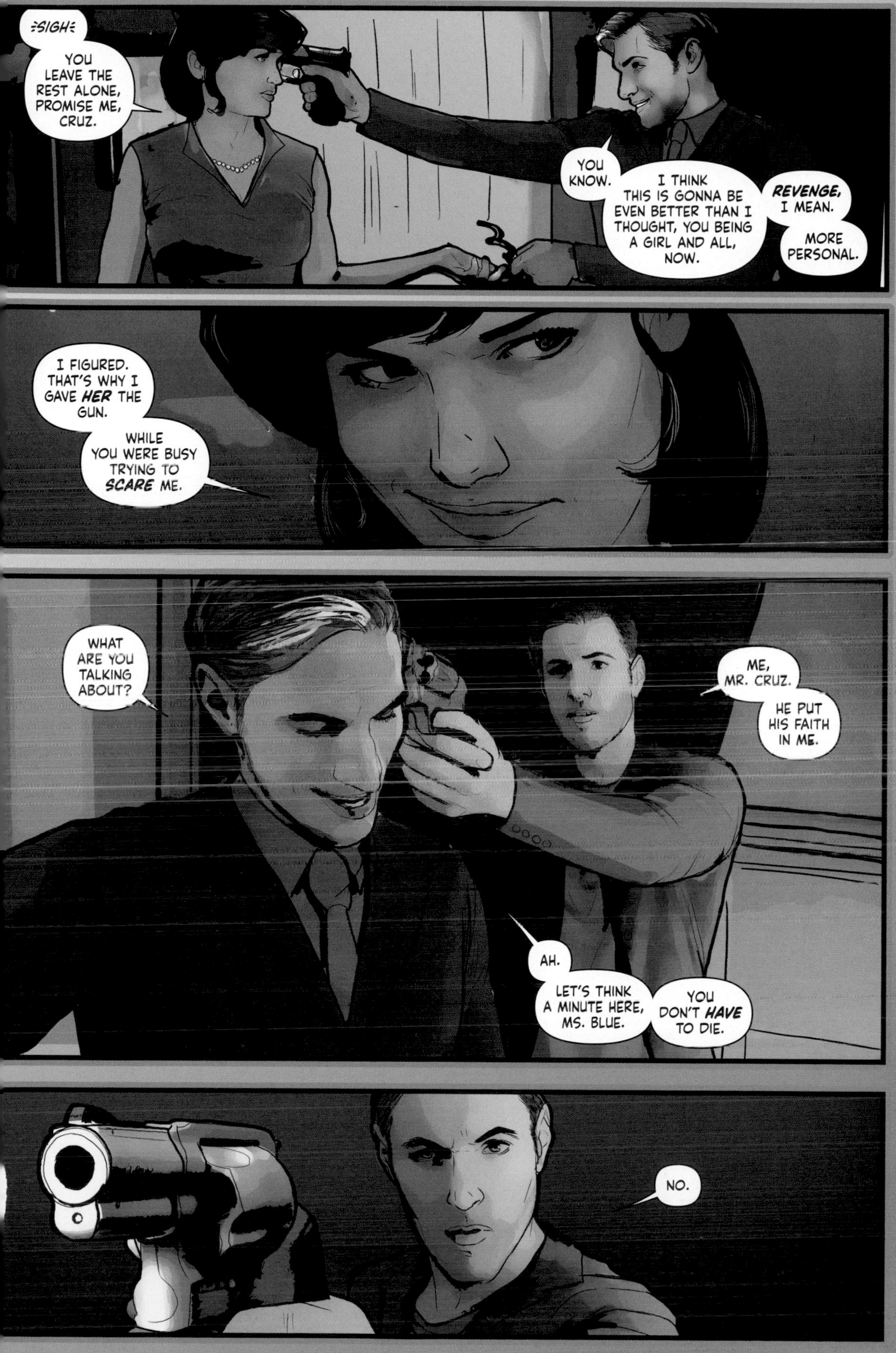

SIGH
YOU LEAVE THE REST ALONE, PROMISE ME, CRUZ.
YOU KNOW.
I THINK THIS IS GONNA BE EVEN BETTER THAN I THOUGHT, YOU BEING A GIRL AND ALL, NOW.
REVENGE, I MEAN.
MORE PERSONAL.
I FIGURED. THAT'S WHY I GAVE HER THE GUN.
WHILE YOU WERE BUSY TRYING TO SCARE ME.
WHAT ARE YOU TALKING ABOUT?
ME, MR. CRUZ.
HE PUT HIS FAITH IN ME.
AH.
LET'S THINK A MINUTE HERE, MS. BLUE.
YOU DON'T HAVE TO DIE.
NO.

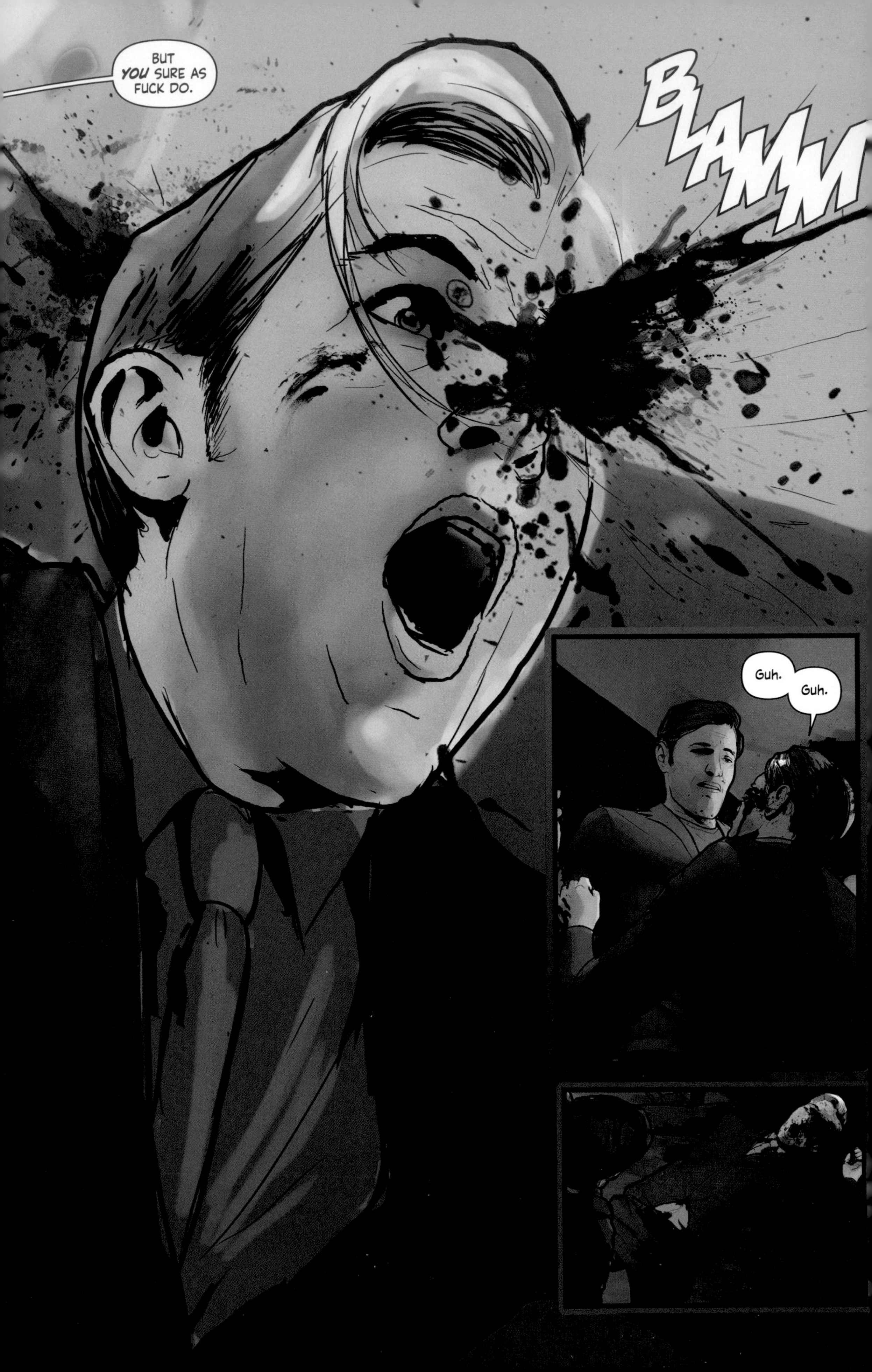
BUT *YOU* SURE AS FUCK DO.
BLAMM
Guh.
Guh.

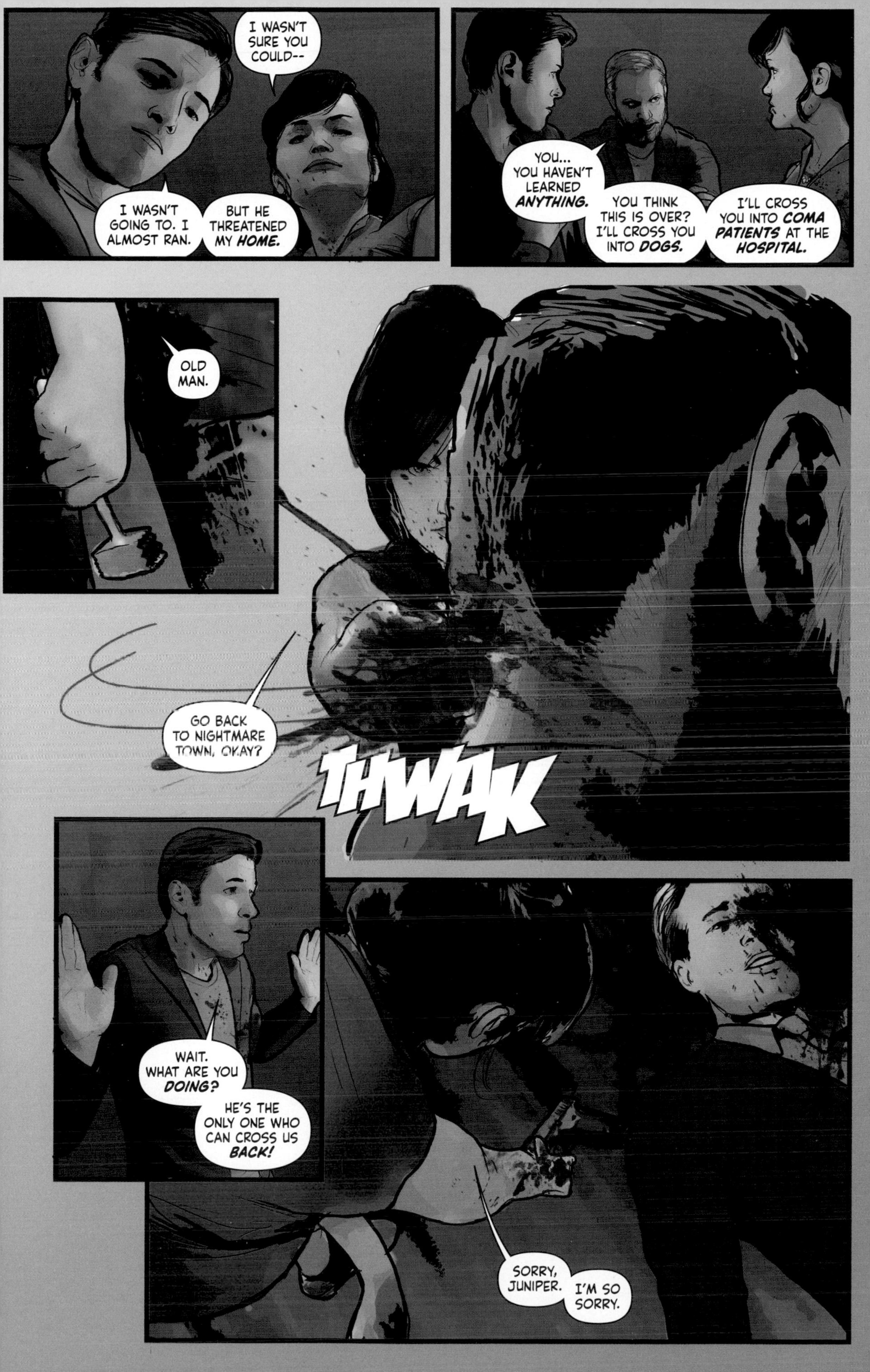

I WASN'T SURE YOU COULD--
I WASN'T GOING TO. I ALMOST RAN.
BUT HE THREATENED MY **HOME.**
YOU... YOU HAVEN'T LEARNED **ANYTHING.**
YOU THINK THIS IS OVER? I'LL CROSS YOU INTO **DOGS.**
I'LL CROSS YOU INTO **COMA PATIENTS** AT THE **HOSPITAL.**
OLD MAN.
GO BACK TO NIGHTMARE TOWN, OKAY?
THWAK
WAIT. WHAT ARE YOU **DOING?**
HE'S THE ONLY ONE WHO CAN CROSS US **BACK!**
SORRY, JUNIPER.
I'M SO SORRY.

I'M NOT GOING BACK. I *LIKE* THIS LIFE.

I DON'T...I DON'T HAVE TO *KILL.* I DON'T HAVE TO BE *AFRAID.*

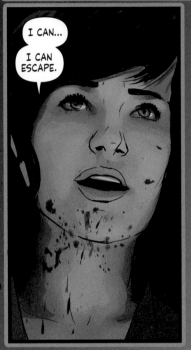

I CAN... I CAN ESCAPE.

IF YOUR--*MY*--OLD BODY IS DEAD...

I CAN'T EVER, I CAN'T EVER BE SWITCHED *BACK.*

CASON. YOU WERE NEVER A GOOD MAN.

BUT YOU WERE NEVER A *TERRIBLE* MAN, EITHER.

YOU REALLY WANT TO *STOP* BEING YOU?

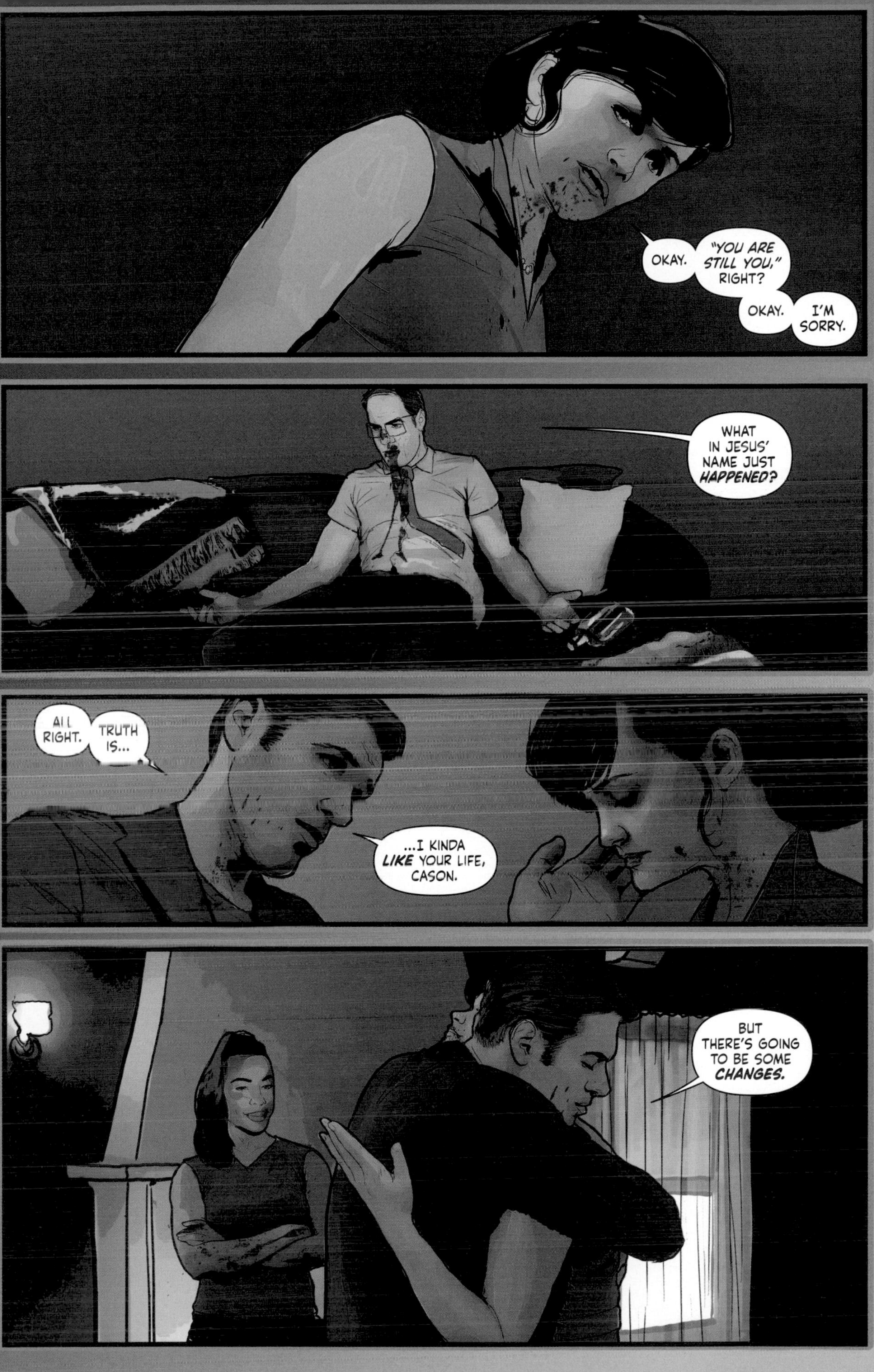

OKAY.
"YOU ARE STILL YOU," RIGHT?
OKAY.
I'M SORRY.
WHAT IN JESUS' NAME JUST HAPPENED?
ALL RIGHT.
TRUTH IS...
...I KINDA LIKE YOUR LIFE, CASON.
BUT THERE'S GOING TO BE SOME CHANGES.

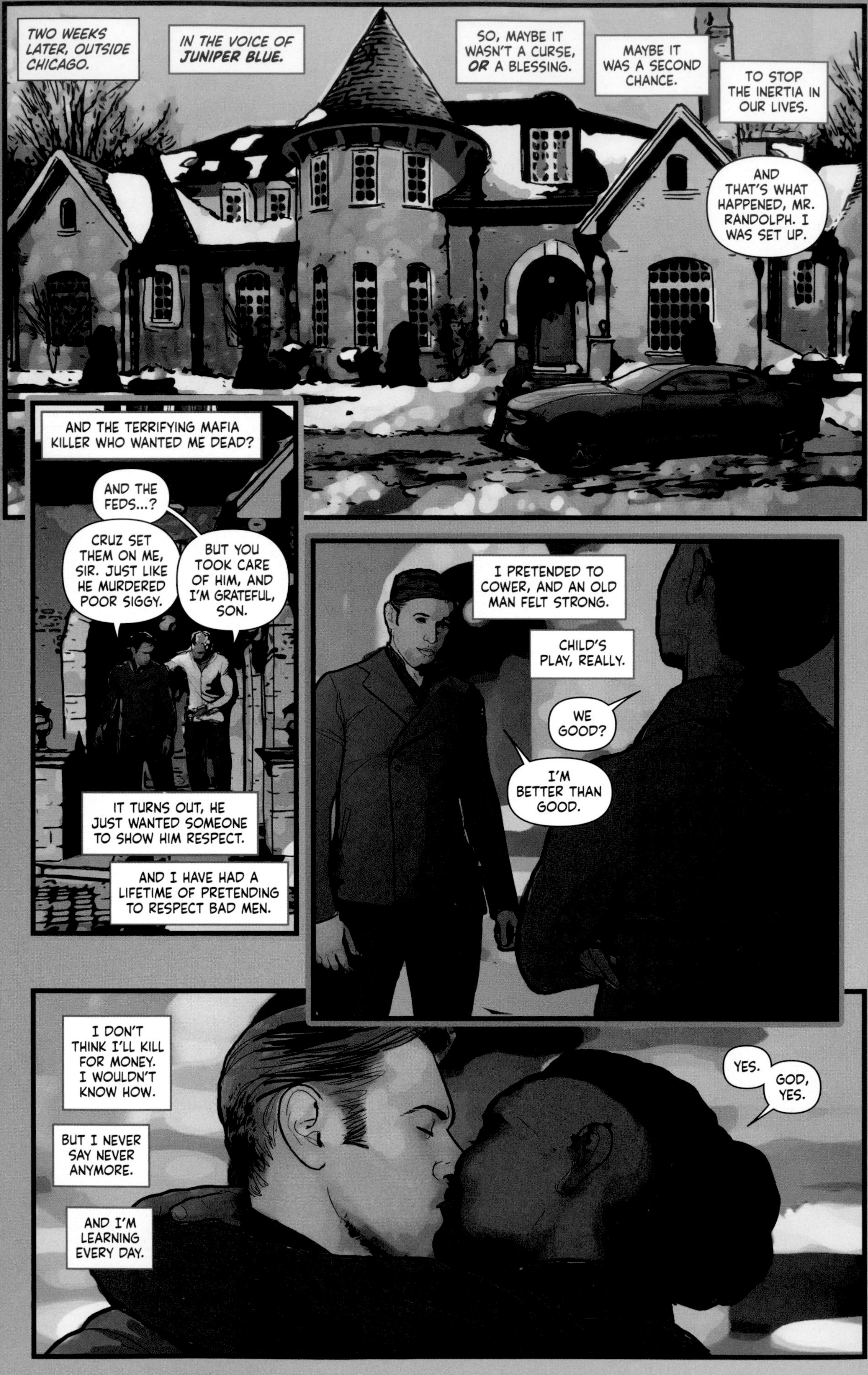
TWO WEEKS LATER, OUTSIDE CHICAGO.
IN THE VOICE OF JUNIPER BLUE.
SO, MAYBE IT WASN'T A CURSE, OR A BLESSING.
MAYBE IT WAS A SECOND CHANCE.
TO STOP THE INERTIA IN OUR LIVES.
AND THAT'S WHAT HAPPENED, MR. RANDOLPH. I WAS SET UP.
AND THE TERRIFYING MAFIA KILLER WHO WANTED ME DEAD?
AND THE FEDS...?
CRUZ SET THEM ON ME, SIR. JUST LIKE HE MURDERED POOR SIGGY.
BUT YOU TOOK CARE OF HIM, AND I'M GRATEFUL, SON.
IT TURNS OUT, HE JUST WANTED SOMEONE TO SHOW HIM RESPECT.
AND I HAVE HAD A LIFETIME OF PRETENDING TO RESPECT BAD MEN.
I PRETENDED TO COWER, AND AN OLD MAN FELT STRONG.
CHILD'S PLAY, REALLY.
WE GOOD?
I'M BETTER THAN GOOD.
I DON'T THINK I'LL KILL FOR MONEY. I WOULDN'T KNOW HOW.
BUT I NEVER SAY NEVER ANYMORE.
AND I'M LEARNING EVERY DAY.
YES.
GOD, YES.

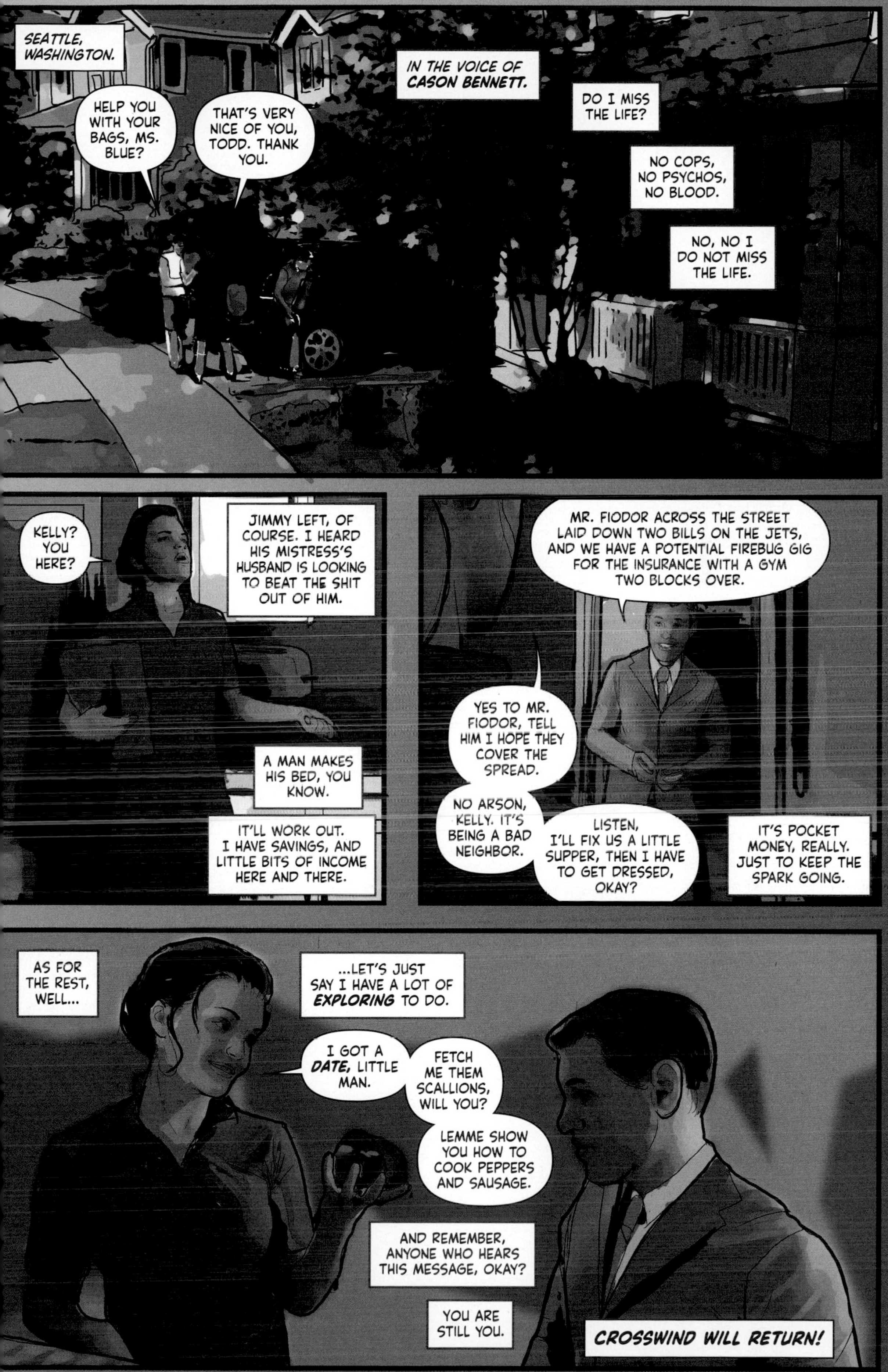
SEATTLE, WASHINGTON.
HELP YOU WITH YOUR BAGS, MS. BLUE?
THAT'S VERY NICE OF YOU, TODD. THANK YOU.
IN THE VOICE OF CASON BENNETT.
DO I MISS THE LIFE?
NO COPS, NO PSYCHOS, NO BLOOD.
NO, NO I DO NOT MISS THE LIFE.
KELLY? YOU HERE?
JIMMY LEFT, OF COURSE. I HEARD HIS MISTRESS'S HUSBAND IS LOOKING TO BEAT THE SHIT OUT OF HIM.
A MAN MAKES HIS BED, YOU KNOW.
IT'LL WORK OUT. I HAVE SAVINGS, AND LITTLE BITS OF INCOME HERE AND THERE.
MR. FIODOR ACROSS THE STREET LAID DOWN TWO BILLS ON THE JETS, AND WE HAVE A POTENTIAL FIREBUG GIG FOR THE INSURANCE WITH A GYM TWO BLOCKS OVER.
YES TO MR. FIODOR, TELL HIM I HOPE THEY COVER THE SPREAD.
NO ARSON, KELLY. IT'S BEING A BAD NEIGHBOR.
LISTEN, I'LL FIX US A LITTLE SUPPER, THEN I HAVE TO GET DRESSED, OKAY?
IT'S POCKET MONEY, REALLY. JUST TO KEEP THE SPARK GOING.
AS FOR THE REST, WELL...
...LET'S JUST SAY I HAVE A LOT OF EXPLORING TO DO.
I GOT A DATE, LITTLE MAN.
FETCH ME THEM SCALLIONS, WILL YOU?
LEMME SHOW YOU HOW TO COOK PEPPERS AND SAUSAGE.
AND REMEMBER, ANYONE WHO HEARS THIS MESSAGE, OKAY?
YOU ARE STILL YOU.
CROSSWIND WILL RETURN!

Cat Staggs is dedicating this story to

Abbie Staggs
aka "Tucker"

March 2003 - December 2017

TRESPASS

Which is the bigger sin, in the eyes of heaven, do you suppose?

Is it arrogance, or oblivion?

Arrogance can make a fool an emperor, make him deem himself above all creatures and worth of every bit of unearned good fortune. Arrogance can make a killer think he is a good man, a user of men can feel he is being charitable in his theft..

And yet, to be oblivious...to be oblivious means putting yourself not just in front of others, but ALONE in front of others, as if they did not even exist. To be in a film, pretending victimhood while discounting others' pain.

I remember the first time I realized I was God.

I had a cat that loved me and a dog that loved only my mother. The dog bit me when I tried to pet it, and drew blood from my innocent young hand, a scar I carry to this day.

So I brought the wind and made two monsters.

A dog that meowed and a cat that loved my mother, but that she was allergic to.

The dog never again licked her hand, and my mother had my father tie the cat in a sack and throw it in the river.

Arrogance versus oblivion.

Cats and dogs.

I have loved few persons and I have lost them all. And the most beloved of them all died alone. I do not forgive.

God does not forgive.

Arrogance and oblivion.

Both are inexcusable, both result in throwing pain and unkindness into the world, both are celebrated by the unworthy and the ignorant.

I am alone. I am solitary, that is to be my lot in my remaining time.

But I think of that cat, that bit me in another shell. And I remember how I begged to ride with my father to the river. I think he thought I would try to talk him out of it. And when he flung the sack into the river, I think he mistook my giggling for tears.

I will not be bitten unanswered again.

I have a gift, and I acknowledge that there is no kind way to use it. So I will use it unkindly, as I am certain that is God's will.

And he works through me, now.

AND ARROGANCE AND OBLIVION HAD BEST BEWARE.

For I have many sacks, and there are always more rivers.

Her daughter was different. At age three, she walked the three miles to the nearest lake to swim and explore. She could not be stopped. "She'll touch the stars, that girl," said her grandmother.

And now, here she was, Commander of the U.W.V. BENEFACTOR, a Stallion-class exploratory and research vessel, as powerful and fast as any of the renowned galactic reconnaissance ships before her, even those piloted by the legends that had inspired her journey.

She had yet to "touch the stars," of course. But this was as close as any human had yet dared. ~~If her family could see her now!~~

She could have had a safe career. She was attractive, raven-haired with piercing eyes. And she was smart, though those around her didn't always recognize this quality, often to their own dismay as she outmaneuvered them in various ways.

But she had no interest in safety, and comfort tended only to make her Uncomfortable, the longer it lasted. Her home had been nurturing, but her six weeks in Boot Camp had been the happiest she had ever been. Until now, until this promotion, and this maiden journey.

With her own ship. With her hand-picked crew.

Commander Louisa May Alcott.

First in her clan to leave Terra.

She rarely even thought of her village anymore. That wasn't home. Even the SHIP wasn't truly home.

The stars. The STARS were her home.
~~And she promised never to leave.~~

"Commander, we're being hailed," said Ensign Farley, one of the youngest of an already young crew. "Source is unknown."

~~She couldn't help but notice his attractive face and form.~~ She snapped into action. There were no Colonnade ships in this quadrant. Being hailed meant hostile intent, almost certainly!

"Scan the vector for vessels, Ensign. And put the call on the monitor," she said, rising from her chair. Her crew looked to her for strength and experience. But the truth was, in all her journeys, she had never had any contact with an alien race at all. She would never show that to her people, however.

At once, the front of the command room seemed to fade, and was replaced by a hideous ~~grinning face~~ smirking visage…it was a Thalarion War Scourge, she recognized it at once. They'd been taught not to judge by appearances, but the sharpened fangs, the hairless pate, and the cruel serpent's eyes were hard to take, just the same.

The Thalarions, even the name made her inexperienced crew tremble. They had been the most sophisticated and brutal slavers in the galaxy, but had become zealots over a spiritual awakening that had taken centuries to complete. Now their religious fervor forced them to hunt down and destroy every race they deemed 'sinful.'

And EVERY race, but their own, was deemed 'sinful!'

The Scourge looked at her through the holographic display, in open contempt. ANYTHING could be a sin to this creature, and any SIN…meant ~~DEATH~~ immediate DESTRUCTION!

She straightened her smart tunic and addressed the being, mustering all the courage and dignity she could. "I am Commander Alcott of the U.W.V. BENEFACTOR, traveling under the flag of peace and exploration. May I ask who it is that I am addressing?"

The Thalarion hissed. "You'll speak when SPOKEN to by a holy SCOURGE of THALARION, Commander of Harlots!"

She refused to rise to his anger. "Our charter permits us exploratory rights through this vector, Ambassador of Thalarion. We respect your authority but as clearly stated in our treaty—"

"SILENCE," hissed the hideous creature. "Your crew and ship are FORFEIT until we may set an INQUIRY upon you, to determine your VIRTUE, or lack thereof!"

She sat, trying to appear calmer than she really was. She had heard stories of these… 'inquiries.' They made the Spanish Inquisition look tame!

"I see. And what is the penalty, should we fail your little test, Ambassador?"

"DEATH BY SCOURGE," he cackled ~~delightedly~~, ~~amusedly~~, evilly.

This is terrible. The words won't DO anything.

I had this story in my head, and it all sounds so STUPID.

STUPID, STUPID, STUPID.

I can't even do this right.

I can't even do this right.

Sometimes I hate what's in my head.

KELLYB: Dude, you there

RILEYSMILES: Yeah, what's up?

KELLYB: I have to talk to you. Got a second?

RILEYSMILES: Okay. Rena's making spaghetti and she thinks she's Gordon Ramsey or something.

KELLYB: Something's wrong here, man. Really wrong.

RILEYSMILES: You need to come over? You need us to come get you?

KELLYB: Let me think.

RILEYSMILES: It's not your dad, is it?

KELLYB: No. Yes.

KELLYB: Shit, I don't know.

KELLYB: It's HER. Juniper. My step.

RILEYSMILES: K, you don't like her. This is not news. Just avoid her, all right?

KELLYB: No, it's not that. Listen. Just…just fucking listen for a minute, okay?

KELLYB: It's like this. When my dad first brought her home to meet me…..I actually felt kinda sorry for her. She was so quiet and my dad, you know what an asshole he is, he just pushed right over her like he does with everybody.

RILEYSMILES: Okay…?

KELLYB: And she didn't seem to have any way to stand up for herself. She's pretty, and I know she's smart, but she acts like she's just, just worthless, I guess.

RILEYSMILES: Dude. I don't like your dad, either, but maybe this works for them.

KELLYB: It doesn't, though. She's unhappy, since they got married, she never smiles anymore, not ever.

RILEYSMILES: K, my mom's at her boyfriend's and my thirteen year old SISTER is making supper. Nobody's family is perfect.

KELLYB: It's more than that. A couple days ago, I came home, she was cooking, I mouthed off a bit, and she slapped me in the face.

RILEYSMILES: WTF? WTF? WTF?

KELLYB: I know, but hang on. She talks different, like, like everything was an act up until now.

KELLYB: Like a different person. Like an ALIEN.

RILEYSMILES: Okay, you're just bullshitting me now.

KELLYB: Or like a guy in a movie. Scarface, something like that. And there's more.

KELLYB: You know those jackwaffles Terry and Corey stole my bike, right?

RILEYSMILES: Sure.

KELLYB: Riley, she chased them down and ran them over with my dad's SUV.

RILEYSMILES: ...

KELLYB: Yeah. Kicked the shit out of our obnoxious neighbors, too. Didn't raise a SWEAT.

RILEYSMILES: DUDE. I think I'm in love with your STEP.

KELLYB: I don't know what to do.

KELLYB: Everything she says, it's impossible...it's crazy.

KELLYB: But it WORKS.

RILESMILES: Okay. So, say this is all true. What are you going to DO?

KELLYB: She says I'm her consigliere.

KELLYB: She says she's going to get me a new wardrobe.

KELLYB: And then?

KELLYB: Then I'm asking someone to the PROM.

AUTHOR'S NOTE: CROSSWIND has been in my mind for a while, now. One of the most strangely fortuitous things to happen during the creation of this story was completely unexpected. I'd been invited to a panel on trans issues in comics for the New York City Comic Con, because of the then-recent inclusion of a trans character in my BATGIRL run. But the panel took an interesting detour, as the moderator/organizer, **CHARLES BATTERSBY**, talked about some of the latent (or blatant) transphobia that often occurred in 'body-swap' stories. Part of the goal of CROSSWIND was to avoid all that, and I'm very thankful to Charles for clarifying some of those clichés and tropes, so that we could do a book that tried to be more inclusive, and more aware than that. This is an interview I conducted with him by email just a few weeks ago. Thank you, Charles, CROSSWIND is better for your work and wisdom.

—**GAIL SIMONE**

GS: First, Charles, if I could ask, could you simply introduce yourself to readers, tell me a little bit about yourself?

CB: I'm a Writer/Actor who has worked in theater, TV, animation, and video games. For fun I'm a cosplayer. I've been out of the closet as transgender for 25 years, and cosplay was one of the things that helped me feel comfortable about living openly. In 2011, I organized my first panel at a convention, and it was about trans issues in video games. Since then I've presented similar panels and talks about gender identity in comic books, theater, and cosplay. Much of my own writing deals with themes of gender identity.

GS: And can you explain to us how trans representation came to be an issue of passion for you?

CB: I was aware that I was "Different" when I was small child, but we didn't have the word "Transgender" back then, and terms like transsexual or transvestite were considered dirty words that children shouldn't hear. I had to learn about people like me from popular entertainment during my childhood in the 70s and 80s.

Unfortunately, back then, there was a trend of using trans characters as villains. One actor, Christopher Morley, had a bountiful career playing cross-dressing villains. There was always the moment when the sexy lady assassin was de-wigged and revealed to be a cunning master of disguise, or a demented psychopath! This plot twist was used in an episode of Charlie's Angels that I saw once, forty years ago, and it still sticks with me.

There was also a liberal use of drag for comedic effect. A then-unknown Tom Hanks starred in a sit-com based entirely around a flimsy excuse to get a couple of guys in drag every episode. I recall an episode of Mork & Mindy where Mork created a failed clone of Mindy that was a man in drag. Of course M*A*S*H* had Klinger crossdressing so he could be discharged from the army.

Even as a child I understood that these characters weren't like me. These were people who were forced to change gender because of implausible plotlines, or because they were generically "Crazy". But these depictions stuck in my memory, because they were the closest thing I ever saw to a person like myself. As an adult I learned that transgender people could be perfectly sane, and dignified. And, by the 90s, they were being depicted that way in the media more often. Even movies like "The Crying Game" were a big step up compared to most of the representation we had in the 70s and 80s.

I still kept an eye out for movies, comics, and games that used gender change as a plot device, or featured poorly written trans characters. I became a walking archive of obscure comic storylines dealing with gender identity. Did you know that The Martian Manhunter had never shapechanged into a female Martian until *Justice League Task Force* issue #7? Did you know that Nomad went undercover as a crossdresser to catch a transphobic serial killer in Albuquerque? I do! Those factoids and countless others are burned into my memory.

GS: I remember your thoughts on body switch stories, and how they often seem to turn to casual transphobia for casually cruel comedy. What do you think it is about the body swap genre that is the most problematic?

CB: Body swap storylines can be a great way to depict how a transgender person feels. Of course the best way is have a trans protagonist, but in a body swap story the characters are literally trapped in the wrong the bodies.

Writers usually overlook the transgender theme and focus on sexism, often with good intentions. A sexist man learns what it's like being a woman, while a sexist woman learns that being man is hard too. However the writers don't realize that both characters are really learning what it's like to be transgender.

A man who has been magically zapped into a woman's body isn't experiencing life as a cisgender woman, he's experience life as a transman who hasn't transitioned yet!

Something else that always gets overlooked in these stories is the idea of the characters using hormones and surgery to change their sex back. The writers seem to assume that, if a cursed monkey paw caused them to swap bodies, then the heroes have no alternative but to spend the rest of the story hunting down another magic monkey paw.

It's also rare that we see a trans character get bodyswapped with a cisgender person. The bodyswap story would be completely subverted if one character is delighted with their new body and doesn't want to swap back. The BBC superhero show *Misfits* did a storyline like this, where a trans character gained the power to swap genitals with other people. Sometimes against their will.

A bad example would be a recent episode of *Law & Order: SVU* where a trans teen is killed in a hate crime. At first, the episode shows a great of sensitivity to the daily harassment that trans people have to endure, but the second half of the episode became a debate about giving harsh sentences to teen offenders. This resulted in the unfortunate implication that hate crime laws should not be used against young people who attack trans kids.

GS: And finally, what would you like to see more of in all media, including comics?

CB: Some of the best stories about transgender characters are written or produced by trans people, and have trans actors playing trans characters. It would great if producers would seek out trans writers/co-writers for stories that deal with trans characters, or gender-switch storylines.

I would also love to see trans actors playing characters that are not specifically written as trans. As an actor myself, I find that I'm often considered for roles as a crossdressing man, a drag queen, or a trans woman, but casting agencies won't consider me for "Waitress" or "Woman #2", or even a female extra in a crowd scene.

Comics are an interesting medium for trans characters. When people are in the early stages of their transition, there might be subtle differences between them and a cisgender person; nearly imperceptible distinctions in body language, voice, and facial features. This raises the unique issue of how a comic book artist can depict these differences without being exaggerated or offensive? How could a letterer imply that a trans character's voice is subtly different?

It also raises the question of should artists draw a trans character differently than a cis character? There are, no doubt, strong opinions on both sides!

Writers also like to depict the transition as an instantaneous "Sex Change Operation" where John completely transforms into Jane in a single procedure. In reality trans people spend years on hormones, and usually get multiple surgeries. In a comic book story that takes 36 issues to play out, should an artist depict gradual changes in a transitioning character's appearance?

GS: Thank you, Charles. I know you couldn't have been aware at the time, but the passion and grace you displayed at your panel has really informed this book. Can you tell me where people can find out more about you?

CB: People can see more about my writing, acting, and cosplay at **www.CharlesBattersby.com**.

I can also be found on **Twitter at @Charlesbatterb**.

Much of my own writing involves trans characters, or themes of gender identity. I'm always happy to see theater companies do my play "The Astonishing Adventures of All-American Girl & The Scarlet Skunk" which has a transgender vigilante as a lead character. I'm also dying to do a reboot of the first transgender superhero, Madam Fatal, if anyone from Warner Bros, DC Comics, or The CW is reading this...

CONFIDENTIAL

EYES ONLY HERITAGE PROGRAM TRANSCRIPT
8/13/17

DOCKET 179991BA SESSION TWO, GREY SITE "FORAGER."
Two Agents Present

AGENT A: So, Mr. Benitez-

SUBJECT: Bennett.

AGENT A: Pardon?

SUBECT: My name's Bennett. Either you call me by my name or we're done here.

AGENT B: (laugh, unintelligible comment)

AGENT A: Oh, well, excuse the fuck out of me, Mr. Bennett. You want to change your name to sound more Anglo, that's your business.

AGENT B: This asshole-

AGENT A: No, it's fine, honest. But maybe he should get used to just being called by a number, in his new penitentiary jumpsuit, hey?

AGENT B: Good one.

SUBJECT: Except they don't.

AGENT A: Don't what, Mr. Bennett?

SUBJECT: They don't call us by numbers in the pen. Seems like you should know that, being big-time feds and all.

AGENT A: You're trying to piss me off. Does that seem like a good plan at this juncture, Mr. Bennett?

AGENT B: Here I thought they called you wise guys.

AGENT A: Right, right. And here we are, with you on three RICO counts.

AGENT B: And what did you do, wise guy? Where'd you put the payoff?

AGENT A: In your fuckin father's garage.

AGENT B: That may be the shittiest thing I've ever heard.

AGENT A: You know what we can do to your poor blind papa bear, Bennett?

AGENT B: I don't think he's gonna like the food in a (unintelligible) federal prison, do you?

SUBJECT: You're assholes. You're both pussies, talking like that.

AGENT A: Sure we are, Mr. Bennett. You shoot guys for a scumbag like Randolph, and we're the assholes.

SUBJECT: All right. All right. But I got conditions.

AGENT B: Fuck you. Tell your conditions to your cellmate when he's reading you bedtime stories.

AGENT A: Now, now, let's hear him out.

SUBJECT: You can have anyone. I'll be your fuckin rat. But you leave Mika and Del out of it.

AGENT A: Huh.

AGENT B: Wait. Are you serious? Fuck this guy and his conditions.

AGENT A: You got a sweet spot for Cruz's piece, we know that, Bennett. And Del…well, he's nothing. No one gives a shit what happens to him.

AGENT B: Wait. These are all killers, you know that.

AGENT A: You want the tail of the snake or the head, (REDACTED)?

AGENT B: Fuck me, this isn't right.

AGENT A: Anything else, Mr. Bennett?

SUBJECT: Yes. I said I'd do this, and I'll keep my word. But–

AGENT A: Yes?

SUBJECT: That psycho motherfucker Cruz has to die.

AGENT A: I don't know who you think we are. We don't–

SUBJECT: I know exactly who you are. It's this way or no way.

AGENT A: No. We're not having this discussion.

SUBJECT: Either you rat him out to Randolph on some fake bullshit, and let his guys do it, or he accidentally gets tagged in the head by feds by mistake. I don't care.

AGENT A: No. No. This isn't a talk we're having.

SUBJECT: His brains on the fucking floor or you get nothing. I am not looking over my shoulder forever.

AGENT A: Fuck you, Bennett. We'll see you in front of the pissiest, brimstone judge we can find.

SUBJECT: His brains on the floor, or fuck off, shitheads.

AGENT A: I already told you—

AGENT B: Wait.

AGENT A: What?

AGENT B: Let's hear him out.

check out crosswind's official theme song
by singer/songwriter rachel miller,
available now on itunes, spotify, and more!
listen for free at www.rachelmillermusic.com.

 /rachelmillermusic

 @rachelmillermusic

 /rachelmillermusic

 @rachmillermusic

www.rachelmillermusic.com

LAST TESTAMENT

I do not say, "last WILL" and testament. Because of these two, this pair of vapid, selfish creatures, I have nothing to give, and no one to give it to. My home is often a city doorway. My treasures nothing but the discarded refuse of a world that no longer cares.

Because of them. Even their names burn my ears.

Cason Bennett and Juniper Blue.

Because of them, my beloved wife died before I could cross her soul into a healthy body, and now she is given to the void. A void I myself am anxious to wander. It will come none too soon, and then I will find out what it is that I, and the Viziers before me, have been tampering with. I do not believe in God.

But I do believe in the running tally of our misdeeds.

And somehow, we must pay for them.

I will pay for those I have misused. I am ready.

But I want to see those who misused me pay, before that allotted time.

So I have no will, any more than a drowned rat has a home, any more than a dying dog has a family.

And yet, it is a matter of will, after all.

My people cannot cross ourselves, nor cross each other. We are the only creatures on this wretched globe that are absolutely guaranteed but one life. It is a trade we make in exchange for power and the good life it has provided most of us for hundreds of years.

So I have known this day would come. After my wife's death, I made no effort to rebuild my life, to seek the comfort of another's tender love and mercy. I made no attempt to contact the rich and powerful, every one of whom would kneel at my feet to beg for my gift and blessing upon them.

And there is a reason.

It is because I am too old and too sickly to avoid the truth anymore. And the truth is, that even though Bennett and Blue, in their thoughtlessness, caused the delay that let my wife die...

...in the end, ultimately, at the closing of a very dark road, I am the one to blame.

I didn't need to leave her side. I didn't need to go perform miracles for some deluded corporate tyrant who will use my gift only for selfish reasons, only to plunder again young vaginas, and to take more money from those with the least ability to part with it. We used to be the shield of kings and emperors, now reduced to giving salesmen and plutocrats time they did not deserve.

And I didn't leave her for that paycheck, considerable though the figure amounted to be. I left her because I left her because I left her because

Because the hospital sickened me. The doctors, the nurses, they sickened me. And even my beloved wife, with the spider legs of cancer crawling through her, always crawling, never dying...

...she revolted me to my core.

I should have crossed her then, but I needed a perfectly suitable candidate. I wanted someone agreeable in form and temperament. I wanted someone who, when she looked in the mirror, saw something that made her smile. And made ME smile.

I felt I had earned that, you see, after watching her fade with the years and illness.

I had earned nothing. And arriving at the hospital ten minutes too late, I would have let the rest of the world die for one more hour with her desiccated form.

I was a fool. I was a selfish fool. No better than the scum I had used my gifts on over the years.

So I ran, I took the job in Dallas, and was glad to be away from the antiseptic smell, the beeping machines. I enjoyed myself. I told her it was essential.

And she fucking died alone, calling my name. Because I was weak, because I was venal.

I know my wife. I know she searches for me in the void, and that I am already forgiven.

But not from myself. Never from myself.

So I am ready to go. I will not move when the gun is pointed at my head. I leave others of my kind, less broken, more hardy, to continue our work and legacy. I am ready to find my wife.

But there are two cursed beings on the skin of this filthy world who must suffer first.

And suffer they shall. May it teach them wisdom I never acquired.

- VOX

ALTERNATE
COVERS

Issue #1 variant cover design

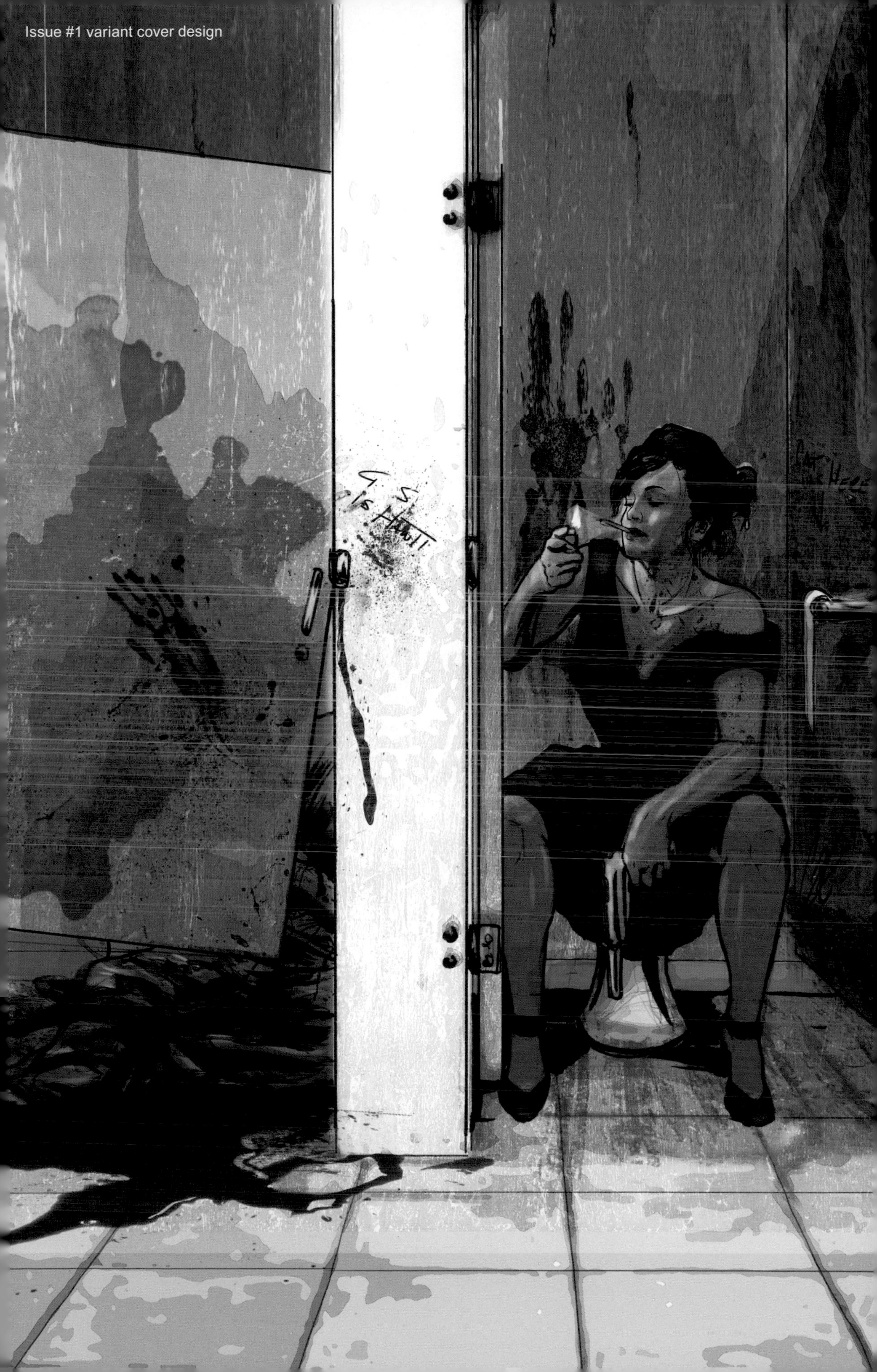

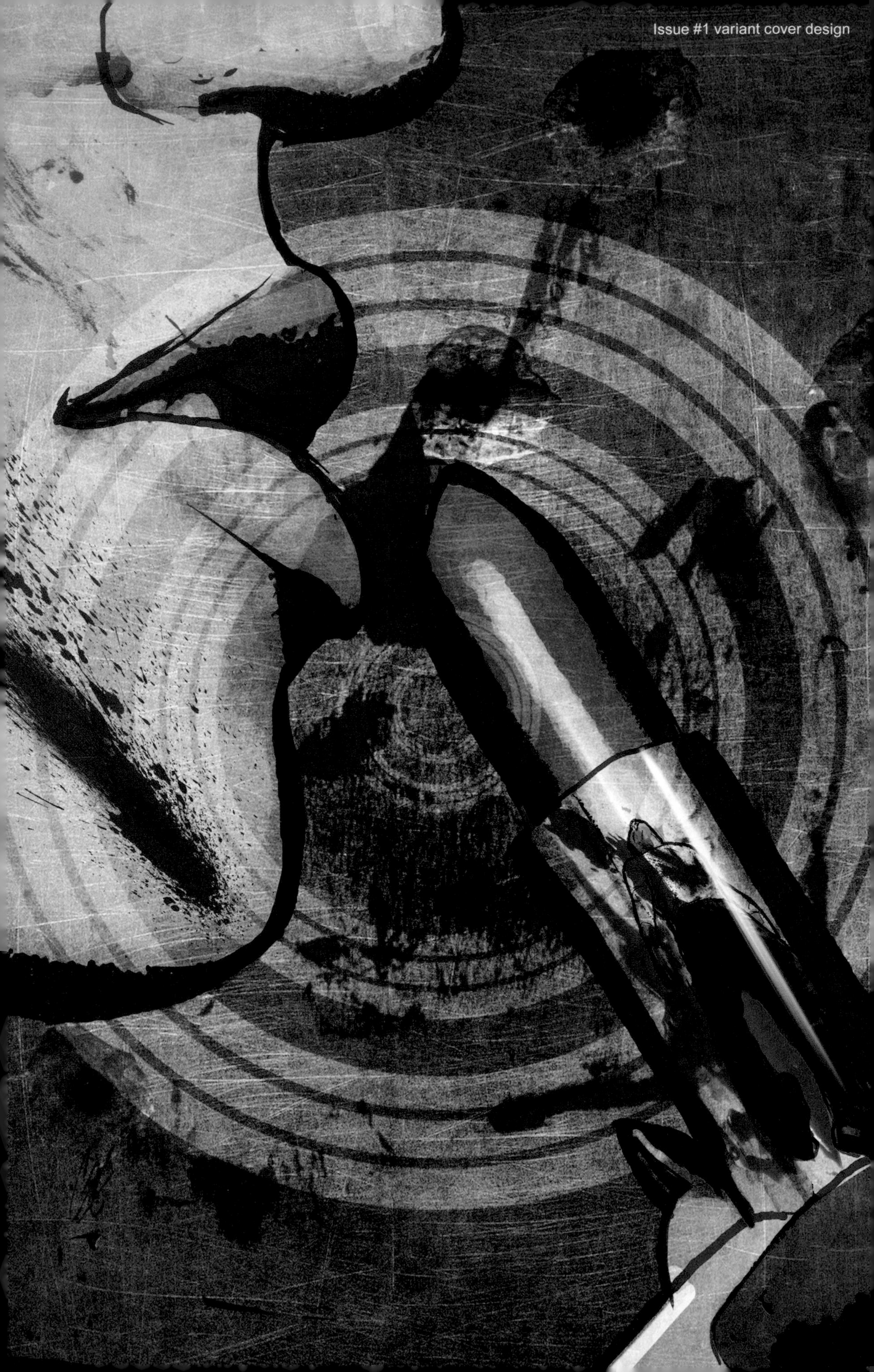

Issue #1 variant cover design

Issue #1 variant cover design

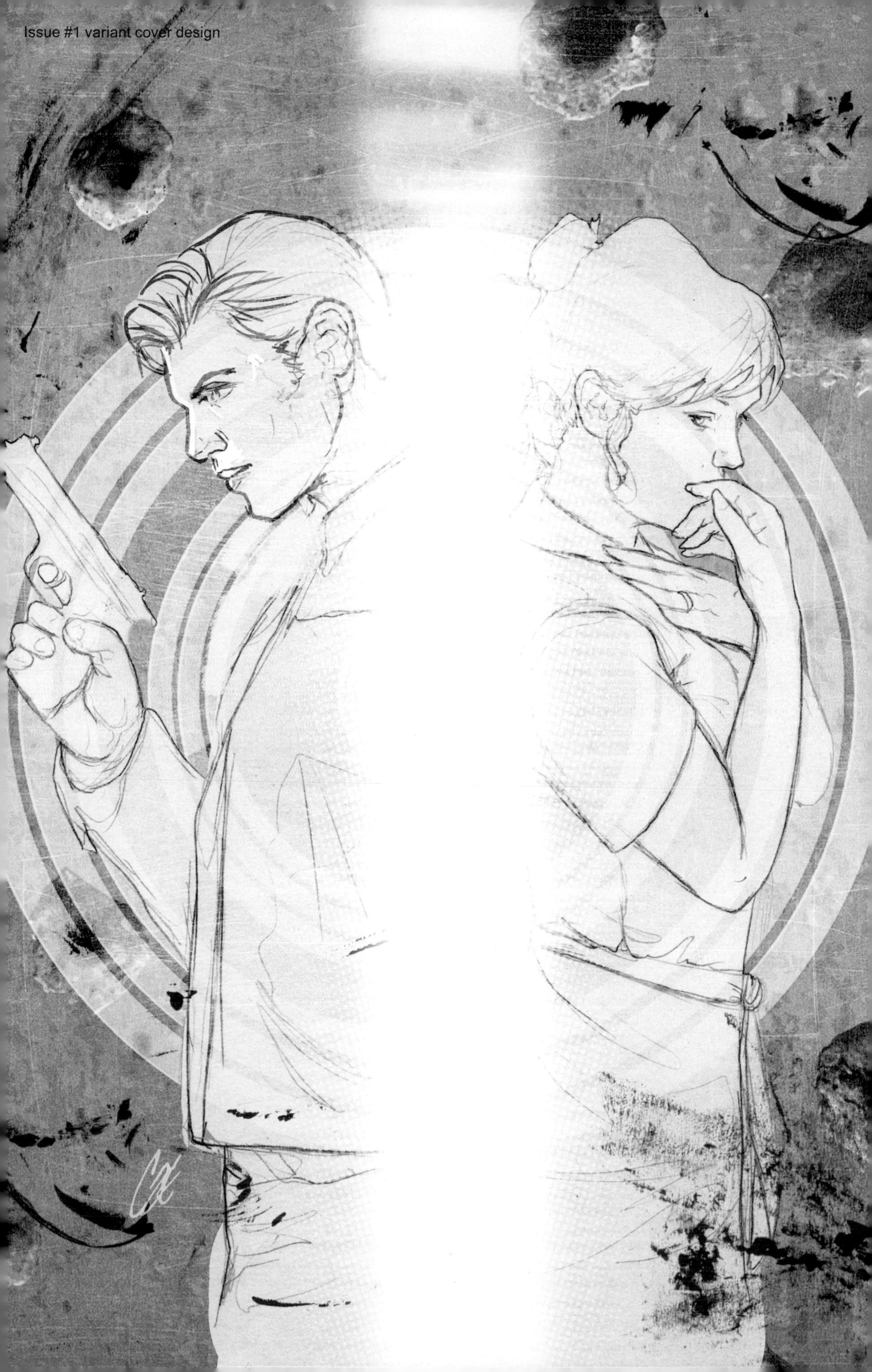

Issue #1 San Diego Comic Con variant cover design

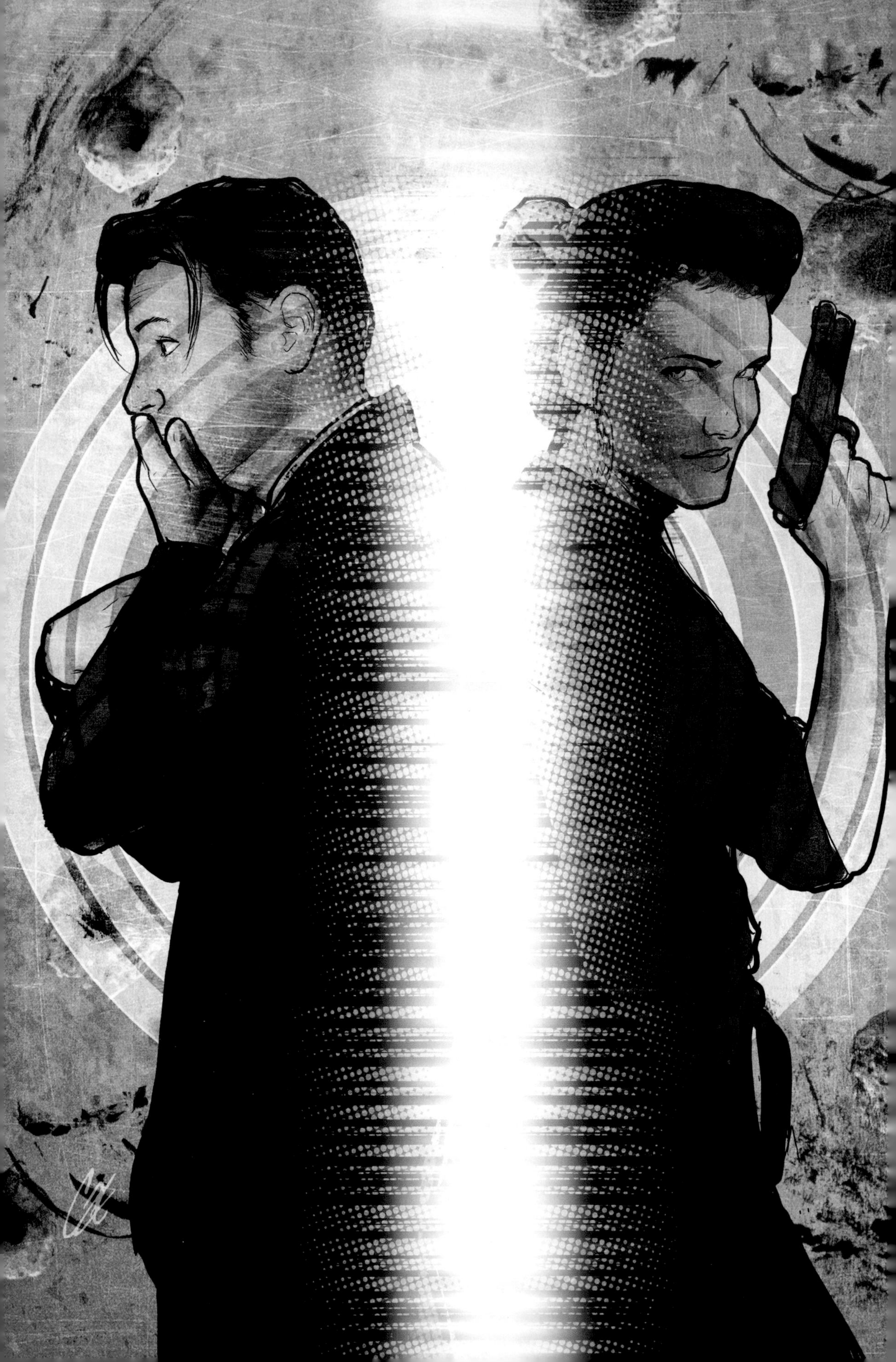

Unpublished Issue #1 variant cover design

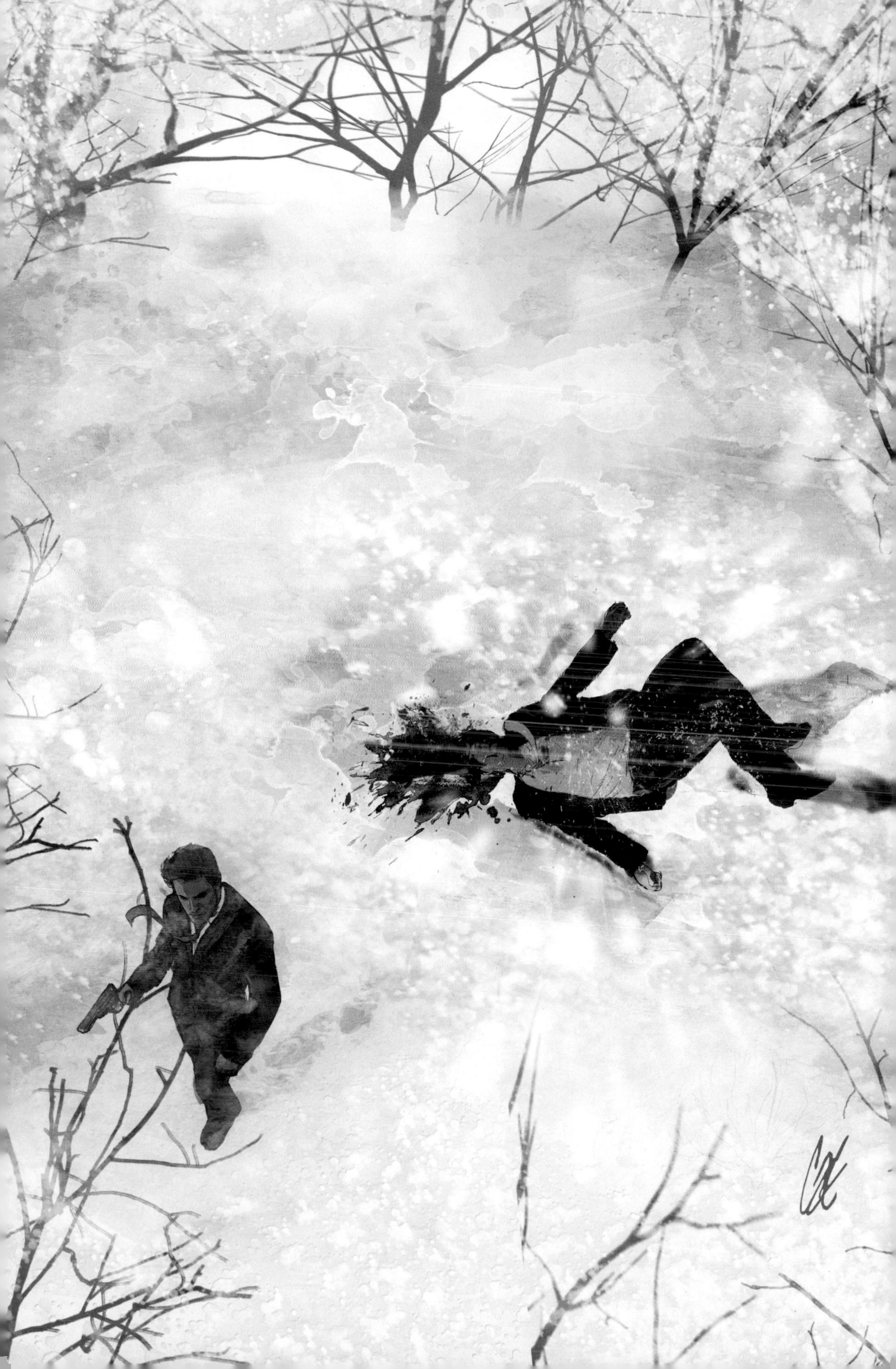

"Pride Month" Issue #1 variant cover design

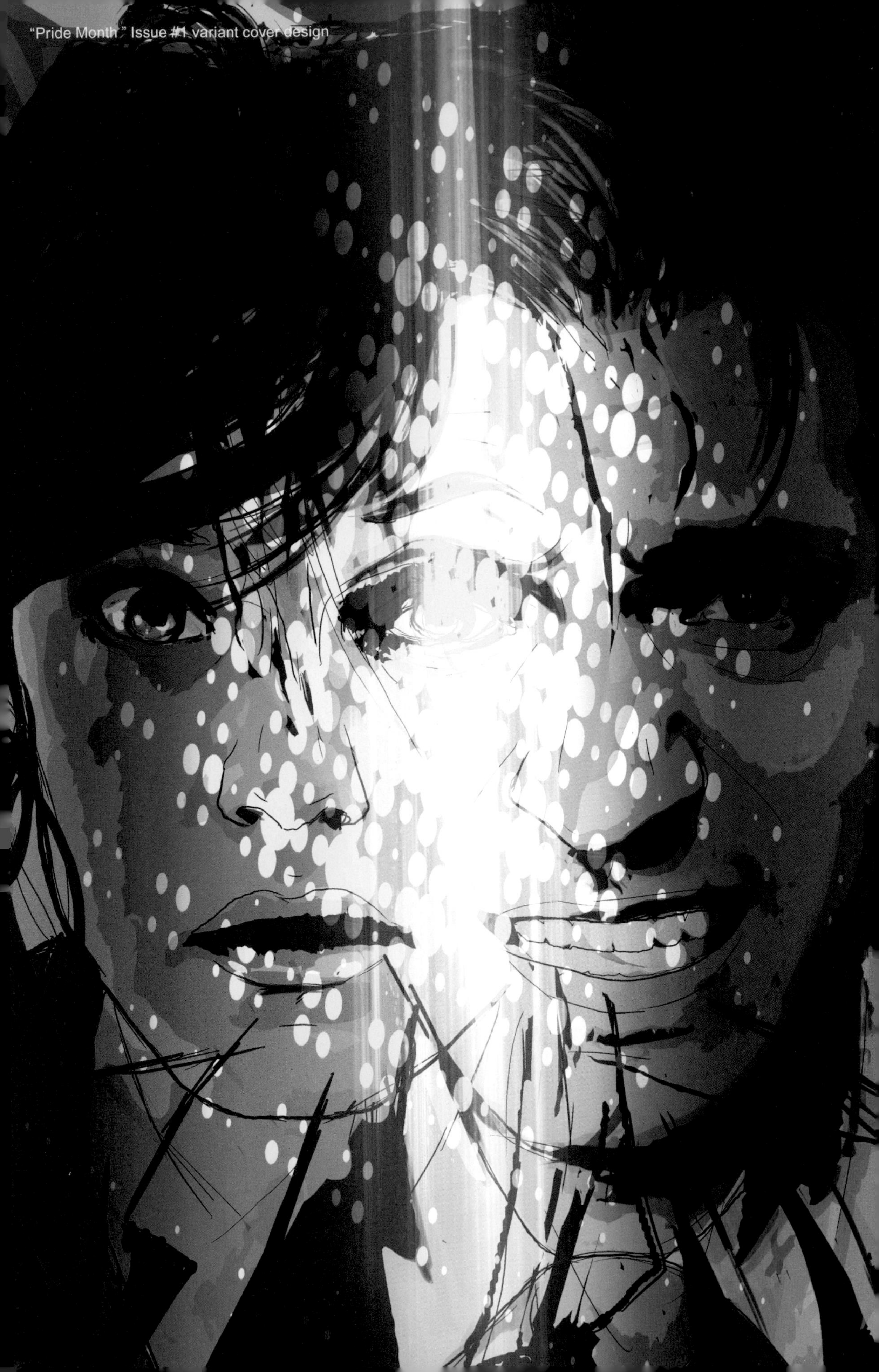

"Images of Tomorrow" Issue #2 variant cover design

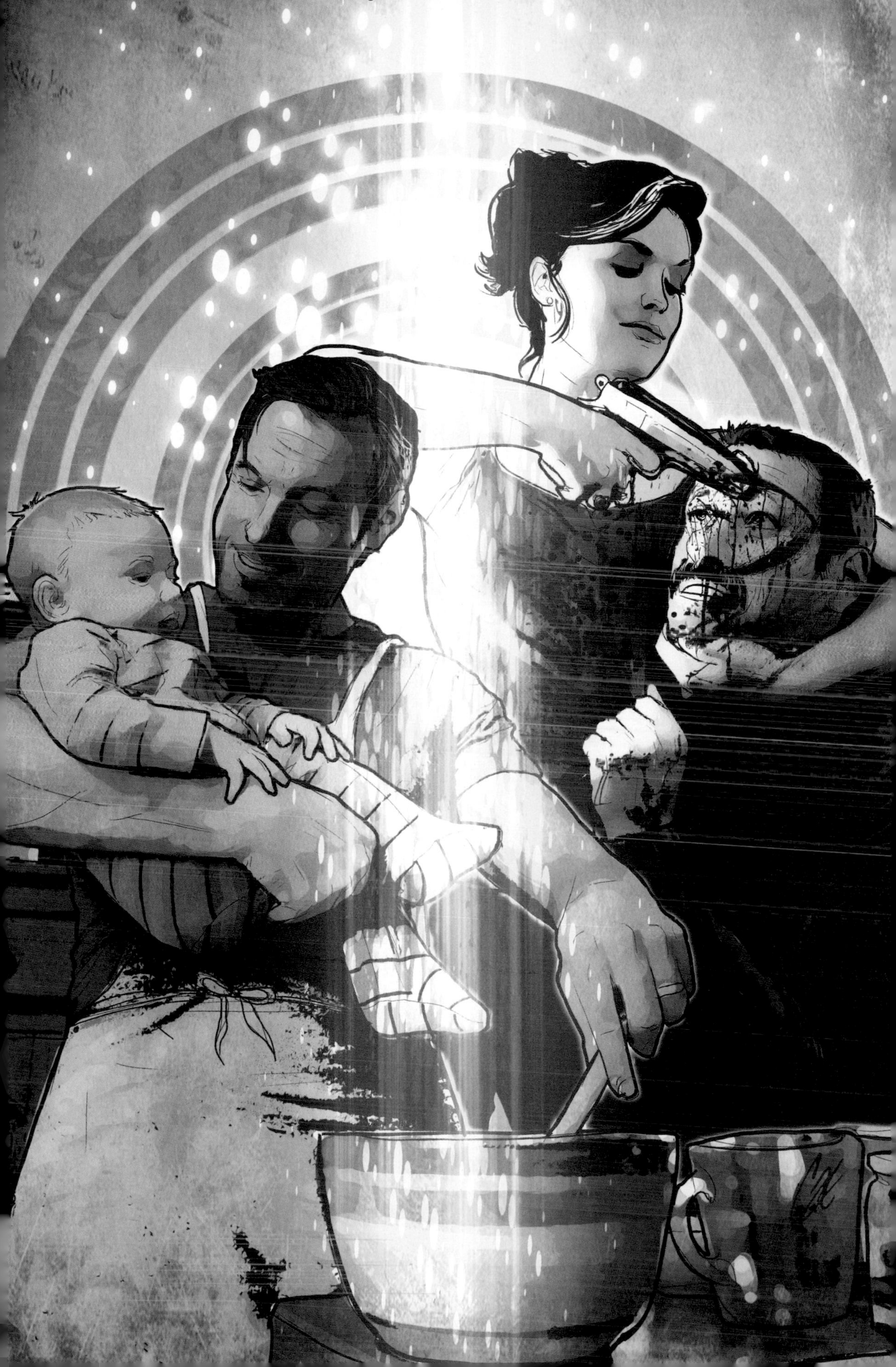

"The Walking Dead Tribute" Issue #5 variant cover design

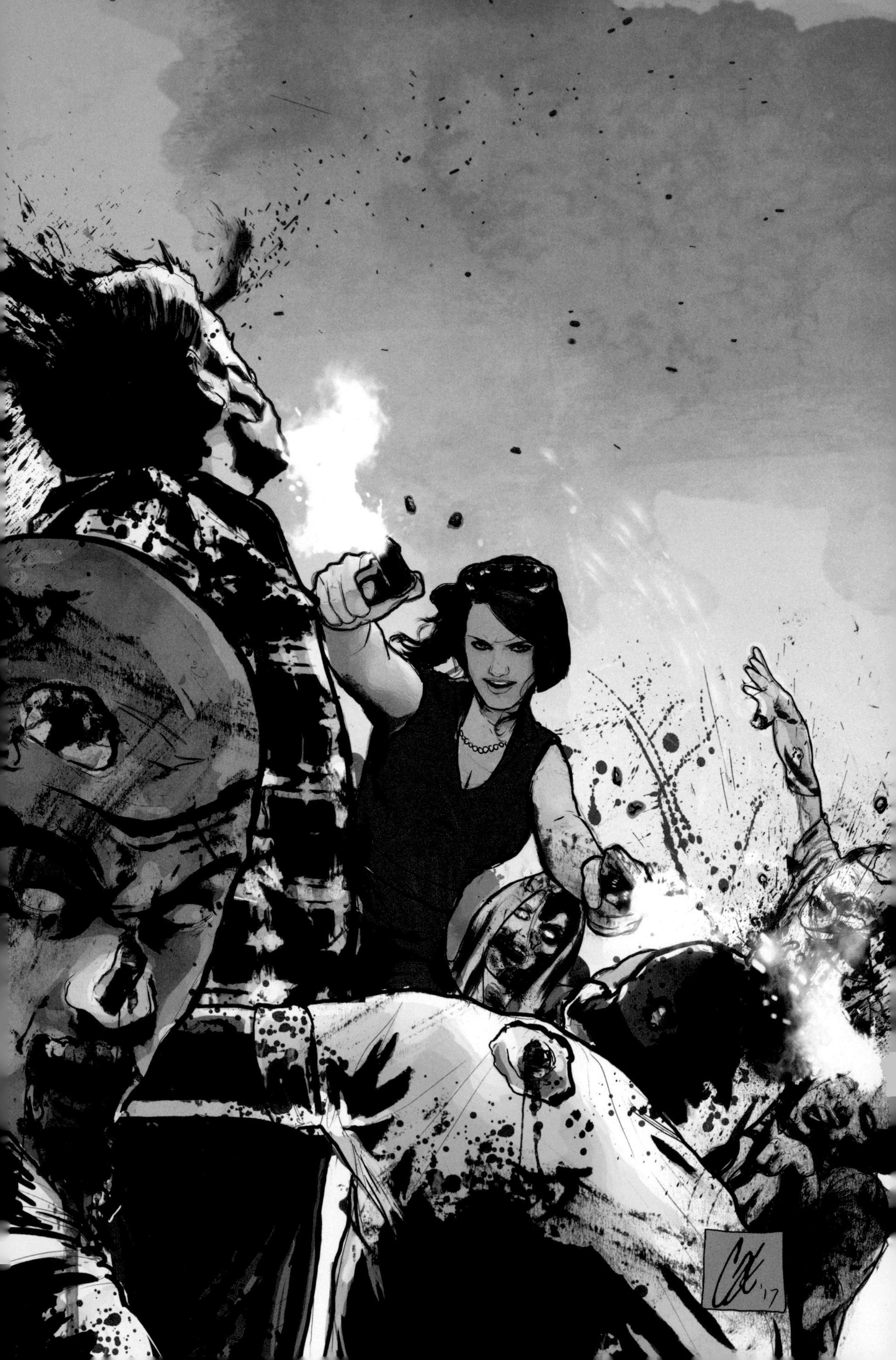
'17

Unpublished "banned book" variant cover design

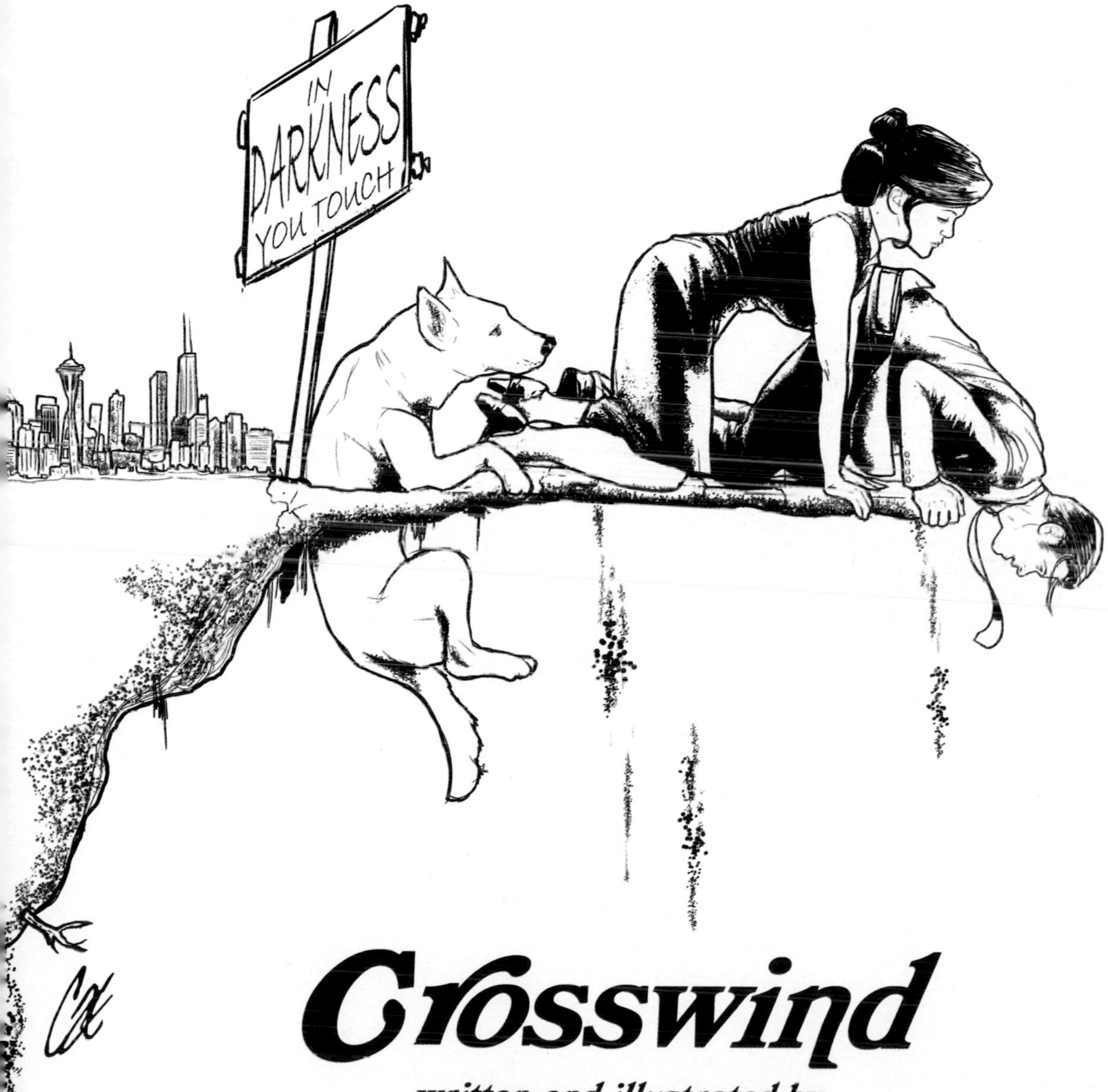
IN DARKNESS YOU TOUCH

Crosswind

written and illustrated by

Gail Simone & Cat Staggs

PENCIL +INK

FROM DESCRIPTIONS TO DRAWINGS

CASON RAY BENNETT is a handsome, mid-twenties hitman, with elegant but casual style. He spends money to look good, but wants to look casual and a bit wind-swept at the same time. He's good and he knows it...he wears black suits with an immaculate shirt underneath, collar unbuttoned, shined shoes and stylish sunglasses. When he sits in a chair, he spreads his arm across the back, crosses his legs...he never looks uncomfortable, intimidated, or ill at ease.

JUNIPER ELANORE BLUE is a lovely, but somewhat frazzled, Seattle housewife. She's attractive and fit from working out to keep her distracted husband's attentions...but she doesn't look people in the eye and her body language is often drawn inward. She has a sexy core, but it is so battered and bullied by the people around her that she doesn't show it easily, she wants to be free and creative and formidable, but she looks at her feet and has her arm across her body, holding her other arm at the bicep, as her standard pose.

CRUCIFIX is a tall, slender red-haired freckled man, who never smiles, his eyes are cold and black as death, he looks like a pale angel of doom. When he shows up at your door, you are about to die. He makes no friends, he is suspicious of everyone, and his defining trait is loyalty to the five families. Anyone who betrays them dies screaming.

Please note that these are early descriptions, the characters evolved considerably as we discovered them.

— CASON —

— JUNIPER —

— CRUZ —

ISSUE #3, PAGE EIGHTEEN:

PANEL ONE: Juniper looks back, not even looking at the furious Anthony.

ANTHONY: I will fuck your ass right UP, you goddamn whore!

JUNIPER: Sure you will, sport.

JUNIPER: You got that thing, Kelly?

PANEL TWO: Her hand takes the handle of the saute pan.

JUNIPER: Good man.

PANEL THREE: She SMASHES the pan into the head of Anthony, ringing his bell to Cleveland and back. Chaz, right behind him, looks stunned.

FX: WHAAAMM

CHAZ: What the FU—

PANEL FOUR: She brings up the pan, HARD, bottom side up, under Chaz's chin, knocking his head back like he was hit with a sledgehammer.

CHAZ: GuRKK.

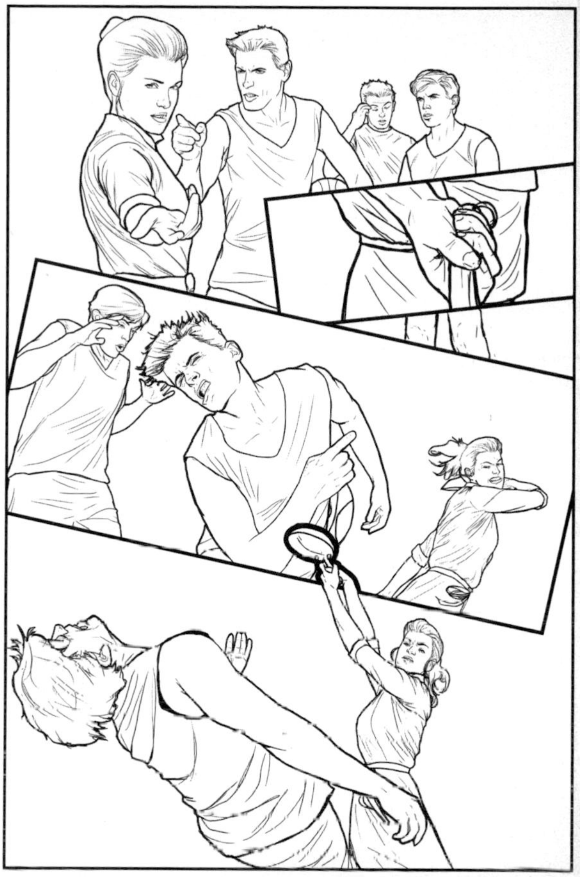

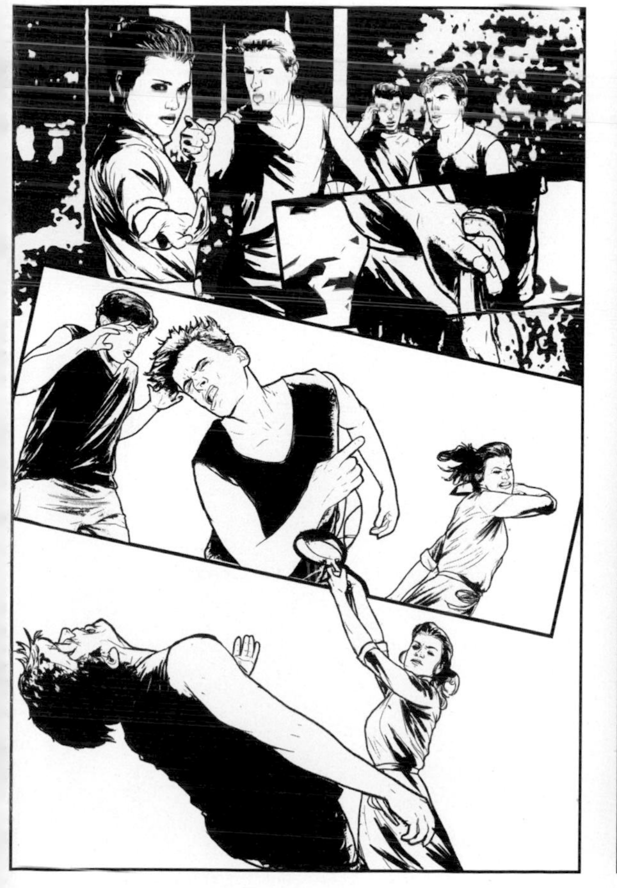

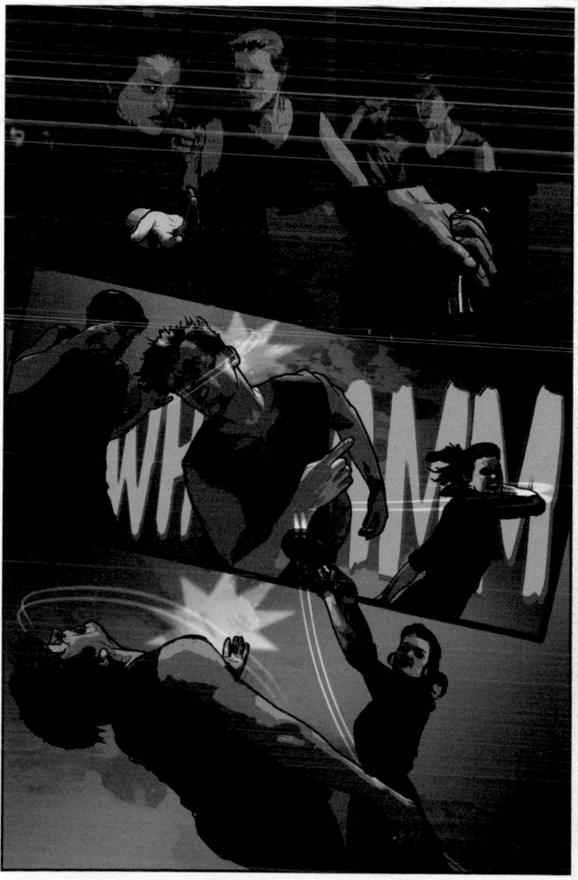
WHAAMM

ISSUE #4, PAGE SIXTEEN:
Mostly Silent page, people trying to sleep.

PANEL ONE: Juniper lays on her bed, a copy of the book THE STARS OUR DESTINATION on her nightstand, she's awake, looking up at the ceiling.

PANEL TWO: Cason, clearly restless, on his own swanky bed.

PANEL THREE: Jim, sleeping uncomfortably on the couch.

PANEL FOUR: Cruz, on his own bed, smiling, holding a gun in each hand, crossed on his chest.

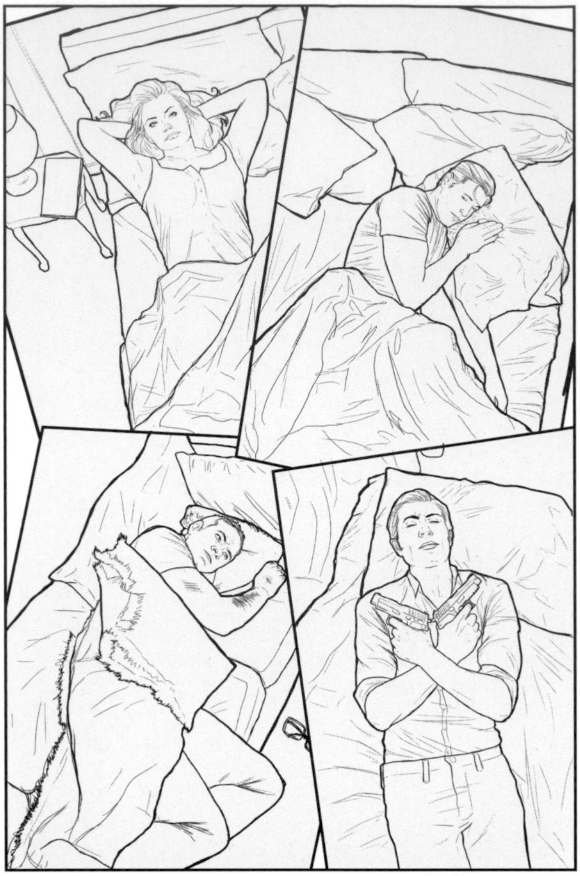

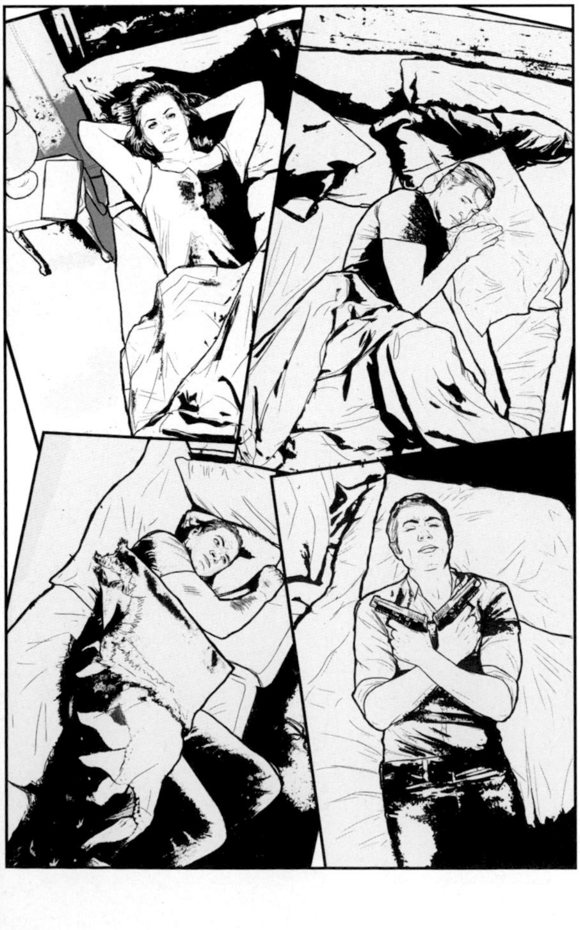

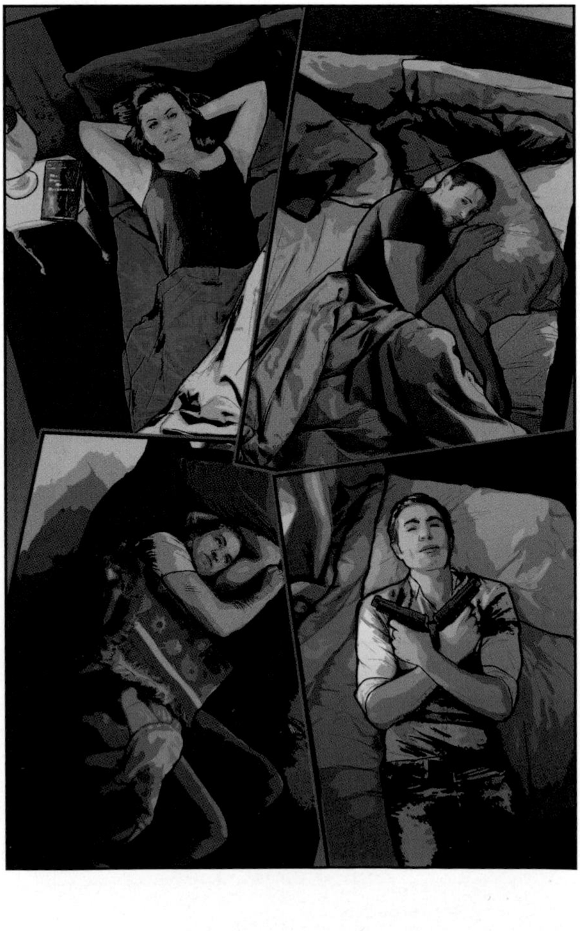